What Truth Is

What Truth Is

Mark Jago

OXFORD
UNIVERSITY PRESS

OXFORD
UNIVERSITY PRESS

Great Clarendon Street, Oxford, OX2 6DP,
United Kingdom

Oxford University Press is a department of the University of Oxford.
It furthers the University's objective of excellence in research, scholarship,
and education by publishing worldwide. Oxford is a registered trade mark of
Oxford University Press in the UK and in certain other countries

© Mark Jago 2018

The moral rights of the author have been asserted

First Edition published in 2018

All rights reserved. No part of this publication may be reproduced, stored in
a retrieval system, or transmitted, in any form or by any means, without the
prior permission in writing of Oxford University Press, or as expressly permitted
by law, by licence or under terms agreed with the appropriate reprographics
rights organization. Enquiries concerning reproduction outside the scope of the
above should be sent to the Rights Department, Oxford University Press, at the
address above

You must not circulate this work in any other form
and you must impose this same condition on any acquirer

Published in the United States of America by Oxford University Press
198 Madison Avenue, New York, NY 10016, United States of America

British Library Cataloguing in Publication Data

Data available

Library of Congress Control Number: 2018933073

ISBN 978–0–19–882381–0

Links to third party websites are provided by Oxford in good faith and
for information only. Oxford disclaims any responsibility for the materials
contained in any third party website referenced in this work.

Dedicated to all the strong women of the world

First amongst them, my mum

Contents

Acknowledgements	ix
Introduction	1

I Truth and Making True
1. Truth: Substantial or Insubstantial?	19
2. Arguments for Truthmaking	53
3. Truthmaker Maximalism	81

II Truthmakers
4. States of Affairs	105
5. Everything and Nothing	131

III The Truthmaking Relation
6. Truthmaking and Grounding	175
7. The Logic of Truthmaking	207

IV Propositions and Paradoxes
8. The Nature of Propositions	233
9. Dealing with Liars	279
Appendix: Proof Theory	321

Bibliography	323
Index: Authors	349
Index: Terms	351

Acknowledgements

This book grew out of an interest in the metaphysics and logic of truthmaking. During my first teaching job at Nottingham, my then colleague Gonzalo Rodriguez-Pereyra published one of the most important papers on truthmaking, 'Truthmaking, Entailment, and the Conjunction Thesis' (Rodriguez-Pereyra 2006b). What struck me most about the paper, apart from the wonderfully clear and compelling metaphysical arguments, was that it could be developed with a logical semantics. Gonzalo had set out truthmaking principles for conjunction, disjunction, and entailment, argued for (or against) on metaphysical grounds. So what kind of logic did these principles generate? What should the model theory look like? I started to play around. During this time, Gonzalo was a wonderful mentor, with endless patience for my endless mistakes.

Just over a year later, David Armstrong temporarily joined the Nottingham department, and we co-taught an MA class (on Truth and Truthmakers, naturally). In preparing the class, we spoke a lot about his views on truthmaking (or rather, he spoke and I listened). I learnt a lot from him in six months. The last time I saw David was at the Australasian Association of Philosophy conference in Melbourne, 2009. To my surprise, he remembered me, took me to lunch, and asked how my thoughts on truthmaking were coming along. Well, here they are, David! Sorry you didn't get to see them. I like to think he would approve of what I've got here, in outline if not in detail: a staunchly realist, Aussie-inspired take on reality.

The research which makes up this book began with work with Stephen Barker on negative states of affairs. Since no respectable journal wanted to publish a paper on negative states of affairs, I had ample opportunity to develop our initial ideas. Once you have negative states of affairs, you're not that far from universal and negative existential states of affairs. Then you've got all you need for a theory of truthmaking. So I returned to the ideas I'd been discussing with Gonzalo about the metaphysics of truthmaking.

At this time, I was living in Australia, and weird and wonderful logics were everywhere. What would a logic of truthmaking look like? I had little idea and stumbled around plenty, but got set on my feet through discussions with Greg Restall, Dave Ripley, Graham Priest, and Zach Weber.

I had no plans for a book on truth, and didn't particularly want to write a book on truthmaking, worrying that it was (by 2013 or so) a topic on which too much had been said already. Deflationism ruled; 'correspondence' theories seemed very much out of fashion. Yet an idea nagged: if you have truthmakers aplenty in your realist metaphysics, plus an independent characterisation of what makes them truthmakers, then why not analyse *being true* in terms of *having a truthmaker*?

What sealed the deal was realising that this identification of truth with truthmaking gives us a way of dealing with the paradoxes of truth. I'd co-organised two workshops on *Propositions and Same-Saying* with Albert Atkin and Rachael Briggs, which generated very helpful discussion on the nature of propositions with Dave Chalmers, Kit Fine, and Jonathan Schaffer, as well as with Albert and Rachael. I was lucky enough to be able to discuss the paradoxes of truth with Dave Ripley, Lionel Shapiro, and Elia Zardini, who've written some of the most impressive and interesting recent papers on the subject. I thought my truthmaking approach offered something simpler, with better metaphysical justification and fewer logical costs.

All that remained was to put all these ideas together. Here's the result.

Many of the ideas discussed here were presented, in various stages of development, in talks at conferences and workshops: Utrecht philosophy department seminar, 19 May 2017; *Ground, Essence & Modality* conference, Helsinki, 8 June 2016; *The Metaphysics of Grounding* workshop, Dresden, 30 April 2016; *The Lightness of Being* workshop, Uppsala, Sweden, 16–17 November 2015; *Aboutness* workshop, Hamburg, 3–4 August 2015; *Midsummer*

Philosophy Workshop, Edinburgh, 30 June 2015; *Truth & Logical Consequence* workshop, Nottingham, 10 June 2015; *Discourse and Philosophy Colloquium*, University of Amsterdam, 17 April 2015; University of Edinburgh Philosophy Research Seminar, 30 January 2015; University of Hertfordshire Philosophy Research Seminar, 13 November 2014; New York Logic Group seminar, 15 September 2014; St Andrews research seminar, 16 November 2013; Melbourne logic seminar, 12 November 2010; *Australasian Association of Logic* conference, Sydney, 2–4 July 2010; University of Sydney Current Projects seminar, 17 May 2010; ANU research seminar, 22 April 2010; *Australasian Association of Philosophy* conference, Melbourne, 5–10 July 2009; Adelaide-Melbourne Logic Axis meeting, Adelaide, 9–10 May 2009; and *Because* conference, University of Geneva, Switzerland, 15–17 February 2008.

I'd like to thank all of the audiences at these talks, who contributed valuable feedback on my ideas. Particular debts of gratitude are owed in this regard to Jamin Asay, Franz Berto, Rachael Briggs, David Chalmers, Alison Fernandes, Kit Fine, Branden Fitelson, Allen Hazen, Ole Hjortland, Dave Ingram, Nick Jones, Jon Litland, EJ Lowe, Penelope Mackie, Peter Menzies, Bryan Pickel, Graham Priest, Greg Restall, Dave Ripley, Jonathan Schaffer, Benjamin Schneider, Jonathan Tallant, Nathan Wildman, and Robbie Williams.

Several early chapters were read at the Nottingham Work-in-Progress seminar. Thanks to all that contributed ideas, particularly Dave Ingram, Penelope Mackie, Jon Robson, and Jonathan Tallant. Aaron Griffith and an anonymous reader carefully read the entire book for OUP and offered me a wonderfully extensive, helpful list of suggestions. You both helped me to improve the text no end; thanks very much! Many thanks also to Jonathan Tallant and Andy Fisher, my heads of department at Nottingham, who have been supportive as I wrote; and to Peter Momtchiloff at OUP, who has been wonderfully encouraging throughout.

Some of the arguments in the book have appeared in previously published articles. §3.3–§3.4 draw on 'Advanced Modalizing Problems', *Mind*, 125(499), 627–42, 2016. §5.2–§5.4 draw on 'The Cost of Truthmaker Maximalism', *Canadian Journal of Philosophy*, 43(4), 460–74, 2013. §5.5 draws on 'Being Positive About Negative Facts' (written with Stephen Barker), *Philosophy & Phenomenological Research*, 85(1), 117–38, 2012. §6.3–§6.5 draw on 'From Nature to Grounding', in *Fundamentality*, ed. Ricki Bliss and Graham Priest, Oxford University Press, forthcoming. §8.2 and §§8.5–8.7 draw on 'Propositions as Truthmaker Conditions', *Argumenta* special issue on *Thinking the (Im)possible*, 2017/18. Finally, §9.7 draws on 'Alethic Undecidability Doesn't Solve the Liar', *Analysis*, 76(3): 278–83, 2016.

As I wrote, the world seemed to turn its back on truth. In the UK, we saw a perfidious Tory government elected, hell-bent on harming the poorest and most vulnerable in society; closely followed by the Brexit vote, and the election of Donald Trump. In each case, established fact was ignored by politicians, the media, and the voting public. Politicians and newspapers could now, it seemed, lie with impunity. We must always remember that the truth is important; it is good for us; and it is valuable for its own sake.

Only one thing is more important in our lives than the truth. The day after I finished writing, Anna and I finally married, and it was the happiest day of my life. Thank you for all the love and support.

Introduction

The Nature of Truth

THIS IS A BOOK about what truth is. It's about the *property* of being true. What features does that property have? What kinds of entity can have that property? What makes an entity have or lack that property? These and similar metaphysical questions will be to the fore throughout my investigation. I'll be less interested in how we talk, or how we think, about truth. My focus is on the property *being true*, rather than the word 'true' or the concept *truth*.

My answer to the question, 'what is truth?' is simple. To be true is to be made true by the existence of a suitable worldly entity. Or rather, it is to stand in the *truthmaking* relation to some entity. Truth arises as a relation between a proposition—the content of our sayings, thoughts, beliefs, and so on—and an entity (or entities) in the world. The property *being true* is an existential property: it is the property *there is an x such that x truthmakes —*. A proposition has this property when it fills the '—' gap. It does this when there is some entity which truthmakes that proposition.

An investigation into truth may focus on the property of *being true*, or on the concept of *truth*, or on the predicate 'is true'. (Asay (2013b, 2014) discusses the importance of the distinction.) My aim in this book is not a to give conceptual analysis of our concept of truth; nor is it to give a definition of our word 'true'. If that were my aim, I'd be guilty of offering you a circular analysis or definition. But it isn't my aim. My aim is to characterise and say something interesting about the property *being true*. I'll do that by first characterising the *truthmaking* relation, which holds between worldly entities and propositions. I'll sometimes express this relation with phrases like 'entity *x* makes propositions ⟨*A*⟩ true'. But don't be misled by the 'makes — true' construction. There are not two elements here, *making* and *truth*. There is a single relation, *truthmaking*, sometimes expressed using the phrase 'makes — true'.

Characterising the *truthmaking* relation is the main task of this book. My aim is not to provide a set of necessary-and-sufficient conditions for truthmaking to hold. Philosophers hardly ever succeed in reducing an important concept–causation, or knowledge, or disposition–to some other, better understood, notions. But they do manage to say interesting, informative (and sometimes, hopefully, true) things about concepts like these. In investigating these concepts, we can come to understand something of their nature, even absent necessary-and-sufficient conditions for their application. We should have the same aim for *truthmaking*. (That said, I do offer a set of necessary-and-sufficient conditions for *truthmaking* in chapter 8. But this analysis depends on my account of what propositions are, which you may or may not accept. I hope to say something interesting about *truthmaking*, independently of any particular theory of propositions.)

From characterising the *truthmaking* relation, it is but a short step to the characterisation of *being true* in terms of *makes true*: the latter is simply the existential generalisation (in the first argument) of the former. Suppose that properties and relations have 'slots', corresponding to the argument places in their linguistic representations. Then *truthmaking* has two slots: the first for the truthmaker (the entity that does the truthmaking), and the second for the truthmade entity, the true proposition. *Being true*, by contrast, has just one slot, for a proposition. We obtain *being true* from *truthmaking* simply by existentially quantifying into the first slot: from — *truthmakes* — to *something truthmakes* —. That, in short, is what truth is.

David Armstrong (2004) suggests a theory of truth in terms of truthmaking very much like this. But it is unclear what kind of theory he intends to offer. He states his theory by saying:

p (a proposition) is true if and only if there exists a T (some entity in the world) such that T necessitates that p and p is true in virtue of T. (Armstrong 2004, 17)

The quoted principle is most often called *truthmaker maximalism*, the thesis that every truth has a truthmaker. (I'll discuss truthmaker maximalism in chapter 3.) The principle has been discussed intensively in the recent literature on truthmaking (see Beebee and Dodd 2005b; Lowe and Rami 2009), but it's rarely treated as a theory of truth. Of the twenty-three papers in the 2015 'state of the art' collection *Unifying the Philosophy of Truth* (Achourioti et al. 2015), for example, none find a central role for truthmaking, and only one (Sher 2015) is a broadly correspondence-to-the-facts-style theory.

In reviewing the situation, Marian David says that 'truthmaker theory is not equipped, and usually not designed, to answer the question "What is truth?"' (David 2016). Asay (2014) argues that a theory of truth should be kept distinct from a discussion of *truthmaking*, for 'the foundational role [truth] plays in our conceptual scheme is not one that needs the aid of any causal or truthmaking powers' (2014, 162; see also Asay 2013b, chapter 4). Armstrong himself describes his principle, variously, as a 'theory of the nature of truth' and 'a necessary and sufficient truth-condition for truth' but 'not ... a definition' (Armstrong 2004, 17). My project here is not merely to give truth-conditions for 'is true', or to state a condition which holds whenever something is true. (That's how the quoted principle is often understood.) I'm with Armstrong, at least when he talks of a 'theory of the nature of truth'. But rather than expressing this theory as a biconditional, as Armstrong does, I want to understand it as a claim: the property of *truth* is identical to the property of *being truthmade by something*.

This truth-as-truthmaking approach bears some resemblance to the old *correspondence* theory of truth of Russell (1905/1994, 1906, 1912, 1940) and Moore (1901). If 'correspondence' means only that for each truth, there exists some related worldly entity, then the theory I'm offering *is* a correspondence theory of truth. As Armstrong says, 'correspondence demands a correspondent, and a correspondent for a truth is a truthmaker' (Armstrong 1997, 14). But if 'correspondence' implies a one-to-one correspondence between truths and things in the world, then I'm out. Your existence makes many truths true: *that you exist*, *that a person exists*, *that something exists*, *that either you exist or I exist*, and many more. But equally, one truth may have many truthmakers: you and I are each perfectly good truthmakers for *that either you or I exist*, as is the pair of us. So correspondence in some nebulous sense: yes. One-to-one correspondence between truths and worldly entities: not here.

We'll have to work hard to make this truth-as-truthmaking theory attractive; even to make it plausible. Why should there be anything to say about what truth is, other than that, in each case, it's true that *A* if and only if *A*? Why should truths have to relate to a worldly entity at all? It's true that Bertie is snuffling when he's snuffling; but why should there be some further entity, the state of affairs *that Bertie is snuffling*, that makes that truth true? And even if there is in this specific case, why think the same goes for *every* truth? Even if there's a state of affairs *that Bertie is snuffling*, it's a further step—and a big one at that—to think that there's some entity in the world that makes it true that no Hobbits exist. I'll discuss these issues—of truth, truthmaking, and truthmaker maximalism—in Part I of the book (chapters 1–3).

If we're going to make a theory of truth in terms of truthmaking plausible, we'll need to say what kind of entity the truthmakers are. I'll develop the line that they are (typically) states of affairs. So what are states of affairs? How does a particular and a property, or some particulars and a relation, get together to make up a state of affairs? Do states of affairs also make true truths such as 'there are no Hobbits'? And if so, how? Do we need *negative* states of affairs, and if so, what *are* they, metaphysically speaking? These are the issues I take up in Part II (chapters 4 and 5).

We then come to questions about the *truthmaking* relation itself. What kind of relation it is? What properties does it have? How can we think about it in precise, logical terms? How (if at all) does it relate to the notion of *metaphysical grounding*? I'll take up these issues in Part III (chapters 6 and 7).

At this point, with these questions answered, we have a theory of truth on our hands. But we can say more. As well as saying what truth is, and how a truth gets to be true, we can say what *kind* of thing truths are. Thoughts, beliefs, sentences, utterances: these can all be true or false. But there is a more basic kind of entity, which we can use to understand whether a thought, belief, sentence, or utterance is true or false. Thoughts, beliefs, sentences, and utterances all have a *content*. They express that such-and-such is the case. That entity—the content they express—is a *proposition*. When I think and then say that Bertie is adorable, and when you come to believe that he is, what I think and say, and what you believe, all have in common the content *that Bertie is adorable*. We believe the same thing, the same proposition; and it's that proposition that my utterance expresses.

Propositions are the *primary* bearers of the truth-values. Propositions are the things that are true, or false, in the first instance. A true belief is a belief with a true proposition as its content; a true utterance is an utterance which expresses a proposition that's true. But what are propositions? Does having a theory of propositions help us solve problems and paradoxes created by truth? I take up these questions in Part IV (chapters 8 and 9).

Which Approach: Metaphysical or Logical?

Stewart Shapiro writes that:

> There are two bodies of philosophical literature on truth. One of these is concerned with the metaphysical nature of truth (or whether it has such a nature). Authors defend and attack varieties of truth-as-correspondence, truth-as-coherence, deflationism, and the like. ... The other body of literature concerns the paradoxes. It seems that there is very little overlap between these bodies .... (Shapiro 2009)

My aim in this book is to combine these approaches. Metaphysical approaches to truth need to address the truth-theoretic paradoxes, most famous of which is the Liar paradox, 'this sentence is not true'. If a theory of truth doesn't address the paradoxes, then the threat of incoherence looms large. But equally, we shouldn't approach a solution to the paradoxes without considering what truth is. If we were completely metaphysically unconstrained, the paradoxes would be much less hard. Without the T-scheme, for example, the Liar paradox won't go through. But we seem to be metaphysically committed to the T-scheme, on the grounds of what property *truth* is. It is only by combining both metaphysical and logical modes of investigation that we get a full and satisfactory picture of what truth is.

And more than that: each approach can learn from, and draw support from, the other. I'll argue for a certain view of propositions (chapter 8) and argue that it gives us the best response to the paradoxes (chapter 9). That theory of propositions makes essential use of some metaphysical notions, including truthmaking. If I'm right, and it really is the best logical solution to the paradoxes, then that is a strong argument in favour of that metaphysical approach.

Realism and Anti-Realism

It's sometimes said by philosophers that a theory of truth settles the question of *realism*: of whether the world exists independently of our knowledge, beliefs, or thoughts. And it's often said that a theory of truthmaking carries a commitment to realism. According to Armstrong, 'To demand truthmakers for particular truths is to accept a realist theory for these truths' (Armstrong 2004, 5), for 'realism about the truth of a particular true proposition [is] the contention that its truth is determined by something that lies outside that proposition' (Armstrong 2003, 12). Bigelow feels that, without truthmaking, 'I find I have no adequate anchor to hold me from drifting onto the shoals of some sort of pragmatism or idealism' (Bigelow 1988, 123). Heil takes truthmaking to be 'a central tenet of realism' (Heil 2003, 61).

I think that's a mistake. A theory of truth tells us what *truth* is; but it needn't tell us whether truths must be known, or knowable, by creatures like us. Similarly, a theory of truthmaking is, in principle, compatible with different positions along the realist/anti-realist spectrum. We may hold that truths require truthmakers but that the truthmakers are brought into existence by our thoughts or other kinds of conceptual activity, for example. Here I agree with Asay:

> The realism/anti-realism debate does not consist in whether or not the truths of some domain have truthmakers, but rather what the nature or character is of those truthmakers. Simply having truthmakers is not sufficient for realism. (Asay 2012, 378)

Let's take a specific theory as an example. Suppose, with Berkeley (1710/1995), that material objects are no more than constructions from our perceptions. That is, material objects exist all right, but they're mental constructions. They're not 'out there' in the world, independently of our thinking about them, as we usually think they are. That's a paradigm anti-realist theory of objects. (I'm using 'anti-realist' here to mean, roughly, that things are mind-dependent. I'm not using 'anti-realist' in the *eliminativist* sense, saying that such-and-such entities don't exist at all.) Nevertheless, Berkeley has truthmakers for truths about material objects—at least, for those truths such as *that Bertie is snuffling*. My perceptions exist and, for Berkeley, they make it true that Bertie is snuffling. Now, I don't think for one minute that that's the right picture of material objects. But our theory of truth—merely saying that to be true is to be made true—doesn't tell us that.

Truthmaking and realism are independent doctrines. Nevertheless, debates about truth have played a part in the question of realism. Many versions of global anti-realism hold that truth is epistemically constrained or essentially knowable. The idea underlies much idealist, phenomenalist, and other anti-realist thought. Berkeley (1710/1995), Kant (1781/1998, A146/B185) (with respect to appearances, as opposed to things in themselves), Mill (1889), Ayer (1936), and

Dummett (1978) all seem to subscribe to the *knowability principle*: that all truths are knowable (by us, or by some idealised version of us). The principle may be motivated by worries about radical deception, leading to meaning skepticism (Putnam 1979, 1981; Button 2013). I don't know whether any of this should be taken a claim about the nature of truth. We can formulate the intended content of 'truths are knowable' without mentioning truth: for any proposition A, if A then we (or someone like us) can know that A. Whatever is the case is knowably the case. The principle concerns the nature of reality, in the first instance, and the nature of truth only as a consequence.

It is no part of the nature of truth, or of reality, that what is true is knowable. Suppose it were: if A then it's possible to know that A. Nevertheless, there's some truth A that isn't known by anyone. So, by assumption, that truth is knowable: it's possible to know that (A and no one knows that A). But that isn't possible at all. For in that supposed possibility, someone knows that A, and yet also knows that no one knows that A. What she knows must be the case and so, in that supposed possibility, someone knows that A and yet no one knows that A: contradiction.

This simple argument, due to Church (2009) and Fitch (1963), is immensely powerful. It shows that not all truths are knowable, and hence that it is no part of the nature of truth to be knowable. (The argument may seem like a logical trick at first, but on careful inspection the reasoning is impeccable (Williamson 1993). It's effective even if one accepts intuitionistic rather than classical logic (Percival 1990); even if we think that knowledge doesn't distribute over conjunctions (Williamson 1993); and even if we think, with Linsky (2009), that knowledge claims should be expressed in a typed logic (Jago 2010). It's this argument, rather than any consideration of what truth is, that puts me firmly in the realist camp.)

Just what this argument tells us about realism and anti-realism is moot. It shows us that any viable anti-realism has to avoid entailing the knowability principle (or else allow that all truths are in fact known). Perhaps this can be done (Hand (2009) and Jenkins (2009) offer suggestions), although I'm skeptical. Regardless, you'll no doubt notice my realist inclinations throughout this book.

What if realism is the best philosophical stance in some but not all cases? What if there are objective facts of the matter, out there in the world, in some domains of enquiry but not in others? The realist stance on material objects—that they exist independently of whether we think about them, and independently of what we know about them—seems very plausible. But what about truths about what's funny, or what's artistically valuable? Wright (1992, 1996, 2001) and Lynch (2009, 2001) argue that we require different truth properties in different domains of discourse, corresponding to different ways of being true (Pedersen and Wright 2013). I reject this *alethic pluralism* (§§1.5–1.7): there is but one property of *being true*, and that's the one identical to *having a truthmaker*.

Outline of the Book

Chapter 1: Substantial or Insubstantial?

I'll begin by contrasting the two main contemporary approaches to truth. The first claims that truth consists in relating to the world in the right way. A proposition is true when it 'corresponds to the facts', whatever that may mean. I'll call this approach, which encapsulates many different theories, the *substantial* approach to truth. (Sher (2016) gives an overview of substantial approaches.) The second approach finds substantial theories to be far too heavy-duty. The proposition *that A* is true if and only if *A*. That's it: there's nothing more to say about what truth is. In particular, there's no need to go heavy-duty and get ourselves caught up with 'correspondence' or 'facts' or any of that. This approach takes truth to be an *insubstantial* property.

In this chapter, I'll present two reasons for thinking that the insubstantial approach won't work. I'll argue that truth is a substantial property. I'll also discuss the issue of alethic pluralism, mentioned earlier: is there just one property of truth, or a plurality fulfilling the *truth* role?

Chapter 2: Arguments for Truthmaking

This chapter focuses on arguments that have been given for thinking that truths need to be made true. I'll argue that these arguments are, for the most part, question-begging. We can't establish that truths *need* truthmakers unless we first know what *truth* is. So my strategy *isn't* to argue that, given the nature of truth, truths must be made true. Instead I'll argue, on metaphysical grounds, that the world contains states of affairs. And, given that states of affairs exist, certain propositions will correspond to them. Those states of affairs then make those propositions true. Our reason for believing in truthmaking is because the world is made up a certain way.

I'll then argue that, if every truth has a truthmaker (as I claim in chapter 3), there is an argument to best explanation identifying *being true* with *having a truthmaker*.

Chapter 3: Truthmaker Maximalism

If there are states of affairs, and some propositions correspond to those states of affairs in the right way, then some truths are made true. But are all truths made true? If not, then the analysis of truth in terms of truthmaking cannot be correct. So a weight is placed on the idea that all truths are made true. This is *truthmaker maximalism*. Why believe it? I'll provide an argument that all propositions are made true. This is a general argument, establishing that all truths have a truthmaker, but it doesn't tell us what kind of entity those truthmakers are. That is the task of chapters 4 and 5.

Chapter 4: States of Affairs

States of affairs play a prominent role in truthmaking theory. But what are they? What is their nature? Are they made up of particulars, properties, and relations? If so, how? How are they associated with language and thought? I consider three approaches to the issue. On one view, particulars, properties, and relations are combined by a *fundamental tie* into states of affairs. On another approach, states of affairs are primitive entities without constituents. A third view holds that, whilst states of affairs are combinations of properties and particulars (or of relations and particulars), there is no additional ontological tie between them. In this chapter, I'll develop and contrast these three theories.

Chapter 5: Everything and Nothing

By this point, I've offered a metaphysical account of states of affairs such as *that Bertie is adorable*. These make the corresponding propositions true in a very simple way. But there are many truths—such as *that Bertie is not a rhinoceros* and *that there exist no Vulcans*—which do not seem amenable to this analysis. Given that we've established that all truths are made true, we now need to ask: what makes such truths true? I survey the suggestions. I divide these into two camps. There's the *parsimonious* approaches, which try to explain how such truths are true without introducing special new entities. Then there's the *plenitudinous* approaches. These concede that extra entities are required to make such truths true. I'll narrow down the options to just one: such truths are made true by negative states of affairs.

Negative states of affairs are the bad boys of metaphysics. But I'll argue that we can make sense of them, and that they are good to have around. I'll offer two accounts of what they are, metaphysically speaking.

Chapter 6: Truthmaking and Grounding

So far, we've covered which truths are made true (all of them!) and by what (states of affairs); but we've said relatively little about the truthmaking relation itself. What kind of relation it is? What properties does it have? When does a truthmaker for one proposition thereby get to be a truthmaker for some other, related proposition? And what relation, if any, does truthmaking bear to the metaphysical notion of *grounding*?

I'll argue that truthmaking is closely aligned to a particular kind of grounding relation between entities (typically, states of affairs). And

I'll argue that the kind of grounding in question is a matter of the natures of objects and properties. This approach tells us something about the nature of truthmaking, and hence of truth. It also hints that truthmaking bears a close relation to the nature of propositions, which I'll investigate in chapter 8.

Chapter 7: The Logic of Truthmaking

In this chapter, I present *truthmaker semantics*. A formal semantics can help us systematise intuitions about the truthmaking relation, and that's the aim here. Truthmaker semantics can be seen as a refinement of possible worlds semantics, with applications where possible worlds semantics can be applied, but without many of the issues faced by possible worlds semantics.

Following Fine (2014, 2016), I distinguish two related notions of truthmaking: *exact* and *inexact*. Exact truthmaking holds when a truth is true precisely in virtue of the entity in question. Inexact truthmaking extends this notion: an inexact truthmaker for a proposition is one which contains, as a part, an exact truthmaker for that proposition. For each notion, I present a logical semantics and investigate the entailment relation to which it gives rise. The logic of inexact truthmaking turns out to correspond to a well-understand logical system: first-degree entailment. But the logic of exact truthmaking is new and surprising. On that logic, conjunctions do not entail their conjuncts. This feature makes the logic highly unusual. I investigate some of its features and provide a characterisation theorem, which characterises the semantic notion of exact entailment in purely syntactic terms.

Chapter 8: The Nature of Propositions

The truthmaking relation is closely aligned to metaphysical grounding, itself closely aligned to the natures of the grounded entities (chapter 6). So, we should expect truthmaking to bear a close relation to the metaphysical natures of the truths. Truths are propositions, and so we should expect there to be a close relation between our theory of truthmaking and our theory of what propositions are.

This theory of truthmaking suggests a simple yet powerful theory of what propositions are. They are entities constituted by their possible truthmakers (and perhaps their possible falsemakers, too). They are built from actual and possible states of affairs, in a way that tells us, very precisely, what would count as a truthmaker for that proposition, were it to exist.

Chapter 9: Dealing with Liars

Many theories of truth cannot deal with the truth-theoretic paradoxes, which include the Liar, 'this sentence is not true'. That in itself is an argument against such theories. Now that I've offered a theory in terms of truthmaking, I must show how it avoids these paradoxes. I'll begin by reviewing some attempts to solve the paradoxes by changing the underlying logic used to generate the problem. I'll argue that the revisions required are too severe. Instead, we should look to our theory of truth. If truth is truthmaking, as I've claimed here, then we can investigate the paradoxes in terms of truthmaking. For truthmaking reasoning to get a grip, there must be some proposition to be made true. So we can make progress by asking: what propositions do the paradoxical sentences express?

On the theory of propositions set out in chapter 8, the Liar sentence doesn't express any proposition at all. Propositions are constructed from possible truthmakers. But no state of affairs can possibly make the Liar true, and so the Liar doesn't express a proposition at all. This blocks the paradox. Moreover, this solution is immune to 'revenge' arguments, for all such arguments must focus on some content expressed. The same goes for the other paradoxes. I suggest that the truthmaking approach is the only adequate, stable response to the paradoxes. That, in itself, is a strong argument in its favour.

Notation

Throughout the book, I'll use standard logical notation (to the extent that such a thing exists!) with

'$\neg$' '$\wedge$' '$\vee$' '$\rightarrow$' '$\exists$' '$\forall$' '$\in$'

being the symbols for *negation* ('not'), *conjunction* ('and'), *disjunction* ('or'), *implication* ('if ... then'), *existential* and *universal quantification* ('there exists' and 'for all'), and *set membership* ('is a member of'), respectively. I'll use

'$\sqsubseteq$' '$\sqcup$'

for the *mereological* notions of *parthood* ('is a part of') and (the derivative notion of) *mereological sum* (or *fusion*), respectively. Other notation will be explained along the way, as it is introduced.

I'll use the italic letters '*A*', '*B*', '*C*' and so on as placeholders for English sentences. When I write 'blah blah blah *A*', you can insert any English declarative sentence you like in place of the '*A*': what I say should hold for any choice of sentence in place of '*A*'.

Since I'll frequently be talking about sentences, I'll employ the convention that sentences in single quotation marks are mentioned, rather than used (i.e., I'm talking about those quoted sentences, rather than asserting their content). When necessary, the single quote marks will also act as the Quine-quotes: ⌜ ⌝. (If you know why that's important, then you know enough to work out when single-quotes are used as Quine-quotes! If not, don't worry about it.) When it's obvious that sentences are being mentioned rather than used (for example, when discussing deductive relationships between sentences), I'll drop the quote marks: I'll write '*A* ⊢ *B*' rather than "'*A*' ⊢ '*B*'". (This is a logician's convention, often used but rarely mentioned.)

It is also useful to have some notation for the proposition *that A* (for any sentence '*A*'). It's become common to use angle brackets '⟨ ⟩' to denote propositions. This is somewhat unfortunate, since that notation is already used in mathematics to denote ordered *n*-tuples (sequences). But since I'll talk often of propositions and rarely of sequences, I'll follow the philosophers' convention of '⟨A⟩' for 'the proposition *that A*'. I'll use the alternative notation '⟨⟨ ⟩⟩' for ordered tuples (sequences) of entities. It's also useful to have some shorthand notation for 'the state of affairs *that A*', for which I'll use '[A]'.

OK, let's get on with it.

I Truth and Making True

1
Truth: Substantial or Insubstantial?

One of the biggest questions in the metaphysics of truth is whether truth is a substantial property. Does truth have a metaphysical nature, in virtue of which we can characterise what truth is? I say so. But deflationists say not: they claim truth is insubstantial. So I'll begin with deflationism: what the theory says (§1.1), how it needs to be formulated (§1.2), and why it doesn't work (§1.3 and §1.4). I'll then discuss pluralism about truth, which holds that truth is substantial in some cases but insubstantial in others (§1.5). This approach, too, has its problems (§1.6) and, I claim, we're better off with a univocal account of truth (§1.7).

1.1 Deflationism

DEFLATIONISTS HOLD that there's no big mystery to truth. We all agree that 'Bertie snuffles' is true if and only if Bertie snuffles, and similarly for any other sentence we might put in place of 'Bertie snuffles'. That much is common to nearly all theories of truth. Deflationists distinguish themselves by saying that's *all* there is to truth. Truth is the property, or concept, defined by all these instances of the *T-scheme*, which we might state (as a first attempt) as follows:

(T) '*A*' is true if and only if *A*.

That's all there is to truth. There's no big mystery, according to the deflationist.

In this chapter, I'm going to give two arguments against deflationism. The first claims that the deflationist breaches sound principles concerning *identity determination* (§1.3). I call this the *identity problem*. The second is that deflationism can't deal with the Liar paradox (§1.4). But I'm jumping ahead. We first need to be clear on the various theories which fall under the label 'deflationism'.

Deflationism is built around an equivalence between a statement that such-and-such is true, and a statement of what it takes for that truth to be true:

(ES) x is true if and only if y

In (T) above, these statements are given as sentences: "A' is true' and 'A', respectively. What is the status of this equivalence? Is it analytic, or otherwise necessary, or merely a material equivalence? What kind of entity features as the truth on the left-hand side of the equivalence? Is it a sentence, or a proposition, or something else? That is, do we form the left-hand side of the equivalence using a name for a sentence or a name for a proposition? And what exactly are we defining: a property, a concept, or something somehow 'thinner' than that?

Let's start with the final question: what kind of entity (if any) is the deflationist trying to define? Consider two truths:

(1.1) Anna knits wonderfully

(1.2) Usually placid Lenny barks at anything with wheels.

They have nothing in common, except they're both true. They have that in common. So, I would say, they have *something* in common, and that something is *being true*. That's a property, as I use the term, for a property is just something that different things can have in common. As Stoljar and Damnjanovic (1997) say,

> since [these propositions] are both true, we can say that they both have the property of being true. In this sense, the

deflationary theory is not denying that truth is a property: truth is the property that all true propositions have. (Stoljar and Damnjanovic 1997)

(I'll say more about properties, and why we should believe in them, in §2.4.)

I needn't insist that my deflationist opponent agree with me. She may say instead that she is analysing the *concept* of truth, or the predicate 'is true', as it's found in English. Of those deflationists who agree that they're interested in a property of truth, some say this is a 'purely logical' property. And by that, they mean that there's nothing to say about its nature, other than what we get from all instances of their preferred version of (ES). All I need for the first argument below (§1.3) is that there are propositions involving *truth*. Whatever kind of entity the deflationist takes *truth* to be, it's hard to deny that.

Next, what of the status (analytic, necessary, or otherwise) of the equivalence scheme? If it isn't necessary, then some instance is possibly false. Is it really possible for 'Bertie snuffles' to be true even though Bertie doesn't snuffle? Yes: those words could have meant something else. We (or other possible beings) could have used the words 'Bertie snuffles' to mean that Donald Trump is a moron. If that possible situation is otherwise much like ours, and Bertie never snuffles in that situation, then 'Bertie snuffles' is true in that situation, even though Bertie is not snuffling.

This isn't what we meant, of course, when we originally asked whether the equivalence scheme is necessary. We were asking whether it's necessarily true *holding fixed what our words mean*. We might try to express this idea as follows:

($T_{English}$) '*A*' is true in English (as it actually is) if and only if *A*.

Or we might instead go for:

(T_{prop}) The proposition *that A* is true if and only if *A*.

Both approaches attempt to hold fixed a content in evaluating whether it is true or otherwise in possible situations. (I'll discuss whether they are successful below.)

When the content of the truth in question is held fixed, it seems there is no possible situation in which one side of the equivalence is true and the other false. It cannot be true that Bertie is snuffling unless Bertie is in fact snuffling, and if it's true that he is, then he is. So we should take the equivalence scheme to be necessarily true. Deflationists may, in addition, take the equivalence scheme to be an analytic truth. (If it's analytic, then it's necessary, but the converse doesn't hold.) They offer it as a definition of truth (or of the predicate 'is true'), and definitional truths are analytic, if any are. I'm going to argue that the deflationist is in trouble, whatever status she thinks the equivalence scheme should have.

Finally, what should go in the place of '*x*' in '*x* is true' on the left of the equivalence scheme? Suppose it's a name for a sentence: call this view *sentential deflationism* (Vitola 1998). The sentential deflationist isn't interested in putting any old sentence-name on the left: she doesn't want to have to come up with an equivalence of the form 'Dave is true if and only if ...', where 'Dave' is a name for my favourite sentence. Instead, she's interested in forming sentence-names by placing sentences in quotation marks. Then, she can use the named sentence on the right-hand side of the equivalence, as in (T) above.

Following Quine, the view is sometimes called the 'disquotational' theory of truth'. He writes that, 'by calling the sentence ['Snow is white'] true, we call snow white. The truth predicate is a device of disquotation' (Quine 1986, 12) and that 'truth is disquotation' (Quine 1987, 213). Quine's view is a descendent of Frank Ramsey's brief remarks on truth (Ramsey 1927, 157–9), sometimes called 'the redundancy theory of truth'. Ramsey writes that "it is true that Cæsar was murdered' means no more than that Cæsar was murdered' (1927, 157). Ramsey thus takes (T) to be an analytic truth.

In what follows, I'll focus on sentential deflationism. We've already seen that this approach does not provide us with a necessary equivalence. But it does not even provide a materially adequate equivalence in all cases. When Emma calls from Sydney, she truthfully says, 'It's hot here'. But the corresponding instance of (T) is:

(1.3) 'It's hot here' is true if and only if it's hot here.

Well, as I write in England in winter, it certainly isn't hot here. So the right-hand side of (1.3) is false. If (1.3) were true, it would follow that 'it's hot here' is not true either. But (as said by Emma in Sydney) it is true. So (1.3) is false.

One might think the problem arises because we're talking about a sentence being true or false without specifying the relevant context. Rather than saying "it's hot here' is true", and leaving at that, we should instead specify the context in which it's true, giving us equivalences of the form:

(1.4) x is true in context c if and only if A.

But in order to guarantee that (1.4) is true, the context c must be the context of utterance (of the relevant instance of (1.4)). If the utterance is made as I write it, then the context of utterance is the one in which I am writing. That context has MJ as its agent (the author of the utterance), Tuesday 10 May 2016 as its time, and Nottingham as its place. This gives us instances of (ES) of the form:

(1.5) 'A' is true in context (MJ, Tuesday 10 May 2016, Nottingham) if and only if A.

Such instances are materially true biconditionals (and they are necessarily true if we add *English* to the context).

But such instances do not define *truth* (or 'is true'), for they are restricted to my context, here and now (and to sentences in English). They define 'is true-in-English for MJ on Tuesday 10 May 2016 in Nottingham'. That is not a particularly interesting concept to define (even for me, here and now). The deflationist intends to capture a notion of truth usable by for all language, any time and any place (and presumably in any given language too). Note that we can't move to this general concept of truth by universally generalising on the context. That will generalise only the left-hand side of the scheme, and so will give us materially false instances.

The mistake in this approach is that it attempts to capture truth-in-a-context for a given sentence. But we are interested instead in truth, simpliciter, of the content of a sentence-in-a-context. It is not a sentence, but rather what a use of that sentence says, on which we should focus. So deflationists do better to formulate their approach in terms of propositions, rather than sentences.

1.2 Deflationism with Propositions

Let's leave deflationism-with-sentences behind, and take a look at the version formulated in terms of propositions. The equivalences are formulated using a name (or other term) for a proposition. I'll write '⟨A⟩' for the proposition that A, so we obtain equivalences such as

(1.6) ⟨Bertie snuffles⟩ is true if and only if Bertie snuffles.

We don't need to say 'true in English', or relativize to a context of utterance, because a proposition already encodes all of this information: it is what is conveyed by a particular utterance in a particular context.

This looks to be a more promising deflationist approach. In general, the propositional deflationist takes truth to be implicitly defined by all instances of the following scheme:

(1.7) ⟨A⟩ is true if and only if A.

When the biconditional is taken as necessary (but not analytic), Horwich (1998) calls this the 'minimalist theory of truth'. I'll stick with 'propositional deflationism'.

I'll now argue that this approach is too limited in its scope: it accounts only for those propositions expressible in English. (I'll argue for this below.) Yet there are more truths than we can express (in English, or in any other natural language). For each real number r, it's true that r is a real number; and each such truth is distinct from the corresponding truth for each other real number. So there are non-denumerably many truths about real numbers, only a countable number of which can be expressed in English (or any other natural language).

To see why a theory based on (1.7) is limited to truths expressible in English (or any other natural language), first suppose that the theory consists of all English *sentences* of the form given by (1.7). That is, we take (1.7) to be an axiom schema, and the theory to be all of its instances (and nothing more). Then clearly, only those propositions expressible in English will be accounted for in the theory. So this can't be the right way to go.

Instead, the propositional deflationist can take her theory to consist of all *propositions* of the form indicated in (1.7). That is, her theory consists of all propositions ⟨⟨A⟩ is true if and only if A⟩. Since these propositions are not formulated in terms of English sentences, the theory then seems to account for the truth of propositions not expressible in English.

On further inspection, however, this attempt fails. We explained which propositions make up the theory in terms of the '⟨−⟩' construction, which we implicitly understood as follows: '⟨A⟩' denotes the proposition that A. That explanation relies on the proposition in question being something we can express. In effect, we have formed a name for that proposition from the sentence 'A'. Rather than enclosing it in quotation marks, as the sentential deflationist (or disquotationalist) does, we enclosed it in the proposition-name-forming marks, '⟨' and '⟩'. This limits the account to propositions expressed by the sentences over which the metavariable 'A' ranges.

The propositional deflationist should instead say that her theory concerns a *function*, from propositions to biconditional propositions, such that if the input is ⟨A⟩ then the output is:

(T-PROP) ⟨⟨A⟩ is true if and only if A⟩

Horwich (1998, 19) takes his 'minimalist' (propositional deflationist) theory to consist of all the outputs from this function.

To make sense of this proposal, we need to know more about what kind of entity the deflationist takes propositions to be. Are they sets of possible worlds, structured entities, or something else entirely? She should not take them to be sets of possible worlds. Each instance of (T-PROP) is a necessary truth and there is but one necessary set-of-possible-worlds proposition: the set of all possible worlds. So if the deflationist were to formulate her account in terms of possible world propositions, there would be just one instance of (T-PROP). The (T-PROP)-forming function would be a constant function on propositions, mapping each $\langle A \rangle$ to the set $\{w \mid w \text{ is a possible world}\}$. But neither that constant function, nor that single proposition, helps us explain what *truth* is. (Horwich (1998, 29–31) is clear that the propositions of his theory are not sets of possible worlds. His theory requires infinitely many instances of (T-PROP).)

The deflationist should not take the propositions of her theory to be *pleonastic* entities, either. The pleonastic account holds that 'propositions are shadows of sentences', brought into existence by 'something-from-nothing transformations' (Schiffer 2003, 71). An example of such a transformation takes us from

(1.8) Bertie is snuffling

to the 'pleonastic equivalents'

(1.9) That Bertie is snuffling is true;

(1.10) It is true that Bertie is snuffling.

In (1.8), 'Bertie' is the only singular term. But both (1.9) and (1.10) contain the singular term 'that Bertie is snuffling', which refers to a proposition. Schiffer's idea is that, although such transformations introduce new entities (propositions, in this case), they are *conservative extensions* to any theory. That means (roughly) that if we extend a theory T to a larger theory T' via such transformations, then nothing statable in the vocabulary of T is entailed by T' but not by T. (See Schiffer 2003, 54–57 for refinements on this definition.)

A deflationist cannot accept this account of propositions for precisely the reason she cannot accept instances of (1.7) as exhausting her account of truth. The truths outstrip the truths expressible in language. Pleonastic propositions are 'shadows of sentences', and so are too few in number to capture all the truths.

The best option for the deflationist is to take propositions to be structured entities. One version of this view comes from Russell (1903), in a letter to Frege:

> I believe that in spite of all of its snowfields Mont Blanc itself is a component part of what is actually asserted in the proposition "Mont Blanc is more than 4000 meters high." We do not assert the thought, for that is a private psychological matter; we assert the object of the thought, and this is, to my mind, a certain complex (an objective proposition, one might say) in which Mont Blanc is itself a component part. (Russell 1904/1980, 169)

On this account, the proposition *that Anna loves Bec* is a structured entity containing Anna herself, the relation *loving*, and Bec herself, in that order. Russell soon changed his mind (Russell 1905), but his briefly held idea has become influential. King (1995, 1996, 2012), Salmon (1986, 2005), and Soames (1987, 2008) each defend a version of the view. An alternative account takes propositions to be structures containing *Fregean senses*: modes of presentation of worldly entities, rather than the entities themselves. (Indeed, Frege (1904/1980, 163) had expressed that view to Russell, prior to the letter quoted above.)

Let's use the term *semantic value* to denote whatever entity a term contributes to the proposition expressed by an utterance. Russellians hold that semantic values (of names and predicates, at least) are particulars, properties, and relations, whereas Fregeans take them to be the senses of those terms.

King (1995, 1996, 2012) argues that the structure of structured propositions is provided by the syntactic structure of the corresponding sentence. The sentences

(1.11) Bertie snuffles

(1.12) Bertie loves Anna

have the structures

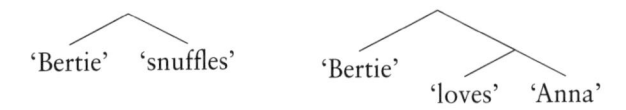

```
    ⌒                    ⌒
'Bertie'  'snuffles'   'Bertie'   ⌒
                               'loves'  'Anna'
```

respectively. King thinks of the propositions they express as complexes in which the semantic values of the terms (Anna and Bertie, the *snuffling* property, and the *loving* relation) are structured by these tree-like relations:

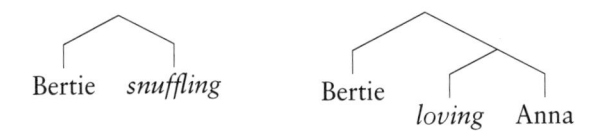

```
   ⌒                     ⌒
Bertie  snuffling     Bertie   ⌒
                            loving  Anna
```

The Fregean approach to structured propositions is very similar, except that we find Fregean senses, or modes of presentation, in place of the Russellian's particulars, properties and relations. So the Fregean versions of the above structures are:

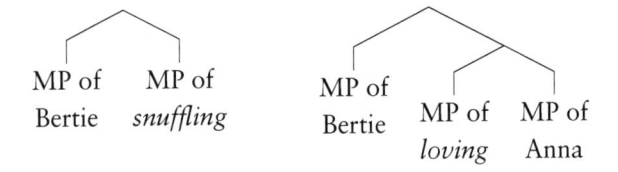

```
    ⌒                       ⌒
 MP of   MP of           MP of    ⌒
 Bertie  snuffling       Bertie  MP of   MP of
                                 loving  Anna
```

Note that Bertie, Anna, *snuffling*, and *loving* each have multiple modes of presentation, and so the phrases 'MP of Bertie', 'MP of Anna', and so on are intended as indefinite, not definite, descriptions.

I think, with Lewis (1970), that these structures are best understood as ordered tuples, themselves understood as sets. (If we think in terms of sentence structure, we are thinking of sentence *types*, understood as sequences of word types; and the best way to understand sequences is as sets.) King (2012) and Zalta (1989) disagree. I won't assume this identification in what follows.

Let's return to the deflationist's account. It should be clear that the structured approach to propositions, whether Russellian or Fregean, suits her purposes well. The structure involved is relatively fine-grained. Each account allows for distinct but logically equivalent propositions. Even very closely related propositions, such as ⟨A ∧ B⟩ and ⟨B ∧ A⟩, will be treated as distinct entities, on a structured approach. So the deflationist's function from each ⟨A⟩ to the corresponding instance of (T-PROP) will be non-trivial, and there will be infinitely many such instances. In short, both the Russellian and Fregean versions of structured propositions seem to be good ways to spell out the deflationist strategy.

How should we understand the function from propositions to instance of (T-PROP), given that those propositions are structured entities? An instance of (T-PROP), ⟨⟨A⟩ is true iff A⟩, has ⟨A⟩ as a constituent *on the right of the biconditional*. (Compare: ⟨A ∧ B⟩ has ⟨A⟩ and ⟨B⟩ as constituents, but is not notated '⟨⟨A⟩ ∧ ⟨B⟩⟩'.) The constituent on the left of the biconditional is a proposition, ⟨⟨A⟩ is true⟩, which itself has ⟨⟨A⟩⟩ as a constituent. On the Fregean interpretation of structured propositions, this is a mode of presentation of the original proposition, ⟨A⟩.

(It may help to think of the '⟨ ⟩' notation on the model of quotation marks. 'Emma', the name, is a constituent of the sentence 'Emma is a Sydneysider', which is about Emma, the person. So '"Emma" is a marvellous name', a sentence about the name 'Emma', doesn't have 'Emma' as a constituent. Rather, it contains '"Emma"', a name for a name. In just the same way, ⟨⟨A⟩ is true⟩ contains ⟨⟨A⟩⟩.)

If the (T-PROP)-instance ⟨⟨A⟩ is true iff A⟩ is a function of ⟨A⟩, and the former has ⟨⟨A⟩⟩ as a constituent, then ⟨⟨A⟩⟩ must be a function of ⟨A⟩. So by the extensionality of functions, ⟨⟨A⟩⟩ = ⟨⟨B⟩⟩ if ⟨A⟩ = ⟨B⟩. This puts pressure on the Fregean interpretation, since in general, a proposition will have many distinct modes of presentation. There is, in general, no canonical function from propositions to modes of presentation of those propositions. Button (2014) runs an argument along these lines, concluding that the deflationist must formulate her theory in terms of Russellian structured propositions.

The worry can be overcome if the Fregean deflationist formulates her theory in terms of a function from *modes of presentation* of a proposition to instances of (T-PROP). This option is made available because, on the Fregean view, each mode of presentation (together with a circumstance, or possible world) uniquely determines its denotation (if it has one). So, holding the actual world (or actual circumstances) fixed, we can formulate a function f from Fregean modes of presentation to their denotations. Now let S be any mode of presentation of a proposition $\langle A \rangle$ (so that $fS = \langle A \rangle$). We can define a further function p on such modes of presentation, such that $pS = \langle S$ is true if and only if $fS \rangle$. Given the Fregean notion of a proposition, this is the instance of (T-PROP) corresponding to $\langle A \rangle$.

The Russellian interpretation handles the worry in a more straightforward way. On the Russellian view, a proposition about an entity e contains e itself. In particular, a proposition about proposition $\langle A \rangle$ will contain $\langle A \rangle$ itself. As a consequence, $\langle \langle A \rangle \rangle = \langle A \rangle$ on the Russellian view. This neatly dissolves the worry.

In sum, the Russellian and the Fregean notions of a proposition are the only live options for the deflationist. The Russellian deflationist formulates her theory of truth in terms of a function from propositions to instances of (T-PROP). The Fregean deflationist, by contrast, should formulate her theory in terms of a function from modes of presentation of propositions to instances of (T-PROP).

1.3 The Identity Problem

So far in this chapter, I've been focusing on what the deflationist's theory of truth should look like. Now I'll move on to a criticism of deflationism. I'll present two main arguments. First, the deflationist theory is incompatible with core metaphysical principles about identity. (Strictly speaking, this argument is aimed at deflationists who take truth to be an entity of some kind, such as Horwich (1998). But, as I argued above, that is a very minimal assumption.) Second, the deflationist theory is inconsistent. This argument will appear in §1.4. (Bar-On et al. (2000) offer a further interesting argument against deflationism, which I won't discuss here.)

Let's recap some important points we've learnt about deflationism. It must be stated in terms of propositions, and those propositions must be structured entities with constituents of some kind. (That's because, to state her theory, the deflationist needs to quantify over constituents of those propositions.) Structured propositions may, but need not, be set theoretic entities: we can leave it open just what notion of structure is involved. The constituents are either particulars, properties and relations; or they are senses (modes of presentation) of various entities. In the former case, we have Russellian propositions; in the latter, we have Fregean propositions.

Whatever the exact nature of these structured propositions, their identity is determined by their constituents being structured as they are. If they are set-theoretic tuples, then their identities are determined purely by their constituents. If there is some primitive structure-forming relation or operation involved, then a proposition's identity is given by its constituents plus the relation or the operation involved in structuring them. Whatever the account, each constituent of a proposition will contribute to the identity of the proposition involved. Change but one constituent and you change the proposition in question.

As a consequence, the identity of each constituent must be fully determined independently of the propositions in which it appears. We can think, metaphorically, of creating a proposition by taking some suitable entities and placing them in a suitable structure. To do that, we'd first need a stock of suitable entities to act as the constituents. Those entities have to be fully determinate things in their own right. (Of course, we don't create propositions at all. Propositions aren't created in a causal way. The metaphor of creation is about what metaphysically determines what, or what fixes the identity of what, and not about what causes what.)

This principle causes havoc with the deflationist's theory, regardless of whether she opts for Russellian or Fregean propositions. Let's first consider how the problem arises in the case of Russellian propositions. On the Russellian version, the deflationist's theory of truth includes all Russellian propositions which are instances of (T-PROP). That theory wholly determines what property *truth* is. Each proposition in the theory plays a role in fixing which property *truth* is. Deflationists accept this. If we missed out on some instances of (T-PROP), or if we included additional propositions, then we would have fixed some other property, not *truth*. So each instance of (T-PROP) partially determines which property *truth* is.

The problem is that, on the Russellian version of deflationism, the property *truth* also partially determines the identity of each instance of (T-PROP). On the Russellian view, ⟨⟨A⟩ is true⟩ contains both the proposition ⟨A⟩ and the property *truth*. Each instance of (T-PROP) is a biconditional structure which contains this proposition and hence which contains (at some level of its structure) the property *truth*.

To illustrate: if propositions are tuples and BICON is the semantic value of the material biconditional 'if and only if', then an instance of (T-PROP) is the tuple:

$$\langle\!\langle \text{BICON}, \langle\!\langle \langle\!\langle \langle A \rangle, truth \rangle\!\rangle, \langle A \rangle \rangle\!\rangle \rangle\!\rangle$$

(To understand the notation here, recall that '⟨A⟩' denotes a proposition, whereas '⟨⟨·⟩⟩' is the notation for tuples.) Each such (T-PROP) instance partially determines the identity of *truth*, which in turn partially determines the identity of each instance of (T-PROP). But that's precisely what the logic of partial determination rules out.

Here's a specific instance of the problem, which brings the issue out sharply. Take the class of all instances of (T-PROP). Call it $\mathcal{T}$. (This is the deflationist's theory of truth, although that is inessential to this instance of the problem.) $\mathcal{T}$ itself has a number of properties. It's a class, for example. So ⟨$\mathcal{T}$ is a class⟩ is true. This result needs to be delivered by the relevant instance of (T-PROP):

(1.13) ⟨⟨$\mathcal{T}$ is a class⟩ is true if and only if $\mathcal{T}$ is a class⟩.

On the Russellian view, that proposition contains $\mathcal{T}$, which itself contains that very proposition. This rules out the view on which propositions are set-theoretic entities (for membership chains must be well founded). But even if propositions do not contain their constituents in the same way as sets contain their constituents, the basic problem remains: we cannot have proposition (1.13) partially determining the identity of $\mathcal{T}$ whilst $\mathcal{T}$ partially determines the identity of proposition (1.13). So the Russellian version of deflationism is untenable.

It won't help the deflationist to insist that there's no such thing as the class of all instances of (T-PROP). We could take instead the mereological fusion of all such instances; or we could quantify plurally over them. In each case, an analogous problem can be formulated. We can even formulate a version of the problem (although not so cleanly) by focusing on single instances of (T-PROP). Let $\langle T \rangle$ be any instance of the (T-PROP) scheme. Then $\langle T \rangle$ partially determines the identity of the property *truth* and *truth* partially determines the identity of $\langle T \rangle$. But that is unacceptable.

One could try to block this conclusion by insisting that partial identity determination may have symmetric instances, in which x partly determines y's identity, and y partly determines x's. (That is a version of *metaphysical interdependence* (Bliss 2014; Thompson 2016b), which I'll discuss a little more in §6.5.) I don't know of any theory of propositions which can accept this result. But even if there are such theories, this is a substantive thesis about the metaphysical nature of truth: that it is metaphysically interdependent on certain other entities. Deflationists, at pains to deny that truth has any substantial nature, have no business with such theories.

On the face of it, this problem should not affect the Fregean version of deflationism. On that view, Fregean senses are the constituents of propositions. So the property *being true* is not a constituent of $\langle\langle A \rangle$ is true$\rangle$ and similar propositions. Rather, such propositions are structures containing modes of presentation of $\langle A \rangle$ and of *being true*.

But the problem, in a related form, rules out this version of deflationism. On the Fregean version, modes of presentation of *being true* partially determine the identity of propositions (the instances of (T-PROP)) which determine what truth is. So the identity of *being true* is partly determined by modes of presentation of *being true*. But quite generally, this cannot be. For some entity y to be a mode of presentation of some entity x, we require that the identity of x be fully determined independently of y. Otherwise, no sense could be made of y being a mode of presentation *of* x. So, in particular, *being true*'s identity cannot be determined, even in part, by its modes of presentation. So the Fregean version of deflationism is untenable, just as the Russellian version is.

(It's not out of the question that someone will offer a theory on which entities may depend for their identity on their modes of presentation. But as above, applying that theory to the nature of truth results in a substantial thesis about what truth is, and deflationists have no business there.) These were the only options for the deflationist: the Russellian and the Fregean routes. Both are untenable. So deflationism itself is untenable.

1.4 Paradox

Time now for my second case against deflationism: it is inconsistent. This argument is independent of the one above. It's a familiar argument, based around the Liar paradox. Nevertheless, I'll argue, deflationists haven't found a satisfactory solution. The problem is right at the heart of deflationist approaches, for the inconsistency is generated by the key player in their theory, (T-PROP):

(T-PROP) $\langle\langle A \rangle$ is true if and only if $A\rangle$

Deflationist theories may differ on what they add to the (T-PROP) instances; but there's nothing you can add to an inconsistent theory to make it consistent.

The problem is that certain instances of (T-PROP), together with standard logical reasoning, generate contradictions. The most famous case is the liar sentence, 'this very sentence is not true'. (T-PROP) says that the proposition expressed by the liar sentence is true if and only if it is not true. So if it is true then it is not true; and if it is not true, then it is true. Either way, contradiction ensues; and the only bit of logic involved was *modus ponens* on each direction of the 'if and only if' in (T-PROP).

The liar is a problem for everyone, threatening any theory of truth with inconsistency. But it hits the deflationist particularly hard. She must avoid paradoxical instances of (T-PROP) in stating her theory but, I'll argue, she has no way to do this. She may not even be able to state her theory at all.

What responses are available to the deflationist? For that matter, what responses are available to any of us? One is to deny the logical steps involved in generating the contradictory conclusion. But that move is hard. Logicians have long investigated what would have to go in order to restore consistency, and the answer is: an awful lot. (I'll discuss revisionary theories in detail in chapter 9.)

Another option is to deny that (T-PROP) really does have an instance saying that the liar is true if and only if it is not true. Given that (T-PROP) is formulated in terms of propositions, this would be the case if there were no liar proposition, saying of itself that it is not true. The problem with this suggestion is that, given the deflationist's use of structured propositions (plus other plausible assumptions), there *must* be such a proposition.

To see why this is, let's first consider the parallel argument showing that there must be a liar sentence. Gödel (1931) used an ingenious construction to show that, in languages powerful enough to represent their own syntax (so that they can name their own sentences), there will exist self-referential sentences. His own example was a sentence that says of itself that it is not provable. Shortly after, Carnap (1934) realised that the argument generalises. So long as a language can represent the *diagonal function*, which maps an open sentence Ax to the sentence $A(\ulcorner Ax \urcorner)$, there will be some sentence B such that $B \leftrightarrow A(\ulcorner B \urcorner)$ is a theorem. In particular, we can take Ax to be $\neg \text{True}(x)$. Then B is a sentence equivalent to $\neg \text{True}(\ulcorner B \urcorner)$, saying of itself that it is not true. The equivalence $B \leftrightarrow A(\ulcorner B \urcorner)$ is a fixed point of the diagonal function. Carnap realised that the fixed point theorem tells us that B must exist. (Gaifman (2006) is a good source on the history of this idea.)

Now let's apply this idea to the deflationist's propositions. We can think of structured propositions as sentences written in a special ontological language, whose names are particulars (or senses thereof) and whose predicates are properties and relations (or senses thereof). So to generate a liar-like proposition Gödel-style, we'll need some trick to represent propositions as name-like propositional constituents. But the deflationist is up to her eyeballs in such tricks. The left-hand side of (T-PROP)-instances say, of some proposition $\langle A \rangle$, that it's true. We notated this as the proposition $\langle \langle A \rangle$ is true$\rangle$. In effect, the deflationist uses a proposition which names another, saying that the named proposition is true. So, reasoning Gödel-style, there'll be a proposition $\langle A \rangle$ which contains as a constituent a name, $\langle \langle A \rangle \rangle$, for itself.

We can run the same argument Carnap-style, using the fixed point theorem. All we need for this is that the deflationist's language of propositions represents the diagonal function. But of course it does: it's true that the diagonal function is a function, so there must be an instance of (T-PROP) whose left-hand side says precisely that. Then the fixed point theorem guarantees that there's a Russellian proposition $\langle \lambda \rangle$ equivalent to $\langle \langle \lambda \rangle$ is not true$\rangle$. Plugging that proposition into (T-PROP) then gives us the proposition $\langle \langle \lambda \rangle$ is true if and only if $\langle \lambda \rangle$ is not true$\rangle$, which quickly descends into explicit contradiction.

At this point, you might well be thinking something like the following. *Hang on, Jago. You're telling us that the deflationist is in a pickle because of liar propositions. But, at some point in this book, you're going to give us a theory of truth. So won't the problem come back to bite you, too? And if you have a solution, why can't the deflationist use it too?*

That's a good thought to have. Anyone claiming to have a theory of truth should say why the liar doesn't KO the theory right at the start of the match. But here's the crucial point. Later on, in chapter 8, I'm going to explain what propositions are using *truth* and *truthmaking*. To understand propositions, I'll argue, we first have to understand the nature of truthmakers. I'll then argue that, with propositions so understood, we avoid the liar. (Indeed, I think this is the only way to avoid the liar.) But this is an explanation the deflationist can't accept, for it commits us to a substantial, non-deflationary theory of truth. Horwich (1998, 41–2) concedes the crucial parts of the problematic reasoning. He doesn't give up on large chunks of logic; and he doesn't say that truth can't apply to propositions or that there is no liar-like proposition. Rather, he concedes that not all instances of (T-PROP) are part of the deflationist's theory. So we need to know: which instances of (T-PROP) are part of her theory? It's worth quoting what Horwich says in full:

> it suffices for us to concede that certain instances of the equivalence scheme [(T-PROP)] are not to be included as axioms in the minimal theory, and to note that the principles governing our selection of excluded instances are, in order of priority: (a) that the minimal theory not engender 'liar-type' contradictions; (b) that the set of excluded instances be as small as possible; and—perhaps just as important as (b)—(c) that there be a constructive specification of the excluded instances that is as simple as possible. (Horwich 1998, 42)

My reaction on reading this for the first time was a dejected *oh*. We aren't going to be told exactly what the theory is? All we get is its general shape, and the hope that there's some method out there, yet to be discovered, for saying exactly what's in the theory. The theory is certainly deflationary—of one's expectations, if nothing else. (See also Marques 2016.)

But worse than that, conditions (a) and (b) conflict. Consider this version of the liar paradox:

(ABOVE) ⟨The proposition below is not true⟩

(BELOW) ⟨The proposition above is true⟩

If (ABOVE) is true, then (BELOW) is not true. But if (BELOW) is not true, then (ABOVE) is not true. So (ABOVE) is not true if it is true. But if (ABOVE) is not true, then (BELOW) is true, and hence (ABOVE) is true after all. Either way, we have a contradiction.

Notice how we needed both instances of (T-PROP), one for (ABOVE) and one for (BELOW), to generate the contradiction. Remove any one of those instances, and the problem goes away. (There'll be other liar-like problems lurking, but not this particular instance.) So which instance of (T-PROP) should we reject? One must reject one; there's no reason to favour one over the other; but rejecting both would violate (b), for we'd then be rejecting more than is strictly necessary.

It might be that, following Horwich's conditions (a) and (b), we end up with *multiple* theories of truth. One of those theories gives up on (T-PROP) for (ABOVE), and another gives up on (T-PROP) for (BELOW). Then there will be uncountably many deflationary theories of truth (for there are uncountably many such liar-like cases). If the deflationist takes this approach, then she has to give up on her ambition of defining a single, unified property of *truth* (or even a single, unified predicate 'is true'). Rather, she'll have to say that there's (uncountably) many truth-like properties, no one of which is any more deserving than the others of the name 'truth'. But deflationists are typically monists about truth (Dodd 2013).

One particularly bad consequence of the approach is this. If there are distinct truth-like properties $truth_i$ and $truth_j$, then we expect there to be truths$_i$ about $truth_j$ and, similarly, truths$_j$ about $truth_i$. But there can't be too many of these, otherwise the liar will come back to bite us. There must be gaps (compared to what we expect) in how the different $truth_i$ properties interact. But then it looks like the deflationist project is radically and irreparably incomplete. In the next section, we'll see other problems for theories with multiple truth-like properties.

1.5 Pluralism about Truth

Let's move on from deflationism. Truth isn't an insubstantial property. It involves relations between propositions and entities in the world. Question: does truth always involve such relations? Or only in certain cases? Is the substantial, relational notion suitable for analysing truth across the board? Or is a more subtle approach required?

Suppose we accept that there's a state of affairs *that Bertie is snuffling* and that this is intimately connected with making ⟨Bertie is snuffling⟩ true. We might then think that this relationship between proposition and state of affairs accounts well for that truth. But then we notice that this kind of explanation seems better suited to some truths than others. Bertie stands before us in all his glory, snuffling and wheezing and wagging his tail. We can get a grip on what it takes for a proposition to correspond to him and the ways he is. It's harder to see how truths about justice, or fashion, or whether a joke was funny, correspond to the world in the same way.

Fashion is notoriously fickle. What's in one day is out another. What's fashionable seems to be set by a complex pattern of trend-setters and early-adopters. But it also seems that one gets to be a trend-setter by being fashionable in the first place: it's not a job with a fixed set of prerequisites. So on what, ultimately, do truths about fashion depend? Nothing so substantial as Bertie and his snuffling, one might think. One might even think that there's little more we can say about the various ups-and-downs of mullets, sailor outfits, and Jacobean ruffs than this: it's true that they're fashionable if (and because) they're fashionable. If so, the deflationist's approach (previous worries notwithstanding) looks good in this context. Perhaps the same goes for truths about justice and humour.

(For the record, I don't side with any of this. Truths about humour do relate to substantial facts, albeit facts partly involving us. But I want to see where this opposing thought takes us.)

Someone attracted to this line of reasoning might go for *pluralism* about truth (Wright 1992, 1996, 2001, 2003). She'll hold that what goes for truth in one domain of discourse might not hold in other domains. When talking about physical objects, correspondence might be the best explanation of truth; when talking about justice, or humour, or fashion, a lightweight deflationist approach might be more appropriate. Pluralism about truth holds that there is no single property (or concept) of truth. There might be *correspondence truth*, *deflationary truth*, *truth-as-stable-evidence*, and perhaps many other kinds of truth out there.

In the debate between substantial and deflationary theories of truth, pluralism may seem to get the best of both worlds. Truth is substantial where correspondence with reality is an appropriate notion; but otherwise, truth is insubstantial. Yet for all its advantages, pluralism isn't the way to go. In what follows, I'm going to focus on Wright's (1992, 2001, 2003) account of pluralism, since I find it the best motivated and most developed account. But similar problems affect other pluralist accounts.

Let's focus on two domains of discourse, a 'heavyweight' one, in which there are mind-independent states of affairs, and a 'lightweight' one, in which (according to the pluralist) there are not. (The 'heavyweight'/'lightweight' terminology is from Pedersen and Wright 2013.) We might take discourses about medium-sized material objects and humour as examples. To each domain, the pluralist associates a truth property. So we have $truth_{heavy}$, which, let's suppose, requires a truth to be related to a mind-independent state of affairs; and $truth_{light}$, which doesn't. Lightweight truth might consist in coherence, or superassertability, or something else entirely. If you like, you could pick one of these notions and read it in place of '$truth_{light}$'. The particular definitions we give here aren't too important, so long as the two properties make conflicting demands on a proposition's truth.

For Wright, a predicate gets to be a truth-predicate by obeying a number of platitudes, including the T-scheme (1992, 34; see also 2001, 760 and 2003, 271–2). But suppose both $truth_{heavy}$ and $truth_{light}$ obey the T-scheme across the board:

(1.14) $\langle A \rangle$ is $true_{heavy}$ if and only if A;

(1.15) $\langle A \rangle$ is $true_{light}$ if and only if A.

We can then quickly conclude that $\langle A \rangle$ is $true_{heavy}$ if and only if $\langle A \rangle$ is $true_{light}$, for any $\langle A \rangle$. In other words, $truth_{heavy}$ and $truth_{light}$ will coincide: whatever is true in one way will also be true in the other way. Moreover, if (1.14) and (1.15) are necessary truths, then it will be necessary that $truth_{heavy}$ and $truth_{light}$ coincide. But this is precisely what the pluralist doesn't want to say, for she denies that some truths (e.g., about fashion or humour) are true in the heavyweight, correspondence way.

So $truth_{heavy}$ won't obey the T-scheme across the board; and neither will $truth_{light}$. Each will obey a version of the T-scheme restricted to that property's domain of discourse. (So $truth_{heavy}$ will obey the T-scheme for propositions about material objects, say, whereas $truth_{light}$ will obey the T-scheme for propositions about humour.)

There's a major problem with this approach. Logical entailment (as usually understood) requires truth to be preserved from premises to conclusion. This presents no problem to the pluralist approach when premises and conclusion of an entailment belong to the same domain of discourse. But what about when they do not? Suppose $\langle A \rangle$ and $\langle B \rangle$ are propositions from different domains of discourse, which are subject to different truth-properties. How, then, are we to account for the valid inference from $\langle A \rangle$ to $\langle A \vee B \rangle$, from $\langle A \wedge B \rangle$ to $\langle A \rangle$, or from $\langle A \vee B \rangle$ and $\langle \neg B \rangle$ to $\langle A \rangle$?

The pluralist has two options here. She may say that there's some specific truth-property, of a kind with $truth_{heavy}$ and $truth_{light}$, which is preserved from premises to conclusion in an entailment. Alternatively, she may say that, in addition to the specific truth-properties, there's also a generic truth-property, which is possessed by any proposition whenever it possesses some more specific truth-property. She will then claim that it is the generic truth-property, and not any of the specific ones, which is preserved from premises to conclusion in a valid entailment. (Wright (2013) discusses these options.)

Suppose the pluralist opts for the former view: for each valid inference, there is some specific truth-property which is preserved from premises to conclusions. (It need not be the same specific truth property for each valid inference.) Since each specific truth-property attaches to some domain of discourse, this option requires that the premises and conclusion of each valid argument all belong to the same domain. So, immediately, this constraint forces the pluralist's hand.

Consider *disjunction introduction*: the inference from ⟨A⟩ (or from ⟨B⟩) to ⟨A ∨ B⟩. Suppose ⟨A⟩ belongs to a lightweight domain, subject to *truth*~light~, and ⟨B⟩ to a heavyweight domain, subject to *truth*~heavy~. Since ⟨A⟩ entails ⟨A ∨ B⟩, the latter must also belong to the lightweight domain. But since ⟨B⟩ also entails ⟨A ∨ B⟩, ⟨A ∨ B⟩ must also belong to the heavyweight domain. In general, ⟨A ∨ B⟩ will belong to whichever domains ⟨A⟩ belongs to, plus whichever domains ⟨B⟩ belongs to.

Already, this result feels suspect. We said above that each truth-property obeys a restricted T-scheme, limited in each case to a specific domain. If ⟨A ∨ B⟩ belongs to both the lightweight and the heavyweight domain, then we have:

(1.16) ⟨A ∨ B⟩ is true$_{light}$ if and only if A ∨ B

(1.17) ⟨A ∨ B⟩ is true$_{heavy}$ if and only if A ∨ B

and hence ⟨A ∨ B⟩ is true$_{light}$ if and only if ⟨A ∨ B⟩ is true$_{heavy}$. But clearly, this is not the case. Suppose ⟨A⟩ is true$_{light}$ but ⟨B⟩ is false$_{heavy}$. Then ⟨A ∨ B⟩ is true because of ⟨A⟩'s truth: it is true$_{light}$, but not true$_{heavy}$. ⟨B⟩ is false$_{heavy}$ and (by hypothesis) ⟨A⟩ is not the kind of proposition for which there exist mind-independent states of affairs. Then there is no mind-independent state of affairs to which ⟨A ∨ B⟩ corresponds, and so ⟨A ∨ B⟩ is not true$_{heavy}$, contrary to the pluralist's restricted T-scheme.

A pluralist could avoid this specific issue by denying the T-equivalences linking ⟨A ∨ B⟩ to any specific truth-property. She will retain the domain-specific T-equivalences only for logically atomic sentences. In their place, she can hold that ⟨A ∨ B⟩ possesses whatever truth-properties that ⟨A⟩ and ⟨B⟩ possess individually. (This is to move further away from the standard T-scheme as a means for characterising truth.)

This move requires an analysis of the truth-properties of each logically complex proposition, analogous to the clause just given for disjunction. Let's consider conjunction: what truth-properties will ⟨A ∧ B⟩ have, given that (let us suppose) ⟨A⟩ is true$_{light}$ and ⟨B⟩ is true$_{heavy}$? Is it true$_{light}$? Is it true$_{heavy}$? Is it some other kind of truth?

This is the issue at the heart of Tappolet's (1997) *problem of mixed conjunctions*. When ⟨A⟩ is a lightweight truth and ⟨B⟩ a heavyweight truth, we do not want to say that ⟨A ∧ B⟩ is a heavyweight truth in the same way that ⟨B⟩ is. ⟨B⟩'s truth carries ontological commitment to a mind-independent state of affairs, according to the alethic pluralist: it is true if and only if there exists a a mind-independent state of affairs *that B*. But ⟨A ∧ B⟩ is not like this. By assumption, there is no mind-independent state of affairs *that A*, and so there's no mind-independent state of affairs *that A ∧ B*.

Neither should we say that ⟨A ∧ B⟩ is a lightweight truth, in the way that ⟨A⟩ is. Lightweight truths are those made true in some way other than by correspondence to a mind-independent state of affairs. Suppose ⟨A⟩ belongs to a domain where truth consists in coherence (or superassertability, or facts about our potential responses, or something like that). ⟨A ∧ B⟩'s truth isn't like that. To be true, it requires ⟨B⟩ to be true, and ⟨B⟩ requires a mind-independent state of affairs. So ⟨A ∧ B⟩ too requires a mind-objective state of affairs, *that B*, to exist. Coherence (or superassertability, or facts about our potential responses) alone won't suffice for ⟨A ∧ B⟩'s truth. It is neither a lightweight nor a heavyweight truth.

Cotnoir (2009) argues that the problem can be resolved without commitment to a generic truth-property. His suggestion proceeds by first considering truth-properties for negations and disjunctions. He argues that ⟨¬A⟩ is true (or false) in whichever way ⟨A⟩ is false (or true): thus ⟨¬A⟩ belongs to whichever domains ⟨A⟩ belongs. He also accepts that a disjunction ⟨A ∨ B⟩ is true in whichever ways ⟨A⟩ or ⟨B⟩ are individually. Thus, ⟨A ∨ B⟩ belongs to all those domains which contain either ⟨A⟩ or ⟨B⟩.

The second step in Cotnoir's proposal, based on the De Morgan law connecting conjunction and disjunction, is to take ⟨A ∧ B⟩ to belong to the same domains as ⟨¬(¬A ∨ ¬B)⟩. Cotnoir finds the idea 'promising',

> as it does not generate a generic truth property, it requires no distinct truth property for compounds, and it treats all truth-functional connectives in a unified way. (Cotnoir 2009, 478)

44 TRUTH: SUBSTANTIAL OR INSUBSTANTIAL?

Cotnoir's suggestion treats each of $\langle A \vee B \rangle$, $\langle \neg A \vee \neg B \rangle$, $\langle \neg (\neg A \vee \neg B) \rangle$ and $\langle A \wedge B \rangle$ as belonging to the same domains as each other. These are all the domains to which either $\langle A \rangle$ or $\langle B \rangle$ belong. But this is just the situation we considered above. If $\langle A \rangle$ belongs to a lightweight domain and $\langle B \rangle$ to a heavyweight domain, then $\langle A \wedge B \rangle$ will belong to both the lightweight and the heavyweight domain. It will be both true$_{\text{light}}$ and true$_{\text{heavy}}$. But as we just saw, $\langle A \wedge B \rangle$ is neither true$_{\text{light}}$ nor true$_{\text{heavy}}$. So Cotnoir's suggestion can't be maintained.

This problem runs deep for the alethic pluralist. I can't see how she can avoid Cotnoir's suggestion. Domains of discourse, and the corresponding truth properties, are supposed to reflect something like the general topic of the proposition in question. But the De Morgan rules preserve topic, as does double-negation elimination. The semantic relationship between $\neg (A \vee B)$ and $\neg A \wedge \neg B$ is as tight as can be: 'not either' is just a different way of expressing 'not the one and not the other'. Similarly, 'not both' is a way to express 'either not one or not the other'. Indeed, I think it's highly plausible that $\langle \neg (A \vee B) \rangle$ is the same proposition as $\langle \neg A \wedge \neg B \rangle$; and that $\langle \neg (A \wedge B) \rangle$ is the same proposition as $\langle \neg A \vee \neg B \rangle$. (See chapter 8 for a defence of this view.) The difference in these expressions is merely syntactic. But I needn't insist on this point: either way, there cannot be a difference in domain between $\langle \neg (A \vee B) \rangle$ and $\langle \neg A \wedge \neg B \rangle$, or between $\langle \neg (A \wedge B) \rangle$ and $\langle \neg A \vee \neg B \rangle$.

The same goes for $\langle \neg \neg A \rangle$ and $\langle A \rangle$: there can be no difference in domain here. We might even think that $\langle \neg A \rangle$ belongs to whichever domain $\langle A \rangle$ does. 'That's not funny' is a claim about humour just as much as 'that's funny' is. Call this principle the *strong domain principle for negation*. We then have the following domain principles:

(D$_\wedge$) $\langle A \wedge B \rangle$ belongs to the same domains as $\langle \neg (\neg A \vee \neg B) \rangle$;

(D$_\vee$) $\langle A \vee B \rangle$ belongs to the domains of $\langle A \rangle$ plus the domains of $\langle B \rangle$;

(D$_\neg$) $\langle \neg A \rangle$ belongs to the same domains as $\langle A \rangle$;

But with these principles in place, $\langle A \wedge B \rangle$ will belong to whichever domains $\langle A \rangle$ belongs, plus whichever domains $\langle B \rangle$ belongs. To see this, suppose that ⟨A⟩ belongs to some domain d, and reason as follows:

⟨A⟩ belongs to domain d	assumption
⟨¬A⟩ belongs to domain d	($D_\neg$)
⟨¬A ∨ ¬B⟩ belongs to domain d	($D_\vee$)
⟨¬(¬A ∨ ¬B)⟩ belongs to domain d	($D_\neg$)
⟨A ∧ B⟩ belongs to domain d	($D_\wedge$)

The same goes for ⟨B⟩'s domains. This establishes that ⟨A ∧ B⟩ belongs to whichever domains ⟨A⟩ belongs, plus whichever domains ⟨B⟩ belongs.

One might object to the strong negation principle ($D_\neg$) on the basis that, in general, existential claims and negated existential claims are different beasts. One might think that the former, but not the latter, place alethic demands on worldly entities; and one might take this as evidence that ⟨A⟩ and ⟨¬A⟩ can differ in their domains. Suppose that's right. Nevertheless, there must be some relation between ⟨A⟩'s domains and ⟨¬A⟩'s domains. Whatever that relationship is, it must allow that when negation takes us from one domain to another, a further negation will bring us back to where we started. If negating a proposition takes us from a domain d to a domain d^*, then a further negation must take us back to the original domain, d. In other words, $d^{**} = d$. So we can drop ($D_\neg$) and formulate a weaker domain principle for negation, as follows:

($D_\neg^*$) There is a function $*$ on domains such that (i) ⟨A⟩ belongs to d if and only if ⟨¬A⟩ belongs to d^*; and (ii) $d^{**} = d$.

Now we can derive the previous result, in the absence of the stronger negation principle ($D_\neg$), as follows:

⟨A⟩ belongs to domain d	assumption
⟨¬A⟩ belongs to domain d^*	($D_\neg^*$)

$\langle \neg A \vee \neg B \rangle$ belongs to domain d^* (D$_\vee$)

$\langle \neg(\neg A \vee \neg B) \rangle$ belongs to domain d (D$_\neg^*$)

$\langle A \wedge B \rangle$ belongs to domain d (D$_\wedge$)

Since the same reasoning applies to $\langle B \rangle$, this shows that $\langle A \wedge B \rangle$ belongs to whichever domains $\langle A \rangle$ belongs, plus whichever domains $\langle B \rangle$ belongs.

To sum up, the alethic pluralist is committed to treating conjunctions as belonging to the domains of their conjuncts. If $\langle A \rangle$ is a lightweight truth (only) and $\langle B \rangle$ a heavyweight truth (only), $\langle A \wedge B \rangle$ will come out as both a lightweight and a heavyweight truth. But (as above) this is precisely what an alethic pluralist should avoid saying.

Unlike in the case of disjunctions, we cannot address this 'mixed conjunction' problem by further restricting the T-scheme. The problem is that mixed conjunctions cannot be true in the ways their conjuncts are true. They must be true in some further way. They will possess a specific truth-property not possessed by their conjuncts. But then, there will be no specific truth-property preserved in the inference from $\langle A \wedge B \rangle$ to $\langle A \rangle$. In short, the alethic pluralist cannot maintain that there are specific truth-properties preserved from premises to conclusion in each valid entailment.

1.6   Alethic Pluralism and Generic Truth

To account for valid entailments, alethic pluralists are forced to accept a generic truth-property, $true_g$. Some alethic pluralists, including Wright (1992) and Edwards (2009), want to avoid this result. (Wright holds that 'there is a single concept of truth, and the property it presents can vary from area of discourse to area of discourse' (Wright 2013, 128), but denies that the concept of truth is a further property.) Other pluralists, including Cotnoir (2009, 478–9), aren't worried by a generic truth-property.

The pluralist can hold that a sentence possesses $true_g$ only in virtue of possessing some other (non-generic) truth-property, which hardly makes those non-generic truth-properties dispensable. She might hold that logically complex propositions never possess a domain-specific truth property. Rather, she'll say that atomic propositions are generically true if they have a specific truth property, and that generic truth (and falsity) bubble up from conjuncts to conjunctions, and from disjuncts to disjunctions, in the usual way.

How does alethic pluralism stand, given that it must accept a generic truth-property? That generic property is possessed by all truths, regardless of the domain of discourse to which they belong. Generic truth doesn't care about what constitutes the truth in question: correspondence to mind-independence states of affairs, correspondence, superassertability, or whatever. It cares only that some appropriate domain-specific criterion of truth is satisfied. A proposition is generically true when there's some features of the world—mind-independent states of affairs, facts about our reactions, facts about language, or whatever—which bear the right relationship to that proposition. In other words, generic truth requires the existence of appropriate features of the world. It's an existential property. That property sounds a bit like the one I outlined in the Introduction: the property which attaches to a proposition ⟨A⟩ when there exists some feature of the world which makes ⟨A⟩ true. We need to investigate this point in some detail.

It is useful, at this point, to compare this approach—alethic pluralism with a generic, existential truth property—to Michael Lynch's *functionalism* about truth (Lynch 2009). Lynch, like the standard pluralist, holds that there are distinct truth-like properties, corresponding to distinct domains of discourse. But he also characterises a generic notion of truth, using the following principle:

(GT) ⟨A⟩ is true if and only if ⟨A⟩ has a property that plays the truth-role. (Lynch 2009, 72)

This notion of truth is an existential notion: it applies to a proposition when there's some specific truth-property possessed by that proposition.

One might be tempted, at this point, to think that the three live views under consideration—alethic pluralism with a generic truth property, Lynch's functionalism, and my preferred truth-as-truthmaking view—are just notational variants of one another. What the first account calls generic truth, the second calls functional truth, and the third calls truthmade truth. There's something to that thought, but I don't accept it. The theory I'll present and defend in the rest of the book is unashamedly *monist* about truth: there is but one truth-property, the property of *having a truthmaker*.

For the truth-as-truthmaking theorist, truth is an existential property, asserting the existence of a truthmaker. That existential quantifier is fully general: it doesn't care what kind of entity the truthmaker is. Wherever there's a quantifier, there can be restricted uses, as in 'there's no Vegemite *in the cupboard*', or 'there's no Vegemite *in the shop*'. These express different contents, to be sure, but not different *kinds* of existence. Vegemite exists in precisely the same way, whether in the cupboard, the shop, or wherever.

Similarly, we might restrict the quantifier in 'is made true by some entity' to the domain of mind-independent states of affairs involving medium-sized dry goods. In that sense, we get a domain-specific truth property. But propositions with this property aren't true in a different way to truths in different domains, just as the Vegemite in the cupboard doesn't exist in a different way to the Vegemite in the shop. Rather, Vegemite exists; some in the cupboard, and some in the shop. Similarly, truths in different domains are true, simpliciter, some in one domain, some in the other.

This suggests that talking of 'domains of discourse' is a red herring when discussing truth. There are different kinds of entity out there: some spatiotemporal, some not; some causal, some not; some whose existence and qualitative profile is independent of us, some not. These distinctions concern the natures of these entities, and not the property of *truth* that attaches to the true propositions about them.

1.7 Going Substantial

The view I'll present and defend in this book is monist about truth: there is but one property of truth, and it's the property of being made true by some entity or other. This approach isn't consistent with alethic pluralism, Wright-style, nor with Lynch's functionalism. My real beef with alethic pluralists and functionalists concerns their insistence that, when it comes to truth, one size won't fit all. They say that one substantial notion of truth won't cover all kinds of discourse. Their generic notion of truth has no inherent nature; it's merely the property of possessing some specific truth property or other. The truth-as-truthmaking theorist, by contrast, finds a unified nature to truth. I'll end this chapter by defending the idea that truth has a unified, substantial nature.

Let's go back and see why pluralists and functionalists think that truth cannot have a unified, substantial nature. Lynch (2009) finds a *scope problem* for correspondence theories of truth (including, presumably, the truth-as-truthmaking theory). He imposes the following restriction on theories of truth:

> a given mental state has G-ish content if the proposition that is that content has Gs as its subject. A correspondence theory ... will seem likely as [a] theory of truth for such states only when we can establish
>
> *Responsiveness:* Mental states with G-ish content are causally responsive to an external environment that contains Gs. (Lynch 2009, 32)

In other words, according to Lynch, a correspondence-style theory is plausible only when we're talking about parts of the causal order. When we make assertions about non-causal entities, some other (non-correspondence) account of truth is required.

There is indeed a deep question about how we can think about, and come to know about, non-causal entities (including non-causal properties). Numbers, pure sets, and mathematical functions are stock examples of non-causal entities. If they are, then how we gain mathematical knowledge is rather mysterious. This in turn makes it hard to see how we express propositions with mathematical content. This point is tangential to our discussion of truth, however. Recall that truth is primarily a property of propositions. Given a target proposition, we want to know, in what would its truth consist? How we come to express that proposition, or know its truth, is a further matter. One beautiful feature of the truth-as-truthmaking approach is that, in general, it doesn't require anything of us, our minds, our knowledge, or our abilities. It allows that there are truths that we don't know, that we won't know, and that we couldn't possibly know. In the general case, if we have objects and properties in the relevant domain of discourse, then we have propositions and states of affairs reflecting that subject matter; and when we have both, matching up in the right way, we have truth.

Lynch requires that correspondence-style theories be restricted to causally efficacious subject matter. This smacks of the kind of anti-realism that requires that truths must be knowable, at least in principle: if A, then it is knowable that A. But this position is ruled out by the Church-Fitch argument (Church 2009; Fitch 1963). In short, if A implies that A is knowable, then A implies that A is known. But this is absurd, since some truths aren't known; so not every truth is knowable. (I discussed this position, and the Church-Fitch argument, in a little more detail in the Introduction.) So we should reject Lynch's proposed restriction on correspondence-style theories of truth, and allow the truth-as-truthmaking account to fly free.

There's a second, and perhaps more general, reason for pluralists and functionalists to hold that a correspondence-style theory of truth won't work across the board. They hold that, in some domains of discourse, there are no objective, substantial states of affairs to which truths can correspond. Wright's (1992) example of truths about humour fit this style of argument. In some cases (goes the claim), there's just no fact of the matter whether a given joke is objectively funny or not.

Claims such as these are primarily claims about the kinds of properties the world contains. The specific claim is that the property *being funny* is not one that attaches to entities (jokes, stories and so on) independently of us and our (actual or potential) reactions. It's a claim about the nature and possession-conditions of *being funny*. Let's say, for argument's sake, that *being funny* attaches to entities based on how ideal humour-appreciators would typically react in ideal humour-conditions. (Now, I don't pretend to understand exactly what that might mean. It, or something like it, must mean something concrete if the Pluralist's objection is to get off the ground; so let's roll with it for the time being.)

When a joke is funny, it has that property. There's a state of affairs *that the joke is funny*. If that analysis of *being funny* is right, then the state of affairs's existence depends on the potential reactions of those ideal humour-appreciators in ideal situations. But why is this a bar to a correspondence theory? Why, in particular, can't we say that that state of affairs, strange and reaction-dependent as it is, is what makes it true that the joke was funny? There's no requirement in the notion of truthmaking, or in the truth-as-truthmaking proposal, that the truthmaker be an objective, mind-independent entity.

There would be a problem here for the truth-as-truthmaking proposal (and for any correspondence-style theory) if there simply was no state of affairs *that the joke was funny* in existence. But why think that? The objection must be that, as the property concerns potential responses, it is not the kind of property whose possession gives rise to actually existing states of affairs.

This line of thought is misguided. Suppose we fully spell out each component of the view, giving us a clear handle on what what constitutes ideal humour-circumstances and ideal humour-appreciators are. (Perhaps they are more rational, consistent versions of us.) Their responses will depend on what they think (and perhaps on whatever sub-personal processes are occurring in their brains). If physicalism holds, then there's objective physical conditions which determine what each will think, and hence what each will say, in response to a given joke.

Perhaps the physical world is non-deterministic enough at the macroscopic level, such that there's no fact of the matter about how each ideal humour-appreciator will react. Perhaps the ideal humour-appreciators will react in diverse ways (that's likely), so that there's no fact of the matter about their collective reactions. But then, according to the analysis of humour we're humouring, the joke isn't funny. We need be concerned only with the case in which it's true that the joke is funny and, in that case, the account says the ideal humour-appreciators will react in a certain way to it. That being the case, there must be a physical basis—a set of physical states of affairs—which determines that they will react in that way. Those physical states of affairs will be objective and mind-independent. They can act, collectively, as the truthmaker for our truth that the joke is funny.

Notice that there's no claim here that we can reduce the concept *being funny* to objective physical concepts. We don't even require that there's a type-type determination between the physical and the funny. It's most probable that very different physical setups give rise to funniness. What we should take from Wright's humour example, at most, is that the conceptual analysis of humour stops with facts about us. We can't analyse the concept of humour without mentioning us and our potential reactions. But that line is compatible with facts of humour being determined, metaphysically, by diverse, objective, and substantial physical facts.

1.8 Chapter Summary

Deflationism should be stated in terms of propositions (§1.2). But this leads to the identity problem (§1.3): the property *truth* partially fixes the identity of the propositions which fix the identity of *truth*. This can't be. That was my first argument against deflationism. The second argument was that deflationism can't deal with the Liar paradox (§1.4). So deflationism should be rejected. Truth requires substantial, metaphysical notions. I also rejected pluralism about truth (§1.5). Pluralism collapses, unless it accepts a generic truth predicate (§1.6). But once that is accepted, the pluralist's data is better accommodated in terms of a univocal, existential truth-property (§1.7).

2
Arguments for Truthmaking

The theory of truth I'm proposing analyses truth in terms of truthmaking. But why think that truths need to be made true by entities in the world? That's a key question in this project. There are no quick, easy arguments in favour of truthmaking (§2.2 and §2.3). My strategy will be to argue that properties and relations exist (§2.4) and, from there, to argue in favour of states of affairs (§2.5). Once we've got these in our ontology, it's but a short step to argue that they are truthmakers for the corresponding propositions (§2.6).

2.1 Why Truthmaking?

THE TRUTHMAKER principle says that, when a proposition is true, something in the world makes it true. It's fair to say that the principle is popular amongst philosophers; or at least, that it is widely discussed. A google search for 'truthmaking' gave me around 109,000 hits; 'truthmakers' gave me 42,700. Given this current wave of popularity, we might expect to find arguments in favour of it rather easily. Prepare to be disappointed! Direct arguments for the truthmaker principle are few and far between.

Let's look at what David Armstrong, perhaps the foremost modern defender of the truthmaker principle, has to say in its favour. In a 1991 article, arguing that classes are states of affairs, he says:

> suppose *a* is *F* ... What is needed is something in the world which ensures that *a* is *F*, some truth-maker or ontological

> ground for *a*'s being *F*. What can this be except the state of affairs of *a*'s being *F*? (Armstrong 1991, 190)

This passage occurs right at the start of Armstrong's article. Note how he wields the truthmaker principle but doesn't offer any argument for it.

Maybe we should look instead at Armstrong's systematic presentation of his truthmaker theory: his 2004 book, *Truth and Truthmakers*. Near the start, Armstrong describes how C. B. Martin introduced him to the idea of truthmaking. Armstrong presents the *phenomenalist* view that material objects are nothing but permanent possibilities of sensation. The view makes use of certain counterfactual statements about what sensations one would have in certain circumstances. Armstrong notes that 'neither of us [Armstrong or Martin] had any sympathy for this view, but it was in the air at the time. The question for us was how it was best argued against' (Armstrong 2004, 1). Martin's answer evidently had a deep impact on Armstrong's thought:

> Martin asked a simple question that seemed to go to the heart of the problem. Suppose that the required counterfactual propositions are indeed true. What are the truthmakers for these truths? Must there not be *some way that the world is* in virtue of which these truths are true? *What is it?* How does the world make these truths true? (Armstrong 2004, 1)

Yet again, truthmaker principle is wielded—this time, as an argument against phenomenalism—but again, no argument is given for it. This is on the very first page of *Truth and Truthmakers*. No argument for the truthmaker principle precedes this passage and, as far as I can see, no argument is given later on either.

How can the truthmaker principle have gained such popularity, if it's so hard to find a direct argument in favour of it? Here are some speculations (which, I should add, are mere speculations about the sociology of contemporary philosophy; nothing much hangs on them). The truthmaker principle articulates something that's at the heart of many realist world views. 'Realist' can mean many things in philosophy. I mean something like this: the world exists, and is the way it is, independently of the way we think about it. Realists think that's the case for most, or possibly all, matters under discussion. If so, then there are truths and falsehoods about those matters, independently of our knowledge. Truths are objectively true, even if we don't know they are true, and in some cases even if we cannot know they are true. That's a very rough criterion, but it should be enough to give a flavour of the kind of philosopher I'm thinking about.

For realists of that description, truths are true because of how the world is, in some specific way. That specific way is part of the world; it's something that exists; and it makes that truth true. This seems to be the thought Russell articulates in his *Lectures on Logical Atomism*:

> When I speak of a fact ... I mean the kind of thing that makes a proposition true or false. ... It is important to observe that facts belong to the objective world. They are not created by our thoughts or beliefs except in special cases. (Russell 1985, 6–7)

So, given realist inclinations, the truthmaker principle is attractive. That's no argument for the truthmaker principle, of course. One would first have to argue for realism, and then argue that there is indeed a definite connection between realism and the truthmaker principle. To complicate matters, I don't think that the truthmaker principle can be used to *articulate* what a realist's commitment is. Certain kinds of anti-realists—idealists about material objects or numbers, for instance—may accept a truthmaker principle. (I touched on this topic in the Introduction.) Idealists, in the sense that I'm using the term, believe that material objects or numbers really do exist, but are mind-dependent entities. Material objects are constructions from our actual or possible perceptual experiences; numbers are constructions from our mathematical thoughts. Those idealists might then take those constructions (or states of affairs involving them) to be truthmakers. So the truthmaker principle, as articulated so far, carries no commitment to realism (in the sense of a mind-independent reality).

2.2 Catching Cheats

It is often said that 'the point of the truthmaker principle ... is to rule out dubious ontologies' (Sider 2003, 40). Merricks (2007, 36) is explicit:

> Catching cheaters is a principal motivation for [the] Truthmaker [principle]. Moreover, Truthmaker is of interest in this book largely because it threatens to rule out this or that philosophical theory. So let us better equip Truthmaker to catch cheaters. (Merricks 2007, 36)

Armstrong's motivation for the truthmaker principle (§2.1) seems closely related to Sider's point. Do such thoughts contain an argument for the truthmaker principle? If so, it will go something like the following.

(DODGY) Theory *T* is dodgy. We want to pin down exactly what's wrong with it. The best explanation of *T*'s dodginess is provided by the truthmaker principle. So, we should accept the truthmaker principle.

This style of argument has been aimed at phenomenalism for its ungrounded possibilities of sensation (Armstrong 2004, 1–2); Rylean dispositionalism for its ungrounded behavioural dispositions (Armstrong 2004, 2–3); Quinean nominalism for its ungrounded predications (Armstrong 1997, 115); the Molinist account of freedom for its ungrounded counterfactuals (Lewis 2001, 614); and presentism for its ungrounded truths about past and future (Sider 2003, 36–7).

The argument isn't intended to be valid. It's offered as an inference to the best explanation. That way of reasoning seems good in scientific contexts. We often reason that, if some scientific theory provides the best explanation of the observed phenomena, then we should believe that theory. And let's just grant, for the moment, that truthmaker theory does provide the best explanation of why a given metaphysical theory looks dodgy. Still, we might ask, who is this argument meant to persuade? DODGY-style reasoning may persuade you if you first believe, on independent grounds, that a given theory is dodgy. But if you have an independent reason to reject that theory, why appeal to truthmaker theory (via DODGY-style reasoning) at all? As Merricks (2007) says, the truthmaker principle 'is no less a controversial philosophical theory than are the theories with which it clashes' (2007, xiv).

Perhaps we should think of the truthmaker principle as a unifying explanation, given a range of metaphysical theories we find dodgy. We might have different specific arguments against each theory, but suspect that there's some general reason why they all fail. We might then appeal to the truthmaker principle as a unifying explanation for their various failures. There's something to this line of thought. But it will justify the truthmaker principle only to the extent that we're sure that those theories all go wrong in the same way. (Schaffer (2010b, 6), for one, 'doubt[s] that all these cases are alike'.) None of these considerations will move someone who doesn't buy the independent arguments against phenomenalism, Rylean dispositionalism, presentism, and so on. So unless you already have a reason to reject those theories, you're unlikely to find this motivation for the truthmaker principle very appealing.

2.3 Grounding

As a rule, philosophers who've used or discussed the truthmaker principle haven't argued directly for it. The most direct argument I've seen in the literature comes from Gonzalo Rodriguez-Pereyra, as follows (2005, 25):

(2.1) Truth is grounded.

(2.2) Grounding is a relation.

(2.3) Relations link entities.

(2.4) Therefore, truth is grounded in entities.

To deny (2.1) would be to say that truth is ungrounded, and hence a primitive matter. Saying that truth is primitive, in this sense, is to say that there's no important connection from the ways of the world to what's true. A proposition is simply true or false, and there's no more to say on the matter. That view is rather implausible. It must hold either that ⟨Bertie is snuffling⟩ could be true even when Bertie isn't snuffling; or else that it's a massive cosmic coincidence that ⟨Bertie is snuffling⟩ is true just in case Bertie snuffles. Both views are implausible.

To emphasise the point, Rodriguez-Pereyra notes that

> the idea that truth is grounded is so compelling that has seemed acceptable to philosophers like W. V. Quine, Paul Horwich, and Crispin Wright, who cannot be suspected of trying to advance the cause of truthmakers. (Rodriguez-Pereyra 2005, 22)

It's sometimes said that Frege held that truth is primitive. But he didn't hold the view I've just described. Instead, he held that the concept *truth* (or the word 'true') can't be defined in more basic terms: 'Truth is obviously something so primitive and simple that it is not possible to reduce it to anything still simpler' (Frege 1897/1979, 128–9). His argument for this is baffling:

> If, for example, we wished to say that 'an idea is true if it agrees with reality', nothing would have been achieved, since in order to apply this definition we should have to decide whether some idea or other did agree with reality. Thus we should have to presuppose the very thing that is being defined. (Frege 1897/1979, 128–9)

Why would checking whether an idea agrees with reality presuppose truth? Our supposed definition tells us that the idea is true *if* it agrees with reality; but that doesn't stop us checking for agreement with reality without presupposing this definition. But even if 'true' or the concept *truth* is indefinable, it doesn't follow that it's a primitive matter whether a proposition has the property of truth. It would mean only that we couldn't re-express such situations in more basic terms.

A philosophical view can get quite radical about a given subject matter and still firmly hold that the truths about that subject matter are grounded. Nominalists about mathematics say that numbers don't exist. But they still hold there are truths of the form '5 + 7 = 12'. They don't say those truths are ungrounded, primitive truths (otherwise, they'd have no principled reason for holding that '5 + 7 = 12' is true whilst '48 + 97 = 12' is false). They can't say that such truths are grounded in numbers, since they deny there are any numbers. Rather, they say those truths are grounded elsewhere: perhaps, in facts about how many material objects there are. (That's not an ontological commitment to numbers, by the way.) For the mathematical nominalist, explaining how '5 + 7 = 12' is grounded is a tricky matter. Why does she bother? Only because her alternative, that truths ungrounded and primitive, is implausible. So (2.1) is on firm ground.

Premise (2.3) is equally plausible. By *entity*, Rodriguez-Pereyra simply means any thing, of any kind, concrete or abstract, particular or universal. A relation is something that *relates* entities together (although see Ladyman and Ross 2007 for an alternative picture). If a relation R did not relate things together, there would be no difference between a situation in which R is instantiated (or otherwise 'in play') and a situation in which it exists but is uninstantiated. Yet there is such a difference; hence relations relate. So (2.3) is unavoidable.

Premise (2.2) is the obvious target for those who want to resist Rodriguez-Pereyra's conclusion. Why must grounding be a relation, according to Rodriguez-Pereyra? To get us on side, he asks us:

> if grounding is not a relation—what is it? That is, how can the truth of the proposition that the rose is red be grounded in the rose's being red if grounding is not a relation? What is it, then, for the proposition that the rose is red to be true because the rose is red? (Rodriguez-Pereyra 2005, 27)

But asking 'what is it?' is entirely the wrong question. If you deny that grounding is a relation, you'll also deny that it's any other kind of thing. Instead, you may take 'grounds' or 'makes true' to be *sentential connectives*, like 'and' or 'it is necessary that'. This is the position Fine recommends:

> My own preference is to treat *ground* as a sentential operator like 'or' or 'if—then—'; it combines with different sentences (those indicating the grounds and what is grounded) to produce a sentence (specifying the relationship of ground). (Fine 2012c, 3; see also Fine 2012b, 46)

On this approach, there is no *grounding* relation, and in that sense, we do not have entities to identify as the grounds of such-and-such.

In a similar way, Melia (2005) argues that we can accept truthmaking-talk without there being a *truthmaker* relation between propositions and entities in the world. We can say things like 'Bertie snuffling makes true the sentence "Bertie is snuffling"'; or 'Bertie snuffles makes true ⟨Bertie snuffles⟩'. We get truthmak*ing* without truthmak*ers*. Here, 'makes true' is being understood as an operator, rather than as a predicate picking out a relation. (Hornsby (2005) makes a similar point against Rodriguez-Pereyra.)

So Rodriguez-Pereyra's opponent can deny that *ground* is best understood as a relation; and, what's more, she can provide a detailed logical theory to back up her claim (Fine 2012c). So Rodriguez-Pereyra's direct argument isn't the way to argue for the truthmaker principle, understood as a claim relating true propositions to truthmaking entities.

The same point applies to another of Rodriguez-Pereyra's arguments for the truthmaker principle. Rodriguez-Pereyra considers an opponent who claims that truths are made true, not by entities, but by the ways things are. But different truths (about, say, a rose) are made true by different ways the rose is:

> What makes true that the rose is red is that it is *red*, while what makes true that the rose is light is that it is *light*. ... the proposition that the rose is red is true in virtue of the rose's being a certain way, namely being red, while the proposition that the rose is light is true in virtue of the rose's being a different way, namely being light. (Rodriguez-Pereyra 2005, 23)

He then argues that this commits us to the reality of ways as truthmakers:

> to distinguish ways presupposes that we can identify them, count them, and quantify over them. But if one can identify, count, and quantify over ways, then ways exist. That is, ways, which are truthmakers, are entities. So we are back to [the truthmaker principle], which claims that true propositions are made true by entities. (Rodriguez-Pereyra 2005, 23)

It's certainly true that, if we genuinely quantify over ways, then ways exist. But the crucial error in Rodriguez-Pereyra's argument is the assumption that ways, if they exist, are truthmakers. His opponent may say, following Melia, that the way the rose is, namely being red, makes true ⟨the rose is red⟩, with 'makes true' understood as a connective, not a relation. The sentential connective view may be maintained even if there are entities which, on the relational view, count as truthmakers.

As a consequence, there is no shortcut to the (relational) truthmaker principle. In order to argue that truths are made true by entities, we must take the long road. Here I agree with Merricks (2007), when he says that

> what we should say about truth's dependence on being turns on what we should say about being as much as it turns on what we should say about truth. (Merricks 2007, xiv)

We must first establish that there exist entities suitable to act as truthmakers. Then we must show that those entities do, in fact, make truths true. I'll attempt the first task by arguing, first, that we are ontologically committed to properties and relations (§2.4); and, second, that possessing a property or standing in a relation consists in the existence of a state of affairs (§2.5). That is no small task, and the discussion here will be brief. The second task is much simpler, for there is a short and convincing argument from the existence of states of affairs to their acting as truthmakers (§2.6).

2.4 From Ways to Properties

Bertie is many ways. Can we capture this idea without committing ourselves to the existence of those ways? Let's try. We can list the ways Bertie is: he's snuffling; he's adorable; and so on. Then we can say: that's it. That list of ways Bertie is exhausts what we can say about Bertie. This strategy reminds us of the deflationist's approach to truth (§1.1). We deflate the notion in question (*ways*, at present) by listing the instances and saying that there's nothing further to the concept.

Ways do more work than this, however. Bertie and John Prescott have something in common: they're both portly. There's something they have in common. Of course, there are also many differences between Bertie and Prescott. Perhaps the differences outnumber what they've got in common. But how can any of this be so, unless there is some *thing* that Bertie and Prescott have in common? And to account for their differences, mustn't there be further *things* that they do not have in common? It seems that we've quantified over (and counted) their similarities and differences. But then, as Rodriguez-Pereyra (2005, 23) says, 'if one can identify, count, and quantify over ways, then ways exist'.

This move may be too quick. Nominalists (about properties) may need to use quantifiers to capture our talk about ways. What isn't obvious is that the quantifiers they use imply that ways are things. Nominalists may use *second-order quantifiers* to quantify into predicate position. From 'Bertie is snuffling', we can replace the predicate 'is snuffling' with a predicate variable 'X', and then bind this with a second-order quantifier '$\exists X$' as follows: '$\exists X$ Bertie X'. We can then say that Bertie and John Prescott have something in common as follows: $\exists X$(Bertie is $X \wedge$ John Prescott is X).

For this move to have any value to nominalists, they must deny at all costs that '$\exists X$' says 'there exists some property', and they must deny that '$\exists X$' is understood as ranging over a domain of properties. But this is a hard task. The simplest reading of '$\exists X$' is 'for some way of being', or 'for some property'. Our nominalist may insist that, by 'object' or 'entity', she means only those things in the range of the *first-order* quantifiers. This is just to stipulate a meaning for 'object' or 'entity', so that it doesn't include properties (or whatever the second-order quantifiers range over.) That's to say that properties exist, but they're not entities. Or more accurately: there are no things (objects, entities) that are properties. But so what? The concession that there are properties is bad enough for the nominalist.

Moreover, it's hard to see how this nominalist can express the claim she wants to defend, that there are no things that are properties. What she denies is that there is some first-order thing identical to some second-order thing. But, given her chosen tools of second-order logic, she can't express this thought. The only reasonable attempt, $\neg \exists x \exists X(x = X)$, isn't a well-formed sentence of her chosen logic (or of any other, so far as I know). So, it turns out, the nominalist taking this route cannot even say that there are no things that are properties. She says there are properties, and can't deny that they are things. She can't assert that they are things either, of course. She has an expressive lacuna. To deny that there are properties (in a way that denies what's central to the realist's view), nominalists shouldn't think that second-order quantification offers a way out.

Melia (2005) offers us an interesting alternative, based on his nominalist-friendly account of truthmaking without truthmakers (§2.3). For

> if ... it is legitimate to have truthmaking without truthmakers, then the way is clear for the sensible nominalist to deal with the problematic quantification and reference to properties. (Melia 2005, 80)

The idea goes like this. What Bertie and John Prescott have in common is that they are both portly. So, for Melia, Bertie is portly and John is portly makes it true that Bertie and John have something in common. Since Melia's nominalist makes sense of 'Bertie is portly' without appeal to a property of *portliness*, she thereby makes sense of 'there is something Bertie and John have in common' without appealing to portliness.

Melia has shown us the moves a nominalist should make in a particular case, and has gestured towards a general nominalist strategy. If what a and b have in common is that both are Fs, then we avoid ontological commitment to that something by saying:

(2.5) a is F and b is F makes it true that there is something a and b have in common.

Similarly, if a and b are both F, G, and H, then we can say

(2.6) a is F and a is G and a is H and b is F and b is G and b is H make it true that there are at least three things a and b have in common.

How should we express the general strategy? Let's explore claims of the form 'there is something x and y have in common'. We might be tempted to give the strategy as follows:

(2.7) For any x and y: if there is some F such that x is F and y is F, then x is F and y is F makes it true that there is something that x and y have in common.

This is precisely what nominalists should not do, however. (2.7) makes use of a second-order existential quantifier, 'there is some F', which (as I just argued) commits us to the existence of properties. (And besides, if second-order quantifiers were nominalistically suitable tools, then nominalists wouldn't have any need for Melia's strategy.)

A better nominalist strategy is to drop the second-order quantifier from (2.7) and rely instead on all instances of the form:

(2.8) For any x and y: if x is F and y is F, then x is F and y is F makes it true that there is something that x and y have in common.

There is a deep problem for this approach. However long this list of instances, it will be too short. Suppose the list is a list of sentences, or particular utterances. Then the list is countable. But things are more ways than that, because there are more than countably many things, and each is unique in some way—even if only because it is not identical to any of those other things.

Will our nominalist accept that there are uncountably many things? The nominalist we've been considering says that there are no properties. She's free to accept the existence of mathematical entities; she needn't be a nominalist about mathematics. If she accepts there are mathematical entities, then she'd better accept there are uncountably many of them. But what if she is a nominalist of both kinds? Then she won't agree with me that there are uncountably many numbers. What about spacetime points, or regions? She may not believe in those either; or she may believe they exist but say they're dependent on other concrete objects, such that there are only finitely many. If our nominalist takes this route, she won't accept that there are uncountably many of anything.

This nominalist is ontologically frugal in the extreme. She won't accept literal talk of any abstract entity. She won't even countenance talk of *sentences*. She'll accept only that there are spatiotemporally located utterances, some of which resemble others in important ways. Such utterances exist just so long as they've been uttered. There are no unuttered utterances. But this frugality comes with a high cost. Let's return to her (supposedly exhaustive) list of instances of (2.8), now understood as a list of utterances. So the list is not only countable, but *finite*, since only finitely many utterances have ever been made. By hypothesis, every utterance in the list is about something that someone has already talked about, or will talk about.

There are some ways, however, that no one has ever spoken about. Which ways are those? Well, of course I can't name specific ways that haven't yet been named! But consider this. Prior to 1963, 'quark' was not part of our scientific vocabulary. (If you think that 'quark' as used by Gell-Mann and 'quark' as used by James Joyce are the same predicate, then change the date of the example to 1939.) Suppose *a* and *b* are quarks. Then they have something in common: both are quarks. But the relevant instance of (2.8) wasn't then in the list. The nominalist's strategy, in 1963 (or 1939) was radically incomplete. Of course, once prompted, one can always produce the relevant utterance: '*a* and *b* are quarks makes it true that *a* and *b* have something in common'. But that response misses the point. There are ways things are which we don't know about, which we haven't named, and about which we may never utter a word. Then there will never be an instance of (2.8) mentioning such ways. Nevertheless, things which are those ways all have something in common. The nominalist can't account for this.

(Should the nominalist go more extreme, and deny that things are ways of which we haven't yet thought or spoken? That form of extreme idealism is very confused. We discover new features of the world all the time. That's to say we discover things (and ways those things are) which pre-date our discoveries. It isn't our investigations that make those things the ways they are. It's worth noting that my present opponent is an extreme nominalist, and that she has no business going in for this extreme idealism. Idealists hold that certain features of the world depend on our language, or concepts, or thought, or proofs, or computations. So our idealist will happily say that there are properties, numbers, other mathematical entities, spacetime points and so on; but she will hold that they are constructs which depend on us. Contrast this with the extreme nominalist's view, on which there no such things.)

Our nominalist had better back up. Her instances of (2.8) had better go beyond the ways we've named. And, most likely, it will have to go beyond the ways we could name. So she won't write her list in English or any other natural language. Her best bet is to say her theory consists of all *propositions* (many nominalists will shudder) of the form indicated by (2.8).

Now recall what we said in §1.2 about the deflationist's attempt to form such a list of propositions. She had to accept the structured notion (either Fregean or Russellian) of a proposition. The same argument applies here. On the sets-of-possible-worlds account, there is but one instance of (2.8): the set of all worlds. (That's because the nominalist needs to treat (2.8) as a necessary truth, which corresponds to the set of all possible worlds.) By contrast, pleonastic propositions, as 'shadows of sentences', succumb to the argument above: there won't be enough pleonastic-proposition instances of (2.8) to account for all cases of some x and some y having something in common. She needs to formulate her theory in terms of Fregean or Russellian structured propositions.

The Russellian interpretation is not available to the nominalist, however, as Russellian propositions have properties and relations amongst their constituents. But the Fregean conception is hardly any better. Fregean propositions commit one to the reality of Fregean senses. Senses are either *sui generis* abstract entities (the most common interpretation of Frege's view: see, e.g., Burge 1992); or they are 'ways in which we refer to something' (Dummett 1996, 256); or they are constructions from properties. None of these interpretations are suitable for the nominalist's needs.

If we understood Dummett's 'ways in which we refer to something' in terms of definite descriptions, then Fregean structured propositions would collapse into sentences. But, as we have already seen, the nominalist cannot use sentences to capture all instances of (2.8). And clearly, she cannot take Fregean senses to be constructions from properties. But taking them to be *sui generis* abstract entities seems just as bad. Whatever her objection to properties is, it will apply all the more so to senses, so understood. For on that view, for each way a thing can be, there exist multiple modes of presentation of being that way.

The nominalist's attempt, via (2.8), to explain away existential commitment to what x and y have in common has failed. When x is F and y is F, we are ontologically committed to what they have in common: the property *Fness*. (Similarly for relations.) This argument doesn't tell us what properties and relations are, metaphysically speaking. What their nature is won't matter too much in what follows. (Just for the record, my money is on Platonic universals. But what follows is equally available to those who prefer immanent universals, and perhaps even to those opting for perfectly resembling tropes, just so long as they have some way of understanding 'x and y have something in common'.)

2.5 States of Affairs

Anyone who accepts the reality of properties and relations faces a difficult question: *how* do particulars possess properties and stand in relations? It is not enough merely for the relevant particulars, properties, and relations to exist. I exist, as does the property *being a fruit*, but I don't possess that property. Something more is needed. One might think the extra required is *property possession*, or *instantiation*, or *exemplification*. That looks to be a relation between particular and property (or between particulars and relation). But how will this extra relation help? Suppose the *instantiation* relation exists, alongside me and the property *being a fruit*. Still, I don't instantiate *being a fruit*. (We'll come back to this issue in §4.1.)

There's a difference between the situation in which particular and property exist without instantiation, and the situation in which the particular instantiates the property. We've used that quantifier again: there's *some* difference. The philosopher who took this kind of talk seriously and came to believe in properties and relations should take note. Reasoning in the same way, she might come to the conclusion that there's *some thing* that makes the difference between possession and non-possession of a property. That entity captures, in its very existence, the particular's possessing that property. It's the fact, or state of affairs, of that thing being that way. In short, the believer in properties and relations should also believe in states of affairs. The very same reasoning that lead her to believe in properties and relations also leads her to states of affairs. (I'll discuss below whether this reasoning is successful.)

There's an alternative account of property possession, on which we have *a*, we have *F*, and *a* is *F*: and that's all there is to say on the matter. There's no extra entity, *a's being F*. Putting matters in the terminology Quine (1951) used, the link between *a* and *F* is *ideological*, not *ontological*. Many contemporary philosophers find this way of thinking useful. It's costly to a theory to posit needless ontology, but it's also costly to posit needless ideology. Good theories strike a good balance between ontology and ideology.

What does it mean to say that property-possession is ideological, not ontological? It means that we give a theory of what it is for a particular to possess a property which commits to no additional ontology (beyond particulars and properties). The theory of property-possession in question will look rather simple, given that we have particulars, properties, and relations in our ontology (and hence available as objects of quantification):

(POSSESSION) For each property F and particular a: a possesses F if and only if a is F.

We can generalise to cover n-place relations (for $n > 1$), and to cover higher-order cases of one property possessing another (as in, *red is a colour*). That's all there is to say about property possession, according to this approach. The approach is deflationary in the extreme about property possession. The question of how a property is possessed by a particular does not arise, on this view.

I'll now offer three considerations in favour of states of affairs, over the deflationary approach. The first is simple, and appeals to the (property) realist's line on the existence of properties. She says, of some particulars: there are ways those things are; there are things they have in common; and those ways and things are entities. We might argue for states of affairs in the same way, by noting that there are ways the world is. It is currently sunny here; Bertie is wagging his tail. These are some of the ways the world is. These things are not properties or particulars: they are states of affairs. Similarly, we can compare different situations—today's baking sun and yesterday's torrential rain—noting the things they have in common and the differences that exist between them. Again, those things are not properties or particulars. They are states of affairs.

One might respond that these things are properties, ones possessed by the whole world (Bigelow 1996; Stalnaker 1976a). Perhaps that's suggested by the phrase 'ways the world is'. If so, then we have a way of rejecting the argument from *ways the world is* to states of affairs. Nevertheless, someone taking this line is committed to a good deal of the states of affairs ideology. Suppose there exist world-properties, such as *being such that Bertie is adorable*. However we understand the metaphysics of that property, our story must have something to do with Bertie himself. It is not the property of *being such that something with Bertie's qualitative profile is adorable*. The target property is specifically *Bertie-involving*.

How is Bertie, a particular, involved in this world-property? Some story must be told. Perhaps there is some mechanism whereby Bertie and the property of *being adorable* get bound together to form the world-property. That operation takes an n-place relation and n particulars and produces a property, a 1-ary entity, with an argument-place for the world. If it's legitimate to stipulate that there is such an operation, then it must also be legitimate to adopt the same machinery, but with the stipulation that the output is an 0-ary entity: an n-place property or relation 'filled' with n particulars. We may then identify those entities with states of affairs.

This argument doesn't show that the world-property approach is *forced* to accept states of affairs. Rather, it shows that the resources required for the world-property account are capable of delivering states of affairs. A defender of one approach has no grounds on which to object to the other.

The remaining two arguments have stronger conclusions: there must be states of affairs. The first is an argument from causation. At the fundamental level, the world evolves deterministically in accordance with the (time-dependent) Schrödinger equation. Suppose, further, that this evolution involves one total state of the world causally bringing about the next. That is to say, the world's being in state s_1 at time t_1 causes the world's being in state s_2 at t_2. Suppose that's the right way to think of things. Then here's an argument for states of affairs:

(P1) Causes are entities.

(P2) The state of the world at t_1 causes the state of the world at t_2.

(C1) So, the state of the world at t_1 is an entity.

(P3) But it is not a particular or a property.

(C2) So, it is a state of affairs.

The argument for (P1) is similar to our argument for properties (§2.4). Consider a historian who says:

> The causes of the First World War are many and complex. They're quite different from the causes of the Second World War (although they do overlap). But at bottom, all wars have the same cause: men pursuing power.

Here, she quantifies over, counts, identifies, and re-identifies causes. That makes them entities in my book. (P2) is our assumption from above; (C1) follows. For (P3), it seems clear that a state of the world is not a particular. (For one thing, the world has different states at different times, and different possible worlds may be in the very same state.) One may think the state of the world is a (big) property it has. But in general, properties in themselves are not causes. It is something's having (or gaining, or losing) a property that is the cause. Since we've established that the state in question is a cause, it follows that it isn't a property. (C2) follows on the assumption that entities are particulars, properties, or states of affairs.

The third argument in favour of states of affairs is an argument from perception. Perception is a causal relation between the perceiver and some entity. I perceive Bertie. But I also perceive that he's portly. I can perceive the former without the latter. In perceiving Bertie (without perceiving him to be any particular way), I stand in the *perceiving* relation to Bertie. But my second state of perception, in which I perceive that he's portly, is distinct from this state. So it does not consist in my standing in the *perceiving* relation to Bertie. Yet it must consist in my standing in the *perceiving* relation to something, and that something must be suitably related both to Bertie and to *being portly*.

What could that something be, other than the state of affairs *that Bertie is portly*? The relation cannot be to the proposition *that Bertie is portly*, for this proposition exists whether or not Bertie is portly.

Were Bertie to shed his paunch, my visual perceptions of him (in good circumstances) would change correspondingly. The change is reflected in which states of affairs, but not in which propositions, exist. We can explain this only by taking states of affairs as the objects of the *perceiving* relation.

You might find a fourth argument in favour of states of affairs later on in the book. In chapter 8, I'll present an account of propositions which makes essential use of states of affairs. I'll argue that the account has a number of happy features, including a line on the Liar, Curry, and similar paradoxes (chapter 9). In fact, I think this kind of approach is the only adequate, revenge-free solution to those paradoxes. But, I argue, it's available only if one accepts states of affairs. If you buy those arguments, then you have a clear argument from best explanation in favour of states of affairs. However, all of that is many pages away. So, for the time being, I'm content to rely on the three arguments just offered.

These arguments do not tell us anything about what states of affairs are like. They tells us only that they exist. (The first argument, with its talk of a mechanism for forming states of affairs from particulars, properties, and relations, is certainly suggestive of Armstrong's 'fundamental tie' approach (2004; 1997), which I'll discuss in §4.1. But that argument offers no details. It has the form: whatever the world-property approach says, I'll say that too.) So we will need to investigate the metaphysical nature of states of affairs further. That will have to wait until chapter 4.

2.6 States of Affairs as Truthmakers

The final step of the argument for truthmakers is to identify states of affairs as truthmakers. The aim right now isn't to argue that all truths have a corresponding truthmaker. (I think that's true, but the argument for that conclusion will come in chapter 3.) Rather, the aim is to argue that, when there exists a state of affairs *that A*, then that state of affairs makes true the proposition *that A*.

Isn't that obviously the case? Perhaps it is: but not all agree. Recall the Fine-Melia view, on which there is truthmaking but no truthmakers. On that view, 'makes true' is a sentential connective, not a predicate denoting a relation. If that view were correct, then states of affairs do not enter into the analysis of truthmaking. So let me try to convince you that, when a state of affairs exists, it serves as a truthmaker.

Even the most truthmaker-adverse philosopher will admit that entities act as truthmakers for some truths. Here's Melia (2005) again:

> trivially, the sensible nominalist will admit truthmakers for certain truths. Joe, who is nothing more than an individual and so very much part of the sensible nominalist's ontology, is himself the truthmaker for 'Joe exists'. And should it turn out that Joe is necessarily human, then Joe again will also be the truthmaker for 'Joe is human'. (Melia 2005, 69)

In general, an existential truth is made true by its *witness*: the entity it claims to exist. If Melia can accept that, arch opponent of truthmakers that he is, then we all should.

One instance of this general principle is this: if ⟨there exists a state of affairs that A⟩ is true, then it is made true by the existence of the state of affairs *that A*. The existence of a state of affairs, say *that a is F*, is precisely what it is for a to possess F. The assertion *that a is F* asserts is that a possesses the property F, and (given our analysis of property possession) this amounts to the claim that there exists a state of affairs *that a is F*. Putting these points together: the claim *that a is F* makes precisely the same alethic-ontological demand on the world as the claim *there exists a state of affairs that a is F*. From an alethic point of view, the claims are indistinguishable, and hence cannot differ in their truthmakers (if they have any). So, given that the state of affairs *that a is F* is a truthmaker for ⟨there exists a state of affairs that a is F⟩, it follows that the state of affairs *that a is F* is a truthmaker for ⟨a is F⟩. Generalising, if the state of affairs *that A* exists, then it is a truthmaker for ⟨A⟩. That's precisely the result we wanted to establish.

2.7 Truth as Truthmaking

Here's the story so far. Truth is a substantial property (§§1.3–1.4), and there's just one property of truth (§§1.5–1.7). To say that truth is substantial is to say that there's some property which we can identify with *being true*, where that identification forms an informative claim about the nature of truth. The question is: what is that property?

We've also seen that there exist states of affairs (§2.5) and, when there is a state of affairs *that A*, it's a truthmaker for the proposition ⟨A⟩. So there exists a relation, *truthmaking*, and whenever it holds between some existing entity and a proposition, that proposition is true. Suppose further that the converse holds: whenever a proposition is true, it has a truthmaker. (That remains to be argued, in chapter 3.) Then we would have identified a property which, of necessity, is coextensive with *being true*: the property of *having a truthmaker* (or, equivalently, of *being truthmade*).

We can think of this property in terms of existential quantification into the first argument-place of the *truthmaking* relation (as discussed in the introduction). It's the property $\lambda x \exists y(y \text{ truthmakes } x)$. I claim that there's a numerical identity between these properties:

(TaTM) *Being true* is numerically identical to *having a truthmaker*.

This is the *truth as truthmaking* principle. There's a corresponding principle for falsity:

(FaFM) *Being false* is numerically identical to *having a falsemaker*.

Falsity is the flip side of truth. A falsemaker for ⟨A⟩ is whatever truthmakes ⟨¬A⟩. So a full understanding of truthmaking thereby provides an account of falsemaking and thereby of falsity. (Accordingly, I won't always mention falsemaking explicitly in what follows.)

What's my argument for (TaTM)? One approach would be an argument by elimination: take each candidate property for being identified with truth, and show that none but *having a truthmaker* will work. That would make for tedious reading (and pity the writer).

Instead, my argument for (TATM) is an inference to best explanation. To be explained are certain features of truth. The best explanation of these features, I claim, is that *being true* is identical to *having a truthmaker*. What are the features of truth I have in mind, and how can I be so sure they're features of truth? Here's one thing we can be sure of: *being true* is the property expressed by the English predicate, 'is true'. That is so in virtue of how we use 'is true' and, in particular, in virtue of certain platitudes which regulate that use (Wright 1992, 2001).

Here's one of those platitudes: ⟨A⟩ is true if and only if A. (Or rather, any instance of that scheme is a platitude, wherever ⟨A⟩ is a proposition.) That is a feature *being true* must satisfy. This is easily explained by (TATM), for it gives us the following chain of equivalences: ⟨A⟩ is true iff ⟨A⟩ has a truthmaker iff the state of affairs *that A* exists iff A. So (TATM) easily and straightforwardly explains the T-scheme platitudes.

Here's another platitude about truth, governing our use of 'is true': ⟨A⟩ is true because A (Wright 1992, 25–6; Lynch 2001, 747). (Or rather, any instance of that scheme is a platitude, wherever ⟨A⟩ is a proposition.) ⟨Anna's knitting is great⟩ is true because Anna's knitting is great. Even Horwich, clearly no friend of truthmaking, says

> It is indeed undeniable that whenever a proposition or an utterance is true, it is true *because* something in the world is a certain way—something typically external to the proposition or utterance. ... ⟨Snow is white⟩ is true *because* snow is white. (Horwich 1998, 104–5)

It takes a little more work to explain this platitude, because we need to say something about 'because'. One prominent, and highly plausible, theory is that 'because' expresses some kind of metaphysically explanatory relation, or else expresses an operator whose content consists in metaphysical explanations (Schnieder 2010, 2011, 2015). But an explanation relates *explanans* to *explanandum*, on the model of a binary relation, whereas truth is a one-place property.

We can easily explain this using (TATM), for then, underlying the monadic existential property *having a truthmaker* is the binary relation — *truthmakes* —. An entity x stands in its first argument place when the proposition in the second argument place is true in virtue of x's existence. This 'in virtue of' is used canonically to express metaphysical explanations. We may replace 'is true in virtue of x's existence' with 'is true because x exists'. And there we have our explanation for the platitude, having assumed (TATM). I doubt any competing property identification can do that.

Here's yet another platitude governing our use of 'is true': truths depend on the ways the world is. (This is a generalisation about truths, not a schema.) This is easy to explain, given (TATM). The *ways the world is* are states of affairs (§2.5), and *truthmaking* is a dependency relation (§6.3) in which a proposition depends on the existence of some entity (typically, a state of affairs). So, given (TATM), each truth will depend on the existence of some entity (typically, a state of affairs). Again, it is hard to see how any competing property can guarantee that dependency.

Here's a final platitude: the truths correspond to the facts. You might think that's too theoretically loaded to count as a platitude governing ordinary uses of 'is true'. But both Horwich and Wright take it to be a platitude:

> [Horwich's theory] does not deny that truths *do* correspond—in *some* sense—to the facts; it acknowledges that statements owe their truth to the nature of reality. (Horwich 1998, 104)

> The Correspondence Platitude—for a proposition to be true is for it to correspond to reality, accurately reflect how matters stand, "tell it like it is," etc. (Wright 2001, 760)

This platitude too is easily explained, given (TATM). Assuming truthmaker maximalism, for each truth there exists a corresponding state of affairs. And the platitude governing 'fact' is this: it's a fact that A iff A. Thus, we have the following chain of equivalences: $\langle A \rangle$ is true iff there exists a state of affairs *that A* iff it's a fact that A. Generalising, the truths correspond to the facts. Even if competing property identifications can secure that result, I doubt they do so so simply.

Perhaps there are more truth-involving platitudes we could consider. Michael Lynch mentions these: 'truth is a worthy goal of inquiry' and 'truth is worth caring about for its own sake' (Lynch 2004, 19). Both are true, but I don't know how much weight to give them as principles governing our use of 'is true'. If they do, then both principles are analytic, and anyone who denies them doesn't know what 'is true' means. Yet Lynch sets himself the explicit book-length aim (2004, 20) of defending the principles. This suggests to me that they are important principles, but not principles governing our use of 'is true'.

I'm also unsure whether Lynch's platitudes essentially concern truth. I'm tempted to treat the use of 'truth' in 'truth is a worthy goal of inquiry' as a means of generalisation, comparable with 'everything Stephen Fry says is true'. For, strictly speaking, truth itself can't be the goal of an inquiry. An inquiry into whether A does not aim to bring about A's truth. Rather, the aim is *knowledge* that A is true (or at least, *justified true beliefs* concerning whether A). But that aim can be expressed without using 'truth': the goal of an enquiry into whether A is to gain knowledge whether A (or to believe A just in case A). We can generalise by universally quantifying over propositions. Or, more succinctly, we can say that the aim is to believe only what's true. All that we require to secure this use of 'truth' is that it satisfy the T-scheme, and we've already seen that (TATM) underpins the T-scheme.

So (TATM) easily and straightforwardly explains the T-scheme platitudes. I doubt any competing identity hypothesis does. Just suppose, for argument's sake, that some other competitor property is necessary coextensive with *being true*. Suppose it's to do with maximal coherence of propositions. (I really doubt that's so, but just suppose.) How is the hypothesis that *being true* is *being in a maximally coherent set of propositions* supposed to underwrite, say, the T-scheme platitude? We would need to show that ⟨A⟩ belongs to a maximally coherent set of propositions if and only if it's the case that *A*. One might hypothesise that the existing states of affairs are maximally coherent, and hence that the corresponding propositions are. But then we're explaining the link between truth and coherence via corresponding states of affairs: in other words, via *truthmaking*. But then, there's a better explanation: the direct one, in terms of truthmaking.

One might think that *correspondence* is a genuine rival to (TATM), by identifying *being true* with *having a corresponding state of affairs*. I have two objections to this. First, *correspondence* is a symmetrical relation: if *x* corresponds to *y*, then *y* corresponds to *x*. But then, this identity claim cannot hope to explain the second platitude above, that ⟨*A*⟩ is true because *A*. Similarly, this rival identity claim cannot explain why truths depend on the ways the world is. We cannot in general infer from '*x* corresponds to *y*' to '*x* depends on *y*'. If all there were to truth was correspondence, it would be a mystery why truths depend on the world, rather than vice versa.

We could always build more into our notion of correspondence. We could insist that it's not a one-one relation, allowing that many states of affairs may correspond to a single proposition, and a single state of affairs may correspond to many propositions. We could insist that it's an asymmetrical relation, with the direction of travel always from states of affairs to propositions. That doesn't sound like a notion of correspondence to me. In fact, it sounds an awful lot like our *truthmaking* relation. Now, if you want to insist on calling this relation 'correspondence', that's fine with me. But don't think that gives you a competitor to (TATM)!

In short, I doubt that any identity thesis for *being true* can account for all of these platitudes, let alone account for them as easily, as (TATM) does. So, inferring to the best explanation of *being true*'s features, we secure (TATM). *Being true* is numerically identical to *having a truthmaker*. That's the argument.

The argument rests on a crucial premise, that for *every* truth there exists a state of affairs which makes it true. That thesis is known as *truthmaker maximalism*. Establishing this premise will be the topic of chapter 3.

2.8 Chapter Summary

I rejected both the 'cheat catching' motivation (§2.2) and Rodriguez-Pereyra's grounding argument (§2.3) for truthmaking. Neither approach gives us a suitably powerful argument in favour of truthmaking. Instead, I argued for the existence of properties and relations (§2.4), and from there to the existence of states of affairs (§2.5). I then gave an argument that, if states of affairs exist, they act as truthmakers for the corresponding propositions (§2.6). Those arguments, taken together, establish that certain truths have states of affairs as truthmakers. Finally, I argued that, on the assumption that every truth has a truthmaker, there is an argument to best explanation identifying *being true* with *having a truthmaker* (§2.7).

3
Truthmaker Maximalism

If the theory of truth as truthmaking is to be plausible, then all truths must have a truthmaker. This is truthmaker maximalism. *It is a difficult idea to defend (§3.1), and existing arguments for it are not sufficiently strong (§3.2). I'll offer a more powerful argument, showing that the maximalist's opponent is committed to a maximalist ontology (§3.4, §3.6). I consider some objections to the argument in §3.5.*

3.1 Maximalism and Non-Maximalism

I'VE BEEN ARGUING that there exist states of affairs, such as *that Bertie is snuffling*, involving (in some way) particulars, properties, and relations. If there are states of affairs such as these, then they are truthmakers for the corresponding propositions. The proposition ⟨Bertie is snuffling⟩ is made true by the state of affairs *that Bertie is snuffling*; it is true because that state of affairs exists. The truth of the proposition is explained by a relation between the proposition and the state of affairs, and that relation is *truthmaking*.

Are all truths made true in this way, by the existence of states of affairs? David Armstrong (2004) christened the view that every truth has a truthmaker *maximalism*. If maximalism is true, then we are close to establishing my main thesis, that to be true is to be made true by some entity. But it's not clear that all truths have a truthmaker. There's reason to think that some truths can be true without being made true by any entity. And furthermore, there's reason to think that some truths just *cannot* be made true by any entity, because there are no entities capable of making those truths true.

Consider the case of Ern Malley, invented as part of an Australian library hoax. Ern Malley never existed. At the time of the hoax, however, many believed he did exist. What made their belief false, and our belief that Ern does not exist true? What makes it true, now, when we say that Ern Malley never existed? Of such truths Lewis says,

> It seems, offhand, that they are true not because things of some kind *do* exist, but rather because counter-examples *do not* exist. They are true for lack of false-makers. Why defy this first impression? (Lewis 1992, 218–19)

Similarly, Russell says,

> You have a feeling that there are only positive facts, and that negative propositions have somehow or other got to be expressions of positive facts. (Russell 2009, 41–42)

If you're tempted by this line of thought, as Bigelow (1988), Mellor (2003, 2009), and Simons (2005) are, then you won't feel any need to search for truthmakers for all truths. On this view, such truths are true not because something exists, but because something doesn't exist. So they have no truthmakers; rather, their truth arises in a different way to truths like ⟨Bertie is snuffling⟩.

I'll call this view, on which some but not all truths have a truthmaker, *truthmaker non-maximalism*. (I'll formulate a non-maximalist theory in §3.3.) We've already established that some truths have truthmakers, so the real battle is between maximalism and non-maximalism. Motivated by Lewis's idea that truths about what doesn't exist are 'true for lack of false-makers', non-maximalists claim that their theory stakes the best claim to common sense.

There are two paradigms of 'negative' propositions which interest the non-maximalist. The first is negative existential propositions, such as ⟨Ern Malley does not exist⟩. The second concerns non-quantificational propositions: ⟨Bertie is not snuffling⟩. One might adopt Lewis's 'true for lack of false-makers' in response to negative existential propositions (and the equivalent universally quantified propositions) only; or one may adopt the line for all kinds of 'negative' proposition. (Asay and Baron (2012) argue that the former 'modest' form of non-maximalism is unstable, but they rely on some questionable assumptions, such as the controversial *Entailment Thesis* (see §6.2). My argument below applies on either reading of 'non-maximalism'.)

The power in the non-maximalist's arsenal comes from the claim that some truths simply cannot be made true by some entity, for no suitable entities exist. By far the biggest challenge to maximalism along these lines comes from *general* truths, such as 'all Tories are mean-spirited' or 'all Greens care about the environment'; and truths about what does *not* exist, such as truths about Ern Malley's non-existence. (General truths of the form 'all *F*s are *G*s' are equivalent to negated existential claims, 'no *F*s are non-*G*s', and so there is really one issue here, not two.)

What should we say in the case of general truths? Are they the kind of truth that can be made true by some entity? Suppose Anna, Bill, and Cath are all Green Party members who care about the environment. On the metaphysical picture I've developed so far, there are states of affairs *that Anna cares about the environment, that Bill cares about the environment*, and *that Cath cares about the environment*. Suppose there's a state of affairs like that for each and every Green Party member. Those states of affairs together make it true that a certain group of people care about the environment; and that certain group of people are, as it happens, all the Greens. Nevertheless, those states of affairs together do not make it true that all Greens care about the environment.

To see the problem, consider Dave. Dave drives his SUV down the street when he could easily walk or cycle; he leaves his heating on constantly and, when it's too hot, he opens his windows; he frequently takes short-haul flights instead of the train; all his rubbish goes in the non-recycling bin. In short, he cares so little about the environment that, to some of his Green Party friends, he seems to be on a personal mission to speed up global warming.

Dave is certainly not a Green Party member himself. But he might have been. He cares deeply about free education for all and, had this aspect of his political life overcome his environmental carelessness, he might have signed up to the Greens. Consider the alternative situation in which Dave did sign up to the Greens, but hold all the other facts the same. Then the facts about Anna, Bill, Cath, and all our previous Greens caring about the environment would still exist. But they no longer make it true that all Greens care about the environment, since the generalisation is no longer true.

Now let's go back to the actual situation, in which all Greens do care about the environment. Should we now say that the individual facts about Anna, Bill, Cath, and the other original Greens are not, in fact, truthmakers for ⟨all Greens care about the environment⟩? It all depends on what we think the *modal* relationship between a truthmaker and a truth must be. We might think a truthmaker must *necessitate* the truth in question:

(NECESSITATION) If x is a truthmaker for ⟨A⟩ then, necessarily, if x exists then x makes ⟨A⟩ true.

But as we just saw, the individual facts about Anna, Bill, Cath and the other Greens do not necessitate ⟨all Greens care about the environment⟩'s truth. So, if (NECESSITATION) is true, then the facts about the individual Greens cannot together be truthmakers for truths about all Greens. The kind of states of affairs we've discussed so far, of the form *that a is F*, seem unable to do the job. (NECESSITATION) makes it very hard to find truthmakers for general truths, and for that reason makes maximalism a much harder position to defend.

The situation is parallel in the case of existential truths. What makes it true that there are no penguins in the Arctic? A plausible candidate is the Arctic itself. That's not a state of affairs (at least not on the common understanding of states of affairs). But entities like the Arctic can be truthmakers, e.g. for ⟨the Arctic exists⟩, and so it isn't a category mistake to treat the Arctic as a truthmaker for ⟨there are no penguins in the Arctic⟩. Alternatively, we could take ⟨there are no penguins in the Arctic⟩ to be made true collectively by states of affairs *that x isn't a penguin*, for each *x* in the Arctic. (The second approach makes the link with general truths explicit, treating ⟨there are no penguins in the Arctic⟩ on the model of ⟨everything in the Arctic isn't a penguin⟩.)

But again, (NECESSITATION) blocks both suggestions. There could have been penguins in the Arctic, in which case, neither the Arctic nor all the facts about what is actually in the Arctic would make ⟨there are no penguins in the Arctic⟩ true. So, given (NECESSITATION), they are not in fact truthmakers for ⟨there are no penguins in the Arctic⟩. (NECESSITATION) makes it very hard to find truthmakers for negative existential truths, just as it does for general truths.

Given that I'm committed to maximalism, you might expect me to reject (NECESSITATION) at this point (as Briggs (2012) does). It would certainly make my life a lot easier. Yet a simple argument convinces me that (NECESSITATION) is true. The argument proceeds by considering the *nature* of propositions and concludes that, if something makes a proposition true, then that something could not have existed and yet failed to make that proposition true. Here's the argument.

A proposition is, by its nature, the kind of thing that's true or false. But more than that: a proposition is true or false because the world is a particular way. ⟨Bertie is snuffling⟩ is true, not because of how the world is in general, but because, in particular, Bertie is snuffling. It's of the very nature of propositions that their truth or falsity depends on specific ways the world is. We might say that a proposition, by its very nature, sets out the specific ways a world would need to be for that proposition to be true. (More on this in §8.5.)

Specific ways of the world are states of affairs (§2.5). If ⟨A⟩'s nature specifies ways of the world needed for ⟨A⟩'s truth, then those states of affairs are ⟨A⟩'s possible truthmakers. That is all part of the nature or essence of a proposition, I claim. But the nature of a thing is necessary to it. It follows that, for any possible truthmaker *x* for ⟨A⟩, it is necessary that *x* makes ⟨A⟩ true if *x* exists. And since (trivially) any truthmaker for ⟨A⟩ is a possible truthmaker for ⟨A⟩, this principle directly implies (NECESSITATION).

(Note that (NECESSITATION) does not imply that a truthmaker must fix the meaning of a true sentence, as Green (2009) claims it does. What is necessitated is the truth of a proposition, which has a modally fixed content. That's compatible with a modal change in which sentences express that proposition, even in the presence of the same truthmaker.)

The general problem for the maximalist, given (NECESSITATION), is that a truthmaker for (3.1) must necessitate Ern's absence. But how could any entity do that? Metaphysicians are highly suspicious of necessary exclusions, just as they are of necessary connections. (I'll discuss purported absence-necessitators in chapter 5.) The non-maximalist seems to hold the trump card, then, if she can explain truthmaking without positing absence-necessitators.

One might even think that there are possible situations in which we can *guarantee* that there is no suitable absence-necessitating entity. It's possible (goes the argument) for there to be nothing concrete but a solitary electron, *e*. Perhaps it's even possible for there to be no concrete entities at all. That possibility is the *empty world*, the smallest of all possible worlds. Let's focus on the solitary electron world. At that world, there are no penguins, so ⟨there are no penguins⟩ is true there. But *e* doesn't make this true, and since there's nothing concrete there but *e*, there's no entity to make ⟨there are no penguins⟩ true. So, at the solitary electron world, ⟨there are no penguins⟩ is true but lacks a truthmaker (Mumford 2007; Saenz 2014). If that's right, then maximalism isn't necessary. (And it clearly won't help to claim that it's merely a contingent truth.)

This argument doesn't help the non-maximalist. To establish that the solitary electron world is indeed possible, we would first have to rule out the kinds of entity of which some maximalists are fond: absences qua genuine entities, negative facts, and totality facts. (I'll discuss these entities in detail in §§5.4–5.6.) A maximalist who thinks that there are absences-qua-entities, for example, will deny that the solitary electron world (as described) is possible. Instead, she'll say, there's a possible world containing a solitary electron, plus absences of every other concrete thing. But suppose the non-maximalist can rule out all such entities. Then she has no need to appeal to the solitary electron world in her argument against maximalism. Rather, she may say, simply, that there are no entities suitable for acting as absence-necessitators, and hence there are (in fact) no truthmakers for truths like ⟨Ern Malley does not exist⟩ and ⟨there are no penguins in the Arctic⟩.

3.2 Arguments for Maximalism

In this section, I'll consider arguments that have been put forward in favour of maximalism. One strategy is inductive. (This was suggested to me by the great, much missed, E.J. Lowe.) On this approach, we first note that truths like ⟨Bertie is snuffling⟩ are all made true by states of affairs. We note that this class of truths is very broad; it comprises many different subject matters; it includes truths about concrete matters, such as what Bertie is up to, and abstract matters, such as the truth that $1 + 1 = 2$. (We might take the truthmaker for the latter to be the state of affairs *that* $1 + 1 = 2$, or we may take it to be just the numbers 1 and 2, taken together.)

If we judge that this class of truths is sufficiently representative of the truths in general, then we may justifiably infer that *all* truths are like this: made true by some entity in the world. This is an inductive, hence defeasible, inference. Nevertheless, the conclusion will be warranted so long as the induction is good and so long as clear defeaters for the conclusion do not come to light.

This strategy isn't as strong as I'd like. For one thing, once we've brought the problem of general and negative existential truths to light, the class of truths we're proposing to use as an inductive base—those for which we've found a truthmaker—might now seem unrepresentative of the truths as a whole. If it is, then the induction from this base will be a poor argumentative move. But even if the induction is justified to some extent, the conclusion reached is defeasible. Are the cases of general and negative existential truths defeaters for that conclusion? Truthmakers for such truths have been proposed (see chapter 5), but all proposals are highly controversial. Opponents of maximalism have ample material with which to object to this inductive approach. Cameron (2008) suggests an alternative way to argue for maximalism, given that some propositions are made true by what exists:

> Truthmaker theory is a theory about *what it is* for a proposition to be true; it's just not the kind of theory that can apply only in a restricted domain. What possible reason could one have for thinking of some propositions that they need to be grounded in what there is that doesn't apply to all propositions? Why should it be okay for negative truths to go ungrounded and not okay for positive truths to go ungrounded? And if negative truths don't have truthmakers then make no mistake: they *are* ungrounded. It is no good to say that they are grounded in the *lack* of a truthmaker for the positive truth that is their negation. Unless we reify this absence of a truthmaker this is nothing but metaphysical smoke and mirrors. It's totally disingenuous to say that ¬p is true in virtue of the absence of a truthmaker for p unless there is *some thing* that is this absence. And if there *is* such a thing as the absence then it is a truthmaker for ¬p, so maximalism is vindicated. (Cameron 2008, 412)

That's a powerful argument. Nevertheless, the non-maximalist can deny that a proposition without a truthmaker is an ungrounded proposition. Cameron's point holds if *grounding* is a relation between entities, for then, a proposition's truth is grounded just so long as there is some entity which grounds its truth. But, as we saw in §2.3, non-relational theories of grounding are available, such as Fine's (2012c). So long as those theories are viable options, Cameron's argument will not go through.

A better argument for maximalism is as follows. Again, we begin with the truths for which we've found truthmakers, including ⟨Bertie is snuffling⟩. Then we ask: *what is it* for such truths to be true? What is this property they have, that we're calling 'truth'? There's a strong case to be made that, for those truths, their truth consists in their having a truthmaker. That is essential to their being true. It is not merely that they would not be true if they had no truthmaker. More than that: their having a truthmaker is *precisely what it is* for such propositions to be true. If that's so, then it is highly plausible that the property these propositions have, in virtue of which we call them *truths*, is that they each have a truthmaker. In short, for the class of propositions we've identified, to be true is to be made true.

But now suppose that maximalism is false. Then some truths, including general and negative existential ones, are not made true. So they do not have the same *truth* property as ⟨Bertie is snuffling⟩. There must be two (or perhaps more) properties of truth. (Griffith (2015, 1170–1) makes a similar point.) But this is a worrying conclusion. We wanted to find out what *truth* is; and we're now told that there isn't any such property. Rather, there are two truth-like properties, depending on the kind of proposition in question.

We've already seen the problems inherent in pluralist theories of truth (§1.5). So non-maximalists have reason to be worried about this conclusion. Non-maximalists might say, instead, that the cases of general and negative existential truths show that truthmaking is *never* constitutive of truth. Rather, they say, there is one property of truth. It's just that some truths are made true, some are not, just as some truths are good to hear and some are not.

I doubt this argument is strong enough, on its own, to justify maximalism to an impartial party. (Baron et al. (2014) discuss these issues further.) I need a stronger argument for maximalism. And, as luck would have it, I have one up my sleeve! My strategy will be to set out the non-maximalist theory of truthmaking (§3.3), and demonstrate how it is committed to the very entities it finds objectionable in the maximalist's ontology (§3.4). Both sections draw on Jago (2012).

3.3 The Non-Maximalist Account

The non-maximalist holds, with Russell, that 'negative propositions have somehow or other got to be expressions of positive facts' (Russell 2009, 41–2). She takes propositions such as

(3.1) ⟨Ern Malley does not exist⟩

to be true, not because of what does exist, but because of what does not: specifically, because *Ern* does not exist. And by the same token, she takes propositions such as

(3.2) ⟨There are no ducks in my bathtub⟩

to be true because of how things are *not*: (3.2) is true because of the *lack* of ducks in my bath. This contrasts with the negations of (3.1) and (3.2) which, if they were true, would be true because of Ern's existence and because of the existence of ducks in my bath.

Guided by this intuition, the non-maximalist isolates a class of propositions which, if true, are made true by the existence of some entity or other. I will call these the *positive* propositions. (Mellor (2009) calls them the 'primary' propositions.) Typically, it is the negations of these propositions (and the negations of the existentially quantified ones in particular) which are the focus of the debate between the maximalist and the non-maximalist.

The non-maximalist takes propositions such as (3.1) and (3.2) to require no truthmaker in order to be true. As Lewis (1992, 218–19) says, they are true in virtue of the absence of a falsemaker. I will call such propositions the *negative* propositions. They are true 'just in case the truthmaker for the corresponding positive proposition is absent, and it is false just in case it is present' (Kukso 2006, 28). The 'corresponding positive proposition' to a negative proposition ⟨¬A⟩ is ⟨A⟩ and, for a negative proposition ⟨B⟩ not of the form ⟨¬A⟩, the corresponding positive proposition is its negation, ⟨¬A⟩. (One might add that whatever makes ⟨A⟩ true also makes ⟨¬¬A⟩ true and vice versa.) As positive truths may have more than one truthmaker, a non-maximalist should say that a negative proposition is true iff the corresponding positive proposition lacks *any* truthmaker.

The account I will call *simple non-maximalism* takes each proposition to be either positive or negative, with the truth of negative propositions determined in the way just described. Kukso (2006) and Mumford (2007), for example, assume that all truths are either positive or negative. But it is not difficult to see that the simple non-maximalist account is in trouble. For consider the false proposition:

(3.3) ⟨There are ducks in my bathtub ∨ there are no lemons in my fridge⟩

By the non-maximalist's lights, ⟨there are no lemons in my fridge⟩ is a negative proposition, which needs no truthmaker to be true. If there were no ducks in my bath and no lemons in my fridge, ⟨there are no lemons in my fridge⟩ and hence (3.3) would be true, but without a truthmaker (according to the non-maximalist). So simple non-maximalism takes (3.3) to be a negative proposition, and hence false iff its negation

(3.4) ⟨¬(there are ducks in my bathtub ∨ there are no lemons in my fridge)⟩

has a truthmaker. But, by the non-maximalist's own lights, (3.4) is a truth with no truthmaker. If (3.2) has no truthmaker, as the non-maximalist claims, then (3.4) has no truthmaker either. But then, on the simple non-maximalist story, (3.3) comes out true, contrary to our assumption.

Hence the simple non-maximalist strategy of exhaustively classing every proposition as either positive or negative, and analysing the truth of each negative proposition in terms of the absence of any truthmaker for the corresponding positive proposition, is doomed.

To avoid the problem, the non-maximalist should not take every proposition to be either positive or negative. She should allow a class of *derivative* propositions, which derive their truth or falsity from the truth or falsity of more logically basic propositions. (Mellor (2003, 2009) gives an account along these lines.) On this account, a true conjunction ⟨A ∧ B⟩ derives its truth from the truth of both ⟨A⟩ and ⟨B⟩; whereas a false conjunction ⟨A ∧ B⟩ derives its falsity from the falsity of either ⟨A⟩ or of ⟨B⟩. Similarly, a true disjunction ⟨A ∨ B⟩ derives its truth from the truth of either ⟨A⟩ or of ⟨B⟩, whereas a false disjunction ⟨A ∨ B⟩ derives its falsity from the falsity of both ⟨A⟩ and ⟨B⟩. A true negation ⟨¬A⟩ derives its truth from the falsity of ⟨A⟩, whereas a false negation ⟨¬A⟩ derives its falsity from the truth of ⟨A⟩. Similar clauses can be given for existential and universal propositions.

On this account, we analyse a derivative proposition ⟨A⟩ by recursing through these clauses until we have a condition for ⟨A⟩'s truth in terms of positive propositions only. This clause connects ⟨A⟩'s truth or falsity to the presence or absence of truthmakers for those positive propositions.

Call this the *sophisticated non-maximalist account*. It takes all propositions to be either positive, negative, or derivative. (On the definition just given, negative propositions are a special case of derivative propositions. For positive propositions ⟨A⟩, ⟨¬A⟩'s truth is derivative on ⟨A⟩'s lacking a truthmaker and ⟨¬A⟩'s falsity is derivative on ⟨A⟩'s having a truthmaker. Hence, by definition, ⟨¬A⟩ is a negative proposition.) It easily avoids the problem just posed for simple non-maximalism. On the sophisticated account, (3.3)'s truth is derivative either on the existence of a truthmaker for ⟨there are ducks in my bathtub⟩ or on the absence of a truthmaker for ⟨there are lemons in my fridge⟩. Hence the theory tells us, correctly, that (3.3) is true iff either there's ducks in my bath or no lemons in my fridge.

I'll assume that the non-maximalist accepts the sophisticated account, or one similar to it, and so classifies propositions into positive, negative, and derivative. She thus has a theory on which all propositions can be evaluated for truth in terms of the existence or non-existence of truthmakers. If the theory is successful, it shows that one need not assume that all propositions need a truthmaker to be true.

3.4 The Maximalist Strikes Back

In this section and the next, I'll argue that there are (by the non-maximalist's lights) positive truths which nevertheless necessitate negative truths. The key step is to argue that, on the non-maximalist's account, propositions such as

(3.5) ⟨Max knows that Ern Malley does not exist⟩

must be treated as positive propositions. This will be problematic for the non-maximalist, for then she will have to find them truthmakers if true.

First, I'll argue that (3.5) cannot be a negative proposition. Suppose for *reductio* that it is. Then, by definition, its negation

(3.6) ⟨¬(Max knows that Ern Malley does not exist)⟩

is a positive proposition, and hence true iff it has a truthmaker. But this is the wrong result. Given the non-maximalist's ontology, there are numerous ways in which (3.6) could be true whilst lacking a truthmaker.

Here is one such case: the hoax was never run, and no one possesses the concept *Ern Malley*. In this case, (3.6) is true because no one has any beliefs whatsoever about Ern Malley. It's true for the lack of relevant knowledge-constituting beliefs. Since the non-maximalist does not accept absences, negative facts, or totality facts, there's no entity to make (3.6) true. Another case: Max does not exist. Then plausibly, (3.6) is true because Max does not exist. Again, given the non-maximalist's ontology, there's no entity to make (3.6) true. So (3.6) is not negative, hence (3.5) is not positive.

For the remainder of this section, I'll argue that there are strong reasons for thinking that (3.5) and similar propositions are not derivative either, and hence that they are positive. Suppose the non-maximalist claims that every proposition of the form ⟨*x* knows that *A*⟩ is derivative, for every negative proposition ⟨*A*⟩. (In fact, she must say this, if she is to avoid the problem I'll discuss below.) She must then tell us upon which propositions they are derivative. Failing to do so would be dialectically hopeless for the non-maximalist. She charges the maximalist with being unable to provide truthmakers for all truths without invoking (what she takes to be) absurd entities. For a maximalist position to be at all plausible, one must say just what kind of entity makes truths such as (3.1) true. By the same token, a non-maximalist who takes (3.5) to be derivative must say upon which propositions it is derivative.

So, if a non-maximalist claims that every proposition ⟨x knows that A⟩ is derivative, she needs to provide a general method for finding a set of propositions upon which ⟨x knows that A⟩ is derivative. The relation between a derivative proposition and the propositions upon which it is derivative is a necessary one. Hence any method for finding a set of propositions on which an arbitrary proposition of the form ⟨x knows that A⟩ is derivative would effectively provide an exceptionless set of necessary and sufficient conditions for knowledge. There is, however, an excellent reason for thinking that there are in general no such conditions, namely that the extensive literature on the Gettier problem failed to find any. Every proposed analysis of knowledge has met with counterexamples.

(I'm not claiming that an exceptionless set of necessary and sufficient conditions is the goal of an analysis of knowledge. Rather, I'm claiming (i) that the only way to show that all propositions of the form ⟨x knows that A⟩ are derivative is to provide an exceptionless set of necessary and sufficient conditions for knowledge; and (ii) that we have good reason for thinking that this cannot be done.)

The issue here does not concern knowledge *per se*. It arises for any factive operator 'O' and negative proposition ⟨A⟩ such that ⟨OA⟩ is a positive truth. As a consequence, it would not help the non-maximalist to claim that ⟨x knows that A⟩ is derivative on some further factive proposition ⟨OA⟩.

Now let's consider the non-maximalist's options for analysing (3.5). Assume it is true. Then, as a positive proposition, it has one or more truthmakers, according to the non-maximalist. Let t be one of its truthmakers. Given truthmaker necessitarianism (which the non-maximalist accepts), it is necessary that (3.5) is true if t exists. As knowledge is factive, it is also necessary that (3.1) is true if (3.5) is; and it is necessary that Ern does not exist if (3.1) is true. So it is necessary that Ern does not exist if t does: t necessarily excludes Ern's existence. The non-maximalist, just like the maximalist, is committed to entities which necessarily exclude other entities from existence. This is not to say that *t* is a truthmaker for (3.1), despite necessitating its truth. (NECESSITATION) is a necessary but insufficient condition for being a truthmaker. (I'll discuss why it is insufficient in §6.1.) So *t* may be a truthmaker for (3.1), but we can't infer for sure that it is. But either way, the non-maximalist must explain (just as the maximalist must) how it can be that an entity can necessarily exclude Ern's existence. This is just the problem the maximalist faces in trying to find a truthmaker for (3.1): how can anything provide the necessary guarantee that Ern does not exist?

The options for the non-maximalist in explaining how *t* does what it does are just the options the maximalist has in finding truthmakers for negative truths. She might take *t* to involve *Ern's (reified) absence* (Kukso 2006; Martin 1996), or the negative state of affairs *that Ern does not exist* (Barker and Jago 2012; Russell 1903, 1985, 2003), or a *totality state of affairs* (Armstrong 1997, 2004; Russell 1989). (I'll discuss each of those approaches in more detail in §§5.4–5.6.) Alternatively, she might take *t* to be a more familiar kind of entity, and offer an account of how such entities necessitate absences. (I'll discuss such approaches in §§5.2–5.3.)

Whichever option she accepts, the non-maximalist gives up the game against the maximalist. If she accepts reified absences, negative states of affairs, or totality states of affairs into her ontology, then she can no longer claim any ontological advantage over the maximalist. Her trump card, recall, is supposed to be that she explains truthmaking without appeal to exotic absence-necessitating entities. But similarly, if she finds a way to explain how ordinary, ontologically uncontroversial entities necessitate (3.5)'s truth, then the maximalist can appeal to the very same strategy. Either way, the maximalist's ontology is no more demanding or controversial than the non-maximalist's. She has relinquished her main case against the maximalist's ontology.

3.5 Non-Maximalist Replies

The most straightforward response to this argument is to put forward some condition, or set of conditions, on which truths about knowledge depend. One takes up this option by offering a set of conditions which correlate perfectly with the truth of 'x knows that A', for any agent x and any proposition $\langle A \rangle$. Those conditions must be independently necessary and jointly sufficient for knowledge, else the non-maximalist could not say the truth of the knowledge claim depends on those conditions in the way she requires. This is a hard line to maintain, because analyses of knowledge, in the sense of exceptionless necessary and sufficient conditions, have been so prone to counter-examples.

Simpson (2014) takes up the challenge on behalf of the non-maximalist:

> suppose non-maximalists opt for a collection of three propositions, which jointly entail (3.5): A itself [that Ern Malley doesn't exist], B, the proposition that Max believes that Ern Malley does not exist, and C which is the third condition on knowledge. The challenge is to find a condition C which does not entail A, or else is not positive, and such that A, B and C jointly entail (3.5). ... One possible route is a safety account (see e.g. Sosa 1999b) which takes C to be a subjunctive conditional 'Max believes that Ern Malley does not exist $\Box\!\!\rightarrow$ Ern Malley does not exist'. (Simpson 2014, 289–90)

Let's grant with Simpson that condition C, if it exists, won't entail the known proposition. (Simpson's non-maximalist needs that, just to be sure that the kind of argument I ran above can't be run with C in place of (3.5).) Simpson then claims that

> This is enough to answer Jago's challenge, so long as non-maximalists are at least willing to attempt answering Gettier cases. (Simpson 2014, 290)

But the non-maximalist has to do more than be willing to attempt answering the challenge. She needs to find an account which at least stands a chance of offering exceptionless necessary and sufficient conditions for knowledge. But that ain't gonna happen.

Simpson's suggestion for condition C is the safety account of knowledge. There's a variety of accounts under the 'safety' moniker (Pritchard 2005, 2007; Sosa 1999a,b; Williamson 2000). Although they spell out the safety condition in differing ways, the guiding idea is that a belief is safe just in case it could not easily have been false. Sosa makes his condition more precise in counterfactual terms (Sosa 1999b, 146):

(SAFETY) If agent a were to believe that A, then A would be true.

Given the usual possible worlds semantics for counterfactuals, one may interpret SAFETY as saying that, in all of the closest worlds where the agent believes that A, it is true that A. Williamson formulates his notion of safety directly in terms of worlds, so that 'safety is a sort of local necessity' (Williamson 2009, 14). In other words, restricting ourselves to the relevant 'close' worlds only, a belief is safe when it is true in all those worlds. Pritchard (2007, 2009) has a more nuanced (and complicated) notion of a safe belief. He allows that a safe belief may be false in nearby worlds, so long as it remains true in most of the nearby worlds (and in all of the 'very close' nearby worlds).

Why do I claim that safety isn't a good candidate for condition C in an analysis of knowledge? Because safety isn't sufficient for knowledge: one can safely believe that A without knowing that A. It's also plausible that safety isn't necessary either: one can know that A, even though one's belief that A isn't safe. Let me start with the case against the sufficiency of safety.

Suppose an evil scientist has you in a machine that measures your brain activity and that this acts as a trigger. If you believe a certain proposition, $\langle A \rangle$, then the machine will detonate a massive bomb, powerful enough to blow up the whole planet. The brain-reading machine is 100% reliable, but the trigger mechanism, from the brain-reading machine to the bomb, is 95% reliable. You're told to form a belief about (or bet on) whether the bomb will detonate; and, based on no evidence at all, you form the belief that it won't. As it turns out, the evil scientist has programmed the machine to detonate if (but only if) you believe that the bomb will detonate. So the bomb doesn't detonate. Lucky for you (and all of us!) that you formed that belief. If the bomb had detonated, the world would be utterly different in all human-related affairs (since planet Earth would have been blown to smithereens). All such worlds are pretty far from our own (at least, in human-related affairs). All the closest worlds are worlds where the bomb doesn't explode. You could easily have believed that the bomb would explode. But if those worlds are close to ours, then the mechanism must have failed (otherwise they won't be close worlds). So, in all close worlds where you believe that the bomb won't explode, it won't explode. Your lucky belief is safe. But you don't *know* that the bomb won't go off. Your belief was based on no evidence; it was a complete fluke that you got things right. So safety isn't sufficient for knowledge.

The case against safety as a necessary condition for knowledge involves a far less evil scientist. Her machine can affect your beliefs: if the scientist throws a switch, she can hide any pink objects in your line of vision, making the scene appear to you as if there's nothing in your line of vision but the white wall, at which you're now looking. But as things stand, her machine is not affecting your beliefs. Now, you're asked whether there's any pink hippos in your line of vision. You carefully check, and see none; you also see nothing to suggest you're being deceived. You come to believe that there are no pink hippos before you. You have reliable eyesight. Visual conditions are good. You know there are no hippos before you.

As it happens, there are pink hippos wandering around the experimental set-up. By chance, none have walked into your line of vision. But if one had, the scientist would have hit her switch, causing you to hallucinate as if there were no such hippo. Your belief that there are no hippos before you would then have been false. So your belief could easily have been false. Yet we already said that you know, on the basis of your excellent vision, that there are no pink hippos before you. If so, then knowledge doesn't require safe belief.

We might debate the cases; question whether they really are genuine cases of knowledge or knowledge failure; or propose all manner of refinements and further complications to the definition of 'safe belief'. But let's not play that game. There's a number of reasons for thinking that it's a dead end (at least, for the non-maximalist's purposes). First, the kinds of example I've just given are very easy to generate, and appear throughout the extensive literature on knowledge written in response to Gettier's 1963 paper. I think it would be very hard to find a condition on knowledge which avoids all such examples.

Second, even the main advocates of the safety condition—Pritchard, Sosa, and Williamson—see it as a necessary but insufficient condition on knowledge. They wouldn't accept that truths about knowledge are derivative upon truths about safe, true beliefs.

And third, Sosa's and Williamson's defence of safety as a necessary condition must be qualified. Sosa (2009, 2011) allows that there are cases of lucky (and hence unsafe) knowledge, and so doesn't require safety as a necessary condition on knowledge. Williamson (2000, 2009) takes safety to be a *circular* necessary condition on knowledge: whether a world counts as relevant to evaluating safety depends (in part) on what the agent knows. He says, explicitly, that 'the point of the safety conception of knowing is *not* to enable one to determine whether a knowledge attribution is true' (Williamson 2009, 9–10; my emphasis). In short, none of the main defenders of the safety condition think that truths about knowledge depend (in the way we require) on truths about safe belief.

No other account of knowledge does any better than the safety account. So there's excellent reason to think that truths about knowledge don't depend on truths about true belief plus some extra conditions. So (3.5) is not a derivative truth. It must be a positive truth, just as I claimed above.

Skiles (2014) offers an alternative response to the problem of finding condition C. He notes that it needn't tell us anything informative about what knowledge is. We're in the business of explaining truthmaking, not knowledge. His suggestion for condition C is:

(3.7) Max is not in a Gettier scenario

A Gettier scenario is (roughly) any scenario in which a justified true belief fails to count as knowledge.

As things stand, (3.7) is too strong. Max may be in some kind of Gettier scenario, but not one that affects his knowledge concerning Ern. Suppose Max is looking at a clock that happened to stop exactly 12 hours previously. Then he's in a Gettier scenario. But he still knows that Ern doesn't exist: that piece of knowledge is unaffected by the stopped clock. So, in this case, we cannot appeal to (3.7) in a truthmaking analysis of (3.5).

This problem is easily remedied, however. We simply change (3.7) to:

(3.8) Max is not in a Gettier scenario concerning ⟨Ern Malley does not exist⟩.

How should we understand 'Gettier scenario concerning ⟨A⟩'? We might try to pin down precisely which features rule out Gettier scenarios. Suppose the non-Gettier scenarios are those in which belief-forming processes are reliable. Whatever condition we give provides us with an informative condition C on knowledge (e.g., in terms of beliefs being formed by reliable processes). But, as I've just argued, we cannot find any such condition. So this isn't the way to make sense of Skiles's suggestion.

Alternatively, we may take condition C to enumerate all the possible non-Gettier scenarios, so that (3.8) has the content:

(3.9) Max is not in any of the possible scenarios $s_1, s_2, \ldots$.

This approach won't work, however, for a non-Gettier scenario could have been a Gettier scenario. In my current scenario, the clock is working fine. But it could have stopped exactly 12 hours ago. If it had, my current scenario would have been a Gettier scenario (concerning knowledge of the time). So avoiding scenarios $s_1, s_2, \ldots$ (rigidly designated) is insufficient for avoiding a Gettier scenario.

An alternative approach is to pick out Gettier scenarios descriptively. The problem here is that there are innumerable ways in which one can be in a Gettier scenario. The only way to ensure (by description) that Max is not in a Gettier scenario is by saying:

(3.10) If Max justifiably believes that Ern Malley does not exist, and Ern Malley does not exist, then Max knows that Ern Malley does not exist.

Skiles's claim is then that (3.5) depends jointly on (3.10), plus ⟨Max justifiably believes that Ern Malley does not exist⟩, plus (3.1). The claim has the form:

(3.11) ⟨A⟩ depends jointly on ⟨B ∧ C → A⟩, ⟨B⟩, and ⟨C⟩.

But this is implausible. In general, an indicative conditional ⟨B → A⟩'s truth depends in some way on ⟨A⟩ and ⟨B⟩, or on some kind of connection or relationship between them. To illustrate: if the conditional is simply the material conditional, then ⟨B → A⟩ is ⟨¬A ∨ B⟩, whose truth depends on ⟨A⟩'s being false or ⟨B⟩'s being true. But then, ⟨A⟩'s truth cannot also depend on ⟨B → A⟩'s truth. A similar story applies whatever our analysis of the indicative conditional. So Skiles's suggestion cannot be maintained.

3.6 Maximalism Across the Board

Negative existential and general truths are not the only difficult cases for truthmaker maximalists. They must find truthmakers for *all* truths. But it's often held that this claim should be restricted to contingent or synthetic truths (Rodriguez-Pereyra 2005), and perhaps also to truths about the present (Tallant 2009).

I disagree, as I must: if truth is to be understood in terms of truthmaking, then every truth, without restriction, must be accounted for in terms of a truthmaker. I'll discuss what the truthmakers for such truths could be in §5.7, when discussing the metaphysics of truthmakers in general. For now, I will offer a reason for thinking that these truths must have truthmakers (of some kind or other). The argument is just the one from §3.4 above. Consider the following contingent, synthetic, and present-tense truths:

(3.12) ⟨Max knows that sets exists⟩

(3.13) ⟨Max knows that large birds are big birds⟩

(3.14) ⟨Max knows that Jane Austen was born in 1775⟩

These require truthmakers, even on the very narrow version of truthmaker theory restricted to contingent, synthetic, and present-tense truths. Yet those entities necessitate necessary, analytic, and past facts, respectively. Perhaps those entities are states of affairs involving sets, meanings, and relevant bits of the past. But then, it seems, we have entities enough to truthmake necessary and analytic truths, and truths about the past. (The responses and counter-responses to this argument go roughly as they did above, in §3.4 and §3.5.)

3.7 Chapter Summary

I've argued that maximalism is a difficult thesis to defend (§3.1) and that the existing arguments for it are not sufficiently strong (§3.2). I offered a more powerful argument, showing that the non-maximalist is committed to a maximalist ontology (§3.4), and hence that the non-maximalist has no argument against the maximalist. I considered two replies to the argument (§3.5), but concluded that the argument stands. We have good reason to believe that all truths, unrestrictedly, have truthmakers. Just what those truthmakers are, metaphysically speaking, is a further question, and a difficult one. I'll try to answer it in chapters 4 and 5.

II Truthmakers

4

States of Affairs

We've reached the view that states of affairs exist and act as truthmakers for the corresponding propositions. But what are states of affairs, metaphysically speaking? I'll begin to answer this question in this chapter, focusing on the metaphysical nature of positive, logically simple states of affairs, such as that Bertie is snuffling. I'll discuss three approaches (§4.1, §4.2, and §4.3), and argue that all are viable options (§4.4).

4.1 The Fundamental Tie Account

LET'S BEGIN OUR investigation of states of affairs with perhaps the most obvious suggestion: states of affairs comprise a particular and a property (or particulars, in some order, and a relation), somehow tied together to form a unified entity. In this vein, Russell (1903, 1985, 2003) speaks of 'complexes' with 'two kinds of constituents' (Russell 2003, 94): particulars and universals (see also Russell 2003, 89). On Russell's view, 'any time *a* bears the relation *R* to *b* there is a complex "*a* in relation *R* to *b*"' (Russell 2003, 94). Russell also speaks of *facts*, 'which are what they are whatever we may choose to think about them' and which are 'the kind of thing that [make] a proposition true or false' (Russell 2003, 101). 'Fact' and 'complex', in Russell's usage, are evidently synonyms for 'state of affairs', as used here. But he does not say much about their nature, beyond their involving a particular or particulars and a universal (a property or relation) as constituents (2003, 89).

Armstrong (1997) expands on the Russellian picture, taking states of affairs to be composed of particulars and properties, bound together with a 'fundamental tie' (Armstrong 2010). Armstrong's states of affairs are more than the sum of their constituents, however, for it may be that the constituents exist and yet the state of affairs does not (Armstrong 1980, 88–94). He takes those constituents to be what he calls *thin particulars* and *immanent universals*. The latter are properties, multi-located in space and time. The former are particulars 'abstracted in thought from their properties' (Armstrong 1997, 109), leaving only 'the particularity of a particular' (Armstrong 2004, 2004). A 'thin' particular is something like the identity of the particular in question: *what* it is, as opposed to *how* it is.

For present purposes, however, we needn't worry too much about just how Armstrong thinks of these categories. What I'm interested in here is how Armstrong thinks particulars (of any kind) and properties (of any kind) get together to form states of affairs. Armstrong recognises 'a big puzzle in the notion of instantiation', the 'fundamental tie' between particular and property which 'sounds like a relation, but ... seems to go deeper than a relation' (Armstrong 2010, 26–7).

There's a familiar argument against treating the fundamental tie as a relation of *instantiation*. We encountered the argument briefly in §2.5. Suppose instantiation is a relation between particulars and properties. And suppose there's a difference between the existence of two (or more) entities, on the one hand, and the state of affairs which they together compose, on the other. Now consider those original entities, say *a* and *F*, plus the relation of *instantiation*. By hypothesis, there is a difference between those three entities, *a*, *F*, and *instantiation*, and the state of affairs of *a* and *F*'s together instantiating the *instantiation* relation. In other words, the three entities taken together is not the same as *a* instantiating *F*, and so is not the same as the state of affairs *that a is F*. The *instantiation* relation has not helped us to form a state of affairs from its constituents.

(This argument is often called 'Bradley's Regress', after F. H. Bradley. Armstrong cites Bradley's *Appearance and Reality* (Bradley 1897) as the source of the argument (e.g., at Armstrong 2010, 27). In fact, it is hard to find the argument anywhere in Bradley.)

Melia (2005) sums up the situation as follows. Even if we assumed that there was a universal of *instantiation*,

> the semantic function of the predicate 'instantiates' cannot *merely* be to denote the universal—for otherwise the string '*a* instantiates *F*-ness' would be nothing more than a list of denoting terms. (Melia 2005, 68)

But a state of affairs is not merely a list of entities. That's why Armstrong says the fundamental tie 'seems to go deeper than a relation' (2010, 26–7).

So how should we think of the fundamental tie between particulars and their properties? Armstrong describes states of affairs as being *composed* of particulars and properties: they are the constituents of a state of affairs. But this mode of composition is *non-mereological*, Armstrong says. Let's see what this means. A *mereological* composition (or *sum*) of entities *x*, *y*, and *z* is just the whole whose parts are all the parts of *x*, *y*, and *z* (and no more than that). In a sense, the whole is nothing beyond its parts. (Although the whole *is* distinct from the parts, since the whole numbers one, whereas the parts number more than one.) But, says Armstrong, a state of affairs isn't like this. The way a state of affairs's constituents come together must be in a non-mereological way, therefore.

Let's review Armstrong's arguments for thinking this. He offers us two main arguments for this view. The first is as follows:

> What appears to be the decisive argument against this suggestion [that the composition in states of affairs is mereological] is that it is possible that *a* and *F* should both exist and yet *a* not be *F*. (Armstrong 1997, 115)

It takes more to bring a state of affairs into existence than merely bringing its individual constituents into existence. So, says Armstrong, the relationship between constituents and a state of affairs is not the familiar part-whole relationship. This is what Armstrong means by saying that the form of composition involved in states of affairs is not a mereological one.

Armstrong's second argument for thinking that the fundamental tie is a non-mereological mode of composition is as follows:

> If parts are summed mereologically to make a whole, then there can be no more than one whole that they make. If there is such a thing as the sum of *a*, *loving* and *b*, then it is exactly the same thing as the sum of *b*, *loving* and *a*. Armstrong (1997)

But, of course, there are two possible states of affairs that can be made from *a*, *loving*, and *b*. So states of affairs cannot in general be mereological sums of their constituents. (See also Armstrong 1989, 93.)

Both of these arguments make rather large assumptions about the nature of mereological wholes, which aren't accepted by everyone. The first argument assumes that, for any plurality of entities, there is some entity composed of them. This is *mereological universalism* (or *unrestricted composition*), and is highly controversial. It says that any plurality of entities whatsoever, however diverse, however separate in space and time (or even if some are not in space and time at all), form a unified whole. There is an object containing my left little finger, your nose, Socrates, and the number π. Maybe that's the right way to think about things. But many find the consequence absurd.

Suppose we denied unrestricted composition. It won't help to do so by claiming that composition *never* occurs (as Sider (2013a) does). If there are no mereological sums, but there are states of affairs, then states of affairs can't be mereological sums of their constituents. What if we hold instead that some but not all pluralities form a whole? We must then state the conditions under which a plurality does form a whole. But all we could say is that *a* and *F* form a whole just in case *a* is *F*. This defeats our very reason for positing states of affairs: to analyse *a*'s being *F*.

So even though Armstrong's first argument assumes a controversial premise, it seems that the conclusion can be reached without the premise. Those who deny unrestricted composition (as well as those who accept it) have good reason not to treat states of affairs as mereological sums of their constituents. Let's treat this conclusion as provisional, however. I'll offer an account below, in §4.3, which challenges this conclusion, even granting the premise.

(For what it's worth, I accept unrestricted composition, simply because there's no other way to articulate the conditions under which a plurality composes as a whole. So either pluralities never form a whole, or they always do. But clearly, they do sometimes: I have parts and you have parts; this table, this chair, this space, this moment of time all have parts. Conclusion: all pluralities whatsoever compose to form wholes.)

Now let's look at Armstrong's second argument against states of affairs as mereological sums of their constituents. The argument was this: there's only one way to compose particulars and relations mereologically, but more than one way to compose the same entities into states of affairs. So states of affairs aren't mereological compositions of their constituents. This argument also trades on a controversial premise: that given some things, there's only one mereological whole you can form from them. That's a principle of the theory known as *extensional mereology*.

We get extensional mereology by taking the *parthood* relation (as in, x is a part of y) to be reflexive, antisymmetric, and transitive, and insisting on the principle of *strong supplementation*:

(SS) If y is not a part of x, then there is some part z of y which doesn't overlap x (i.e., x and z have no part in common).

If we accept all that, then mereology behaves as an extensional theory: mereological wholes are defined by their parts. There's no way to take some entities and form distinct wholes containing exactly those parts. So if we accept all that, then Armstrong's argument looks good: the difference between *that Anna loves Bertie* and *that Bertie loves Anna* shows us that neither state of affairs is the mereological sum of *Anna*, *Bertie*, and *loving*.

Strong supplementation, and consequently extensional mereology, are very plausible. Non-extensional mereologies are mathematically interesting theories, but it is hard to make sense of two objects which nevertheless have exactly the same parts as one another. (We can't point to states of affairs as counterexamples, since we're trying to establish whether states of affairs can be mereological wholes.) So Armstrong's second argument is persuasive. If states of affairs are composed of particulars and properties at all, then we have good reason to take that composition to be non-mereological.

The picture we have is that the fundamental tie between particular and property is a non-mereological mode of composition. What more can we say to characterise the fundamental tie? Is there just one non-mereological kind of composition (so that the tie is *the* non-mereological kind), or are there many ways to compose some entities non-mereologically? Saying that the tie is not a familiar kind of composition is helpful, as far as it goes, but clearly doesn't enlighten us all that much. We still want to know: just what is this fundamental tie?

Let's see what Armstrong says on the matter. In his last writings on the subject, he offers us 'a new suggestion' (Armstrong 2010, 32). The suggestion concerns the Humean ban on necessary connections between distinct entities, which Armstrong considers 'quite attractive' as a general rule:

> But I am now going to suggest that we could relax it a little. Suppose we allowed there to be necessary connections in re, in the world. In particular suppose we were to postulate an objective necessity holding between particulars and universals. We might well make the connection to be of a limited sort. It might be no more than this. Universals (contingent beings as I think) need not have just the instantiations that they actually have. But they must (an anti-Humean must) be instantiated by particulars, at least once. Particulars (contingent beings) need not have the properties they actually have. But they must (an anti-Humean must) instantiate universals. There would then be a mild necessary connection between particulars and universals, and this would be the 'fundamental tie' that so many metaphysicians have felt it necessary to postulate. Particulars and universals would retain their distinctness while needing connection with the other. (Armstrong 2010, 32–3)

Armstrong's suggestion is that this 'mild' necessary connection between particulars and properties 'explains the mysterious nature of the fundamental tie that holds the constituents of states of affairs together, thus giving us the states of affairs' (2010, 33).

I don't see how Armstrong's suggestion can explain the fundamental tie. Take our state of affairs *that Bertie is snuffling*. Armstrong's 'mild' necessary connection isn't between Bertie and *snuffling*: it isn't between Bertie and any particular property (except, perhaps, the property *possessing some property or other*). The state of affairs is utterly contingent, and so no necessary connection can enter into it. If a necessary connection doesn't hold where the tie does hold, then I can't see how the former can explain the latter.

Even setting this problem to one side, it is hard to explain one obscure notion merely by postulating a necessary connection. The very reason Humeans deny that there are any necessary connections is that they find the notion completely inexplicable. Necessary connections call out for an explanation. A mysterious connection can't be explained solely by saying that there's a necessary connection in the neighbourhood. That is to heap mystery on mystery.

Armstrong's suggestion is best viewed as telling us something about the nature of possible worlds, and not about the nature of states of affairs. The suggestion amounts to this: there's no possible world which contains a particular which doesn't also contain some state of affairs containing that particular; and similarly, there's no possible world containing some property which doesn't also contain some state of affairs containing that property (in 'property position'). That would be the case if possible worlds have states of affairs as their basic building blocks: if, as Wittgenstein had it, worlds are totalities of states of affairs, not of things.

Armstrong accepts exactly this picture of reality, on which 'the fundamental realities that constitute the world and are capable of independent existence are states of affairs' (Armstrong 2010, 26). Accepting this view tells us about the nature of possible worlds. But it tells us nothing about the nature of the states of affairs that make up those worlds. As far as this view is concerned, states of affairs might be primitive entities without internal constituents. (I'll discuss such a theory in §4.2.)

We should set Armstrong's suggestion to one side: it can't help us to understand the nature of states of affairs. We must ask once again: how can we explain the fundamental tie—this strange notion of non-mereological composition—which holds between particulars and their properties?

It might help if we spell out a few properties of non-mereological composition and non-mereological parthood. Let's notate the non-mereological composition of x and y as '$x \wedge y$' and x's being a non-mereological constituent of z as '$x \prec z$'. Then $\prec$ is irreflexive, asymmetric, and non-transitive. Nothing is a constituent of itself; no pair of entities are constituents of one another; and the constituents of constituents of some entity need not be constituents of that entity.

The state of affairs *that Bertie is wheezing* has Bertie as a constituent; but *that (that Bertie is wheezing) is a state of affairs* does not have Bertie as a constituent. But constituents of constituents of some entity may be constituents of that entity: *being a state of affairs* is a constituent of both *that s is a state of affairs* and *that (that s is a state of affairs) is a state of affairs*. So $\prec$ is non-transitive, not intransitive.

This relation $\prec$ fails the analogue of *strong supplementation*:

(4.1) If $y \not\prec x$ and $x \neq y$ then there is some $z \prec y$ which is not a constituent of, and has no constituent in common with, x.

It fails this principle because there may be upper bounds, but no unique upper bound, for a pair x, y with respect to $\prec$. In principle, x and y can be non-mereologically composed in distinct ways: $x \wedge y$ and $y \wedge x$. Then we have $x \wedge y \not\prec y \wedge x$ and $x \wedge y \neq y \wedge x$ but both x and y are constituents of $y \wedge x$, and so (4.1) is false.

A non-mereological composition $x \wedge y$ is an upper bound of x, y with respect to $\prec$ (that is, $x, y \prec x \wedge y$). But we cannot define $x \wedge y$ as the least such entity: given that $\prec$ does not satisfy (4.1), there may be no such entity. The operator $\wedge$ is non-commutative ($x \wedge y \neq y \wedge x$ for some x, y) and anti-associative (($x \wedge y) \wedge z \neq x \wedge (y \wedge z)$ for any x, y, z).

We may allow that some properties can instantiate themselves: *being a property* is a case in point. Then, setting $x = y =$ *being a property*, we have $x \wedge y = x \wedge y$. But the example may be misleading: it might be that properties are arranged in a hierarchy, such that a property can be instantiated only by entities lower in the hierarchy. (There may be properties *being a level-1 property*, *being a level-2 property*, and so on.) If that's right, then $\wedge$ is anti-commutative: $x \wedge y \neq x \wedge y$ for any x, y. It's fair to say that, from a mathematical point of view, $\prec$ and $\wedge$ are not particularly interesting. Pursuing the mathematical approach to uncovering their properties won't get us very far.

We've been trying to understand what the nature of the fundamental tie is: what is it for a property and a particular to compose, non-mereologically, a state of affairs? Perhaps the best we can say is this: the fundamental tie is philosophically and mathematically opaque. There's very little we can say about it, philosophically or logically.

Now, that in itself isn't an argument against the view. At some point in our philosophical theory, there's going to be concepts that we can't say much about. But of course, it would be far better if we could avoid working with such opaque concepts. So, for all we've said so far, Armstrong's approach remains a live option. We haven't ruled it out. But if we come up with an alternative theory, which goes further in explaining the metaphysical nature of states of affairs and coheres well with our other philosophical commitments, then that alternative theory may well be preferable to Armstrong's.

4.2 The Primitivist Account

Let's consider a different approach to states of affairs. Skyrms (1981) develops an idea he finds in Wittgenstein's *Tractatus* into a metaphysics of states of affairs. Skyrms writes:

> Wittgenstein's truly daring idea was that the ontology of the subject (nominalism) and the ontology of the predicate

(platonism) were both equally wrong and one-sided; and that they should give way to the ontology of the assertion. We may conceive of the world not as a world of individuals or as a world of properties and relations, but as a world of facts—with individuals and relations being equally abstractions from the facts. (Skyrms 1981, 199)

On this view, states of affairs are not made up of constituents of some other ontological category (not objects; not properties). Rather, they are metaphysically primitive and unstructured:

Facts [i.e., states of affairs] are primitive entities. Nevertheless we can say something about their nature in terms of the way in which we classify them. An atomic fact can be completely characterized by a relational-classification (e.g. is-a-loves-fact) and its coordinate object-classifications (e.g. with John standing in the first place of the loving relation and Mary in the second).

(It isn't easy to square this idea with Wittgenstein's notion that states of affairs are 'configuration[s] of objects' (1921/1922, §2.0272). But never mind: Skyrms's project isn't Wittgenstein exegesis, but rather, the development of the interesting idea just quoted.)

An immediate issue with this suggestion is: if states of affairs are primitive, how do we associate these entities with particulars, properties, and relations? What it is about two primitive states, x and y, that tells us that each is a *redness* state, or a John-involving state? What makes one way of classifying the primitive states of affairs in terms of particulars, properties, and relations right, and another way wrong? And what can it mean for the particulars associated with a state of affairs to stand in the first (or the second, or ...) place of the associated relation? That would seem to require a structure of argument places, which primitive structureless entities don't have.

Skyrms says relatively little on these issues. In response to the central question of how we associate particulars, properties, and relations with primitive states, he says:

The way we break things up depends on what objects and relations we take as being most *generally* useful in characterizing the world. This determination is made by *science*, not logic. ... Science judges which are the fundamental objects and relations of the world. This is a *pragmatic* evaluation. (Skyrms 1981, 201)

The idea, I take it, is that some ways of associating primitive states with particulars, properties, and relations are more useful to us than other ways. If there's a unique most useful way of carving things up, then that's the way we should. If several such ways are equally as good, then we can pick any of those ways. There's no independent fact of the matter as to which way is right. So ultimately, according to Skyrms, our identifying a particular primitive entity as the state of affairs *that Bertie is snuffling* is a pragmatic matter.

But here's a curious fact. Suppose we also pick out a different primitive entity as the state of affairs *that Bertie is sleeping*, and another still as the state of affairs *that Anna is snuffling*. We re-use pieces of language (names and predicates) when we pick out different primitive states. Why so? Is it that they have something in common with our original state, that makes it right or useful to re-use a name like 'Bertie' or a predicate like 'snuffling' in the new cases? It seems wildly implausible to say that there's nothing about the two states, in virtue of which we describe both using 'Bertie'. As Turner says, 'if all reality supplies is an infinite list of brute necessary connections, how did we get a priori, productive access to them?' (Turner 2016, 41). It seems, on Skyrms's view, that

> There are no general features of reality for us to pick up on, whether in a cognitively transparent way or not, that would let us evaluate the quasi-validity of novel arguments we had never seen before. (Turner 2016, 41)

Our ability to identify and re-identify states of affairs as involving Anna or Bertie, and to draw useful inferences from them in a systematic way, can't be a cosmic coincidence. Skyrms has a problem making sense of these features of our language use and inferential practices.

The problem is not (merely) about how we do or should carve up the world using bits of language. Rather, the problem is to explain how we are so successful in attaching words for particulars and properties to things that are, metaphysically, nothing of the sort. There must be something about those primitive, structureless states in virtue of which our choices are correct, or justified, or more useful than other possible choices.

Turner (2016) takes up that explanatory challenge. His response is to think of states of affairs in terms of geometrical structures, together with a systematic way of understanding certain geometric features in the familiar subject-predicate way. In Turner's hands, concepts such as *having Bertie in the 1st argument place*, or *being a snuffling-state*, are analysed in purely geometrical terms.

To illustrate some of the central ideas in Turner's approach, consider the square in figure 4.1. Think of each sentence 'Rxy' as a state of affairs. Notice how the horizontal line labelled 'a' features all the states of affairs in which a appears in R's first argument place (and similarly for the other horizontal lines). The vertical line labelled 'a' features all the states of affairs with a in R's second argument place (and similarly for the other vertical lines). The diagonal features states of affairs in which one entity fills both of R's argument places.

If we begin with R, a, and b, it's easy to see how to construct this geometrical arrangement. Turner's idea is to work in reverse: begin with the geometrical arrangement of primitive states and (using notions like 'line' and 'diagonal') recover talk of the 'constituents', R, a and b.

Turner axiomatises his theory, using two primitive geometrical relations and an *orientation function* (which I'll say something about below). Geometrical models of the theory (combined with an orientation function) have the following property: picking out certain geometrical structures in a specified way is guaranteed to single out a unique state of affairs. Indeed, we can systematically map predicates 'R' and names 'a', 'b' onto geometrical structures such that (again, given an orientation function), 'Rab' picks out a unique state of affairs, the one we think of as *that Rab*.

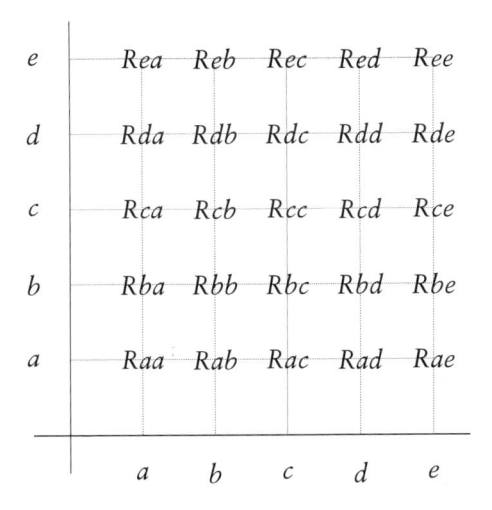

```
e  |  Rea   Reb   Rec   Red   Ree

d  |  Rda   Rdb   Rdc   Rdd   Rde

c  |  Rca   Rcb   Rcc   Rcd   Rce

b  |  Rba   Rbb   Rbc   Rbd   Rbe

a  |  Raa   Rab   Rac   Rad   Rae
   |_____
       a     b     c     d     e
```

Figure 4.1: STATES OF AFFAIRS MAPPED GEOMETRICALLY

Turner's achievement is remarkable. It is not at all obvious that geometrical structures on primitive states of affairs can be systemically associated with a first-order language with the usual subject-predicate structure. Turner shows—and formally proves—that it can be done. His full account is precise and complex: I can't hope to do it justice here. But this brief sketch should provide enough information about the shape of Turner's approach to allow us to raise some issues.

The first issue concerns Turner's geometric relations. They hold between primitive states of affairs. It might be that states $s_1, \ldots, s_5$ form a straight line, which is parallel to the line formed by $s_6, \ldots, s_{10}$. On Turner's story, these geometrical relationships—*forming a line*, *being parallel to*—are not of a kind with the non-fundamental relations holding between particulars, such as *liking* or *being taller than*. The latter group of relations are derivative on the basic states of affairs and their geometrical arrangement. The geometrical relations holding between states of affairs, by contrast, are primitive and metaphysically fundamental; they are not derived from further states of affairs.

As a consequence, if states $s_1, \ldots, s_5$ form a line, then there is no state of affairs *that* $s_1, \ldots, s_5$ *form a line*. Rather, there exists just those states $s_1, \ldots, s_5$, which, nevertheless, form a line. So on reflection, we should not talk about there existing relations like ... *form a line*. Turner puts the position as follows:

> When I said there were some relations, that was a mere *façon de parler*. There are just the facts [i.e., states of affairs]. But the facts are externally structured. They are systematically related to each other, and we can speak informatively about how they are related to each other. Ultimately, I will write down a sober metaphysical theory. That metaphysical theory will have predicates — relational predicates — that I use to say metaphysically serious things about how these facts are interrelated. But using these predicates doesn't commit me to there being *relations* ... (Turner 2016, 22)

Recalling Quine's (1948) idea that predicates are mere ideology—which Armstrong (1978) dubs 'ostrich nominalism'—Turner describes someone who accepts the theory as 'an ostrich about her quasi-geometric predicates' (Turner 2016, 22).

I argued in §2.4 that nominalism across the board isn't tenable. So Quine's ostrich nominalism is out: one cannot be an ostrich about all predicates. But that argument doesn't prohibit being an ostrich about some predicates. Indeed, since Turner relies on just two primitive geometrical predicates, we can be sure that his approach avoids the worry I raised there.

The issue, rather, is that Turner doesn't provide us with a unified analysis of predication. Some predications will be treated ontologically, by being associated with a state of affairs. Others will be treated ideologically, with no corresponding ontology. We find all the metaphysically derivative predications in the former category, and all the primitive geometrical predications in the later. How much of an issue is this (if it's an issue at all)?

It depends on what we want from a theory of states of affairs. Some, including Armstrong (1997), posit states of affairs in order to explain what it is for particulars to possess properties and stand in relations.

On this view, a theory of states of affairs provides an ontological analysis of predication. If that's what we want a theory of states of affairs to do, then that theory should apply to all predications. But Turner's theory doesn't do that and so (if that's what we want a theory to do) it isn't the one for us.

Turner's aim isn't to give an ontological analysis of predication, however. Rather, he is exploring whether the ways the world appears to be can be grounded in primitive, structureless states of affairs. That aim doesn't require a state of affairs corresponding to each true predication. Some of those predications might be truths stipulated by the theory itself.

My view is that (other things being equal) a theory which explains predication trumps one which doesn't; and (again, other things being equal) a theory which explains predication in a uniform way trumps one that explains it in disparate ways. That point will feature when we come to weigh up the viable options. It isn't in itself a reason to reject Turner's account.

Let's turn to another worry with Turner's account. As a first pass, the worry is this. On Turner's theory, the state of affairs *that a is F* could have been some completely different state of affairs, say, *that b is G*. There's nothing about any state of affairs itself that makes it *that* state of affairs, rather than some other. Indeed, there's nothing about Turner's entities, in and of themselves, that makes them states of affairs at all. All of that depends on their being geometrically arranged with respect to one another. The objection is that states of affairs can't be like that. Rather, the state of affairs *that a is F* must be essentially and intrinsically, in and of itself, the state of affairs *that a is F*.

As it stands, this objection isn't right. For Turner, the states of affairs exist in *logical space*. The geometrical relations between them extend through logical space, and so extend over distinct possible worlds. In moving from world to world, those geometrical relations do not change. As a consequence, those geometrical relations between states of affairs hold of necessity. So, Turner can say, the worry just raised never gets off the ground.

I disagree. To appreciate the thought behind the objection, we need to understand a little more of Turner's theory. Its centrepiece is an axiomatic geometrical system. Those axioms have many models (just as logical axioms or scientific laws do). Each such model is a model of all logical space, and hence each such model fixes what is possible and necessary (relative to that model). For Turner, there is a unique *intended model*, which captures what is really the case. What is really possible (or necessary) is what is possible (or necessary) according to the intended model.

But this move stands in tension with the following observation. When one devises a theoretical system or theory of some kind, one thereby sets up a notion of possibility (and necessity), in terms of what is allowed by (and what is required by) that system or theory. When we lay down a system of laws of nature, for example, we thereby give criteria for *nomic possibility and necessity*. What is nomically possible (gives those laws) is whatever is consistent with the laws; what is nomically necessary (gives those laws) is whatever is entailed by those laws. Similarly, when we lay down logical laws, we thereby give criteria for *logical possibility and necessity*. And by the same token, when one lays down a system of metaphysical laws, one thereby gives a criterion for metaphysical possibility and necessity. In general, we get a notion of possibility from a theory by holding fixed its axioms (or rules, or other posits), and seeing what they allow.

When a metaphysical system stipulates that metaphysical possibility and necessity is to be understood relative to the intended model, we have conflicting criteria. On the one hand, metaphysical possibility is given by the possible worlds of the intended model; on the other, it is given by consistency with the laws of metaphysics. These criteria conflict when there are models of the metaphysical laws which correspond to no world of the intended model. In our present case, they conflict because there are models of Turner's geometrical axioms which differ from the intended model on how the primitive states are related.

We can resolve the tension (in general, and to some extent) by distinguishing between different notions of possibility: we may even allow different notions of metaphysical possibility. One such notion is given by the worlds of the intended model. On this notion, alternative geometrical arrangements of primitive entities are not genuine possibilities. Nevertheless, there is a broader notion of genuine possibility: whatever is allowed whilst holding Turner's axioms fixed. In this sense of possibility, alternative geometrical relationships between primitive entities are possible. Each geometrical model satisfying Turner's axioms gives a genuine possibility, in this sense of 'possibility'.

Those models differ on how the primitive entities are related to one another, and hence differ on which of those primitive entities is (say) the state of affairs *that a is F*. It might be that, in one such model, primitive entity s_1 is the state of affairs *that a is F*, whereas in another such model, s_2 is the state of affairs *that a is F*. Being the state of affairs *that a is F* is a role played by a primitive entity relative to a model. Given this broader sense of possibility, the actual state of affairs *that a is F* could have been the state of affairs *that b is G*, as in the original objection. And that is not a happy conclusion to draw for a defender of states of affairs.

Turner may respond by denying that there's a genuine sense of possibility corresponding to his geometrical models (or, equivalently, to consistency with his axioms). Or he may bite the bullet and accept that a given state of affairs could have been some other state of affairs. The first option is unattractive on methodological grounds. Someone who denies this sense of possibility is then under pressure to reject other senses of possibility which deviate from *how the world could have been*, including the nomic, logical, mathematical, conceptual, and epistemic notions of possibility. A blanket ban on all such notions is unattractive.

The problem with the second option is that the concept of a state of affairs just doesn't allow that a given state of affairs could have been some other state of affairs. We identify states of affairs by what they make the case: for something to be the case just is for a given state of affairs to exist. That is the very nature of that state of affairs. But given that, there is no possibility—not even a conceptual or epistemic possibility—of a gap between a state's identity and what it makes the case. It is conceptually necessary that *being that a is F* fixes a state's very identity, rather than being a role with different potential occupiers. So this issue is a genuine worry for Turner's proposal.

In sum, Turner's account is as precise and detailed as we could wish a theory of states of affairs to be. It trumps Armstrong's non-mereological theory in many respects. Although it introduces more theoretical primitives than Armstrong's view, each of Turner's primitives are fully axiomatised, whereas Armstrong's notion of non-mereological composition is opaque. However, Turner's view seems to conflict with what I take to be a conceptual truth about states of affairs: that the state of affairs *that a is F* is necessarily, by its very nature, the state of affairs *that a is F*. Neither theory is clearly better than the other.

4.3 The Mereological Account

The two approaches we've looked at so far might seem to exhaust our options. Either states of affairs are primitive, or else they're built in some special, non-mereological way from particulars, properties, and relations. In this section, I will revisit a thread from §4.1, where we encountered Armstrong's arguments against the simple view on which states of affairs are mereological sums of particulars, properties, and relations. If those arguments can be met (and I think they can), we would certainly have a worthwhile theory: states of affairs would not require any mysterious fundamental tie, but neither would they be primitive, constituent-less entities.

The idea is to take the state of affairs *that Fa* to be no more than the mereological sum of property F and particular a, which I'll write '$F \sqcup a$'. I'll call this the *mereological account* of states of affairs. If this approach is coherent, those who believe in states of affairs can benefit greatly in ontological and ideological parsimony. If one accepts the ontologically primitive entities of the theory—particulars, properties, and relations—then the mereological theory's states of affairs incur no additional ontological cost, beyond that already incurred by unrestricted mereological composition. And, given acceptance of mereology theory, states of affairs incur no additional ideological cost. For these reasons alone, the mereological theory is worth investigating.

(Since we can argue for unrestricted composition on independent grounds, this shouldn't count as a cost to the theory. Indeed, it is moot whether there is a cost at all. Lewis (1991, 82) argues that 'the new commitment [to mereological wholes] is redundant, given the old one [to the parts]'.)

Armstrong's two arguments against the idea were as follows. First, a particular and a property may exist without that particular having that property. By contrast, the mereological sum of particular and property exists whenever its parts do, and so the state of affairs cannot be the mereological sum of particular and property. Second, a relation and some particulars may sum into just one mereological whole, whereas they may form multiple states of affairs: *that Rab* is not the same as *that Rba*. So again, a state of affairs cannot be a mereological sum.

I indicated in §4.1 that both arguments rely on assumptions about how mereology works. Those assumptions are *mereological universalism* (the whole exists whenever the parts do) and *extensionality* (distinct wholes differ in their parts). Nevertheless, both assumptions are very reasonable. In fact, mereology is at its best as a comprehensible theory when both assumptions are in play. I accept both assumptions. So let's suppose Armstrong's conclusions are right: for each particular and property there exists a unique sum of that particular and property. How, then, can I even suggest that states of affairs might be mereological sums?

Consider the idea that there are unrealised possibilities. You might have picked some other book to read right now. I could have been a musician rather than a philosopher. Had things gone differently in the distant past, conscious life may never have evolved on Earth. These are all unrealised possibilities. There are lots of possibilities like this. But now consider that thought very seriously: *there are* such unrealised possibilities. What are they? Well, in some sense, they're states of affairs, much like the current states of affairs *that you're reading this book*, *that I'm a philosopher*, and *that there's conscious life of Earth*. But in another sense, the former group of states of affairs are very unlike the latter group. The latter states of affairs actually obtain: they all relate to how our reality actually turned out. The former, by contrast, relate to how things merely could have gone.

This line of thought suggests that there are states of affairs which do not obtain. They exist all right—there *are* such unrealised possibilities—but they do not contribute to making up the world around us. This line of thought holds that there is a vast plurality of states of affairs, only some of which make up the actual world. The remainder make up various merely possible worlds. Such states of affairs are the unrealised possibilities: the unfulfilled dreams, lucky escapes, and wild scenarios that never came to pass.

This thought allows the approach to deal with Armstrong's first worry: I exist, as does the property *being a musician*, but I'm not a musician, so there's no state of affairs *that MJ is a musician*. Or rather, we should now say that there's no obtaining state of affairs *that I'm a musician*. But there is a state of affairs *that MJ is a musician*, the sum of me and the property *being a musician*. That state of affairs is an unrealised possibility, a state of affairs which obtains at some merely possible world. (I'll consider a variation on Armstrong's first worry, as well as his second worry, below.)

Whenever we have particulars and properties, we have the corresponding states of affairs, only some of which obtain. To make sense of this idea, we need to factor this abundance of states of affairs into discrete, well-behaved worlds. It is very natural to think of worlds as being in some way made up of states of affairs. Let's say, as a first attempt, that a possible world is a collection of states of affairs, meeting certain conditions (with the nature of a 'collection' and the precise conditions to be spelled out at a later date). We will want to rule out a particular possessing conflicting properties, given some prior notion of conflict. We will require that $F \sqcup a$ and $G \sqcup a$ (the mereological sums of F and a, and of G and b, respectively) belong to a collection only if F and G do not conflict. We then identify possible worlds with the collections of states of affairs meeting our conditions. We might then ignore the deviant collections, giving them no role in our system. Or we might identify them with *impossible* worlds.

We can't think of these collections of states of affairs as mereological sums. (At least, we can't if we adopt classical extensional mereology). For if we did, there would be no difference between the (toy) world containing the states of affairs *that a is F* and *that b is G* and the (toy) world containing the states of affairs *that b is F* and *that a is G*. Both would be the sum $F \sqcup a \sqcup G \sqcup b$. But these worlds are different, so they cannot be sums of states of affairs. (Of course, no possible world contains so few states of affairs anyway.)

Instead, we can take worlds to be nonempty sets of states of affairs. But wait! Wouldn't that make possible worlds abstract entities, on a par with numbers, functions, and other mathematical entities? We want worlds (or this world, at least) to be concrete entities, just as physical as the ground beneath our feet.

Why is it that philosophers tend to think of sets as wholly abstract entities, existing nowhere and nowhen, standing in such stark contrast to spatiotemporally located concrete entities such as you and me? One reason is that *pure* sets—sets built from nothing but other sets—are paradigmatic mathematical entities, and it's common (for those who believe in mathematical entities at all) to think of them as being outside time and space. How else could they give rise to immutable mathematical truths? But what we're interested in here are the *impure* sets and, in particular, those built from concrete spatiotemporal entities. So our question is: is a set of concrete entities, such as the set containing me and you and your copy of this book, an abstract entity or a concrete one? Does it exist outside time and space? Is it akin to mathematical entities like pure sets, numbers, and functions? (And if so, in which ways?) Or should it be grouped along with the concrete entries which make it up?

Lewis (1991) is keen to emphasise that nothing we know for sure about sets depends on taking them to be abstract entities, outside time and space. Instead, he suggests, we could take a singleton $\{a\}$

to be located wherever and whenever the material object *a* goes (Lewis 1991, 1993). And, similarly, we could take the pair $\{a, b\}$ to be located (possibly discontinuously) wherever and whenever the material objects *a* and *b* are individually. As Lewis says, 'we go much too fast from not knowing whether [sets] are [spatiotemporally located] to thinking we know they are not' (Lewis 1993, 13).

Do we have any positive reasons for thinking that sets containing spatiotemporally located entities are themselves spatiotemporally located? Perhaps. If you're a presentist, you think that Ada Lovelace—mathematician, key contributor to the development of computers, and daughter of Byron—existed but exists no longer. You should say the same for singleton, {Ada}. It existed when Ada did, but if it still existed, you could infer Ada's existence too, contrary to your presentism. So, by presentist lights, some sets are located (in time at least). I'm not a presentist. But I do think it's a conceptually coherent view, and it's a view many philosophers accept. So, by implication, taking {Ada} to be a temporally (or even a spatiotemporally) located entity is conceptually coherent, and is a view that many philosophers should accept.

It's at least plausible that sets are spatiotemporally located when they have spatiotemporally located members. In particular, it's plausible that sets of concrete states of affairs are themselves spatiotemporally located. So it's at least plausible that concrete possible worlds are sets of states of affairs. Whilst I don't have an argument which convinces me that this theory is correct, I think it's worth investigating the view further.

A world collects together what is the case, according to it. So let us say that *a* is F, according to world *w*, just in case some state of affairs *that a is F* is a member of *w*. This is so just in case $F \sqcup a \in w$. Then $F \sqcup a$ will be spatiotemporally located whenever *a* is and so world *w* too will be spatiotemporally located whenever *a* is. Worlds will come out as concrete entities. Phew! As a consequence, worlds (thus conceived) overlap quite literally. It is precisely the same particulars, properties, relations, and states of affairs that may be found across distinct worlds.

Now we can consider a variant of Armstrong's first objection to the mereological view which I didn't deal with adequately above. The claim is that, if x and y are parts of world w, then their sum $x \sqcup y$ is also a part of world w. If so, and if states of affairs are sums, then *that Fa* is a part of w whenever a and F are. But now suppose that states of affairs *that Fb* and *that Ga* obtain, relative to w. Then, the argument goes, F and a are parts of w, and hence so is *that Fa*. But this is absurd, for an *Fb*-and-*Ga* world need not be an *Fa*-world.

This consequence does not follow, however. Given the mereological account, states of affairs are members, not parts, of worlds. To obtain a similarly worrying conclusion from the mereological account, we would need to add an additional premise:

(4.2) If x and y are parts of members of world w, then their sum $x \sqcup y$ is also a member of world w.

But this is not in the least plausible. A world is a specific collection of things. Parts of things in that collection need not be in the collection. By analogy: the current team is a collection of players. Anna is one of the players, but her left foot is not. Another analogy: an inventory of the Dali collection will include *Persistence of Memory*. Not included in the inventory is a small bit of canvas, which is nevertheless a part of *Persistence of Memory*. Quite generally, parts of members of x needn't be members of x. The objection doesn't worry the mereological account.

We must now consider the case of relational universals and the states of affairs in which they feature. Such states of affairs feature two or more particulars. If those particulars feature in those states of affairs as mereological parts, then there is no intrinsic difference between the state of affairs *that Rab* and the state of affairs *that Rba*. States of affairs, if mereological sums, are unordered entities. This seems flatly to contradict the obvious fact that there are non-symmetric relations R, such that *Rab* may hold without *Rba* holding. This was Armstrong's second objection to the mereological view.

The best way to address the problem is to think of a state of affairs *that Rabcd* as the sum of R with the *sequence abcd*. That sequence is not merely the sum of *a*, *b*, *c*, and *d* (there are 24 such sequences, but only one such sum). It is essential to this view that we treat a sequence *abcd* as a single object. As Quine says (of ordered pairs):

> It is central to the purposes of the notion of ordered pair to admit ordered pairs as objects. ... the very point of the ordered pair is its role of object—of a single object doing the work of two. (Quine 1960, 257)

The same goes for sequences in general. So the mereological account needs to give a story of what sequences are. It cannot do so by invoking various relations holding between the sequenced particulars, for that would require a prior explanation of non-symmetric relations: precisely what is to be explained! Nor should the mereological theory take there to be some primitive sequence-forming operation, for the resulting theory would be just as opaque as the notion of non-mereological composition (§4.1).

The best option for the mereological theory is to take sequences to be sets, via Kuratowski reduction: the sequence xy is $\{\{x\}, \{x,y\}\}$ and, for any sequence σ, the sequence $x\sigma$ is $\{\{x\}, \sigma\}$. (I argued above that sets of located entities are themselves located. Thus the sequence *abcd* will be located exactly where *a*, *b*, *c*, and *d* are located.)

Here is a worry for this view. Shouldn't *that Anna loves Bec* involve Anna and Bec (the material entities) directly, rather than sets containing them? All parties should agree that the way in which *that Anna loves Bec* involves Anna and Bec somehow captures Anna and Bec in that specific order. It is then an open question how to treat 'Anna and Bec in that order'. The suggestion here is to adopt an ontological interpretation: what *that Anna loves Bec* involves is the entity: *Anna and Bec in that order*. That entity is the Anna-and-Bec-involving entity which puts Anna first, Bec second; it is the sequence: Anna, Bec (identified with the set $\{\{Anna, \{Anna, Bec\}\}$).

$\{Anna\}$ is certainly distinct from Anna, and $\{\{Anna, \{Anna, Bec\}\}$ is certainly distinct from Anna and Bec together. Nevertheless, $\{Anna\}$ is intimately connected with Anna, in that she alone gives $\{Anna\}$ its identity. Indeed, the Kuratowski reduction of sequences is suggestive:

{Anna} may be thought of as the entity *Anna first* (as in, *Anna first, Bec second*). On this reading, what *that Anna loves Bec* involves is (i) the *loving* relation, and (ii) the concrete collection of *Anna first* and *Bec second*. But then, *that Anna loves Bec* does indeed involve Anna and Bec in an appropriate way.

(One curiosity of this view: a collection $\{x, y\}$ is *y second* when collected with *x first*; it is *x second* when collected with *y first*; and it is merely a collection otherwise. So $\lambda x.being\ x\ second$ is an extrinsic property, whereas $\lambda x.being\ x\ first$ is intrinsic. That's a curiosity, but not an objection.)

In summary, the view under consideration treats states of affairs as intrinsically ordered entities in virtue of having sequences as parts. Sequences of spatiotemporally located entities are themselves spatiotemporally located entities, and hence so are the states of affairs involving them, just as we expect them to be.

4.4 Comparing the Approaches

I've discussed three accounts of the nature of states of affairs: the fundamental tie account (§4.1), the primitivist account (§4.2), and the mereological account (§4.3). Which is best? Each is coherent; each has its advantages and disadvantages; each provides a workable metaphysics of states of affairs. We could continue our investigation of truth and truthmaking with any of these accounts in place. I needn't settle on one of them.

Nevertheless, it's worth discussing their comparative merits before moving on. The fundamental tie account faces the objection from opacity (as discussed in §4.1). That sets up the account for a fall: it's likely to be trumped by a similarly coherent but less opaque account. Yet it is the only account discussed here compatible with a strict actualist metaphysics, on which everything that exists actually exists. Both the primitivist and the mereological account accept the existence of non-actual states of affairs. If that's an absolute deal-breaker in your metaphysics, then you should accept the fundamental tie account, opaque as it is.

The primitive account of state of affairs is elegant and powerful, but (of course) it comes with ideological and metaphysical costs. A cost of the mereological account is that we have to think of worlds as located sets of states of affairs. But if we accept that impure sets in general can be located, then that's not so big an issue. The mereological account has the advantage—uniquely in theories of states of affairs—that it requires no theoretical primitives over and above those to which we're already committed.

Much of what follows (chapter 5 aside) is equally compatible with these three accounts of states of affairs. So feel free to select your preferred theory. Or, if you're undecided, we can go forward with a theoretical 'black box' account of states of affairs in mind: they're whatever entities make true propositions such as ⟨Bertie is snuffling⟩.

4.5 Chapter Summary

I've presented three approaches to (positive, logically simple) states of affairs: the fundamental tie account (§4.1), the primitivist account (§4.2), and the mereological account (§4.3). All three are viable options. Each have their advantages and disadvantages (§4.4), and none emerges as the outright best account.

5

Everything and Nothing

What should we say about the 'difficult' cases of truthmaking, involving general and negative existential truths, modal truths, counterfactual truths, analytic truths, and temporal truths? The toughest cases are the general and negative existential truths. I'll argue that we can't account for them without introducing new bits of ontology (§5.2 and §5.3). Armstrong's totality states of affairs are not the best option (§5.4). Negative states of affairs are a better bet (§5.5), although their metaphysical analysis is difficult (§5.6). I'll discuss the remaining cases—modal truths, counterfactual truths, analytic truths, and temporal truths—in §5.7.

5.1 Maximalism and Necessitation (Again)

FOR EVERY TRUE proposition, there must be some entity whose existence necessitates the truth of that proposition. That conclusion is entailed by two key principles about truthmaking, which we met in §3.1:

(MAXIMALISM) For every truth, there is some entity which makes that truth true.

(NECESSITATION) If x is a truthmaker for $\langle A \rangle$ then, necessarily, $\langle A \rangle$ is true if x exists.

These do not define what truthmaking is, but they do place heavy constraints on our theory. I've argued that both theses are true. How can our ontology back up these claims? In particular, what kind of entity could necessitate

(3.1) ⟨Ern Malley does not exist⟩

(5.1) ⟨all Greens care about the environment⟩

(5.2) ⟨there are no penguins in the Arctic⟩

(5.3) ⟨there are no Vulcans⟩

and other 'difficult' truths such as these?

If an entity is to make such propositions true, then it necessitates an absence: of Greens who don't care about the environment, of Arctic penguins, of Ern Malley, or of Vulcans. I previously (§3.1) called such entities *absence-necessitators*. Then part of our worry is this: the story so far requires absence-necessitators, but (supposedly) there can be no such entities.

To be sure, this is not the whole of the worry for the maximalist. For even if some entity x necessitates ⟨A⟩'s truth, it does not follow that ⟨A⟩ is true in virtue of x. Yet the phenomenon of absence-necessitation (if it is indeed a phenomenon) calls out for ontological explanation. And it seems highly likely that an ontological story about absence-necessitators will provide entities which explain why such truths are true, rather than false.

To make that point, let's consider the kinds of absence-necessitators that have been proposed in the literature. I introduced these briefly in §3.4. We find talk of *absences*, considered as genuine entities (Kukso 2006; Martin 1996). On this view, there are general entities such as empty spaces and voids, and there are specific entities such as *the absence of Ern Malley*. We also find talk of *negative states of affairs* (Barker and Jago 2012; Russell 2009), sometimes called 'negative facts'. These are states of affairs such that *that Bertie is not speedy*, *that penguins do not live in the Arctic*, and perhaps also, *that there exist no Vulcans*. Finally, we have Armstrong's *totality states of affairs* (Armstrong 1997, 2004), *that so-and-so are all the Fs*. A totality state of affairs might be *that Anna, Bec, ..., are all the Greens*. The idea is that this state of affairs, plus all the particular states of affairs about Anna, Bec, and so on caring about the environment, will necessitate that all Greens care about the environment.

I'll discuss these options in detail in §5.4 and §5.5. For now, the point is this: if there were such entities, then we could reasonably claim that they serve as truthmakers for negative (including general and negative existential) truths. If there is such an entity as *the absence of Ern Malley*, it is perfectly suited as a truthmaker for (3.1). If there is a negative state of affairs *that Bertie is not speedy*, then it is perfectly suited as a truthmaker for ⟨Bertie is not speedy⟩. And if there are totality states of affairs, they seem well placed (in combination with particular positive states of affairs) to make true general truths such as (5.1). This is how their proponents see those entities. So, as I see things, the problem of absence-necessitators is at the heart of the more general problem of general and negative existential truths.

The problem for these proposed absence-necessitators is that absences-qua-genuine-entities, negative states of affairs, and totality states of affairs are generally thought to be 'really peculiar' (Cameron 2008, 413), or 'too weak to bear much metaphysical weight' (Fox 1987, 206). The worry is sometimes put by insisting that *genuine existence is positive* (Molnar 2000, 84–5), whereas absences, negative states of affairs, and totality states of affairs are all 'negative' entities and hence not genuine parts of existence.

It's unclear exactly what Molnar means by calling reality 'positive' (see Parsons 2006). But I don't doubt that there's an issue here. Absences, negative states of affairs, and totality states of affairs seem to be very different kinds of entity to those we're used to. Certainly, philosophers past and present have been adverse to such entities. Russell (who accepted negative states of affairs) notes that:

> One has a certain repugnance to negative facts, the same sort of feeling that makes you wish not to have a fact "*p* or *q*" going about the world. You have a feeling that there are only positive facts, and that negative propositions have somehow or other got to be expressions of positive facts. ... When I was lecturing on this subject at Harvard I argued that there were negative

facts, and it nearly produced a riot: the class would not hear of there being negative facts at all. (Russell 2009, 41–2)

It's hard to imagine philosophers rioting, particularly at Harvard in 1914. But we get the picture: as a general rule, philosophers don't like negative states of affairs, or other kinds of negative entity. And even absent a definition of 'negative entity', there's a presumption that, whatever negative entities are, they're bad news.

So there is a presumption that, if we have to account for absence-necessitators, then it's best to do so using the ontological resources we've already got. To some extent, that's true of any philosophical analysis: best to avoid positing new ontology, if at all possible. That rule of thumb has to be balanced with other requirements. We also want a systematic theory which doesn't posit basic, unexplained truths, or otherwise explain new cases in totally ad hoc ways. Sometimes, new ontology is required. But in the case of absence-necessitation, the scales come tipped heavily against new ontology.

Parsimonious maximalists attempt to account for general and negative existential truths without positing any new ontology. They do without absences-qua-entities, negative states of affairs, totality states of affairs, or any other custom-designed absence-necessitators. Rather, they think that far less exotic entities will do the job, provided that we think about them in the right way.

Below, I'll discuss two broad approaches to parsimonious maximalism. The first approach (§5.2) takes ordinary particulars or states of affairs as truthmakers for the difficult negative truths. I'll consider suggestions along these lines by Russell (2009) (influenced by Demos (1917)), Cheyne and Pigden (2006), Lewis (2003), and Lewis and Rosen (2003). The second approach (§5.3) takes the entire world as the truthmaker for all the difficult negative truths. In this category, we find suggestions by Cameron (2008) and Schaffer (2010b).

I'll argue that these approaches fail. We can't be parsimonious maximalists. Truthmaker maximalism requires entities beyond the ordinary: absences, negative states of affairs, or totality states of affairs. I'll discuss these options in §5.4 and §5.5.

5.2 Maximalism with Ordinary Entities

Option 1: Incompatibility

I'll begin with an account that crosses many people's minds when thinking about truthmakers for negative truths. It was raised when Russell gave his lectures on logical atomism at Harvard in 1914, defending the existence of negative states of affairs (§5.1). Subsequently, an audience member, Raphael Demos, wrote a reply to Russell (Demos 1917), arguing that negative states of affairs aren't needed. Rather, a negative proposition ⟨¬A⟩ should be analysed as asserting that 'an opposite of ⟨A⟩ is true', or 'some ⟨B⟩ is true which is an opposite of ⟨A⟩' (Demos 1917, 196; notation changed).

Russell (2009, 42–5) discusses this approach, charitably interpreting Demos's 'opposite of' as meaning 'incompatible with'. Russell gives the example of his white chalk. Since ⟨the chalk is white⟩ is true, and that proposition is incompatible with ⟨the chalk is red⟩, this analysis correctly treats ⟨the chalk is not red⟩ as true. (Note that the analysis needs Russell's 'incompatible with' and not Demos's (1917, 191) 'opposite of' or 'inconsistent with': *red* is not the opposite of *white*, and '*x* is red' is not logically inconsistent with '*x* is white'.) Demos's idea seems to be that the explanation doesn't appeal to negative states of affairs, and hence negative states of affairs aren't required in the explanation of truth.

Russell complains that, interpreted this way, the approach 'makes incompatibility fundamental and an objective fact, which is not so very much simpler than allowing negative facts' (Russell 2009, 44). I'm not sure this objection will stick. A defender of the approach could reply that nothing makes it the case that ⟨A⟩ and ⟨B⟩ are incompatible (when they are). Or alternatively, she could say that the identities of ⟨A⟩ and ⟨B⟩ themselves make ⟨A⟩ and ⟨B⟩ incompatible.

I don't want to dwell on whether this is the right approach to propositions such as ⟨the chalk is not red⟩. What we need to know is whether the approach will generalise to our difficult cases, including (3.1), (5.1), (5.2), and (5.3). What positive state of affairs is incompatible with the existence of Vulcans? What positive state of affairs is incompatible with the existence of Ern Malley? There are such states of affairs. For example, the states of affairs *that I know there are no Vulcans* is incompatible with the existence of Vulcans. But my knowledge isn't what makes (5.3) true. My knowledge is metaphysically too far downstream for that.

You might think that, if we list out all the positive states of affairs concerning the Arctic, then these together will be incompatible with there being penguins in the Arctic, and hence that these positive states of affairs are what make (5.2), ⟨there are no penguins in the Arctic⟩, true. But for reasons familiar from §5.1, there isn't genuine incompatibility here. Suppose the positive states of affairs we've listed detail everything that occupies the surface of the Arctic, region by region. Polar bears here; snow there; thin air elsewhere with no mention of penguins. But still, these states of affairs remain compatible with the existence of Arctic penguins, for the Arctic could have been a bit bigger, with that extra bit of Arctic being home to some penguins.

Where there are genuine incompatibilities between propositions, we might be able to account for corresponding negative truths in terms of positive states of affairs. But the approach won't generalise, because in many of our problem cases, we don't have incompatibilities of the right kind.

On reflection, this incompatibility approach is little better than a restatement of our original problem from §5.1: how can any entity necessitate the absence of another? If x necessitates the absence of y, then x and y must be incompatible with each other. Incompatibility of this kind is just mutual absence-necessitation. So if our task is to understand and explain absence-necessitation, we clearly can't help ourselves to a notion of metaphysical incompatibility. That merely restates the problem.

Option 2: Entities As They Are

Cheyne and Pigden (2006) offer a different approach to the problem. They suggest we think of ordinary entities *as they actually are*. They consider Plato's adversary, Theaetetus, and the proposition that he isn't flying. What makes this true, they say, is *Theaetetus as he (actually) is*, for 'if Theaetetus *were* flying this fact would not exist' (Cheyne and Pigden 2006, 259).

They reason similarly in the case of negative existential truths:

> Consider the great big positive fact (or collection of facts) *S223 as it (actually) was on 4/7/05*. ... Now our claim is that the existence of this fact—*S223 as it (actually) was on 4/7/05*—necessitates or *makes true* the proposition that there was no hippopotamus in the room. For (necessarily) if there had been a hippopotamus in the room, this fact—*S223 as it (actually) was on 4/7/05*—would not have existed. Instead there would have been some other hippopotamus-involving fact. (Cheyne and Pigden 2006, 255)

On this treatment, *S223 as it (actually) was on 4/7/05* is a collection of positive states of affairs only (Cheyne and Pigden 2006, 249), and makes true ⟨there was no hippo in S223 on 4/7/05⟩. That being so, you might wonder how this approach makes progress on the previous suggestion. The answer is, it doesn't.

Cheyne and Pigden's reasoning makes a crucial mistake in its handling of the description 'S223 as it (actually) was on 4/7/05'. Clearly, if there had been a hippo in S223, then S223 would not have been as it actually was. But that doesn't imply that the collection of positive states of affairs they have in mind wouldn't have existed. S223 could have been a bit bigger, with a hippo in the extra bit. All the positive states of affairs concerning S223 would remain the same, but there'd be some added. The description 'S223 as it was on 4/7/05', used in that possible context, would then pick out the larger collection of states of affairs. S223 as it was on 4/7/05 would then not be the referent of 'S223 as it was on 4/7/05'. But that doesn't imply that S223 as it was on 4/7/05 (the collection of states of affairs) would cease to exist (just as the teacher of Aristotle wouldn't have ceased to exist, had he ceased teaching Aristotle).

(Note that inserting 'actually' into the description doesn't help at all. For 'S223 as it actually was on 4/7/05' picks out, in any possible context, the actual-world collection of states of affairs if they exist.

It is a *rigid* description. But this makes no difference to the argument. Considered as a collection of states of affairs, S223 as it actually was on 4/7/05 is just S223 as it was on 4/7/05. And as we've already seen, that collection of positive states of affairs is compatible with there being an S223-dwelling hippo.)

Parsons (2006) objects to Cheyne and Pigden's account in a slightly different way. Cheyne and Pigden say,

> the (first order) way the universe actually is (a very large and complex fact, but a positive fact nonetheless) makes it true that there are no unicorns. (Cheyne and Pigden 2006, 257)

But Parsons replies that

> the following world is possible: a world containing two island universes, one of which is configured just as *our* universe is configured (and which contains no unicorn), the other of which is not so configured, and which contains unicorns. In that world, the truthmaker that Cheyne and Pigden are talking about exists, and unicorns exist. (Parsons 2006, 594–5)

So again, Cheyne and Pigden's proposed truthmaker, the way the universe actually is, won't do.

Parsons's objection is an instance of the kind I discussed above. Our universe is, in fact, all there is. (Or at least, it's all there actually is.) But this fact is not entailed by the positive facts about how the universe is. Unless we explicitly include some negative or totality state of affairs, *that the universe (as it is) is all there is*, then we can't rule out situations like the one Parsons has in mind.

It's worth noting, however, that Parsons's objection leaves the door open for Cheyne and Pigden to reply. They may hold that island universes are not possible. (They may follow Lewis (1986) in taking a possible world to be a maximally spatiotemporally connected entity, for example.) That would rule out the possibility of Parsons's envisaged scenario. But the general line of objection from above would remain untouched. Purely positive states of affairs about things as they are do not necessitate the kind of truth Cheyne and Pigden have in mind.

Option 3: Qua-Entities

Cheyne and Pigden's *things as they are* approach is a neat idea but, as it stands, it will not work. There's a better way to make good on the idea, however, due to Lewis (2003). In outline, the idea goes like this. What makes

(5.4) ⟨this lemon is juicy⟩

true? Why, this lemon! But the lemon could have been dry. 'Could' is a highly context-sensitive term, however. If there are contexts in which such cases are not genuine possibilities, the lemon will necessitate (5.4)'s truth. How can we get into such contexts? For Lewis, we need only bring the lemon's juiciness to conversational salience. One way to do this is by picking out the lemon *qua* juicy. So for Lewis, the lemon qua juicy (which is just the lemon itself) will make (5.4) true.

This may sound like so much linguistic jiggery-pokery. To determine whether it is, we need to look more closely at Lewis's theory of modality and how it supports this notion of truthmaking. For a long time, Lewis rejected truthmaker theory on the grounds that 'the demand for truthmakers just is a demand for necessary connections' (Lewis 1999, 219), which conflicts with his Humeanism. The latter requires that, for any two possible entities x and y, a duplicate of x must be able to co-exist with a duplicate of y (Lewis 1986). In particular, a duplicate of whatever makes (5.3) true must be able to co-exist with a Vulcan. But how could this be, if a truthmaker for ⟨A⟩ must necessitate ⟨A⟩'s truth?

Later on, Lewis noticed a way of reconciling truthmaking with Humeanism (Lewis 2003). According to his counterpart theory (Lewis 1971, 1986), something can be essentially *F* without being intrinsically *F* (i.e., even if some intrinsic duplicate of that thing is not *F*). On Lewis's story, I am identical to my body, yet I'm essentially a person, whereas my body isn't: it could have been a mere lifeless lump. Since the counterpart relation is one of similarity, which is a matter of contextual salience, attributions of essential properties vary with context. Picking me out *qua person* raises my personhood to salience, creating a context in which only people are my counterparts. In those contexts, we can truthfully say 'I'm essentially a person'.

Lewis (2003) treats truthmaking in a similar way. The truthmaker for ⟨this lemon is juicy⟩ is the lemon, *qua* juicy. That entity is just the lemon, insofar its juiciness is raised to salience (the effect of the '*qua* juicy' locution). It is perfectly consistent, in some other context, to hold that the lemon might not have been juicy.

In their postscript to Lewis's (2003) paper, Lewis and Rosen (2003) extend the idea to cover negative existentials. They take (5.3) to be made true by the world, *qua* unaccompanied by Vulcans. For more specific negative existentials, such as

(5.5) ⟨there are no hippos in the lake⟩

we get more specific truthmakers: in this case, the lake, *qua* unaccompanied by hippos. This approach is parsimonious. (The lake *qua* unaccompanied by hippos is just the lake; and similarly for the other cases.) It's also (by design) compatible with Lewis's Humeanism, which many take to be an advantage.

The Lewis-Rosen view faces a serious triviality objection, however. As Lewis recognises (2003, 32), it would be absurd to claim that Elvis, *qua* unaccompanied by Vulcans, is what makes (5.3) true. Elvis has nothing whatsoever to do with whether there exist Vulcans. What is the difference between this 'cheap trick' (Lewis 2003, 32) and the genuine account? It is this, says Lewis: in the genuine account, the invoked counterpart relations must 'rest upon similarities that strike us as having at least some importance' and 'rest predominantly upon intrinsic similarity' (2003, 33).

Even with this restriction in place, we can run a triviality objection. Consider all those perfect intrinsic duplicates of Elvis. Each is exactly similar to Elvis himself in many, many respects of intrinsic similarity. (This remains the case even if we restrict 'respects of similarity' to natural properties.) Now select from the Elvis duplicates those that are unaccompanied by Vulcans. They remain exactly similar to Elvis in many, many respects, but differ extrinsically from Elvis in one respect (namely, they are unaccompanied by Vulcans). So 'intrinsic duplicate of Elvis, unaccompanied by Vulcans' is a way of selecting counterparts which rests *predominantly* (albeit not totally) on intrinsic similarity, just as Lewis requires.

By Lewis's lights, picking out Elvis qua intrinsically as he is and unaccompanied by Vulcans determines a suitable context in which to treat Elvis as a truthmaker for (5.3). And if Elvis can be a truthmaker for (5.3)—which, after all, has nothing whatsoever to do with Elvis—then just about any entity can be a truthmaker for just about any true proposition. But that's absurd. Triviality has not been avoided. A theory along these lines would be maximalism in name only: it would do no useful work. We need to look elsewhere.

5.3 The Whole World

We shouldn't give up on parsimonious maximalism just yet. There's a further idea we haven't yet explored, which takes the whole world as the truthmaker for our problematic negative truths. I'll consider two theories which take this approach, due to Cameron (2008) and Schaffer (2010b).

Option 4: The World, Essentially As It Is

Cameron's (2008) account of what makes the negative truths true is a descendent of Lewis and Rosen's view. It's an attempt to overcome the triviality worry raised in §5.2 by rejecting Lewis's multiplicity of counterpart relations. On Cameron's view, the truth of modal ascriptions is independent of the context of utterance (2008, 420): there is a single counterpart relation for all contexts.

The key idea in Cameron's account is that each world (in any context, however picked out) is essentially the way it is. In counterpart theoretic terms, each world's only counterparts are itself and worlds indistinguishable from it. As a consequence, each world couldn't be any way other than the way it is, and so the world's existence necessitates all the propositions true according to it. Accordingly,

Cameron takes each world w to be the truthmaker for each negative proposition that's true according to w. In this way, Cameron's account is both maximalist and parsimonious.

Why think that the world is essentially as it is? Cameron claims that 'the actual world is individuated by what is true according to it' and that 'this amounts to the claim that it has all its properties essentially' (2008, 415). But this isn't the only way to individuate the actual world. If the actual world is the only concrete world, then we can individuate the actual world as being the largest spatiotemporal entity. If there's a plurality of concrete worlds, then we can individuate each in terms of its concrete parts. The latter had better not commit us to treating worlds as being essentially as they are, lest we treat all entities as having all their parts essentially. So I don't find Cameron's positive argument for his view persuasive.

Perhaps we should adopt Cameron's approach on more pragmatic grounds: it gets the job done, without additional ontology. One worry with this approach is that the world as a whole is a severely non-discriminating truthmaker. We expect the following to differ in (at least some of) their truthmakers (as they do on the Lewis-Rosen view):

(5.6) ⟨there are no Vulcans in Sydney⟩

(5.7) ⟨there are no Hobbits in London⟩

These differ completely in their subject matter: one is about Sydney and Vulcans, the other about London and Hobbits. Making (5.6) true requires Sydney to be a certain way, but shouldn't require the non-Sydney part of the world to be any particular way. Similarly, making (5.7) true requires London to be a certain way, but shouldn't require the non-London part of the world to be any particular way. Intuitively, (5.6) is true in virtue of the way Sydney is, whereas (5.7) is true in virtue of the way London is. Cameron's view denies this. Cameron may opt to bite the bullet here, but it is a worry nevertheless.

More tellingly, Cameron's view also faces a triviality objection, somewhat similar to that faced by the Lewis-Rosen theory. Take any actual entity, x. Since there are no unicorns, x is such that there are no Vulcans. Now (and here's the dubious move), stipulate that x has no counterparts but itself. Then, as if by magic, x necessitates the truth of (5.3), ⟨there are no Vulcans⟩. But, as x was an arbitrarily chosen entity, it would be absurd to take x to be ⟨there are no Vulcans⟩'s truthmaker on this basis.

The question for Cameron is this: why is it appropriate to stipulate that the whole world, but not some other entity, has no counterparts but itself?

One might argue that we cannot take an arbitrary x to have no counterparts but itself, since each entity could have been some other way. But Cameron cannot accept this principle in general, since he claims the whole world could not have been some other way. Rather, he explains 'the world could have been some other way' in terms of the parts of the world that could have been otherwise. But we can play that game too. For any x, let w_x be the whole world (considered as a mereological sum) minus x, and stipulate that it has no counterparts but itself. Then, by Cameron's lights, w_x is a suitable truthmaker for every actual truth, and we can explain away 'w_x could have been otherwise' in terms of its parts being otherwise. But again, since x was arbitrary, this theory is absurd. The point is that we have no reason to think that Cameron's is any better.

One might think that what's wrong with the trivial theories, based on picking some arbitrary x as our truthmaker for some truth ⟨A⟩, is that in general x will have nothing to do with ⟨A⟩'s subject matter. In general, *being such that A* does not contribute to x's intrinsic nature. Cameron (2010) argues that such properties are 'suspicious' because they do not make 'a contribution to the intrinsic nature of their bearers at the time at which they are instantiated' (Cameron 2010, 60). In short, a truthmaker for ⟨A⟩ must be intrinsically connected to ⟨A⟩'s truth.

If we accept that principle, then the dubious, arbitrary approaches just mooted are ruled out: an arbitrarily chosen entity will not, in general, be intrinsically such that there no Vulcans. So far so good. But neither is the whole world intrinsically such that there are no

Vulcans. Intuitively, an intrinsic property is one 'which things have in virtue of the way they themselves are', rather than 'in virtue of their relations or lack of relations to other things' (Lewis 1986, 61). Lewis's precise definition has it that x is intrinsically F just in case every perfect duplicate of x is also F (1986, 61–2). But a perfect duplicate of our world need not be such that there are no Vulcans, for that duplicate need not be all there is. Duplicate our world, add some additional bit of spacetime, add Vulcans to the extra spacetime: then we have a duplicate of our world, such that there are Vulcans. So, restricting truthmakers for ⟨A⟩ to entities which are intrinsically such that A, we thereby rule out Cameron's approach.

I cannot see how to draw a clear line between Cameron's approach and the trivial variants on it I've suggested. But these trivialise the notion of truthmaking, just as the Lewis-Rosen approach does (§5.2). So I do not think that Cameron's account is a promising way to make good on parsimonious maximalism.

Option 5: Truthmaker Monism

Truthmaker monism (Schaffer 2010b) is the doctrine that, if ⟨A⟩ has a truthmaker at world w, then w itself is ⟨A⟩'s one and only truthmaker at w (2010b, 307). This view is motivated by Schaffer's *priority monist* metaphysics (Schaffer 2010a,c). On this view, there exists a plurality of entities: the world and all its proper parts. All of those proper parts are ontologically dependent on the one fundamental entity, the world as a whole. Schaffer argues for truthmaker monism by claiming that:

(FUNDAMENTAL) If x is a truthmaker for some ⟨A⟩, then x is a fundamental entity.

Combined with priority monism, this entails truthmaker monism.

In this way, Schaffer can allow that the world is a truthmaker for (5.3), even though it might have co-existed with a Vulcan, as part of a larger world w^+ (2010b, 318). In this case, the counterpart of the actual world is not fundamental (for it is a proper part of w^+) and hence is not a truthmaker at w^+. So whilst Schaffer rejects (NECESSITATION), he accepts:

(NECESSITATION*) If x is a truthmaker of $\langle A \rangle$ then, necessarily, $\langle A \rangle$ is true if x exists and is a truthmaker.

He argues that this is sufficient to establish that any truth is grounded. Let's grant this point. Then (MAXIMALISM) is easily satisfied; the theory is parsimonious; and all without invoking essential properties or implicating counterparts (Schaffer 2010b, 322).

The key question for Schaffer is: why think (FUNDAMENTAL) is true? Schaffer gives a number of arguments in its favour. He argues that 'truthmakers need to be restricted to fundamental entities to ensure the right order of explanation' (Schaffer 2010b, 319), that is, from being to truth and not vice versa. But, as Schaffer himself acknowledges (2010b, 319–20), all that we need to get the order of explanation right is that the more fundamental explains the less fundamental. Morrissey the cat's existence explains why ⟨Morrissey exists⟩ is true, but not vice versa, because Morrissey is more fundamental than that truth. Morrissey is far from being a fundamental entity, and so this argument does not support (FUNDAMENTAL).

Schaffer also argues that 'the restriction to fundamental entities is needed if any 'cheaters' are to be caught' (2010b, 319). I raised doubts in §2.2 about 'cheat-catcher' arguments for truthmaking. But even if cheat-catching is important, the argument isn't persuasive, because at least some 'cheaters' can be caught without appeal to (FUNDAMENTAL). The case against presentists is that they (supposedly) can't find any entities, fundamental or otherwise, to act as truthmakers for truths about the past or the future.

What about other cases of 'cheat-catching'? In making his case, Schaffer focuses on 'Rylean behaviourism, with its *brute dispositions*' (2010b, 319). Schaffer's point is that (FUNDAMENTAL) is required to rule these out. I don't agree. Someone who takes a disposition to be 'brute' is taking it to be ungrounded, hence fundamental. Such entities won't be ruled out by (FUNDAMENTAL). In short, neither the presentist case nor the brute dispositions case of cheat-catching provides support for (FUNDAMENTAL).

Without (FUNDAMENTAL), the argument from priority monism to truthmaker monism does not go through. ⟨Morrissey exists⟩ may be grounded in Morrissey's existence, even if Morrissey is not a fundamental entity. Morrissey is clearly the most relevant entity to the truth of ⟨Morrissey exists⟩. The same goes for each entity x and the proposition that x exists. So (FUNDAMENTAL) should be rejected in favour of a ubiquity principle:

(UBIQUITY) Every entity is a truthmaker for some proposition.

Given (UBIQUITY), (NECESSITATION*) implies (NECESSITATION). So Schaffer's account fails (NECESSITATION*), in just the way it fails (NECESSITATION). The actual world might have co-existed with a Vulcan (as part of a larger world), whilst remaining a truthmaker (for some proposition or other), contradicting (NECESSITATION*). But without (NECESSITATION*), Schaffer does not have a solution to the problem of negative truth (§5.1). Our quest for a solution must turn elsewhere.

5.4 Totality States of Affairs

The parsimonious maximalist accounts we've discussed all have fatal problems. The moral I want to draw is that truthmakers for negative truths don't come cheaply. To account for those truths in truthmaking terms, we need to expand our ontology with dedicated truthmakers. The contenders are Armstrong's totality states of affairs (1997, 2004), negative facts (Barker and Jago 2012; Russell 2009), and absences (Kukso 2006; Martin 1996). In this section, I'll consider totality states of affairs.

Armstrong analyses totality states of affairs as follows. There is a relational universal, *Tot*, which relates a mereological sum of things s to a property F just in case s is the sum of all Fs (Armstrong 2004, 73). *Tot*'s relating the sum of all hamsters to the property *being a hamster* is the totality state of affairs *that such-and-such are all the hamsters*. If there are *n* hamsters, then this state of affairs serves as the truthmaker for 'there exist exactly *n* hamsters'. *Tot*'s relating the sum of all first-order states of affairs to the property *being a first-order state of affairs* is the totality state of affairs *that such-and-such are all the first-order states of affairs*. This state of affairs serves as a truthmaker for all truths not made true by one of the first-order states of affairs, such as ⟨there are no flying hamsters⟩.

How does the approach apply to general truths, such as ⟨all ravens are black⟩? Armstrong identifies 'two totalities: the mereological whole of the black ravens and the mereological whole of the ravens' (2004, 74), and claims that ⟨all ravens are black⟩ is true 'if and only if the two totalities are identical' (2004, 74). But this is false, in general. The sum s_1 of all concrete entities is identical to the sum s_2 of all concrete *mereological atoms* (that is, entities with no proper parts). Yet not all concrete entities are mereological atoms.

Armstrong could avoid the problem by treating *Tot* as a relation between a set, rather than a mereological sum, of entities and a property. This avoids the problem because a set, unlike a sum, allows for unique decomposition. There's only one correct answer to 'what are the members of set *X*?', whereas there is, in general, no unique answer to 'what are the parts of sum *s*?'. But the suggestion fails for another reason: a variant on Russell's paradox.

If a totality state of affairs features a set of *F*s for every property *F* (simple or complex), then there must be a set corresponding to each such property, containing all and only the *F*s. But consider the complex property *being an x which is not a member of itself*. Any theory which asserts the existence of a set corresponding to this property—including the variation on Armstrong's theory we are now considering—is internally inconsistent. So we cannot amend Armstrong's original theory in this way.

Another option is to take *Tot* to be a polyadic relation, relating together each individual *F* plus the property of being *F*. A totality state of affairs will then have the form $Tot(x_1, x_2, \ldots, F)$, where $x_1, x_2, \ldots$ are all the *F*s. But, on metaphysical grounds, I doubt that there can be such relations. If anything is essential to a given relation *R*, it is the number of things related together by R. Indeed, this is a point I took from Armstrong himself (private communication). One could argue that, for each ordinal κ, there is a unique κ-adic totality relation Tot_κ. But not only is this move ontologically extreme, it also rejects Armstrong's insistence that exactly the same Tot relation is involved in each totality state of affairs (Armstrong 2004, 73).

There's another kind of worry for Armstrong's totality states of affairs, as follows. The totality state for a property F will somehow involve all the Fs (as a sum, a set, or individually), plus F itself, plus Tot. But consider the property *being a state of affairs*. The corresponding totality state should then include all states of affairs. But it too is a state of affairs, and so it must include itself. This just isn't possible, whatever 'include' may mean. States of affairs, on Armstrong's view, are non-mereological compositions of constituents. Their identity is determined by their constituents (and the way they are composed). So the constituents of a state are metaphysically strictly prior to the state itself.

It follows immediately that no state is part of what determines its own identity, and hence no state is amongst its own constituents. By the same reasoning, a state cannot be a mereological part or a set-theoretic member of one of its constituents. So, whatever the constituents of totality states are (mereological sums, sets, or individual entities), there cannot be a totality state corresponding to each property. (In particular, there cannot be one corresponding to *being a state of affairs*). The concept of Tot was introduced by description: it is the relation of *totalising*, which holds between a property and all the entities which possess it. The objection shows that there cannot be any such relation.

One can overcome this objection by moving to a *typed* theory, with a distinct totalising relation Tot_i for each order i of states of affairs. (First-order states contain no totality relation; $i + 1$-th-order states contain Tot_i.) But a typed theory doesn't provide enough totality states for the maximalist. Take the case of Anna. She's just finished reading *Truth and Truthmakers* and become a big fan of totality states. In fact, they're now her favourite kind of entity:

(5.8) There's no kind of state of affairs Anna likes more than a totality state of affairs.

That's a contingent negative existential truth. On Armstrong's theory, it has a totality state of affairs as a truthmaker. The property in question is *being one of Anna's most favourite states of affairs* and the totality in question is the collection (sum, set, or plurality) of all her favourite states of affairs. That collection includes states of every order. Since each totality state sits at some particular order, there's no totality state which collects them all together. Consequently, there's no totality state to act as truthmaker for (5.8), and so maximalists can't accept this typed account of totality states.

I've given two arguments against Armstrong's account of totality states of affairs. They lead me to the conclusion that there is no such relation as *Tot*; and even if there was it would not provide enough totality states to give truthmakers for all truths. So the maximalist had better look elsewhere.

5.5 Negative States of Affairs

The remaining options for making good on truthmaker maximalism are to include either negative states of affairs or absences, considered as genuine entities, in our ontology. I'll consider both options together, for there's a clear relation between absences and negative existential states of affairs. (In fact, I'll propose that we understand the former in terms of the latter.) Negative states of affairs (like all entities described as 'negative') get a bad press: see Cameron (2008), Fox (1987), Molnar (2000), and Mumford (2007). But when we examine the arguments against them, we find them lacking. (What follows draws on joint work with Stephen Barker in Barker and Jago 2012).

Mumford (2007) doubts that the concept of a negative state of affairs is even coherent. He worries that a negative state of affairs 'sounds like an absence of a fact, and an absence is nothing at all' (2007, 46). If the claim is just that absences do not exist, it begs the question agains the defender of absences. If the claim is that absences, by their nature, are non-existents, then it is mistaken. Anyone who believes in absences-as-entities will distinguish sharply between the absence—an entity that exists—and of what it is an absence: Vulcans, penguins in the university lake, or Ern Malley. The absence of Vulcans isn't itself a Vulcan, so there's no conflict in saying the absence exists.

In §5.1, we met a related worry, held by many and articulated by Molnar (2000, 84–5) as follows. Everything that exists is positive; but negative states are not positive, and so are debarred from the realm of being. What does it mean to call some entity 'positive' or 'negative'? In general, I have no idea, and Molnar doesn't say either. Does 'negative entity' mean an entity described in negative language? Hopefully not: I'm often described in negative language, but thankfully, I'm not one of the entities Molnar wanted to rule out.

Perhaps 'negative entity' means an entity whose very being or essence can be captured only by using negative language. That chimes well with how we talk about negative states or absences: we get at what they are only by using phrases like 'that such-and-such isn't F' or 'such-and-such's non-existence'. But if this is all 'negative entity' means, Molnar's argument is puzzling. Why should the fact that we talk about would-be entities in a certain way imply that they cannot exist? (Parsons (2006, 591–2) also expresses doubts about the coherence of describing entities as 'positive' or 'negative'.)

Molnar's thought seems to be that negative states or absences would constitute a special kind of existence, *the negative kind*, distinct in kind from the way in which everyday entities exist. Molnar's claim is then that there is but one kind of existence. That's a claim I find very attractive. As I see things, *existence* is a completely basic, indefinable philosophical concept. Admittedly, it's certainly possible to give a coherent story on which there are multiple notions of existence. But I find that approach unmotivated. So, whilst one could respond to Molnar by making sense of different kinds of existence, I prefer to accept his line that there is but one kind.

I claim that both negative and positive states of affairs exist, and they exist in precisely the same sense of 'existence'. Those states may be fundamental entities, or they may be non-fundamental constructions from other entities. If we take states of affairs to be metaphysically fundamental (as on the primitivist view from §4.2), then we are saying that there are (at least) two kinds of fundamental entity: the positive and the negative states of affairs. But to say that there is more than one fundamental kind of entity is not to say that entities in each category come with their own special kind of existence. The standard model of particle physics posits sixteen kinds of fundamental particle. It doesn't tell us that there are sixteen kinds of existence. Rather, it tells us that there are sixteen fundamental kinds of particle, all of which exist in precisely the same sense as each other. The same could be said for different kinds of states of affairs.

Here's another objection against negative states of affairs. The objection begins with Armstrong's line that 'whatever truthmakers are postulated should make some sort of causal/nomic contribution to the working of the actual world' (2004, 39). But, the objection goes, negative states contribute nothing to the workings of the world, and so don't exist (Molnar 2000).

One might dispute Armstrong's and Molnar's premise here. (Presumably, Armstrong means that *concrete* truthmakers should contribute to the causal/nomic workings of the world. We should not object to sets or numbers merely on the basis that they are non-causal.) But a stronger response is to grant the premise and show that Molnar's conclusion doesn't follow.

First, consider some causal claims. The Liberal Democrats lost nearly all their seats in the 2015 UK General Election because people didn't vote for them. The holes in Anna's eardrums cause her hearing problems. When I forgot to water my tomatoes, the lack of water caused their untimely demise; my failure to water them was to blame. I once saw a modular wine-rack system, priced by the hole. Those holes nearly caused a hole in my bank account.

Dowe (2009) argues that 'causation by absence cases' violates the principle from Special Relativity that no signals can travel faster than the speed of light, and hence cannot be considered as genuine cases of causation. Dowe interprets that principle as entailing that all effects occur within the forward lightcone of the cause. Suppose I have been transported to a galaxy far, far away (outside my tomato plants' forward lightcone). Then, Dowe says, my being in that distant galaxy can't be what causes the plants to die (without violating Special Relativity). But this worry misinterprets the claim. What causes the plants to die, I say, is the negative state *that I did not water the plants* (or, if you like, the absence of the event of my watering them). That state (or absence) is located with the plants, just as the absence of penguins in the lake is located in the lake (and not wherever the penguins are). The cause is co-located with the effect, so there can be no violation of Special Relativity.

Here's another way in which negative states of affairs contribute to the material world. Donuts are material objects. The thing about donuts is that they have holes. If you fill the hole with dough, there is no longer a donut. The hole, just like the donut, is a part of reality. We can count, quantify over, and refer to donut-holes, just as we can donuts, so we should treat them as entities. A donut-hole is a specific absence (of donut-dough), insofar as it is appropriately surrounded by donut-dough. (Not all absences of donut-dough are donut-holes!) That absence is part of the donut's physical make-up. It is part of what constitutes the donut. And in that way, specific absences (as negative existential states) contribute to the material world.

Casati and Varzi (1994) try to resist this conclusion, by taking holes to be immaterial entities. Yet we can perceive holes (and gaps, dents, and the like); this strongly speaks against their being immaterial. Lewis and Lewis (1970) also resist the conclusion, identifying holes with hole-linings (the inner surfaces of the surrounding material). But this view is hard to maintain. Filling a hole with a different material can destroy the hole whilst preserving the surrounding surfaces. So holes are not surrounding surfaces.

Here's one more way in which negative states of affairs contribute to the material world. I can see Bertie, and this reassures me that he exists. I can hear that he's barking and see that he's restless. I am not merely seeing Bertie; I am seeing that he is certain ways, and his being those ways amounts to the existence of the corresponding states of affairs. They are what I see. But I can also see that Bertie isn't speedy; I can see he isn't a leopard; and I can see that he's not sharing a room with a hippo. I see that Bertie, or the room, or the world, isn't a certain way. That things aren't those ways consists in the existence of negative states of affairs.

On this view, I see the negative states of affairs *that Bertie isn't a leopard* and *that there is no hippo in the room*. Here's an argument for that conclusion. *Visual perception* is (or at least involves) a causal relationship between the perceiver and the perceived entity. My seeing Bertie is (or involves) a causal relation between Bertie and me. My seeing that Bertie is restless is (or involves) a causal relation between the state of affairs *that Bertie is restless* and me. And similarly, my seeing that Bertie isn't speedy is (or involves) a causal relation between the state of affairs *that Bertie isn't speedy* and me. Causal relations require concrete, spatiotemporally located relata. Hence Bertie, *that Bertie is restless*, and *that Bertie isn't speedy* are all concrete, spatiotemporally located entities.

One may object that such 'perception of negative' cases are really inferences from perceptions of positive states of affairs. We perceive that things (positively) are thus and so and, from that information, infer that such-and-such is not the case. Some but not all 'perception of negative' cases can be explained this way (Farennikova 2013).

Close your eyes and slowly run your fingers across the table top. As your fingers cross its edge, what do you feel? The only way I can describe what I feel is this: the sudden *absence* of the table. That feeling is important for haptic edge detection: you know where the edge is when you feel a change in your fingers, from the presence to the absence of the table. You might infer *here is the edge* from the change in feeling. But from what positive sense of touch could you infer that change? The change is phenomenally irreducible: it is the movement from feeling presence to feeling absence.

We can say something similar about visual edge detection. Your visual systems identify the edge of the table based on the (relatively) visually homogenous visual data presented by its surface, contrasted with a sudden change in visual data. The relevant information here is the sudden change in visual data. We identify the region corresponding to that change with the table's edge. Now, it might be that the visual data correspond to positive state of affairs. But perception of the sudden change in data can be explained through their comparison: *here* the data are so-and-so, whereas *here* they are not. Perception of the sudden absence of homogenous data is an integral feature of edge perception. Visual perception of material objects involves perception of negative as well as positive facts.

Visual edge detection is a very fast process. A cricketer driving off a fast bowler bowling at 90mph has around 445 milliseconds from the ball leaving the bowler's hand to the time of impact. In that time, she must first track the ball's flight (which involves visual edge detection), before taking a large stride forward and bringing her bat through. She commits to her shot within around 200 milliseconds of the ball being released. Inference is too slow a process to play a role here. As Farennikova (2013, 451) argues, 'seeing absence seems to be an indispensable part of our experience of the world'.

I've offered three ways in which negative states of affairs contribute to the material world: through causation, through material constitution, and through the role they play in perception. These features are interrelated and are all good reasons to believe in negative states of affairs.

5.6 The Nature of the Negative

The concept of negative states of affairs is coherent, and we have good reason to believe in them. But what are they, metaphysically speaking? How costly is it to add them to our ontology? My aim in this section is to take each of the theories of positive states of affairs from chapter 4 in turn, and see whether it can support a theory of negative states of affairs.

The Fundamental Tie Account

Suppose we adopt the fundamental tie approach to (positive) states of affairs (§4.1). The fundamental tie is an opaque notion: there's very little we can say about its nature, other than that it binds together objects, properties, and relations to form the corresponding states of affairs. The fundamental tie is an ideological addition to our theory. We don't introduce the tie as a new piece of ontology. Rather, we use the concept to describe states of affairs and the associated particulars, properties, and relations. But suppose we're OK with all that, in the case of positive states of affairs.

We can make a similar move in the case of negative states of affairs. We introduce a new bit of ideology, a further fundamental tie. We use this new concept to talk about the way things aren't. That is, we think of this new tie as binding together a and F when a isn't F. Call this the negative fundamental tie. That concept is just as opaque as the positive fundamental tie. There's very little we can say about it, other than that the negative state of affairs *that a isn't F* consists in a and F being bound together by the negative fundamental tie. But if that opacity is not an overriding objection in the case of the positive tie, then it is not an overriding objection in the case of the negative tie either. That is the line for which Stephen Barker and I argue in Barker and Jago 2012.

Introducing the positive tie to our ideology is a cost, and introducing the negative tie is a further cost. No one likes opaque bits of ideology, and so those costs must be taken seriously. The point we make in Barker and Jago 2012 is that, if we accept the positive fundamental tie, then we're already amenable to taking on such costs. Accepting the negative tie is more of the same, from the perspective of the cost it incurs.

One looks to offset theoretical costs with theoretical benefits. These include the means to validate truthmaker maximalism, and hence to support the theory of truth I've been advocating. I've argued that truthmaker theorists should be maximalists (chapter 3) and that other attempts to validate maximalism fail (§§5.2–5.4). If we accept that much, then we should at least accept that the negative fundamental tie will play a useful role in our theory.

The negative fundamental tie brings other benefits, too. As discussed in §5.5, we can identify absences with negative existential states of affairs. The absence of a hippo in this room is the state of affairs *that there is no hippo in this room*.

In Barker and Jago 2012, we analyse this state of affairs in terms of the complex property *being-a-hippo-in-this-room* and the higher-order property *being instantiated* being negatively tied together. This move allows us to analyse concepts such as *absence*, *hole*, *edge*, and so on. We can be realists about absences, holes, and edges. That's theoretically appealing because we often identify, name, count, and quantify over absences, holes, and edges. Non-realist theories have to paraphrase or otherwise explain away such talk, which is notoriously hard to do (see §5.5). The realist approach is semantically the most straightforward, and perhaps the only one that fully accounts for our use of these concepts. That's a strong reason in favour of it, and by implication, in favour of the negative fundamental tie.

One feature of this account is its commitment to uninstantiated properties. For any possible property F, if nothing is F, then there exists the state of affairs, *that nothing is F*, analysed as F and *being instantiated*, negatively tied together. This approach requires F to exist. I take this to be a commitment of any theory on which properties are individuated independently of their bearers, including the present approach.

The Primitivist Account

We encountered the primitivist approach to positive states of affairs in §4.2. The basic idea, recall, is that atomic states of affairs are primitive entities. They do not have particulars, properties, and relations as constituents. Rather, the states of affairs are the basic entities, from which particulars, properties, and relations are abstracted.

The best-developed version of the theory is Jason Turner's geometric framework (Turner 2016), which we also met in §4.2. On this theory, the class of positive states of affairs *that Rxy*, where x and y take their values from a, b, c, d, and e, can be graphed geometrically, as in figure 5.1:

There are two simple ways to extend the theory to include negative states of affairs. The first goes via negative properties and relations.

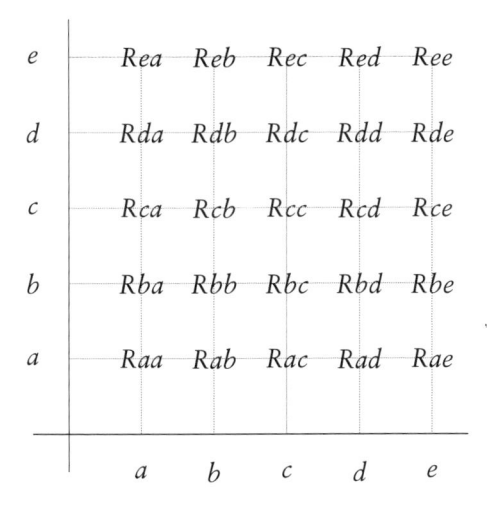

```
e  |—— Rea —— Reb —— Rec —— Red —— Ree

d  |—— Rda —— Rdb —— Rdc —— Rdd —— Rde

c  |—— Rca —— Rcb —— Rcc —— Rcd —— Rce

b  |—— Rba —— Rbb —— Rbc —— Rbd —— Rbe

a  |—— Raa —— Rab —— Rac —— Rad —— Rae
   |_____
        a      b      c      d      e
```

Figure 5.1: STATES OF AFFAIRS MAPPED GEOMETRICALLY

We introduce a new theoretical primitive ∗ which maps quality spaces to quality spaces, such that $S^{**} = S$. (A quality space is a line, square, cube, hypercube, ..., like the square shown above.) Each n-dimensional quality space corresponds to an n-ary property or relation. The square above corresponds to the binary relation, R. In the extended theory, we take quality space S^* to correspond to property/relation R^* just in case S corresponds to R. We then think of states of affairs involving R^* as the negations of the states of affairs involving R. So, if Rab is the positive state of affairs *that Rab*, then *that R*ab* is the negative state of affairs *that a isn't R to b*.

The second approach is to introduce to each state of affairs a polarity. To do this, we now associate each $n + 1$-dimensional quality space with an n-ary property or relation. The additional argument place is occupied by a polarity, a 'switch', 0 or 1. States of affairs with polarity 0 are the negative states of affairs; those with polarity 1 are the positive ones. On this approach, we can represent a monadic property F (taking a, b, c, d, and e as its possible values) as a rectangle, as in figure 5.2.

158 EVERYTHING AND NOTHING

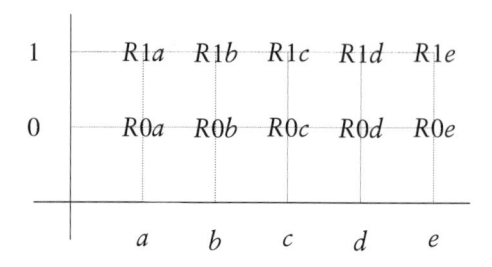

```
1  ┤── R1a    R1b    R1c    R1d    R1e

0  ┤── R0a    R0b    R0c    R0d    R0e
   │
   ┼─────────────────────────────────
        a      b      c      d      e
```

Figure 5.2: POSITIVE AND NEGATIVE STATES OF AFFAIRS

On either approach, the axiomatic theory will need to be strengthened, to ensure the incompatibility of Rab and R^*ab (or $R1ab$ and $R0ab$), and to guarantee the necessity of $Rab \vee R^*ab$ (or $R1ab \vee R0ab$).

Both approaches inherit the benefits and costs of Turner's geometrical approach to primitive states of affairs. But the second approach seems committed to treating 0 and 1 as particulars, just like all the other 'labels' on the axes, a, b, c, and so on. This is hard to justify metaphysically. The negativity of a negative state of affairs is, if anything, a way that that state of affairs is. So the first approach is perhaps the better of these two. If you're tempted to adopt Turner's theory for positive states of affairs, then one of these extensions to that theory is a good way to accommodate negative states of affairs.

The Mereological Account

Finally, we come to the mereological approach to states of affairs from §4.3. The approach, recall, takes states of affairs to be mereological sums of particulars, properties, and relations. Thus all combinations of those elements into states of affairs exist. The theory then divides the existing states of affairs into discrete possible worlds. This is the most radical approach of the three, since it requires us to re-think our notion of what a world is.

I don't see that there is any acceptable way to extend this theory to include negative states of affairs. Here are two suggestions, both of which are problematic. On the first, we accept that there are negative as well as positive properties and relations. Negative states of affairs are then those mereological sums which include a negative property or relation. This is similar to one of the extensions I just suggested to Turner's primitivist account of states of affairs. However, there are good reasons for a defender of the mereological view to reject this modification of it.

That theory attempts to remove the mystery from states of affairs, by analysing them in terms of a widely accepted and formally axiomatisable notion: mereological summation. The suggestion now is that we add a primitive notion of negative properties and relations. By some distance, that is not a widely accepted notion. And in taking the negativity of negative properties and relations to be a primitive matter, we cannot offer an informative axiomatisation of the notion. So a defender of the basic mereological view of states of affairs should reject this modification.

The second suggestion for extending the basic mereological view is this. On the basic view, worlds are taken to be sets of states of affairs. On the extended view, we take worlds to be pairs of sets of states of affairs. By definition, the first of the pair tells us what obtains, whereas the second of the pair tells us what is not the case, relative to that world. So, if world w is a pair $\langle\langle w^+, w^-\rangle\rangle$, with $F \sqcup a \in w^+$ and $G \sqcup b \in w^-$, then a is F, and b isn't G, relative to w.

On this view, there is no intrinsic difference between the positive and the negative states of affairs. Whether a property-and-particular sum counts as a positive or a negative state of affairs, relative to world w, depends on its membership of w^+ or w^-. From a purely semantic point of view, this approach is elegant and useful. It treats worlds as akin to *double propositions*, which I'll discuss in §8.5.

From a metaphysical point of view, however, the view is problematic. A state of affairs is supposed to *make* the relevant propositions true. It should necessitate their truth. But the suggestion cannot accommodate this idea. For a state of affairs s may make true a proposition $\langle A \rangle$ relative to w_1, and yet make true its negation, $\langle \neg A \rangle$, relative to w_2. Moreover, and quite aside from truthmaking considerations, it is hard to believe that a state's positivity or negativity is neither essential nor intrinsic to it. A positive state of affairs *that Fa* is, by its nature, about *a* being *F*. It is both essential and intrinsic to *that Fa* that it is a positive state of affairs. So a defender of the basic mereological view of states of affairs should reject this modification to the view as well.

In short, the fundamental tie and primitivist theories of positive states of affairs can each be extended to accommodate negative states of affairs. The mereological account, however, cannot. If one initially favoured the fundamental tie account as a theory of positive states of affairs, then it remains your best bet when extended to cover negative states of affairs. Similarly, if you initially favoured the primitivist account, then it remains your best bet for negative states of affairs.

5.7 More Tough Cases

I've been arguing that we can account for negative existential and general truths, in terms of negative states of affairs. But these are not the only 'difficult' cases for the truthmaker maximalist. We must also find truthmakers for modal and counterfactual truths, analytic truths, and truths about the past and the future. These are tough cases. Merricks (2007, chapters 5–7), for example, argues that modal truths, truths about the past or future, and subjunctive conditional truths, have no truthmakers. (Baron et al. (2014), Bennett (2011c), and Hawley (2011) discuss these arguments further.) Yet in §3.6, I gave a general argument, claiming that these truths all have truthmakers. In order to make good on that conclusion, I now need to show what kinds of entity could act as truthmakers for those truths.

Modal Truths

Some philosophers think the truthmaker thesis should be restricted to contingent truths. In their introduction to *Truthmakers: The Contemporary Debate*, Beebee and Dodd sum up the thought:

> one might wonder whether necessary—and, in particular, *analytic*—truths need truthmakers; an analytic truth, it could

be said, is true *however* the world is, and so is not *made true* by anything. (Beebee and Dodd 2005a, 2)

I find this thought wrongheaded. Perhaps it's a hangover from thinking of truthmaking as a kind of supervenience (or some other modal notion), which becomes trivial in the case of necessary truths. Or perhaps it comes from a way of thinking of a proposition's being truthmade as a kind of demand on the world. Since necessary truths make no particular demands on the world, one might conclude that they're not made true at all.

I disagree. I'm with Merricks, in holding that 'truthmaker theorists should insist that necessary truths have genuine (non-trivial) truthmakers' (2007, 26). Clearly, some necessary truths are made true. For any entity x you like, the proposition saying that x exists depends for its truth on x's existence. If x is a necessary existent (the empty set; some Platonic property; God) then ⟨x exists⟩ is a necessary truth, made true by x itself. Other necessary truths have less exotic truthmakers. The state of affairs *that Bertie is snuffling* makes ⟨Bertie is snuffling⟩ true, and thereby makes true any disjunction with that proposition as a disjunct. Case in point: the necessary truth,

(5.9) ⟨Bertie is snuffling ∨ Bertie isn't snuffling⟩.

(On this basis Mellor (2009) adopts the bizarre view that true disjunctions in general do not have truthmakers.)

More interesting is the question of truthmakers for true statements of necessity, of the general form:

(5.10) ⟨A is necessary⟩

These, it seems, cannot have contingent truthmakers. Bertie's snuffling is what makes (5.9) true, but it isn't what makes it a necessary truth. If it were, it would also make ⟨Bertie is snuffling⟩ a necessary truth, and it clearly doesn't do that.

What makes (5.9) a necessary truth (and what truthmakes the statement that it is necessary) is up for grabs. I'll offer my preferred answer in just a bit. Before that, I want to offer a more ecumenical approach. It goes like this: you tell me your favourite analysis of modality, and I'll give you a truthmaker for anything of the form (5.10). Let's consider some examples.

Suppose you use a Lewisian approach, a plurality of genuine possible worlds, to analyse modal statements. Necessary truth consists in truth according to each of those worlds. So (5.10) may be understood as a universal quantification over possible worlds: all such worlds are *A*-worlds. But, given that we already have an account of truthmakers for universally quantified truths, there is no particular problem here.

Armstrong (2004) argues that Lewis's approach gets the direction of explanation wrong:

> it seems natural and plausible to say that it is the fact that the necessary truth is *itself* necessary that determines its truth in all worlds. This intension determines its extension across possible worlds. The alternative view is a sort of giant regularity theory. The truth is true in each world, and *because* of this it is necessarily true. The direction of explanation here seems quite wrong. (Armstrong 2004, 95–6)

But this 'giant regularity theory' is precisely what Lewis intended. In general, the Lewisian method is to analyse intensional concepts in purely extensional terms, so that 'all there is to the world is a vast mosaic of local matters of particular fact, just one little thing and then another' (Lewis 1986, ix). So, if we add Lewis's strategy on modality to the metaphysics we've developed so far, then we've got truthmakers for modal truths.

Merricks (2007) argues that the Lewisian approach doesn't deliver truthmakers for modal statements. His argument begins by considering what to say about propositions that (by Lewis's lights) are true but not actually true, like:

(5.11) ⟨There exist unicorns⟩

Supposing that unicorns are possible, unicorns exist within Lewis's metaphysics, and so (5.11) has a truthmaker. But it's not actually true. So the existence of a truthmaker doesn't suffice for actual truth. Merricks infers that actual truths need actual truthmakers:

> *That a horse exists* is actually true because it has an actually existing truthmaker. *That a unicorn exists* is not actually true because it fails to have an actually existing truthmaker. ... So I conclude that a corollary of [the truthmaker principle] is that, in general, actual truths have actual truthmakers. (Merricks 2007, 100)

The objection is then that 'Lewis cannot satisfy this corollary' (2007, 100). For if ⟨A⟩ is possible but not actually true, then ⟨possibly, A⟩ is actually true, but (by hypothesis) does not have an actual truthmaker. Its truthmaker is some part of some other possible world. So not all actual truths have an actual truthmaker.

Lewis should feel no pressure to accept Merricks's inference. Take the parallel cases of truths about other times and places. Merricks's reasoning would have us accept that what's true of the here and now should have a truthmaker here and now. That's sensible in the case of an utterance of 'it's raining', but the idea doesn't generalise. 'Socrates died in 399 BCE in Athens' is true, here and now, yet its truthmaker is located in 399 BCE in Athens.

Merricks may ask why it is, for Lewis, that the existence of a unicorn doesn't make (5.11) actually true. Divers (1999) explains that, for Lewis,

> the semantic function of a possibility operator on a non-modal quantificational sentence is always that of quantifying in, by way of a variable that is already reserved for worlds. (Divers 1999, 229)

The actually operator has a similar effect on a non-modal quantificational sentence, binding the implicit world-variable to the actual world. So the claim (as made by us) that (5.11) is actually true has the content:

(5.12) It is true that: in the actual world, there are unicorns.

This content clearly requires an actual-world unicorn to make it true. No special principle is required to rule out otherworldly unicorns as truthmakers for this proposition. Lewis's semantics automatically gives the result that non-actual unicorns do not make (5.11) actually true.

The Lewisian approach is not the account of modality available, of course. We might instead think that there are primitive modal facts. This doesn't mean that any modal truth is a primitive brute fact. A better way to understand the idea of primitive modal facts is by taking certain propositions to be compossible with certain others. On this view, which sets of propositions are compossible is a brute fact. (Adams (1974), Fine (1977), and Plantinga (1974, 1976) offer related approaches to primitive modal facts.)

The fundamental modal facts, on this view, apply to sets of propositions. Of these, the maximal compossible sets of propositions represent ways things could have been. They are the ersatz possible worlds, from which we can easily analyse a given proposition's contingency or necessity. On this view, those primitive compossibility facts are ultimately the truthmakers for all modal truths. In particular, the truthmaker for a proposition ⟨necessarily, A⟩ is the negative existential state of affairs, that no proposition is compossible with ⟨¬A⟩.

Merricks (2007, 102–11) objects to this approach as well:

> Suppose that abstract worlds are maximal possibly true propositions. ... [Then] my being possibly forty feet tall is purportedly reduced to my being represented as being forty feet tall *by some possible world or other*. But this reduction ... says that the way something is—my being possibly forty feet tall—depends on propositions and their relations to truth. This is in direct opposition to the core intuition behind [the truthmaker principle], which is that propositions' relations to truth depend on the way things are, not the other way around. Merricks (2007, 107)

The principle in action here is that my being possibly forty feet tall should not depend in any way on propositions about me. That seems reasonable (although I'll return to the point below). But there's a simple response available. We can take the ersatz possible worlds to comprise maximal compossible states of affairs, as Plantinga (1974, 1976) does, rather than maximal compossible propositions. It's clearly legitimate, in outline, to take my being possibly forty feet tall to depend on possible states of affairs.

Merricks (2007, 108) objects that 'we should unequivocally insist that Plantinga's abstract states of affairs are propositions' because 'the parallels [between them] are so striking'. But it's open for a defender of the view to deny this identification, in which case, Merricks's main objection carries no force. (The more pressing worry for Plantinga's view, as I see it, its how to explain non-actual states of affairs. Do they exist but not obtain? Are they non-existent entities? I discuss the options in detail in §8.6.)

I don't think a defender of propositional ersatz worlds needs to concede so much ground to Merricks. The worry, recall, is that how I possibly am does not depend on propositions about me (2007, 107). For propositions are mere representations of how things are, and how I might have been does not depend on how I am represented as being. But this last point is moot. Just consider what Lewis says about how his genuine worlds represent *de re*:

> Humphrey may be represented *in absentia* at other worlds ... [by their having] as part a Humphrey of its own, a flesh-and-blood counterpart of our Humphrey, a man very much like Humphrey in his origins, in his intrinsic charatcer, or in his historical role. By having such a part, a world represents *de re*, concerning Humphrey ... that he exists and does thus-and-so.
> (Lewis 1986, 194)

If genuine worlds may reduce the *de re* modal property *being possibly F* to *being represented as being F by some possible world*, they surely ersatz worlds can too? One might think that the difference lies in whether Humphrey's otherworldly representative is 'a flesh-and-blood counterpart', as it is for Lewis, or merely some abstract representation of him. Does that matter? Does it matter if the abstract proposition representing Humphrey involves flesh-and-blood

Humphrey himself, as Russellian propositions do (§1.2)? More argument would be needed to show that there is a genuine problem here. As things stand, then, the approach with ersatz worlds possessing primitive modal properties is viable, and provides truthmakers for modal truths.

A third approach to modal truthmakers comes in the form of localised facts about possibility, in the form of specific dispositions. Vetter (2015) shows how to generalise the notion to what she calls *potentialities*, which include an entity's potentiality for things in general to be such that A. On her analysis, it is possible that A just in case something has an iterated potentiality for things to be such that A. (An iterated potentiality is something's potentiality to bring about a further potentiality.) On this approach, it is necessary that A just in case nothing has the iterated potentiality for things to be such that $\neg A$. So, adding Vetter's metaphysics to our own, the truthmaker for a proposition ⟨necessarily, A⟩ is the negative existential state of affairs that nothing has the iterated potentiality for things to be such that $\neg A$.

A fourth option adopts a Finean stance on essence (Fine 1994, 1995, 2005), and takes facts about the essences of things as the grounds for other modal claims (see also Rosen 2010, 121). This approach is localised, in the sense that essences are essences of particular things. It stands to necessity roughly as Vetter's notion of potentiality stands to possibility. (Vetter 2015 contains an interesting discussion of the similarities and differences between her account and Fine's.) For an essence-based account to deliver truthmakers for modal facts, we will have to depart from Fine's preferred metaphysics and construe essences as entities in their own right. On that approach, the essences of particular things, either in isolation or collectively, are the truthmakers for true propositions ⟨necessarily, A⟩.

(A fifth option has it that 'truthmakers for modal truths are facts about our concepts and their conditions of application' (Dyke 2007). I don't suggest that this is a plausible account.)

Each of the first four options provides a plausible account of truthmakers for ⟨necessarily, A⟩. My sympathies lie with the essence-based account. On that view, (5.9) is a necessary truth because of the essences of negation and disjunction. Given the logical natures of negation and disjunction, combining any proposition ⟨A⟩ together with negation and disjunction to form ⟨A ∨ ¬A⟩ produces a logical truth. So those natures, or essences, together make ⟨necessarily, Bertie is snuffling ∨ Bertie isn't snuffling⟩ true.

This approach is in line with Armstrong's (2004, 95–6) objection to the Lewisian approach. (5.9) is true in all worlds because of the natures of negation and disjunction. The extent of possible worlds reflects, but does not determine, that proposition's necessity. Insofar as those natures feature in that proposition, its logical necessity is internal to it, just as Armstrong says it should be. This approach also captures the intuition that drives Merricks's (2007, 102–11) objection to ersatz worlds (discussed above), that how a thing could be shouldn't in general depend on how that thing is represented as being.

I'll discuss the relationship between truthmaking and this notion of essence further in §§6.3–6.4, and apply some of those ideas to the analysis of propositions in §8.2 and §8.5.

Counterfactual Truths

My approach to truthmakers for counterfactuals follows the ecumenical approach used above: give me your favourite account of counterfactuals, and I'll tell you what their truthmakers are. Suppose you think it's got something to do with closeness relations between possible worlds. Then the truthmakers for counterfactuals will involve states of affairs involving those similarity relations. If those worlds are concrete Lewisian worlds, then a state of affairs *that in all the closest such-and-such worlds, so-and-so obtains* might suffice. If they are ersatz worlds, then the truthmakers may also involve primitive modal facts, *that such-and-such propositions are compossible* (as discussed above).

You might think that this is the wrong approach to analysing counterfactuals. No problem: I'm not committed to that approach. You might prefer an account of counterfactuals (or at least, those reporting causal processes) in terms of primitive dispositions (Anjum and Mumford 2014; Mumford and Anjum 2011, 2009). Or you might think that certain counterfactual facts are amongst the primitive modal facts (Lange 2004, 240). Either way, the account provides entities to act as truthmakers for counterfactual truths.

Analytic Truths

Philosophers worry about truthmakers for analytic truths—those truths we take to hold in virtue of their meanings—perhaps even more than they worry about truthmakers for necessary truths. (Russell (2007, 2008) discusses whether the analytic/synthetic distinction can be sustained.) Recall Beebee and Dodd's summary: 'one might wonder whether necessary—and, in particular, *analytic*—truths need truthmakers' (Beebee and Dodd 2005a, 2). It's not unusual for otherwise committed truthmaker theorists to exclude analytic truths from their account. Rodriguez-Pereyra, for example, holds that:

> The truth of the proposition that bachelors are not married does not depend on what reality is like—whatever reality is like, bachelors are not married. In general analytic propositions are not grounded in reality. (Rodriguez-Pereyra 2005, 21)

Again, I find this puzzling. We often take 'analytic truth' to mean something that's true *in virtue of meaning*. It's very natural for truthmaker theorists to understand 'true in virtue of' statements as claims about truthmaking. So why not in this case? Why not say that analytic truths are true in virtue of facts about meaning? Such facts are genuine features of reality and, whether we take them to involve shared patterns of use, or abstract functions from words to semantic values, they are entities available for truthmaking duty.

Armstrong (2004) takes this line on analytic truths:

> The statement [a father is a male parent] is about fathers. But this particular truth about fathers has as its *truthmakers* nothing but the meanings of the words in which it is expressed. In particular 'father' and 'male parent' have *the very same meaning*. ... given all the meanings, all the analytic truths are fixed. (Armstrong 2004, 109)

Accepting Armstrong's line would support my overall approach here: that there's no particular difficulty in finding truthmakers for these 'difficult' cases, once we've provided truthmakers for negative existentials, and so on.

I don't think Armstrong's approach can be right, however. One worry is this. We might think of meaning as something brought into existence by our using words as we do. If so, then there might have been no meaning at all. But still, triangles would had three sides; bachelors would remained unmarried; and vixens would remain female foxes. What makes those propositions true in those possible situations cannot have anything to do with meanings. Other truthmakers would be required. Now, this argument does not show that those truths are not in fact made true by meanings. It shows only that they could have had other truthmakers. Nevertheless, if analytic truths can have truthmakers not involving meanings, then it is plausible that they do in fact have truthmakers not involving meanings. But what?

Quite independently of this worry, I don't think that meanings can be what make analytic truths true. When two words have the same meaning, substituting one for the other does not affect the proposition expressed. The proposition ⟨ostriches are big birds⟩ is identical to ⟨ostriches are large birds⟩. By the same token, ⟨big birds are large birds⟩ is identical to the logical truth ⟨big birds are big birds⟩. But logical truths are not true in virtue of meanings. (At least, they're not made true by the meanings of non-logical concepts like 'big'. The best approach, I think, identifies their truthmakers with the essences of the logical connectives: universal quantification and implication, in this case.) Since ⟨big birds are big birds⟩ is not made true by the meaning of 'big' (or 'large'), neither is ⟨big birds are large birds⟩. In general, meanings are not what make such propositions true.

Surely this conclusion is absurd? After all, analytic truths are, *by definition*, those true in virtue of their meaning. We must untangle some thinking here. The fact that ⟨big birds are large birds⟩ is identical to ⟨big birds are big birds⟩ points to the confusion: the mistake was in classifying *propositions* as analytic or synthetic. Propositions live at the wrong semantic level to be classified in those ways. Meanings belong to (disambiguated) words, not to propositions. Meanings determine propositions but, in so doing, information is lost: given a proposition, we cannot always recover the words or meanings which determined it.

If something is analytic, by contrast, then that entity must be the kind of thing with which we can associate a unique meaning. In saying that *big birds are large birds* is analytic, we are making reference both to the sentence 'big birds are large birds' and to the proposition it expresses (or perhaps to the sentence plus its meaning).

One way to understand 'is analytic' is as an *Abelardian* predicate (Noonan 1991), sensitive to the way in which the proposition is presented. 'Is so-named' is a prime example of an Abelardian predicate. Richard Sylvan was so-named (by himself) because of his love for the Australian bush. We can't infer from this that Richard Routley was so-named because of his love for the Australian bush, even though Routley is Sylvan. The former use of 'is so-named' has the content *is named 'Sylvan'*, whereas the latter has the content *is named 'Routley'*. The predicate picks out different properties, depending on the term preceding it.

Something similar happens with 'is analytic' and 'it is analytic that'. In saying 'it is analytic that big birds are large birds', the content of 'is analytic' makes reference to the way the proposition is presented, via the sentence 'big birds are large birds'. The analyticity claim is true because the sentence's meaning guarantees that it expresses a logical truth. That is the sense in which the truthmakers for analytic truths involve meanings.

Temporal Truths

What to say about temporal truths (abut the past or the future) depends very much on one's metaphysics of time. Eternalists, who hold that past, present, and future all exist, have no trouble finding truthmakers for temporal truths. The past and future exist in just the way the present does, on their view, and so there exist past and future truthmakers, just as there exist present ones. (Charlotte Brontë wrote

Jane Eyre⟩ is made true (now) by the state of affairs *that Charlotte Brontë write Jane Eyre at time t*, together with the fact that time *t* is before the present time.

Finding truthmakers for temporal truths is an issue only for those who deny that the future, and perhaps the past too, do not exist in the way the present does. Presentists, holding that only present entities exist, have offered all kinds of responses to this worry. One option puts forth *Lucretian* properties, such as *having contained sabre-toothed tigers* (Bigelow 1996). Some present entities presently possess that property: Asia, and the world as a whole. Those states of affairs are presently existing entities, so allowed by the presentist's ontology, which can act as truthmakers for ⟨there were sabre-toothed tigers⟩.

It feels something like cheating to deny the past's existence but to allow properties which, in some sense, capture the past (Merricks 2007, 135). Cameron (2010) says such a property 'is suspicious because it points beyond its instances in the sense that a thing's presently having that property tells us nothing about the *present intrinsic nature* of the thing' (2010, 59).

Cameron suggests a variant on the view: the truthmakers for past truths are *temporal distributional properties*. *Being black-and-white striped* is a spatial distributional property, specifying a repeating arrangement of black strips and white strips over the surface of whatever possesses it. Temporal distributional properties do the same, but over time. Cameron thinks present states of affairs involving these properties are suitable truthmakers for truths about the past.

I'm doubtful about these approaches. I don't see how they can account for hecceitistic truths about, say, Jane Austen, given that (according to presentists) there's no such person. Perhaps there's a workaround in terms of hecceitistic properties, like *being Jane Austen* (Ingram 2016a,b). But there again, I'm no presentist. I'm content that Special Relativity gives us excellent reason to believe in the existence of times other than our present. All that matters here is that presentists can bring themselves to accept such entities and, as it happens, many of them do.

5.8 Chapter Summary

Given (NECESSITATION), parsimonious maximalist truthmaking theories look appealing. But such theories cannot be sustained (§§5.2–5.3). So we must accept that maximalism comes at a serious ontological cost. Moreover, given the argument of chapter 3, truthmaker theory in general carries that cost: you can't be a truthmaker theorist without being a maximalist. In the really difficult cases of negative existential and general truths, I've argued that the best approach involves positive and negative states of affairs (§§5.4–5.5). These can be understood either in terms of positive and negative fundamental ties, or by extending the primitivist account of states of affairs (§5.6). Given this ontology, finding truthmakers for the remaining cases—modal, analytic, and temporal truths—posed little problem (§5.7).

III The Truthmaking Relation

6
Truthmaking and Grounding

In previous chapters, I've argued that all truths have a truthmaker, and I've developed an ontological account of what those truthmakers are. They're states of affairs, and they include negative and other logically complex entities. Now it's time to turn our focus to the truthmaking relation itself. What kind of relation is it? What are its logical properties? Can it be defined, or otherwise understood, in more conceptually basic terms? What is its relation to the general concepts of grounding *and* metaphysical determination? *These are the questions I'll try to answer in this chapter.*

6.1 Can Truthmaking Be Defined?

TRUTHMAKING IS the central notion in this book. So, if the approach is to be persuasive, we will need to develop a thorough philosophical understanding of that relation. One line of philosophical investigation is to give a conceptual analysis, or definition, of truthmaking. That project would aim to explain or reduce the concept *truthmaking* to more basic concepts, in terms of a formula of the form:

(6.1) x is a truthmaker for $\langle A \rangle$ if and only if ....

We should expect the equivalence to hold in all conceptually possible situations; and we should expect the concepts that fill in the '...' to be well understood. (They should be at least as well understood as, and preferably better understood than, *truthmaking*.)

I don't hold out much hope for this definitional project in general. It's worth remembering that the *truthmaking* concept is a philosopher's term of art. In this respect, it is unlike the concept *truth*. It is part of a philosopher's job to say something about *truth*, but not so for *truthmaking*. Rather, she may introduce *truthmaking* as a concept to help her explain the general features of the world. If *truthmaking* could be reduced to more basic concepts, then it would serve an intermediary purpose only. Ultimately, it could be done away with. But part of what I'm arguing in this book is that *truthmaking* is a central philosophical concept. Philosophy needs it to help explain the general features of the world. It can't be defined away.

Later on, in chapter 8, I'm going to put forward a theory which will seem in tension with this stance. There, I'll argue for a theory of what propositions are. Given this theory, and given a particular proposition ⟨A⟩, it will be easy to say under what conditions some entity x is a truthmaker for ⟨A⟩. Indeed, it will turn out that, given the ontological resources required for propositions to exist, no further bit of ontology is required for the *truthmaking* relation to exist. But this account will not bring conceptual enlightenment to our investigation of truthmaking in any robust sense. Rather, to make sense of that account of propositions, we first need to understand the concept of *truthmaking*.

Even in the absence of a full conceptual analysis of *truthmaking*, there is lots we can say about the relation. We do this by finding answers to the following kinds of question:

(6.2) What is the relation between *truthmaking* and *necessity*?

(6.3) What is the relation between *truthmaking* and *grounding*?

(6.4) What grounds the state of affairs *that x truthmakes ⟨A⟩*?

(6.5) What truthmakes the proposition ⟨x truthmakes ⟨A⟩⟩?

(6.6) What are the logical properties of the *truthmaking* relation? Is it (ir)reflexive? (a)symmetrical? (in)transitive?

In providing answers to these questions, we will come to have a much better conceptual grasp of *truthmaking*, even though those answers do not add up to a conceptual analysis.

6.2 Truthmaking and Necessity

Let's begin with some attempts to define *truthmaking*. On one approach, to be a truthmaker for a proposition ⟨A⟩ is to necessitate ⟨A⟩'s truth. John Fox, in an early paper on (the contemporary conception of) truthmaking, states the view: 'by a truthmaker for A, I mean something whose very existence entails A', and goes on to add that "necessitates' would perhaps be more felicitous' in place of 'entails' (Fox 1987, 189). More precisely, the idea is this:

(TRUTHMAKING AS NECESSITY) x is a truthmaker for ⟨A⟩ iff, necessarily, ⟨A⟩ is true if x exists.

Fox uses this principle as a definition of 'truthmaker'. The 'only if' direction is the (NECESSITATION) principle from §3.1. I argued there that we should accept (NECESSITATION). It's the 'if' direction of (TRUTHMAKING AS NECESSITY) that's questionable.

From (TRUTHMAKING AS NECESSITY), we can infer the following principle:

(ENTAILMENT) If x is a truthmaker for ⟨A⟩, and ⟨A⟩ entails ⟨B⟩, then x is a truthmaker for ⟨B⟩, too.

The argument is simple: if ⟨A⟩ entails ⟨B⟩, then by definition, it is impossible for ⟨A⟩ to be true without ⟨B⟩ also being true. So any x necessitates ⟨A⟩'s truth only if it necessitates ⟨B⟩'s truth too. So, given (TRUTHMAKING AS NECESSITY), any truthmaker for ⟨A⟩ is also a truthmaker for ⟨B⟩.

We can also reason from (ENTAILMENT) to the controversial right-to-left direction of (TRUTHMAKING AS NECESSITY), as follows. Suppose that, necessarily, ⟨A⟩ is true if x exists. Then it is impossible for ⟨x exists⟩ to be true and ⟨A⟩ to be false, hence ⟨x exists⟩ entails ⟨A⟩. But given that x is a truthmaker for ⟨x exists⟩, (ENTAILMENT) implies that x is a truthmaker for ⟨A⟩.

There's a well-known problem with these approaches: they treat every entity as a truthmaker for every necessary truth (Restall 1996). Any necessary truth ⟨A⟩ is, by definition, necessitated by any entity whatsoever. So, given (TRUTHMAKING AS NECESSITY), you and I and the Eiffel Tower are each truthmakers for ⟨1 + 1 = 2⟩, for ⟨either fox hunting is cruel or it isn't⟩, and for ⟨there is no God⟩. That is highly implausible at best.

Restall (1996, 334) notices an even more serious problem with (TRUTHMAKING AS NECESSITY) and (ENTAILMENT). Suppose we also accept the following principle:

(DISJUNCTION) x is a truthmaker for ⟨A ∨ B⟩ iff either x is a truthmaker for ⟨A⟩ or x is a truthmaker for ⟨B⟩.

The problem is that (TRUTHMAKING AS NECESSITY) and (DISJUNCTION) together entail that every entity is a truthmaker for every truth (Restall 1996, 334).

Suppose ⟨A⟩ is true, and consider any existing entity x. By (TRUTHMAKING AS NECESSITY), x is a truthmaker for ⟨A ∨ ¬A⟩ and so, by (DISJUNCTION), either x is a truthmaker for ⟨A⟩ or x is a truthmaker for ⟨¬A⟩. But x cannot be a truthmaker for ⟨¬A⟩, since ⟨¬A⟩ is false. So x is a truthmaker for ⟨A⟩. Since x and ⟨A⟩ were arbitrary choices, it follows that any existing entity whatsoever is a truthmaker for every truth. But this is absurd. It trivialises truthmaker theory, and cannot be accepted.

I've argued elsewhere that (DISJUNCTION), as stated here, is false (Jago 2009). Briefly, that's because there are (at least) three ways to make a disjunction ⟨A ∨ B⟩ true: by making just ⟨A⟩ true; by making just ⟨B⟩ true; or by containing a part which makes ⟨A⟩ true and a part which makes ⟨B⟩ true (which amounts to being a truthmaker for ⟨A ∧ B⟩.) I'll argue, in §7.2 below, that the third way of making ⟨A ∨ B⟩ true need not make true either ⟨A⟩ on its own or ⟨B⟩ on its own. So (DISJUNCTION), as stated here, fails.

(Moreover, if there are disjunctive states of affairs, then there is a fourth way to make ⟨A ∨ B⟩ true, which also falsifies (DISJUNCTION). For a disjunctive state of affairs may make ⟨A ∨ B⟩ true without making either disjunct, or their conjunction, true.)

Nevertheless, (TRUTHMAKING AS NECESSITY) is not off the hook. Even though (DISJUNCTION) is false, a related principle is true:

(DISJUNCTION*) For all non-disjunctive states of affairs x, x is a truthmaker for ⟨A ∨ B⟩ iff x is a truthmaker for ⟨A⟩, or x is a truthmaker for ⟨B⟩, or x is a truthmaker for ⟨A ∧ B⟩.

Although this is a weaker condition than (DISJUNCTION), it is strong enough for the triviality result. As before, suppose ⟨A⟩ is true. By (TRUTHMAKING AS NECESSITY), any non-disjunctive x is a truthmaker for ⟨A ∨ ¬A⟩. Then neither ⟨¬A⟩ nor ⟨A ∧ ¬A⟩ has a truthmaker (since both are false). So by (DISJUNCTION*), x is a truthmaker for ⟨A⟩. So (TRUTHMAKING AS NECESSITY) and (DISJUNCTION*) together entail that any existing non-disjunctive entity whatsoever is a truthmaker for every truth, which is absurd.

There have been various attempts to respond to these triviality results. One is to limit the scope of (TRUTHMAKING AS NECESSITY) to contingent truths:

(CONTINGENT TRUTHMAKING AS NECESSITY) For contingent propositions ⟨A⟩, x is a truthmaker for ⟨A⟩ iff, necessarily, ⟨A⟩ is true if x exists.

And there is a corresponding entailment thesis, similarly restricted to contingent propositions:

(CONTINGENT ENTAILMENT) For contingent propositions ⟨A⟩ and ⟨B⟩, if x is a truthmaker for ⟨A⟩, and ⟨A⟩ entails ⟨B⟩, then x is a truthmaker for ⟨B⟩, too.

This is the principle Restall (1996, 334) calls *Jackson's Thesis*, after some remarks Frank Jackson makes on truthmaking in Jackson 1994.

The restriction to contingent truths in (CONTINGENT TRUTHMAKING AS NECESSITY) and (CONTINGENT ENTAILMENT) does little to avoid the problem, however. As before, the argument is due to Restall (1996, 334–5). Any contingent x is a truthmaker for $\langle x \text{ exists}\rangle$, which entails $\langle x \text{ exists} \wedge N\rangle$ for any necessary truth $\langle N\rangle$. So, either by (CONTINGENT TRUTHMAKING AS NECESSITY) or by (CONTINGENT ENTAILMENT), x is a truthmaker for $\langle x \text{ exists} \wedge N\rangle$.

Restall then argues that, in general, a truthmaker for $\langle A \wedge B\rangle$ is a truthmaker both for $\langle A\rangle$ and for $\langle B\rangle$. If so, then x is a truthmaker for $\langle N\rangle$. Since x and $\langle N\rangle$ were arbitrary choices, it follows that any contingent entity is a truthmaker for any necessary truth. And as before, given (DISJUNCTION*), triviality soon follows. Given any truth $\langle A\rangle$, any non-disjunctive state x is a truthmaker for $\langle A \vee \neg A\rangle$ and hence, by (DISJUNCTION*), for $\langle A\rangle$, which is absurd.

Restall's argument relies on the following principle:

(CONJUNCTION) x is a truthmaker for $\langle A \wedge B\rangle$ iff $\langle x\rangle$ is a truthmaker for $\langle A\rangle$ and x is a truthmaker for $\langle B\rangle$.

But, as Rodriguez-Pereyra (2006b) convincingly argues, this principle is false. I'll discuss why this is in §7.2 below. For now, it's enough to flag that I don't accept CONJUNCTION, and so I can't accept Restall's argument as it stands.

Nevertheless, there is a strictly weaker conjunction principle, which all should accept, and which allows for a similar argument to Restall's. The idea is that a truthmaker for a conjunction is made up of a truthmaker for each conjunct. It contains truthmakers for the conjuncts, even if it itself is not a truthmaker for those conjuncts. More precisely:

(CONJUNCTION*) x is a truthmaker for $\langle A \wedge B\rangle$ iff x is a sum $y \sqcup z$, where y is a truthmaker for $\langle A\rangle$ and z is a truthmaker for $\langle B\rangle$.

Note that the right-hand side of (CONJUNCTION) implies the right-hand side of (CONJUNCTION*), for $x \sqcup x = x$, but not vice versa.

Given (CONJUNCTION*) and either (CONTINGENT TRUTHMAKING AS NECESSITY) or (CONTINGENT ENTAILMENT), the triviality argument goes as follows. Take any truth $\langle A \rangle$. By (CONTINGENT TRUTHMAKING AS NECESSITY), any contingent entity x is a truthmaker for $\langle x$ exists $\wedge$ $(A \vee \neg A)\rangle$. So by (CONJUNCTION*), x has a part, y, which is a truthmaker for $\langle A \vee \neg A \rangle$. But since $\langle \neg A \rangle$ is false, by (DISJUNCTION*), y is a truthmaker for $\langle A \rangle$. Generalising, any contingent entity x has a part which is a truthmaker for any truth whatsoever. In particular, all contingent mereological atoms (entities with no proper parts) will count as truthmakers for all truths. That is just as absurd as the conclusion of Restall's argument.

I'll discuss (DISJUNCTION*) and (CONJUNCTION*) further in chapter 7. For now, the intuitive appeal of each should be clear. The conclusion to draw is that the restriction to contingent propositions doesn't help: truthmaking still can't be understood in terms of necessitation or entailment.

A second approach to avoiding the triviality results, while remaining within the necessity/entailment approach to truthmaking, is to weaken the notion of necessity or entailment involved. This is the approach Armstrong (2004) recommends for rescuing (ENTAILMENT):

> if [the entailment] principle is to be applied in full generality, then the entailment here cannot be classical entailment. ... The exact limitations to be placed on entailment in the suggested Entailment principle is a technical matter ... and I will simply assume that something is available. (Armstrong 2004, 11)

Weakening a notion of necessity means counting fewer situations as being necessary (or equivalently, as allowing more possibilities). It's common to think of the progression from *nomic* to *metaphysical* to *logical* to *doxastic* necessity as representing ever-weaker concepts of necessity: each admits possibilities the previous notion did not. To avoid the problems mentioned above, the operative concept of necessity has to be weak enough to avoid treating each proposition $\langle A \vee \neg A \rangle$ as a necessary truth. That requires a very weak notion of necessity. Arguably, doxastic necessity could fit the bill (if you allow that someone can fail to believe that $A \vee \neg A$). But clearly that's not going to help the definitional project, since we can't define truthmaking in terms of what people believe.

Nor can we define truthmaking in terms of logical entailment, as usually understood. Logical entailment is a relation between (sets of) sentences, whereas a definition of truthmaking has to connect an entity to a proposition. Some entities have no name, and some propositions are not expressed by any sentence of English (or any countable language; see §1.1). Nevertheless, those entities will be involved in truthmaking relationships. Truthmaking outruns entailment relationships between sentences.

It is not even clear what form such a definition would take. To bring out the issue, let's try this (with the quotes read as Quine-quotes):

(6.7) x is a truthmaker for $\langle A \rangle$ iff 'x exists' logically entails 'A'.

If understood as a universal quantification over entities x and propositions $\langle A \rangle$, then we cannot determine which sentences appear on the right (since we cannot in general infer from an entity to its name, or from a proposition to the sentence which expresses it). If understood as a universal quantification over the sentences on the right, by contrast, then (6.2) is inconsistent. Suppose $x = y$ (but not as a matter of logic). Then 'x exists' entails 'x exists' but 'y exists' does not. So (6.7) entails that x, but not y, is a truthmaker for $\langle x$ exists$\rangle$. Yet since $x = y$, we may infer that y is a truthmaker for $\langle x$ exists$\rangle$: contradiction. So (6.7) will not do.

If truthmaking as logical necessitation/entailment is to work, it must be formulated in terms of a weak necessitation/entailment relation between propositions. To evaluate that approach, we need a logic on the table. Armstrong mentions (perhaps without endorsing) suggestions in Read (2000) and Restall (1996) to borrow a notion of entailment from a *relevant logic* (Mares 2004; Read 1988; Routley et al. 1982). Relevant entailment certainly seems a good candidate for avoiding the problems we met above since, in general, A does not relevantly entail $B \vee \neg B$.

I don't think that suggestion will work. Just about all logics, including all the main relevant logics, support the following equivalences:

(∨∧-EQUIVALENCE) A is equivalent to $A \vee (A \wedge B)$

(∧∨-EQUIVALENCE) A is equivalent to $A \wedge (A \vee B)$

So, defining truthmaking in this way, ⟨A⟩, ⟨$A \vee (A \wedge B)$⟩, and ⟨$A \wedge (A \vee B)$⟩ will be assigned the same truthmakers. But that is the wrong result. Suppose ⟨B⟩ has nothing whatsoever to do with ⟨A⟩. Then truthmakers for ⟨B⟩ cannot be part of what makes ⟨A⟩ true. They may contribute to making ⟨$A \wedge B$⟩ and ⟨$A \vee B$⟩ true, and hence can contribute to making ⟨$A \vee (A \wedge B)$⟩ and ⟨$A \wedge (A \vee B)$⟩ true. So ⟨A⟩ need not have the same truthmakers as either ⟨$A \vee (A \wedge B)$⟩ or ⟨$A \wedge (A \vee B)$⟩.

Avoiding that issue will require a very weak logic indeed, certainly weaker than all the standard relevant logics. Yet *any* logic, however weak, faces a further problem. If it is an adequate logic of truth, it treats ⟨A⟩ and ⟨⟨A⟩ is true⟩ as equivalent propositions. So, given that logic, it will be logically necessary that A whenever the state of affairs *that* ⟨A⟩ *is true* exists. (There's no getting away from such states of affairs: so long as we accept that truth is a property, and that property possession consists in the existence of a state of affairs, then we have states of affairs of the form *that* ⟨A⟩ *is true*.) But then, in defining truthmaking in terms of logical necessitation, *that* ⟨A⟩ *is true* will incorrectly count as a truthmaker for ⟨A⟩. Clearly we can't accept that result. ⟨A⟩'s truth *consists in* the existence of *that* ⟨A⟩ *is true*, so that state of affairs can't be what *makes* ⟨A⟩ true. Nor should we search for a weaker logic still, in which ⟨A⟩ is not equivalent to ⟨⟨A⟩ is true⟩, for such a logic has given up on our concept of truth. (I discuss this point further in §9.6.)

In short, I don't see any way to define truthmaking in terms of either necessity or entailment, logical or otherwise. It's perfectly possible to define a logical system in which A entails B just in case truthmakers for ⟨A⟩ are also truthmakers for ⟨B⟩. In fact, that's precisely the aim of chapter 7. But that notion of entailment won't be of any use in defining truthmaking, because we first need the notion of truthmaking to define that logical system. We'll be able to set down the right principles for that logic precisely because the semantics is given in terms of truthmakers. Clearly, we can't then use that logic to define what we mean by 'truthmaking'.

6.3 Truthmaking and Grounding

The relationship between a truth and its truthmakers is a kind of metaphysical dependence: the proposition's truth depends, in a metaphysical, non-causal way, on the existence of one of those truthmakers. This kind of metaphysical dependence is often called *grounding*.

An understanding of grounding has broad applications throughout metaphysics: to physicalism about the mind (Fine 2012b; Wilson 2016a), to metaphysical fundamentality (Schaffer 2010c), and to what intrinsic properties are (Barker and Jago 2017; Rosen 2010), as well as to the nature of truth and truthmaking (Liggins 2008; Schaffer 2010b). Grounding has also been used in social ontology to analyse the notion of *social construction* (Epstein 2015; Griffith 2017; Schaffer 2016b).

Grounding is often taken to be an *explanatory* relation, in a distinctive metaphysical sense (Jenkins 2013; Thompson 2016a; von Solodkoff 2012). Fine claims that 'investigation into ground is part of the investigation into nature' (Fine 2012b, 76). And indeed, the last few years have seen an explosion of philosophical literature on grounding. (Bliss and Trogdon 2016, Clark and Liggins 2012, and Trogdon 2013 survey the literature. Miller and Norton (2016) and Wilson (2014) are dissenting voices, arguing that there's no need for grounding.)

Following Audi (2012a), Rosen (2010), and Schaffer (2009), I take grounding to be a relationship between entities. Typically, but not always, these are states of affairs. It might be, for example, that the state of affairs *that Anna's brain is in such-and-such configuration* is what grounds the state of affairs *that Anna is in pain*. I will assume that a general claim of this form is the correct way to express 'brain states ground pain states'.

Audi and Rosen think grounding holds only between states of affairs (which they call *facts*). But I don't see why we should restrict the notion. It's quite natural to take *that there exist numbers* to be grounded by specific numbers (and pluralities of numbers), rather than by the states of affairs *that 1 is a number, that 2 is a number*, and so on. (The numbers themselves are candidate grounds because they are numbers essentially. This is not the case in general. Socrates does not ground *that someone is a philosopher*, since Socrates might not have been a philosopher.) So entities other than states of affairs may be grounds.

It is also plausible (if we accept mereological universalism) that mereological sums are grounded in their parts, in the sense that the sum exists in virtue of the parts existing. If so, then entities other than states of affairs may be grounded. So here, I am in agreement with Schaffer (2009): in principle, the *grounding* relation is not fussy about the kinds of entity it deals in.

(Since states of affairs will nevertheless feature heavily in the discussion that follows, I'll use the notation '[*A*]' for the state of affairs *that A*. This helps abbreviate nasty-sounding constructions like 'the state of affairs that the proposition that *A* is true' to '[⟨*A*⟩ is true]'.)

The specific connection I have in mind between grounding and truthmaking is this:

(T-GROUNDING) x is a truthmaker for ⟨*A*⟩ if and only if x grounds the state of affairs *that* ⟨*A*⟩ *is true*.

We can't treat this as a definition of *truthmaking*, however, because it invokes the notion of *truth* and our project is to understand truth in terms of truthmaking.

It is clear, however, that (T-GROUNDING) captures an important relationship between truthmaking and grounding. An important aspect of our investigation into truthmaking involves making sense of this relationship. Accordingly, I'm going to spend some time considering the general notion of grounding. In this section, I'll sketch a theory of grounding and show how, together with the analysis of truth in terms of truthmaking, (T-GROUNDING) can be derived. I'll then (§6.5) discuss some general properties of the grounding relation, and whether they are inherited by truthmaking.

One approach considers grounding to be a kind of *metaphysical causation* (Schaffer 2016a; Wilson 2017). Whilst there's certainly something in that, the idea, taken literally, seems problematic, given that grounding is a necessary relation (Bernstein 2016; Koslicki 2016). I'm going to pursue an alternative approach. I'm also going to assume a univocal notion of grounding. (See Cameron 2015, Koslicki 2015, and Wilson 2016b for discussion.)

Let's begin with four simple cases of grounding: conjunctions, disjunctions, existentials, and sets. These cases are straightforward: conjunctions are grounded jointly by their conjuncts; disjunctions (individually or jointly) by their disjuncts; existentials by their instances; and sets by their members. In these cases, I take it, we have a good grasp on what's going on (Rosen 2010, 117). As Anscome (no friend of this kind of metaphysics) says in the related case of making true, 'disjunctions and propositions with 'some' are somewhat favourable examples for a concept of what makes true' (Anscombe 2000, 1). I'll call these the *logical cases* of grounding.

Here, we can understand 'conjunction', 'disjunction', and 'existential' as applying either to logically complex states of affairs, or to logically complex propositions. We can spell out the former case more precisely as follows: the existence a conjunctive state of affairs is grounded in the joint existence of its conjunct states of affairs (and so on). In the latter case, we mean that the truth of a conjunctive proposition is grounded jointly in the truth of its conjuncts (and so on). I'm going to concentrate here on the case of grounding logically complex states of affairs. (If you don't think there are such things as logically complex states of affairs, pretend I'm talking about propositions.)

These logical cases are central to the general account of grounding I'm going to sketch here: *all* cases of grounding will boil down to these, or so I'll claim. (As these cases are basic, I'm not pursuing a fully reductive analysis of grounding, of the kind given (for 'complete and immediate formal ground') by Poggiolesi (2016).)

Now let's consider some arbitrary non-fundamental property, F. What grounds a thing's possession of F? Equivalently, what grounds the existence (for some a that is F) of the state of affairs *that a is F*? Because F is (by assumption) a non-fundamental property, there must be some ground or other: further facts about a (or about other entities) in virtue of which *that a is F* obtains. Just what these other facts are depends entirely on what property F is. A specification of what F is, is thereby a specification of the *grounding conditions* for F-possession. In saying what F is, we are also saying what it is for something to possess F, and that amounts to giving possible conditions for grounding *that — is F*.

The approach I'm suggesting is similar to Audi's (2012a). He argues that

> Grounding is importantly tied to the natures of properties. Whether two facts are suited to stand in a grounding relation depends heavily upon what properties are involved in those facts. ... let us say that facts are suited to stand in a relation of grounding only if their constituent properties are *essentially connected*. (Audi 2012a, 108)

I agree, to an extent. The nature of a property F—*what F is*—specifies what it takes for something to be F. In this way, Audi and I agree that the nature of F specifies grounding conditions for F-possession.

Let's consider an example. Take Haslanger's ameliorative analysis of the nature of the property, *being a woman*:

> S *is a woman* iff$_{df}$ S is systematically subordinated along some dimension (economic, political, legal, social, etc.), and S is "marked" as a target for this treatment by observed or imagined bodily features presumed to be evidence of a female's biological role in reproduction. (Haslanger 2004, 6–7)

On the account I'm suggesting, an analysis such as this first and foremost tells us what *being a woman* is: it tells us about the nature of the property. But it thereby tells us about the grounding-conditions for states of affairs involving *being a woman*. *That Anna is a woman* is grounded by a complex of further states of affairs involving Anna's systematic economic, political, legal, or social subordination, plus states of affairs involving other people perceiving or imagining that Anna has properties associated with female reproduction.

One way to understand this approach is in terms of *real definition*, brought to prominence in contemporary philosophy by Fine (1994) and Lowe (2012). Lowe understands a real definition as 'a proposition which tells us, in the most perspicuous fashion, *what E is*' or, in the case of merely possible entities, '*what E is or would be*' (Lowe 2012, 104–5). For Fine, a real definition is a proposition (or collection of propositions) true in virtue of the identity of the entity in question (Fine 1994).

Rosen (2010) expresses a similar idea, on which 'reduction or analysis is a relation among propositions, and real definitions of items are given by general schemata for such reductions' (Rosen 2010, 122). The link to grounding, on Rosen's approach, is that 'if p's being the case consists in q's being the case, then p is true in virtue of the fact that q' (Rosen 2010, 122). In particular, Rosen has in mind the case where the real definition of some property F is specified by real definition (q) of being F (p). This case coheres well with Audi's view, if we treat F's real definition as way of specifying its nature. (Koslicki (2012) discusses the relationship between essence and real definition in Fine and Aristotle.)

My own view breaks with Audi's on several crucial points. First, Audi's idea that we have grounding between states of affairs 'only if their constituent properties are *essentially connected*' is too restrictive. The state of affairs [Bertie is adorable] grounds [⟨Bertie is adorable⟩ is true]. But this grounding fact has little to do with the nature of *truth*, and even less to do with *being adorable*. (Griffith (2014, 208) makes a similar point.) The nature of truth specifies that [⟨Bertie is adorable⟩ is true] will be grounded by any truthmaker for ⟨Bertie is adorable⟩. But the nature of truth alone can hardly tell us what those truthmakers are.

Rather, it is the nature of the proposition, ⟨Bertie is adorable⟩, which specifies that [Bertie is adorable] is one of it's truthmakers. It is the combined natures of ⟨Bertie is adorable⟩ and of *being true* which together determine that [Bertie is adorable] grounds [⟨Bertie is adorable⟩ is true]. The moral is that, whilst grounding-conditions for some state of affairs [*Fa*] might be given by the essence *F*, they need not be. In general, grounding conditions for [*A*] may be given by the natures of any of [*A*]'s constituents, individually or taken together.

Perhaps more importantly, I disagree with Audi on the details of the nature-grounding link. How do we get from entities having such-and-such natures to states of affairs being grounded in such-and-such ways? What is it about those natures that implies those grounding conditions? The answer, according to Audi, appears to be: nothing. The link between specific natures and specific grounds is a basic, unanalysable connection. He says:

> it is of the essence of redness that an instance of it can be grounded in an instance of maroonness. ... But note that this does not entail that these properties have complex essences, or any kind of internal complexity that might allow us to say more specifically why it is that they stand in that relation. ... the fact that maroonness is a determinate of the determinable redness is no doubt relevant. But even so, that relation between the properties does not itself hold in virtue of anything about their natures that we could specify except to repeat that they are so related. There is nothing intrinsic to maroonness that explains why it is a determinate of redness, *except* that it is *this color*, i.e., maroonness. (Audi 2012a, 109)

If that's right, then the theory must trade in a huge number of basic, unanalysable necessary connections, from essences to grounds. My worry is not with necessary connections per se. Rather, my worry here is that any attempt at explanation of ground will swiftly come to a halt. Too much is left unexplained.

We can do better. I interpret the analysis (or real definition) of a property *F* as telling us *what F is*, metaphysically speaking. That's step one. To get clearer on this notion, we must bring out an ambiguity, often missed, in 'the nature of *F*'. This can mean: (i) what it takes for something to possess *F*; or it can mean something along the lines of (ii) what the entity *F* is, or what it is essentially like. To bring out the difference, try this: is *being human* essential to (or part of the nature of) *being a woman*? In sense (i), yes: only humans can possess *being a woman*. But in sense (ii), no: *being human* is not a property possessed by the property *being a woman*. In sense (ii), *being a woman* is, by its nature, an abstract, multi-locatable entity, not a woman. Sense (ii) refers to the *constitutive nature* of the property, *being a woman*. (We should, at this point, leave it open whether either property is a *constitutive part* of the other. I'll say more on this idea below.)

It's common to conflate these senses of 'the nature of *F*'. Rosen (2010), for example, notes that 'the canonical form of a real definition should be this: $X =_{df} ...$', but goes on to say that, 'without significant distortion ... Instead of asking, 'What is knowledge?', we can ask: 'What is it for a person to know that *p*?'" (Rosen 2010, 122). This is a shift from sense (ii) to sense (i) of 'the nature of knowledge': from the constitutive nature of *knowing* to its possession conditions.

My interest here is, in the first instance, in the constitutive nature of things: in *what they are*. My claim is that understanding what a property is, in this sense, reveals its possession conditions, and hence explains facts about grounding. An example will make this clearer. A puppy is a domestic dog, less than one year old. I take *being a puppy* to be the conjunctive property whose conjuncts are the properties *being a dog*, *being domesticated*, and *being less than a year old*. The previous sentence specifies the constitutive nature of the property, *being a puppy*. This is the primary way in which I understand 'real definition'.

The immediate grounds for a state of affairs [*x* is a puppy] are: [*x* is a dog], [*x* is domesticated], and [*x* is less than a year old]. These three states of affairs together ground [*x* is a puppy]. They do so because (i) [*x* is a puppy] contains *being a puppy*, (ii) *being a puppy* is a conjunctive property, and (iii) conjunctions are grounded collectively by their conjuncts. Point (iii) involves one of the basic logical cases of grounding from above. These are bedrock in the theory of grounding.

These are the immediate grounds of [*x* is a puppy], but not its only grounds. *Being a dog*, *being domesticated*, and *being less than a year old* are not fundamental properties, and so they too may be analysed as logically complex entities. Each analysis reveals grounding conditions for those properties which (assuming transitivity of grounding) are thereby grounding conditions for *being a dog* also. Each iteration of this process takes us from less fundamental to more fundamental properties. A complete analysis of a property specifies its structure as a logical combination of fundamental properties only. This is its constitutive nature. In this setting, a real definition can be seen as an informative identity statement, with only logical vocabulary and fundamental properties in the definiendum.

I've been arguing that non-fundamental properties should be understood as logically complex entities, and that their grounding conditions should be understood in terms of this complex nature. (Note that this commitment does not assume that each property has a *conceptual* analysis. There is no requirement that the logically complex 'definiens' of a property be finite, or informative to us.) So whenever one instance of property possession grounds another, we should look to the nature of those properties (and perhaps also to the natures of the entities that possess them) for an explanation.

This approach may help us understand other philosophical uses of grounding-talk. Consider the relation between determinable properties and its determinates: *being red* and *being scarlet*, say. This is often characterised in terms of grounding. On the approach I'm suggesting, we should understand the relationship as a consequence of the determinable's logically complex nature. It might be that *being red* is a disjunctive property, containing *being scarlet* as a disjunct. Or it may be that *being red* is an existential property, asserting the possession of some specific shade of red. (Rosen (2010, 128) suggests similar options.)

Both options seem plausible. Suppose we think of colours as dispositions to reflect certain ranges of wavelengths of light. We might think of those ranges as uncountably infinite disjunctions of exact wavelengths, or as existential quantifications over exact wavelengths within the given range. Either way, once we have an ontological 'logical form' for *being red* and *being scarlet*, it will then follow from the basic grounding rules (either for disjunctions or for existentials) that possessing *being scarlet* is a possible ground for possessing *being red*.

A further use for grounding-talk is in explaining the relationship between the mind and the brain. Yablo (1992) comes closest to articulating the kind of explanation I have in mind, when he says that 'mental/physical relations are a species of determinable/determinate relations' (Yablo 1992, 256). As Yablo notes, this approach provides a plausible solution to the mental causation problem, whereby specific brain states seem to 'crowd out' mental states from having any causal impact on behaviour (Kim 1998). In general, 'rather than competing for causal honors, determinables and their determinates seem likelier to share in one another's success' (Yablo 1992, 272). And so, in particular, 'physical determinates cannot defeat the causal pretensions of their mental determinables' (1992, 273).

I find that a convincing response to the exclusion problem. But I disagree with Yablo on what it is for F to be a determinate of G. For Yablo, this is a modal relationship: necessarily, every F is G, but some possible G isn't F (Yablo 1992, 252). On this view, any contingently possessed F is a determinate of any necessary property, such as *being such that $A \lor \neg A$*. This analysis doesn't capture the target notion, on which to be a determinate of G is to be G *in a specific way*. Better to understand F's being a determinable of G in terms of G's logical constitution, as F's being a disjunct or existential instantiation of G. (In the latter case, I have in mind that G is an existential property, which we may represent as $\lambda x \exists y A x y$, and F is $\lambda x A x [^c/_y]$, for c some value of y.)

On the general approach I'm suggesting, non-fundamental properties are built from fundamental ones via logical modes of construction, forming conjunctive, disjunctive, negative, existential, and universal properties. Reality is structured via these logical constructors. On this view, the structure of reality can be analysed through *construction* or *building* relations (Bennett 2011b). The kind of building relations I have in mind involve the construction of logically complex properties (and logically complex states of affairs) from logically more basic ones.

(This approach has some similarities with Wilsch's (2015) *Nomological Account of Ground*, based on *laws of metaphysics*, 'general principles that characterize the individual construction-operations' such as mereological summation (Wilsch 2015, 3301). The principles governing the construction of the logically complex entities in my theory would count as laws of metaphysics for Wilsch.)

How should we understand logically complex properties, metaphysically speaking? I'll briefly outline one approach, based on the *fundamental tie* approach to states of affairs (§4.1, §5.6). On that view, states of affairs have particulars, properties, and relations as constituents. We can think of any state of affairs with a missing particular as a property: *that a is F* without *a* is just *F*; *that a likes b* without *a* is the property of *liking b*. Positively tying either property together with *a* gives us back the state of affairs with which we started. Similarly, removing *a* from *that a isn't G* gives the negative property *being non-G* (the entity which, when positively tied together with *a*, gives *that a isn't G*). And more generally, if we have negative, conjunctive, disjunctive, existential, and universal states of affairs, then we have negative, conjunctive, disjunctive, existential, and universal properties and relations. (For a formal theory of how this works, see Jago 2011.)

So the burden of explanation falls on our account of logically complex states of affairs. Conjunctive states of affairs may be understood as mereological sums of their conjunct states of affairs, and existential states of affairs as containing a higher-order property of *being instantiated*. Moreover, if we have the means to form negative states of affairs, then disjunctive and universal states of affairs may be understood in terms of negative conjunctive and negative existential states of affairs, respectively (Barker and Jago 2012; Jago 2011). On this approach, logically complex properties and relations are built from more basic ones in much the same way that logically complex terms are formed from more basic bits of syntax.

(Similar moves could, I think, be made within Turner's (2016) primitivist account of states of affairs (§4.2) once extended to include negative states of affairs, as in §5.6.)

The approach just sketched provides an account of the grounding conditions for possessing non-fundamental properties and standing in non-fundamental relations. (Fundamental properties and relations are, by definition, not grounded.) This gives us an account of grounding for those cases in which the work is done purely by the properties and relations involved. But there are other cases to consider.

The existence and identity of a non-empty set x is grounded by its members, for example. Above, I took this to be one of the basic 'logical' cases of grounding. This condition is handwritten into the theory, and so is not one of its novel predictions. Nevertheless, the case fits the general form of explanation I've given so far, if we think of set-formation as a logical constructor, along the lines of the logical constructors. The 'analysis' of set x specifies its members, combined in the set-theoretic way: $\{x_1, x_2, ...\}$. (Conceptually, this 'enumeration' stands to the constitutive nature of a set as a logically complex real definition stands to the constitutive nature of a property or relation. But again, this must be understood in an ontic way, potentially outstripping our conceptual resources. Genuine enumerability is not required.) As there is nothing to this 'analysis' of a set beyond specifying its members, there is nothing to ground the existence and nature of that set beyond its members, taken together.

We can tell a similar story for the case of mereological summation. The 'analysis' of a mereological sum specifies the whole in terms of its proper parts. We can treat mereological summation as a kind of ontic conjunction. We can think of particular-particular sums on the model of *term conjunction*, as when we say 'Anna and Bec came to the party'; and we can think of property-property sums on the model of *predicate conjunction*, as in when we say 'Anna is clever and creative'. So why not think of summation as a generalised kind of conjunction, with parts as conjuncts of the whole? If we do, then our conjunction grounding clause will also cover mereological sums. The 'analysis' of a mereological sum then independently implies the correct grounding relationship: mereological wholes are grounded collectively by their proper parts.

We can extend the approach to abstract entities more generally, if we have some understanding of their natures. We may treat 1 as the unique successor of 0, 2 as the unique successor of 1, and so on. So if we have some analysis for 0 (or if we take it as a metaphysical primitive), then we can provide constitutive natures and hence grounding conditions for (facts about) the natural numbers.

The case of material objects is less clear. My view is that material objects do have natures (Barker and Jago 2017; Jago 2016b), but distinct possible entities may share the same nature. If that's right, then the natures of material objects will not suffice for grounding their identities. But even if material objects do have fully individualising natures, this will not suffice for grounding their existence if (as seems plausible) the natures of non-existent entities themselves exist. A presentist, for example, may hold that Socrates' individualising nature still exists, even though Socrates no longer does.

For present purposes, we needn't settle on whether particular objects have individual natures, non-individual natures, or no natures at all. It will suffice that non-fundamental properties and relations come with substantial real definitions, which we can treat as spelling out grounding conditions for the states of affairs involving them.

Now let's apply this general account of grounding to the property *being true*, and to states of affairs involving it. Our thesis is that the nature of truth consists in the existence of a truthmaker. Accordingly, the corresponding real definition identifies *being true* with the existential property $\lambda x \exists y (y \text{ truthmakes } x)$. So, according to this analysis, the alethic state of affairs [⟨A⟩ is true] is to be identified with the existential state of affairs [$\exists y (y \text{ truthmakes } \langle A \rangle)$].

That analysis provides us with a very simple grounding condition for alethic states of affairs. In general, existential states of affairs are grounded by their instances, and since [⟨A⟩ is true] is identified with [$\exists y (y \text{ truthmakes } \langle A \rangle)$], it follows that its possible grounds are all and only the possible truthmakers for ⟨A⟩. Notice that we have now derived our truth-grounding principle,

(T-GROUNDING) x is a truthmaker for $\langle A \rangle$ if and only if x grounds the state of affairs *that $\langle A \rangle$ is true*

from a general theory of grounding and our analysis of the nature of truth. That's an important result, adding justificatory weight to our theory of grounding. It also suggests that we might be able to discover more about truthmaking by investigating general features of the *grounding* relation.

6.4 Grounding Grounding and Grounding Truthmaking

Now that we have an account of grounding on the table, let's use it to investigate important properties of the *truthmaking* relation. Here's the questions (first raised in §6.1) we haven't yet answered:

(6.4) What grounds the state of affairs [x truthmakes $\langle A \rangle$]?

(6.5) What truthmakes the proposition $\langle x$ truthmakes $\langle A \rangle \rangle$?

(6.6) What are the logical properties of the *truthmaking* relation? Is it (ir)reflexive? (a)symmetrical? (in)transitive?

I'll address (6.4) and (6.5) in this section, and (6.6) in §6.5.

We have already seen that there's a very close link between the states of affairs [x truthmakes $\langle A \rangle$] and [x grounds that $\langle A \rangle$ is true]. This suggests that we can pursue (6.4) in terms of a general account of what grounds a state of affairs [x grounds y]. I'll call this the *grounding grounding question*. Here are two potential answers (see Sider 2013b):

(GROUNDED) y grounds [x grounds y]

(GROUND) x grounds [x grounds y]

Let's begin with (GROUNDED). Suppose we have two grounding states of affairs: (i) [x grounds y] and (ii) [y grounds [x grounds y]]. If grounding is transitive, then (i) and (ii) imply that x grounds [x grounds y]. But this is what the opposing account, (GROUND), says! So (GROUNDED) and the transitivity of grounding imply (GROUND).

Now let's turn to (GROUND). This is the view Bennett (2011a) defends:

> Grounding, I claim, is not (only) internal, but *super*internal. A superinternal relation is one such that the intrinsic nature of only *one* of the relata—or, better, one side of the relation— guarantees not only that the relation holds, but also that the other relatum(a) exists and has the intrinsic nature it does. ... I claim that it is the mark of grounding that it is superinternal. That is what makes it *generative*. Everything is settled by the base, by the first relatum(a). (Bennett 2011a, 32–3)

> Given the existence of the ground, nothing else has to happen for it to be a ground, for it to ground what it does. God need not bend down and insert a staple, nor yank a string to unfurl the grounding relation upwards like a sail. The grounding relation is already, automatically present. Indeed, it is perhaps best not to call it a relation at all. (Bennett 2011a, 35)

I have two complaints with this view. The first concerns Bennett's claim that, when it comes to claims about grounding, 'everything is settled by the base' (2011a, 33). This is not so. Suppose it's the case that A but not that B. Then the states of affairs [A] and [$A \vee B$] have the same actual grounds. That's a fact about grounding: *that* [A] *and* [$A \vee B$] *have the same actual grounds*. Call this fact F. Those grounds for [A] can't be what grounds F. For consider a possible situation w in which those grounds for [A] exist, in addition to (independent) grounds for [B]. In w, the grounds for [A] and [$A \vee B$] differ, and hence F does not obtain in w. Since the grounds for [A] obtain but F does not in w, the grounds for [A] cannot be grounds for F. But by assumption, nothing else in the (actual) base grounds F if [A]'s grounds do not. So the base does not settle all the facts about grounding.

The second complaint concerns Bennett's central claim, that x grounds the state of affairs [x grounds y], directly. A ground for the state of affairs [x grounds y] should explain why it is, metaphysically speaking, that x grounds y. But in general, x alone will not do that. To see this, we can take parallel cases with identical grounds:

(6.8) x, y together ground the existence of the set $\{x, y\}$

(6.9) x, y together ground the existence of the mereological sum $x \sqcup y$

Why does the existence of x and y ground the existence of the set $\{x, y\}$? Because, in general, that's what a set is: sets are of collections of things. Why does the existence of x and y ground the existence of the sum $x \sqcup y$? Because, in general, that's what a mereological sum is: sums are comprised of their parts, and no more. These explanations are very similar, but not the same. The former appeals to what it is, in general, to be a set, whereas the latter appeals to what it is, in general, to be a mereological sum. The former would not do as an explanation of (6.9) and the latter would not do as an explanation of (6.8). It is not merely that these differing explanations present some information to us in different ways. They differ crucially in a metaphysical sense: one appeals to the nature of *being a set*, whereas the other appeals to the nature of *being a mereological sum*.

Grounding is supposed to help with, underwrite, or even consist in metaphysical explanation. In particular, the kind of metaphysical explanatory difference underlying (6.8) and (6.9) should be tracked by differences in ground. Consequently, (6.8) and (6.9) themselves should have different grounds. So it is not the case, in general, that x grounds [x grounds y].

So what grounds [x grounds y], if not x and not y? Surely something unrelated to x and y cannot do the job. Let's see what our theory of grounding conditions from §6.3 has to say on the matter. According to that theory, grounding conditions for a state of affairs y are given by metaphysical analysis of y's constitutive nature. If y is a nonfundamental state of affairs [Fa], then the analysis proceeds by asking what it is to possess *Fness*. The answer takes the form of a real definition of *Fness*, which identifies *Fness* with a logically complex structure built, ultimately, from fundamental properties and relations. We can then read off grounding conditions for possessing *Fness*, using the basic grounding clauses for conjunctions, disjunctions, existentials, and sets.

On this theory, grounds are given by the nature of the grounded entity. The metaphysical explanation flows from nature to grounding. So if entities $x_1, x_2, \ldots$ together ground y, then it is y's nature that grounds this fact. [Bertie is a dog], [Bertie is domesticated], and [Bertie is less than a year old] together ground [Bertie is a puppy]. That grounding fact is itself grounded by [Bertie is a puppy]'s nature, which depends on the nature of *being a puppy*. It is because *being a puppy* is, by its nature, the ontic conjunction (mereological sum) of *being a dog*, *being domesticated*, and *being less than one year old*, that facts about being a dog, being domesticated, and being less than one year old together ground *puppy*-states of affairs.

Audi (2012b), Dasgupta (2014b), Fine (2012b), Litland (2017), Rosen (2010), and Trogdon (2013) all offer theories on which essences play a role in grounding the grounding facts. Litland's approach is particularly powerful. He thinks in terms of 'metaphysically explanatory arguments' (2017, 2) from grounding to grounded facts (propositions, on Litland's account). (DeRosset (2013) thinks of grounding in similar terms.) For Litland, these arguments are 'composed from basic explanatory inferences' (2017, 10), such as the inference from A to $A \vee B$, and form a kind of proof system.

As a special case, there are explanations from zero premises (just as there are proofs from zero premises). In these cases, Litland calls the explanans *zero-grounded*. In particular, all grounding facts are themselves zero-grounded. Nevertheless, they are accounted for in terms of the basic explanatory inferences. But what fixes those inferences? Litland's answer is that they 'are part of the essence of items involved in those inferences' (2017, 25). I see no genuine tension between this approach and mine. Where Litland says 'zero-grounded', I say: grounded in the natures of the logical concepts (conjunction, disjunction, and so on.)

We can use the account of grounding to analyse grounding facts about sets and mereological sums, such as (6.8) and (6.9) above. It is the nature of $\{x, y\}$—the fact that it is a set, with members x and y only—that grounds the fact that x and y together ground $\{x, y\}$. What of (6.9)? As we saw in §6.3, treating mereological summation as a kind of ontic conjunction implies that a mereological whole is grounded collectively by its proper parts. We can now add: it is the nature of a whole $x \sqcup y$—its being the sum of x and y only—that grounds the fact that x and y together ground $x \sqcup y$.

This general idea, that the grounded entity's nature is what grounds a specific grounding state of affairs, needs some refinement. That nature, as a necessary entity, will exist even if the grounding states of affairs in question do not. We want to say that the nature of disjunction grounds [[A] grounds [$A \vee B$]], for example. That fact about grounding is necessary, even though [A] is not. How can this be?

We have been using 'grounds' loosely, in a non-factive sense. In this usage, 'x grounds y' does not imply that x and y both exist, and so does not assert that a specific relation holds between x and y (see also Litland 2017). Since I view grounding (proper) as a relation between entities, I will interpret this non-factive usage of 'grounding' in a counterfactual way:

(NON-FACTUAL:) 'x non-factually grounds y' should be understood as: x would stand in the *grounding* relation to y, were x to exist.

If natures are necessary existents, as I've assumed, then the grounding facts they ground must have this counterfactual form. If [Gb] grounds [Fa], then the nature of [Fa] grounds the fact that [Gb] would ground [Fa], were b to be G.

As a consequence, grounding facts proper—those directly involving the *grounding* relation—are not always grounded by a nature alone. They are grounded jointly by the nature of the grounded entity and the existence of the purported ground. A genuine grounding state of

GROUNDING GROUNDING AND GROUNDING TRUTHMAKING 201

affairs [*x* grounds *y*] is grounded jointly by the existence of *x* and the nature of *y*.

In our conceptual investigation of what grounds what, the counterfactual, non-factive notion takes centre stage. To understand the nature of disjunction, for example, we must understand that a disjunctive entity (be it a state of affairs or a proposition) is grounded by its disjuncts. That key conceptual information does not depend on whether either disjunct obtains or is true. In such instances, we are not primarily focusing on specific facts involving the *grounding* relation. Rather, we are interested in which of those facts would obtain, were the relevant relata to exist.

We have our account of what grounds grounding. Now let's apply this to truthmaking. Specifically, the questions I want to answer are:

(6.4) What grounds the state of affairs [*x* truthmakes ⟨*A*⟩]?

(6.5) What truthmakes the proposition ⟨*x* truthmakes ⟨*A*⟩⟩?

Given the very tight relationship between truthmaking ⟨*A*⟩ and grounding [⟨*A*⟩ is true], set out in (T-GROUNDING) in §6.3, I suggest the following principle:

(6.10) *x* grounds [*y* truthmakes ⟨*A*⟩] if and only if *x* grounds [*y* grounds [⟨*A*⟩ is true]].

Suppose that's right. On the account just described, [*y* grounds [⟨*A*⟩ is true]] is (non-factively) grounded in the nature of the alethic state of affairs, [⟨*A*⟩ is true]. I take that nature to involve two aspects: the nature of the proposition ⟨*A*⟩ plus the nature of the property *being true*. So given (6.10), [*x* truthmakes ⟨*A*⟩] too is (non-factively) grounded jointly by the natures of ⟨*A*⟩ and of *being true*. Its factive ground comprises those natures plus *x*'s existence. Given (T-GROUNDING), those entities are thereby joint truthmakers for the proposition ⟨*x* truthmakes ⟨*A*⟩⟩.

This is an important result. Think of it like this: holding fixed the nature of *being true*, a proposition ⟨*A*⟩'s nature determines which entities x make it true. This picture gives us an important insight into the nature of propositions. I'll return to this topic in chapter 8, where I'll use the idea to develop a metaphysical account of what propositions are.

6.5 Reflexivity, Symmetry, Transitivity

There is one question from §6.1 which remains unanswered:

(6.6) What are the logical properties of the *truthmaking* relation? Is it (ir)reflexive? (a)symmetrical? (in)transitive?

One might hope that our account of grounding from §6.3 will shed light on the issue. But two problems frustrate that aim. First, there seem to be no convincing arguments to establish the logical properties ((ir)reflexivity, (a)symmetry, (in)transitivity) of the *grounding* relation (Bliss and Priest forthcoming). Second, even if there were, that would not imply that the *truthmaking* relation shares those properties.

The *standard account* of grounding has it that grounding is irreflexive, asymmetric, and transitive. (On this picture, each grounding chain is a strict order.) The view is often stated, but I've yet to see a convincing argument for it. By contrast, Thompson (2016b) defends a view she calls *metaphysical interdependence*, on which grounding is non-symmetric, and Bliss (2013, 2014) argues that there can be circular grounding chains. Each view allows that entities can mutually ground one another. Jansson (2016) argues that we can account for the appearance of asymmetry without positing a genuinely asymmetric metaphysical relation. Priest (2014) defends a stronger view: everything plays a role in grounding everything else. Grounding is symmetric, on this view. Jenkins (2011) discusses views on which grounding is not irreflexive. Schaffer (2012) argues that grounding is not transitive, and Rodriguez-Pereyra (2015) argues that it is not irreflexive, not asymmetrical, and not transitive.

I suspect the account of grounding offered above supports the standard view. On that view, non-fundamental properties and relations (and perhaps all non-fundamental entities) are built from more fundamental entities via logical constructors, in much the way logically complex terms and sentences are built from more basic bits of syntax. If we take that analysis seriously, it certainly suggests irreflexivity, asymmetry, and transitivity. (Nothing is genuinely constructed just from itself; there are no cycles of construction; and constructions out of constructions out of *xs* are themselves constructions out of *xs*.) But here, we're appealing to our intuitive understanding of construction as a temporal process; who knows whether this holds for the 'vertical' ontic notion?

I'm not going to go into the arguments for and against the standard view here, for the simple reason that it won't help us understand *truthmaking*. The crucial link between truthmaking and grounding, (T-GROUNDING), does not imply that they have the same logical properties. In particular, irreflexivity of grounding does not imply irreflexivity of truthmaking. To see this, suppose that grounding is irreflexive, but that there is an instance:

(6.11) ⟨A⟩ truthmakes ⟨A⟩.

We then infer, using (T-GROUNDING), that ⟨A⟩ grounds the state of affairs [⟨A⟩ is true]. But this doesn't conflict with grounding's irreflexivity, since [⟨A⟩ is true] is not identical to ⟨A⟩. So it's consistent to think that *grounding*, but not *truthmaking*, is irreflexive.

Similarly, asymmetry of grounding does not imply asymmetry of truthmaking. Suppose we have an instance in which distinct propositions ⟨A⟩ and ⟨B⟩ truthmake one another. Then (T-GROUNDING) implies that ⟨A⟩ grounds [⟨B⟩ is true] and that ⟨B⟩ grounds [⟨A⟩ is true]. But this doesn't conflict with grounding's assumed asymmetry, since ⟨A⟩ is not identical to [⟨A⟩ is true] and ⟨B⟩ is not identical to [⟨B⟩ is true].

And again, suppose we have a counterexample to the transitivity of truthmaking:

(6.12) x truthmakes $\langle A \rangle$

(6.13) $\langle A \rangle$ truthmakes $\langle B \rangle$

(6.14) x does not truthmake $\langle B \rangle$

Then by (T-GROUNDING), x grounds [$\langle A \rangle$ is true], $\langle A \rangle$ grounds [$\langle B \rangle$ is true], and x does not ground [$\langle B \rangle$ is true]. But this is not a counterexample to transitivity of grounding, since [$\langle A \rangle$ is true] is distinct from $\langle A \rangle$. The upshot is that *truthmaking* need not be a linear order, even if *grounding* is. (Griffith (2014, 205–6) offers a similar argument.)

We will need to investigate the logical properties of *truthmaking* directly. Griffith (2014, 198) and Rodriguez-Pereyra (2015, 523–5) offer an argument that *truthmaking* is not irreflexive, not asymmetrical, and not transitive. (Tahko (2013) argues against transitivity of what he calls 'truth-grounding', but the argument is flawed, as Rodriguez-Pereyra (2015, 524) notes.) Griffith and Rodriguez-Pereyra each consider the proposition

p: $\langle p$ exists$\rangle$

to be a counterexample to irreflexivity and asymmetry. Since p says that p exists, it is made true by p, itself. That seems undeniable. So the only question is: is there such a proposition?

One might think that there must be: after all, we know that there exist meaningful self-referential sentences asserting their own existence. Since these are true, they must express propositions. But those propositions aren't self-referential. The sentence "'p' exists" expresses the non-self-referential proposition $\langle$'p' exists$\rangle$, asserting that the sentence 'p' exists. So consideration of self-referential sentences doesn't settle the issue of whether there exist 'self-referential' propositions such as p above.

The answer depends on our account of what propositions are. Suppose they are of the non-Russellian structured kind (§1.2), containing representational entities. Then, by the familiar diagonal argument, there will exist a proposition p containing a representational element r which represents p. On that view, there can be no objection to a proposition asserting that it itself exists.

On other views, by contrast, self-reference is ruled out. On the set-theoretic variant of the Russellian view (§1.2), propositions are sets (of sets of sets ...) and represent entities by containing them as members (of members of members ...). Self-reference would then require self-membership (or cyclical membership chains), which is ruled out in standard (well-founded) set theory. On the account of propositions I present in §8.5, self-reference and cycles of reference are ruled out for this very reason. And indeed, that account implies that truthmaking is irreflexive and asymmetrical. But the argument for that will have to wait on the detail of the theory of propositions, in §8.5.

The one case we can settle now is transitivity: truthmaking is not transitive. Existential propositions are truthmade by their instances. So ⟨⟨Bertie snuffles⟩ exists⟩ is made true by ⟨Bertie snuffles⟩, which is in turn made true by [Bertie snuffles]. But [Bertie snuffles] is not what makes ⟨⟨Bertie snuffles⟩ exists⟩ true. That's because ⟨⟨Bertie snuffles⟩ exists⟩ is about the existence of a proposition, and [Bertie snuffles] is not a proposition; so [Bertie snuffles] cannot be a truthmaker for ⟨⟨Bertie snuffles⟩ exists⟩.

One might push back on this point: doesn't our answer depend on what makes a proposition exist? If we thought that ⟨Bertie snuffles⟩ exists (in part) in virtue of [Bertie snuffles], then would this give us reason to think that ⟨⟨Bertie snuffles⟩ exists⟩ is true in virtue of [Bertie snuffles]? (I'll offer a theory of propositions along those lines in §8.5.) Not quite. The problem with this line of thought is that [Fa] *wholly suffices* as a truthmaker for ⟨$Fa \vee Gb$⟩, which in turn wholly suffices as a truthmaker for ⟨⟨$Fa \vee Gb$⟩ exists⟩. But even if [Fa] contributes to ⟨$Fa \vee Gb$⟩'s existence, it cannot be the whole story. [Fa] would be a *partial*, but not a *full*, truthmaker for ⟨⟨$Fa \vee Gb$⟩ exists⟩. So *full truthmaking* (which is the notion in which we're interested here) is not transitive. (Indeed, on the account of propositions I'll defend in §8.5, *truthmaking* is non-transitive, but not intransitive.)

(The issue just raised is puzzling. [Bertie snuffles] is a contingent existent, whereas ⟨Bertie snuffles⟩ is not. It is hard to see how ⟨Bertie snuffles⟩'s existence conditions could rest on anything contingent. I'll return to this difficult issue in §8.6.)

6.6 Chapter Summary

Truthmaking can't be defined in terms of necessity, or entailment, even if we restrict those notions to relevant entities (§6.2). Truthmaking is closely related to grounding (§6.3), and so we can understand truthmaking better by gaining a clearer picture of what grounding is. I proposed a way to understand grounding (§6.3), which explains how facts about truthmaking are grounded (§6.4). We still do not know as much as we would like about the logical properties of the *truthmaking* relation. For that, we will need an account of what propositions are, which will appear in §8.5.

7
The Logic of Truthmaking

In the previous chapter, we began to characterise the logical properties of the truthmaking relation. The aim of this chapter is to take this project further by developing a formal semantics for truthmaking. I distinguish two related notions of truthmaking: **exact** *and* **inexact** *(§7.2). Exact truthmaking holds when a truth is true precisely in virtue of the entity in question. Inexact truthmaking extends this notion. The logic of exact truthmaking is highly unusual (§7.3), and so I'll spend some time investigating it (§7.4). The logic of inexact truthmaking, by contrast, turns out to correspond to a well-understood logical system (§7.5).*

7.1 Truthmaker Semantics

THE AIM OF TRUTHMAKER semantics is twofold. Firstly, it can help us systematise intuitions about the truthmaking relation. Secondly, it has applications in fields beyond metaphysics, just as possible worlds semantics does. Truthmaker semantics can be seen as a refinement of possible worlds semantics, with applications where possible worlds semantics can be applied, but without many of the issues faced by possible worlds semantics. (I discuss those issues in detail in Jago (2014). Applications of truthmaker semantics are beyond the scope of this book. Fine (2012a, 2014, 2017a,b, 2016, 2015) has pursued the topic in detail. Moltmann (2015) discusses a similar approach.)

In developing truthmaker semantics, I will be concerned primarily with two questions:

(7.1) How do the truthmakers of logically complex propositions relate to the truthmakers of their constituent propositions?

(7.2) Under what conditions must truthmakers for some proposition $\langle A \rangle$ thereby be truthmakers for a logically related proposition, $\langle B \rangle$?

These questions are clearly related. Suppose, in answer to (7.1), we articulate principles relating truthmakers for conjunctions to the truthmakers for their conjuncts, truthmakers for disjunctions to the truthmakers for their disjuncts, and so on. This will provide us with an answer to (7.2). And conversely, the way to investigate an answer to (7.2) is by providing a means to determine the truthmakers for a logically complex proposition $\langle A \rangle$, in terms of the truthmakers for its constituent propositions.

Several principles have been proposed as partial answers to these questions (some of which we met previously in §6.2):

(ENTAILMENT) If x is a truthmaker for $\langle A \rangle$, and $\langle A \rangle$ entails $\langle B \rangle$, then x is a truthmaker for $\langle B \rangle$, too.

(DISJUNCTION) x is a truthmaker for $\langle A \vee B \rangle$ iff either x is a truthmaker for $\langle A \rangle$ or x is a truthmaker for $\langle B \rangle$.

(CONJUNCTION) x is a truthmaker for $\langle A \wedge B \rangle$ iff x is a truthmaker for $\langle A \rangle$ and x is a truthmaker for $\langle B \rangle$.

(MINIMALITY) If x is a truthmaker for $\langle A \rangle$, then x is a *minimal* truthmaker for $\langle A \rangle$: there is no proper part y of x ($y \sqsubset x$) such that y is also a truthmaker for $\langle A \rangle$.

(HEREDITY) If x is a truthmaker for $\langle A \rangle$ and x is a part of y ($x \sqsubseteq y$), then y is a truthmaker for $\langle A \rangle$.

(RELEVANCE) If x is a truthmaker for $\langle A \rangle$, then x is wholly relevant to whether $\langle A \rangle$ is true.

There's been plenty of discussion of these principles in the literature, notably by Armstrong (2004), Read (2000), Restall (1996), and Rodriguez-Pereyra (2006b). Much of the discussion relies on intuitive examples about how truthmaking should work. (See, for example, Armstrong 2004, 11 or Restall 1996, 333–4. Note that Armstrong (2004) defines *minimal truthmaker* in a less general way: 'If T is a minimal truthmaker for p, then you cannot subtract anything from T and the remainder still be a truthmaker for p' (2004, 19–20). The definitions are equivalent in extensional mereology.)

My aim here is more systematic. I will offer formal systems with truthmaking at their core, which can adjudicate on these principles. To settle on a semantics, we first need to fix some parameters. Should our semantics verify all, some, or none of the principles listed above? In §7.2, I discuss an important choice-point in the semantics, concerning (HEREDITY), and trace the consequences of that choice for (CONJUNCTION) and (DISJUNCTION). The crucial choice is between an *exact* and an *inexact* notion of truthmaking. (The terminology is due to Fine (2017a, 2016).) In §7.3, I present a semantics for exact truthmaking. This is a highly unusual logical system. I characterise the corresponding notion of entailment in §7.4. In §7.5, I present a semantics for inexact truthmaking, and relate it to more familiar logical systems.

7.2 Truthmaking, Exact and Inexact

It's a lazy Sunday morning. Anna is knitting in the back room, whilst Bertie is snuffling in the garden. What makes it true that Anna is knitting and Bertie is snuffling is the conjunctive state of affairs, the sum of *that Anna is knitting* and *that Bertie is snuffling*. Each conjunct truth is made true by one of these states of affairs, taken individually, so that the conjunction is made true by the combined state of affairs. That much seems straightforward.

One remarkable feature of this simple picture is this: what makes the conjunction true is not what makes the conjuncts true. What makes it true that Bertie is snuffling is not the conjunctive state of affairs, *that Anna is knitting and Bertie is snuffling*. Rather, its truthmaker is just *that Bertie is snuffling*. This point is made forcefully by Rodriguez-Pereyra (2006b):

> The truthmaking relation obtains between a portion of reality and a proposition if and only if the proposition is true *in virtue of* the portion of reality in question. But then what makes a conjunction true need not make its conjuncts true. ... it is not the case that ⟨Peter is a man⟩ is true in virtue of the fact *that Peter is a man and Saturn is a planet*. What ⟨Peter is a man⟩ is true in virtue of is simply the fact *that Peter is man*. (Rodriguez-Pereyra 2006b, 970)

Rodriguez-Pereyra's argument is simple but powerful. Based on these considerations, we should reject (CONJUNCTION): the left-to-right direction does not hold in general. (Van Fraassen (1969, 485) notes a similar point.) As a consequence, we should also reject (ENTAILMENT), which implies (CONJUNCTION), since ⟨A ∧ B⟩ entails both ⟨A⟩ and ⟨B⟩. (We have already seen, in §6.2, that (ENTAILMENT) is problematic. Rodriguez-Pereyra's argument provides an independent reason to reject it.)

For similar reasons, we should also reject (HEREDITY). For (HEREDITY) implies that a conjunctive state of affairs *that A ∧ B* makes true whatever its parts make true. Its parts are the states of affairs *that A* and *that B* (and their proper parts, if they have any), which make true ⟨A⟩ and ⟨B⟩, respectively. But if this were so, (CONJUNCTION) would hold too. So, having rejected (CONJUNCTION), we must also reject (HEREDITY).

A natural response to Rodriguez-Pereyra's argument is this. Sure, ⟨Bertie is snuffling⟩ is not true strictly in virtue of the state of affairs *that Anna is knitting and Bertie is snuffling*. But that state of affairs nevertheless guarantees that Bertie is snuffling, and hence that ⟨Bertie is snuffling⟩ is true. It does this by containing *that Bertie is snuffling* as a part.

The thought here is that, if state x contains as a part a truthmaker for ⟨A⟩, then x itself should count as a truthmaker for ⟨A⟩. That is precisely the content of (HEREDITY). It says that, if we add extra parts to a truthmaker for $\langle A \rangle$, the resulting entity will also truthmake $\langle A \rangle$. But truthmaking is not merely a guarantee of truth (§6.2). If it were, we would be committed to (ENTAILMENT) (given that entailment is a guarantee of truth-preservation from premises to conclusion). But we have reason for rejecting (ENTAILMENT), quite independently of Rodriguez-Pereyra's argument (§6.2). Rather, a truthmaker for $\langle A \rangle$ is a way the world is, in virtue of which $\langle A \rangle$ is true, rather than false. So Rodriguez-Pereyra's point stands.

We may take a more concessive line at this point, however, and admit a plurality of truthmaking notions. In particular, we can adopt the notion of *exact truthmaking*, characterised by the *true in virtue of* locution, but also accept an additional notion of *inexact truthmaking* (Fine 2014, 2016). The latter is characterised in terms of the former: to inexactly truthmake $\langle A \rangle$ is to have as a part an exact truthmaker for $\langle A \rangle$:

(INEXACT TRUTHMAKING) x is an *inexact truthmaker* for $\langle A \rangle$ $=_{df}$ there is some part y of x ($y \sqsubseteq x$) which is an exact truthmaker for $\langle A \rangle$.

So, for example, when a world w contains an exact truthmaker for $\langle A \rangle$, then w itself is an inexact truthmaker for $\langle A \rangle$. Given (MAXIMALISM), it follows that every world at which $\langle A \rangle$ is true is an inexact truthmaker for $\langle A \rangle$. Inexact truthmaking (unlike exact truthmaking) also satisfies (HEREDITY):

(7.3) If x inexactly truthmakes $\langle A \rangle$ and $x \sqsubseteq y$, then y inexactly truthmakes $\langle A \rangle$ too.

Note that exact and inexact truthmaking are not exclusive categories. Indeed, by definition, every exact truthmaker for $\langle A \rangle$ is thereby an inexact truthmaker for $\langle A \rangle$.

Should we follow Rodriguez-Pereyra in holding that only exact truthmaking is to count as truthmaking? Or should we take the more concessive line and work with both notions? The answer very much depends on our purposes. Exact truthmaking is the primary notion, since inexact truthmaking can be defined in terms of exact truthmaking, but, as far as I can see, not vice versa. I take exact truthmaking, *true in virtue of*, to be the notion we should use in metaphysical analysis. Wherever I have used 'truthmaking', without qualification as 'exact' or 'inexact', I always mean 'exact truthmaking'. And so it shall continue in chapters 8–9.

For logical purposes, both the exact and the inexact notions are interesting and worth investigating. I'll do so in §7.3 and §7.5, respectively. The logic of inexact truthmaking is the logic of things that include, but may not be identical to, (exact) truthmakers. So I understand 'inexact truthmaker' as 'thing which includes a truthmaker', and not as denoting a genuine kind of truthmaker.

It is worth noting that this discussion is foreshadowed by van Fraassen (1969). He provides a semantics in terms of set-theoretic representations of states of affairs, which he then uses to define two entailment relations. The first, 'a very tight relationship', is understood as 'whatever makes A true, also makes B true' (van Fraassen 1969, 485). The second is a looser relationship: all the facts containing a fact that makes A true contain a fact that makes B true. The former notion corresponds to *exact truthmaking entailment* (§7.3), the latter to *inexact truthmaking entailment* (§7.5). Van Fraassen's discussion says very little about the former relation, but he does note its central feature: $A \wedge B$ does not exactly entail A (van Fraassen 1969, 485).

Exact truthmaking invalidates (CONJUNCTION). What's more surprising is that, given some plausible additional principles, it also invalidates (DISJUNCTION) (Jago 2009). We can demonstrate this via an argument from (DISJUNCTION) to (CONJUNCTION), via the following principle:

($\wedge$-to-$\vee$) If x is a truthmaker for $\langle A \wedge B \rangle$, then x is a truthmaker for $\langle A \vee B \rangle$.

This principle, combined with (DISJUNCTION), implies the controversial 'only if' direction of (CONJUNCTION). For suppose x is a truthmaker for $\langle A \wedge B \rangle$. Then given ($\wedge$-to-$\vee$), x is a truthmaker for $\langle A \vee B \rangle$ and hence, by (DISJUNCTION), x is either a truthmaker for $\langle A \rangle$ or a truthmaker for $\langle B \rangle$. As $\langle A \rangle$ and $\langle B \rangle$ are arbitrary, it would be absurd to think x is guaranteed to be a truthmaker for just one of $\langle A \rangle$ and $\langle B \rangle$. It must truthmake both $\langle A \rangle$ and $\langle B \rangle$. But if so, the 'only if' direction of (CONJUNCTION) holds.

To establish ($\wedge$-to-$\vee$), we need only the (uncontroversial) right-to-left direction of (DISJUNCTION) plus:

(CONJUNCTION*) x is a truthmaker for $\langle A \wedge B \rangle$ iff x is a sum $y \sqcup z$, where y is a truthmaker for $\langle A \rangle$ and z is a truthmaker for $\langle B \rangle$.

(IDEMPOTENCE) x is a truthmaker for $\langle A \rangle$ iff it is a truthmaker for $\langle A \wedge A \rangle$ iff it is a truthmaker for $\langle A \vee A \rangle$.

The first we met in §6.2. It is justified by Rodriguez-Pereyra's argument above (taking the conjunctive state of affairs *that A* $\wedge$ *B* to be the sum of the states *that A* and *that B*.) But it is equally valid on the inexact notion of truthmaking.

We can demonstrate ($\wedge$-to-$\vee$) as follows. Suppose x is a truthmaker for $\langle A \wedge B \rangle$. Then, by (CONJUNCTION*) left-to-right, x is a sum $y \sqcup z$, where y truthmakes $\langle A \rangle$ and z truthmakes $\langle B \rangle$. So by (DISJUNCTION), y truthmakes $A \vee B$ and, likewise, z truthmakes $\langle A \vee B \rangle$. Then, by (CONJUNCTION*) right-to-left, $y \sqcup z$ (and hence x) is a truthmaker for $\langle (A \vee B) \wedge (A \vee B) \rangle$. So, by (IDEMPOTENCE) for $\wedge$, x is a truthmaker for $\langle A \vee B \rangle$.

That establishes ($\wedge$-to-$\vee$), and hence the link from (DISJUNCTION) to (CONJUNCTION). (In effect, (DISJUNCTION) allows us to strengthen (CONJUNCTION*) to (CONJUNCTION).) So if we accept Rodriguez-Pereyra's argument against (CONJUNCTION), we should also reject (DISJUNCTION). Here, we begin to see the value of developing truthmaker semantics, for Rodriguez-Pereyra (2006b) himself accepts (DISJUNCTION), whilst rejecting (CONJUNCTION).

His response to this issue (Rodriguez-Pereyra 2009) is to reject (IDEMPOTENCE). The first argument he offers for this is as follows:

⟨A ∧ A⟩ is made true by the conjunctive fact *that A ∧ A*. ... But ⟨A⟩ is not true in virtue of the conjunctive fact *that A ∧ A*: it is true in virtue of the fact *that A*. ... It might be thought that the fact *that A ∧ A* just is the fact *that A*. But this makes no sense, because the fact *that A* is not a conjunct of itself. (Rodriguez-Pereyra 2009, 437, notation changed)

This argument fails, on our understanding of conjunctive states of affairs as mereological sums. The state of affairs *that A ∧ A* is the sum of the state *that A* with itself, which is identical to *that A*.

Rodriguez-Pereyra's second argument against (IDEMPOTENCE) is as follows.

Take the propositions ⟨there is at least one muse and there is at least one muse⟩ and ⟨there is at least one muse⟩. The latter proposition is made true by Thalia and is also made true by Clio. It is made true by them separately, not collectively. But since the former proposition is a conjunction, it is collectively made true by the truthmakers for its conjunct. Thus the conjunction ⟨there is at least one muse and there is at least one muse⟩ is collectively made true by Thalia and Clio. Thus it is not true that what makes ⟨there is at least one muse and there is at least one muse⟩ true is what makes ⟨there is at least one muse⟩ true. (Rodriguez-Pereyra 2009, 441)

This argument assumes that distinct witnesses for an existential—in this case, the muses Thalia and Clio—cannot *jointly* or *collectively* make the existential true. On Rodriguez-Pereyra's picture, Thalia on her own is a truthmaker for ⟨there is at least one muse⟩, as is Clio on her own, whereas Thalia and Clio (taken together) are not. But there is no reason to think this.

Thalia and Clio, taken together, have all the properties we expect of a truthmaker for ⟨there is at least one muse⟩. They both necessitate, and are wholly relevant to, that truth. They are not (together) a *minimal* truthmaker for ⟨there is at least one muse⟩, in the sense of (MINIMALITY) above: having no proper part which is itself a truthmaker for ⟨there is at least one muse⟩. But neither are they (together) are minimal truthmaker for ⟨there is at least one muse and there is at least one muse⟩, and so Rodriguez-Pereyra cannot appeal to (MINIMALITY) in his argument. Rodriguez-Pereyra's assumption can't be justified, and so his argument should be rejected. (IDEMPOTENCE) stands, and as a consequence, we may reject (CONJUNCTION) only if we also reject (DISJUNCTION).

There is of course something very appealing about (DISJUNCTION). That's because, although false, it is almost right. The correct principle for disjunction (introduced in §6.2) is this:

(DISJUNCTION*) For all non-disjunctive states of affairs x, x is a truthmaker for $⟨A \vee B⟩$ iff x is a truthmaker for $⟨A⟩$, or x is a truthmaker for $⟨B⟩$, or x is a truthmaker for $⟨A \wedge B⟩$.

As we shall see, both the exact and the inexact truthmaker semantics validates (DISJUNCTION*).

Now let's turn to (MINIMALITY). The formulation above is false, since not all truths have minimal truthmakers at all. ⟨There are infinitely many prime numbers⟩ is made true by any infinite plurality of prime numbers (or by the states of affairs that those numbers are prime). But for every such plurality, there is a sub-plurality which also truthmakes ⟨there are infinitely many prime numbers⟩. A second attempt to capture the restriction to minimal truthmakers is:

(MINIMALITY$_2$) If $⟨A⟩$ has any minimal truthmakers, then all of its truthmakers are minimal.

But this does no better. ⟨There are infinitely many prime numbers ∨ I exist⟩ has a minimal truthmaker: me. Nevertheless, it also has many legitimate but non-minimal truthmakers: each infinite plurality (or sum thereof) of prime numbers.

A restriction to minimal truthmakers (however formulated) is false by definition on the inexact notion. Inexact truthmaking is by definition preserved by adding parts, but minimality is not. One might therefore think that (MINIMALITY) (or some reformulation of it) captures an important distinction between exact and inexact truthmaking. Indeed, one might think that the state of affairs *that*

Anna is knitting and Bertie is snuffling is not an exact truthmaker for ⟨Bertie is snuffling⟩ precisely because it isn't a minimal truthmaker. It contains a proper part, *that Bertie is snuffling*, which is itself a truthmaker for ⟨Bertie is snuffling⟩.

This thought is misguided, however: (MINIMALITY) is false on the exact notion of truthmaking, just as it is on the inexact notion. The argument above shows us why. On the exact notion, $A \wedge B \vDash A \vee B$: all truthmakers for ⟨$A \wedge B$⟩ are thereby truthmakers for ⟨$A \vee B$⟩. In general, truthmakers for ⟨$A \wedge B$⟩ are conjunctive states of affairs, *that $A \wedge B$*. So *that $A \wedge B$* will thereby truthmake ⟨$A \vee B$⟩. But *that $A \wedge B$* is not a minimal truthmaker for ⟨$A \vee B$⟩, since it has a part, *that A*, which truthmakes ⟨A⟩. So (MINIMALITY) is false, even on the exact notion of truthmaking.

Finally, we come to (RELEVANCE). We saw in §6.2 that we cannot define *truthmaking* in terms of relevance plus necessitation. But (RELEVANCE) is phrased in terms of a necessary condition only, and it is certainly a live option. As discussed in §6.2, however, relevance is not an exact notion. We are not interested in the relevant physical causes of a truth, for example. The notion of relevance must be understood metaphysically, in terms of the entities which contribute to determining, or grounding, the truth in question. These are precisely the notions we are trying to understand through our metaphysical investigation of truthmaking. So we cannot build a precise logical semantics from a principle like (RELEVANCE). We can, however, use the notion of relevance to interpret those semantics in a philosophically useful way.

One thing we can say for sure about (RELEVANCE) is that it is rejected by the inexact notion of truthmaking. Suppose x is a truthmaker for ⟨A⟩ but y is completely irrelevant to whether ⟨A⟩ is true or false. Then $x \sqcup y$ is partly, but not wholly, relevant to ⟨A⟩'s truth. Nevertheless, due to (HEREDITY), $x \sqcup y$ is an inexact truthmaker for ⟨A⟩. So inexact truthmakers need not be wholly relevant to the truths in question.

7.3 Exact Truthmaking

In this section, I will present the truthmaker semantics corresponding to the exact notion of truthmaking. This section draws on joint work with Kit Fine (Fine and Jago 2017). I'll use these to define a notion of *exact entailment*, and give some results about exact entailment in §7.4. I'll discuss the truthmaking semantics corresponding to the inexact notion in §7.5.

The characteristic feature of exact truthmaking is that truthmakers for a conjunction are not in general truthmakers for its conjuncts. As above (§7.2), we analyse a truthmaker for a conjunction $\langle A \wedge B \rangle$ as the sum of a truthmaker for $\langle A \rangle$ and a truthmaker for $\langle B \rangle$:

(CONJUNCTION*) x is a truthmaker for $\langle A \wedge B \rangle$ iff x is a sum $y \sqcup z$, where y is a truthmaker for $\langle A \rangle$ and z is a truthmaker for $\langle B \rangle$.

This is, in essence, van Fraassen's clause for conjunction (1969, 484), which has a similar motivation.

We analyse the truthmakers for a disjunction $\langle A \vee B \rangle$ in terms of the truthmakers for $\langle A \rangle$, plus those for $\langle B \rangle$, plus those for $\langle A \wedge B \rangle$. In §7.2, we phrased this principle as:

(DISJUNCTION*) For all non-disjunctive states of affairs x, x is a truthmaker for $\langle A \vee B \rangle$ iff x is a truthmaker for $\langle A \rangle$, or x is a truthmaker for $\langle B \rangle$, or x is a truthmaker for $\langle A \wedge B \rangle$.

Given these principles, truthmakers for $A \wedge B$ are thereby truthmakers for $A \vee B$ (in keeping with our conclusions in §7.2). For the reminder of this chapter, we will ignore the possibility of disjunctive states of affairs. (We do this purely to simplify our logical semantics.)

We need to say something about the falsemakers for conjunctions and disjunctions. But this is straightforward. A falsemaker for $\langle A \wedge B \rangle$ is something which falsemakes $\langle A \rangle$, or $\langle B \rangle$, or else is the sum of such falsemakers; a falsemaker for $\langle A \vee B \rangle$ is a fusion of a falsemaker for $\langle A \rangle$ and a falsemaker for $\langle B \rangle$; and a falsemaker for $\langle \neg A \rangle$ is whatever makes $\langle A \rangle$ true (while a truthmaker for $\langle \neg A \rangle$ is a falsemaker for $\langle A \rangle$).

The truthmaker semantics is defined over a domain of entities, which we typically think of as states of affairs. (Although, as already pointed out (§5.3, §6.2), every entity x whatsoever is a truthmaker for $\langle x \text{ exists}\rangle$.) I'll call the entities in the domain *states*, and assume these states are closed under (pairwise) mereological sums: if s and u are states in the domain, then so is $s \sqcup u$.

Having given an overview of our semantics, it is time to make it more precise. As is standard in formal logic, I'll work with sentences, rather than propositions, and (purely to aid readability) I'll drop quotation marks for sentence-variables in the logical language.

Definition 7.1 (Syntax). Let $\mathcal{P}$ be a set of primitive sentence letters. The language $\mathcal{L}$ is then the smallest set containing $\mathcal{P}$ closed under 1-place $\neg$ and 2-place $\wedge$ and $\vee$. Λ is the set of *literals* over $\mathcal{P}$, i.e. $\mathcal{P} \cup \{\neg p \mid p \in \mathcal{P}\}$. Let $\leq_{\mathcal{L}}$ be any total order on $\mathcal{L}$. We define $\bigwedge\{A_1, \ldots, A_n\} = (A_1 \wedge (A_2 \wedge \cdots \wedge A_n)\cdots)$, where $A_i \leq_{\mathcal{L}} A_j$ iff $i \leq j$. (We shall see below that $\wedge$ is commutative and associative, and so brackets and order of conjuncts is semantically irrelevant.)

Take $\mathcal{P}$ (and hence $\mathcal{L}$ and Λ) to be fixed throughout.

Definition 7.2 (Frames and models). Frames are pairs $\langle\!\langle S, \sqsubseteq \rangle\!\rangle$, where S is a set of entities (states) and $\sqsubseteq$ is a partial order (reflexive, transitive and anti-symmetric), such that each pair $s, t \in S$ has a least upper bound in S, denoted $s \sqcup t$. An *exact truthmaking model* is a structure $\langle\!\langle S, \sqsubseteq, |\cdot|^+, |\cdot|^- \rangle\!\rangle$ where $\langle\!\langle S, \sqsubseteq \rangle\!\rangle$ is a frame and $|\cdot|^+$ and $|\cdot|^-$ are valuation functions from primitive sentences $\mathcal{P}$ to 2^S, closed under $\sqcup$: if $s, t \in |p|^+$ then $s \sqcup t \in |p|^+$, and similarly for $|p|^-$.

Definition 7.3 (Exact truthmaking and falsemaking). Given an exact truthmaking model $M = \langle\!\langle S, \sqsubseteq, |\cdot|^+, |\cdot|^- \rangle\!\rangle$ (which I'll leave implicit), *exact truthmaking* $\Vdash_e$ and *exact falsemaking* $\dashv\!|_e$ relations are then defined by double recursion as follows:

$$s \Vdash_e p \quad \text{iff} \quad s \in |p|^+$$
$$s \dashv\!|_e p \quad \text{iff} \quad s \in |p|^-$$
$$s \Vdash_e \neg A \quad \text{iff} \quad s \dashv\!|_e A$$

$s \dashv\vdash_e \neg A$ iff $s \Vdash_e A$

$s \Vdash_e A \wedge B$ iff $\exists tu(s = t \sqcup u \ \& \ t \Vdash_e A \ \& \ u \Vdash_e B)$

$s \dashv\vdash_e A \wedge B$ iff $s \dashv\vdash_e A$ or $s \dashv\vdash_e B$ or

$\exists tu(s = t \sqcup u \ \& \ t \dashv\vdash_e A \ \& \ u \dashv\vdash_e B)$

$s \Vdash_e A \vee B$ iff $s \Vdash_e A$ or $s \Vdash_e B$ or

$\exists tu(s = t \sqcup u \ \& \ t \Vdash_e A \ \& \ u \Vdash_e B)$

$s \dashv\vdash_e A \vee B$ iff $\exists tu(s = t \sqcup u \ \& \ t \dashv\vdash_e A \ \& \ u \dashv\vdash_e B)$

Given this semantics, no formula is valid (in the sense of being true at all states in all models), and any set of formulae is satisfiable (just consider a state which both truthmakes and falsemakes every primitive p). Instead, the logic is characterised in terms of the entailments it supports. As usual, we treat entailment as the preservation of truth from premises to conclusion. But in so doing, how should we conceptualise our premises? We could treat them *collectively*, so that entailment amounts to preservation of truth from the *conjoined premises* to the conclusion. Alternatively, we could treat our premises *distributively*, so that entailment amounts to preservation of truth from each individual premise to the conclusion. These notions coincide on single-premise entailments, but are not equivalent when we have multiple premises.

When there are no further restrictions on the models we use, the conjunctive approach will give us a nonmonotonic entailment relation. A will conjunctively-entail A, but $\{A, B\}$ will not conjunctively-entail A (since $A \wedge B$ does not, in general, conjunctively-entail A.) Fine (2016) investigates this conjunctive notion of entailment in combination with various restrictions on models. Accordingly, I'll not say any more about it here.

I shall focus on the distributive notion of entailment, abbreviated as '$\vDash_e$', defined as follows:

Definition 7.4 (Exact Truthmaking Entailment). Γ exactly entails A, written $\Gamma \vDash_e A$ iff, for any exact model M and any state s of M, $M, s \Vdash_e A$ whenever $M, s \Vdash_e B$ for each $B \in \Gamma$.

Exact equivalence is defined as two-way exact entailment. As the reader can easily check, exact entailment satisfies the following equivalences and entailments:

$$A \wedge B \dashv\vdash_e B \wedge A$$
$$A \wedge (B \wedge C) \dashv\vdash_e (A \wedge B) \wedge C$$
$$A \wedge (B \vee C) \dashv\vdash_e (A \wedge B) \vee (A \wedge C)$$
$$A \wedge A \dashv\vdash_e A$$
$$A, B \vDash_e A \wedge B$$
$$\neg(A \wedge B) \dashv\vdash_e \neg A \vee \neg B$$
$$\neg\neg A \dashv\vdash_e A$$

$$A \vee B \dashv\vdash_e B \vee A$$
$$A \vee (B \vee C) \dashv\vdash_e (A \vee B) \vee C$$
$$A \vee (B \wedge C) \vDash_e (A \vee B) \wedge (A \vee C)$$
$$A \vee A \dashv\vdash_e A$$
$$A \vDash_e A \vee B$$
$$\neg(A \vee B) \dashv\vdash_e \neg A \wedge \neg B$$

Note that distribution of $\vee$ over $\wedge$ is not an equivalence, for $(p \vee q) \wedge (p \vee r) \nvDash_e p \vee (q \wedge r)$. To see this, take the model:

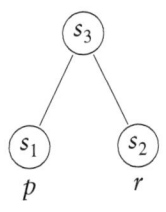

Here, we have $s_1 \Vdash_e p \vee q$ and $s_2 \Vdash_e p \vee r$, hence $s_3 \Vdash_e (p \vee q) \wedge (p \vee r)$, but $s_3 \nVdash_e p \vee (q \wedge r)$. Given the failure of $\vee$ to distribute over $\wedge$, our semantics does not give rise to a $\wedge, \vee$-distributive lattice. This is precisely what makes reasoning about the semantics more difficult (and more interesting) than would otherwise be the case.

Since $\wedge$ is commutative and associative, it is harmless to write $\bigwedge \{A_1, \ldots, A_n\}$ as $A_1 \wedge \cdots \wedge A_n$, and to ignore the ordering $\leq_{\mathcal{L}}$.

7.4 Exact Entailment

The purpose of this section is to present some formal results concerning exact entailment. As with the previous section, it draws on joint work with Kit Fine (Fine and Jago 2017). Readers looking for a non-technical presentation should skip this section; those looking for the highlights only can skip to the end of the section, where I present the main results concerning exact entailment. For brevity I'll skip the proofs here: you can find them all in Fine and Jago 2017.

I'll begin with a precise way to extract from a sentence A a description of the definite ways a truthmaker for A should be. I'll then use these descriptions to provide a syntactic characterisation of exact entailment. Syntactic descriptions of the truthmakers for A take the form of a set of literals. Intuitively, a description $\{\lambda_1, \ldots, \lambda_n\}$ describes a state s which is the sum of states $s_1, \ldots, s_n$, where each s_i truthmakes literal λ_i. I'll call such a description, qua set of literals, a *selection* from A. As selections provide us with a syntactic means to reason about our semantics, it is natural to begin our discussion by constructing a canonical model.

Definition 7.5 (Canonical Model). Let $\mathfrak{M} = \langle\langle \mathfrak{S}^\mathfrak{M}, \sqsubseteq^\mathfrak{M}, |\cdot|^{+\mathfrak{M}}, |\cdot|^{-\mathfrak{M}} \rangle\rangle$ where:

- $\mathfrak{S}^\mathfrak{M} = 2^\Lambda$, the set of all sets of literals;

- $\sqsubseteq^\mathfrak{M}$ is $\subseteq$ restricted to $\mathfrak{S}^\mathfrak{M}$;

- $|p|^{+\mathfrak{M}} = \{\{p\}\}$;

- $|p|^{-\mathfrak{M}} = \{\{\neg p\}\}$.

$\mathfrak{M}$ is clearly a genuine model. Now we can define our notion of a *selection* from A.

Definition 7.6 (Selections). Given a formula A, a set of literals x is a *selection from* A just in case $\mathfrak{M}, x \Vdash_e A$. The set of all selections from A, $\mathcal{S}A$, is $\{x \mid \mathfrak{M}, x \Vdash_e A\}$. We then extend the terminology to sets of sentences Γ: a selection from Γ contains one selection from each $A \in \Gamma$. We define the set of all selections from Γ, $\mathcal{S}\Gamma$, as follows. When $\Gamma = \{A_1, A_2, \ldots\}$ for distinct $A_1, A_2, \ldots$, $\mathcal{S}\Gamma$ is the collection of all sets $\{x_1, x_2, \ldots\}$, for each x_i a selection from A_i.

An equivalent characterisation of $\mathcal{S}A$ is:

$$\mathcal{S}p = \{\{p\}\} \text{ and } \mathcal{S}\neg p = \{\{\neg p\}\}$$
$$\mathcal{S}(A \wedge B) = \{x \cup y \mid x \in \mathcal{S}A, y \in \mathcal{S}B\}$$
$$\mathcal{S}\neg(A \wedge B) = \mathcal{S}\neg A \cup \mathcal{S}\neg B \cup \mathcal{S}(\neg A \wedge \neg B)$$
$$\mathcal{S}(A \vee B) = \mathcal{S}A \cup \mathcal{S}B \cup \mathcal{S}(A \wedge B)$$
$$\mathcal{S}\neg(A \vee B) = \{x \cup y \mid x \in \mathcal{S}\neg A, y \in \mathcal{S}\neg B\}$$
$$\mathcal{S}\neg\neg A = \mathcal{S}A$$

This presentation brings out the similarity between our notion of a selection and van Fraassen's definition (1969, 484) of truthmaking and falsemaking sets.

The following lemma establishes the relationship between A's selections and the states that truthmake A.

Lemma 7.1 (Selection lemma). For any formula A, model M and state s in M:

$$M, s \Vdash_e A \text{ iff, for some } x \in \mathcal{S}A, \ M, s \Vdash_e \bigwedge x$$

We use selections to characterise the syntactic relationship between premises and conclusion in an exact entailment. The conclusion must be built from selections from the premises, in a certain way, in order for an exact entailment to hold. I'll make this relationship precise in the characterisation theorem 7.9 below. Given this theorem, compactness and decidability results are very straightforward.

I'll proceed by showing how to transform a model in to a congruent model. Intuitively, the congruent model takes certain states in the original model and treats them as a single state. The strategy is then to build a counter-model to a purported entailment by identifying all the states which truthmake the premises, and showing that this state does not truthmake the conclusion. The following definitions and lemmas give the details.

Definition 7.7 (Difference and convexity). A state □ is *null* just in case □ ⊑ s for every s. If a null state exists, it is unique, and we reserve the name '▫' for it. States s and u overlap iff some state $t \neq$ ▫ is a part of both: $t \sqsubseteq s$ and $t \sqsubseteq u$. The greatest lower bound of s and u, if there is one, is denoted $s \sqcap u$. The *difference* of states s and u, written $s - u$, is the unique state t (if there is one) such that any v is a part of t iff v is a part of s but does not overlap u. (So, $s - u$ is the $\sqsubseteq$-greatest part of s which does not overlap u, if there is one.) A set of states S is *closed under difference* iff $s - u \in S$ whenever $s, u \in S$. A set of states S is *convex* iff $t \in S$ whenever $s, u \in S$ and $s \sqsubseteq t \sqsubseteq u$.

Note that $s - $▫$ = s$ and $s - s = $▫, for any state s. If S is closed under difference, then $s - s \in S$ for any $s \in S$, and so ▫ $\in S$. For technical reasons, we will occasionally need to rely on models containing the null state. But this is a harmless move for, as the following lemma shows, we can always add the null state to the bottom of a model without changing the model elsewhere.

Lemma 7.2 (Null state). Let $M = \langle\!\langle S, \sqsubseteq, |\cdot|^+, |\cdot|^- \rangle\!\rangle$ and $M^▫ = \langle\!\langle S \cup \{▫\}, \sqsubseteq^▫, |\cdot|^+, |\cdot|^- \rangle\!\rangle$, where $s \sqsubseteq^▫ u$ iff either $s \sqsubseteq u$ or $s = $▫. Then, for any $s \in S$: $M, s \Vdash_e A$ iff $M^▫, s \Vdash_e A$.

Definition 7.8 (Congruence relation). Let $M = \langle\!\langle S, \sqsubseteq, |\cdot|^+, |\cdot|^- \rangle\!\rangle$ be any model with S closed under arbitrary fusions ($\bigsqcup U \in S$ for any $U \subseteq S$) and pairwise difference. Let $C \subseteq S$ be a convex set closed under $\sqcup$. We define an equivalence relation $\equiv_C$ on S as the smallest equivalence relation such that:

(a) If $s, u \in C$ then $s \equiv_C u$; and

(b) If $s \equiv_C s'$ and $u \equiv_C u'$ then $s \sqcup u \equiv_C s' \sqcup u'$.

(Note that there must exist a smallest such relation.) We will write $[s]_C$ for $\{u \mid u \equiv_C s\}$ and boldface **s**, **u**, ... for arbitrary equivalence classes.

The following lemma gives us an equivalent characterisation of our congruence relation, $\equiv_C$.

Lemma 7.3. Let M and C be as above, and let $s \approx_C u$ whenever: either $s = u$; or else (i) there are $c_1, c_2 \in C$ such that $c_1 \sqsubseteq s$ and $c_2 \sqsubseteq u$ and (ii) $s - \bigsqcup C = u - \bigsqcup C$. Then $s \approx_C u$ iff $s \equiv_C u$.

Definition 7.9. Let M and C be as above. We define an operator $\sqcup^C$ on equivalence classes of states by setting $\mathbf{s} \sqcup^C \mathbf{u} = \bigcup_{s \in \mathbf{s}, u \in \mathbf{u}} [s \sqcup u]_C$.

Given two states s and u, we can find the sum of their equivalence classes, $[s]_C \sqcup^C [u]_C$, by taking the equivalence class of their sum, $[s \sqcup u]_C$, as the following lemma establishes.

Lemma 7.4. $[s]_C \sqcup^C [u]_C = [s \sqcup u]_C$.

This feature greatly simplifies the presentation, since we can now identify $\mathbf{s} \sqcup^C \mathbf{u}$ with $[s \sqcup u]_C$, for any $s \in \mathbf{s}$ and any $u \in \mathbf{u}$.

Definition 7.10 (Congruent structures). Let M and C be as above. We transform M into a congruent structure,

$$M^C = \langle\!\langle S^C, \sqsubseteq^C, |\cdot|^{+C}, |\cdot|^{-C} \rangle\!\rangle$$

where:

- $S^C = \{[s]_C \mid s \in S\}$

- $\mathbf{s} \sqsubseteq^C \mathbf{u}$ iff $\mathbf{s} \sqcup^C \mathbf{u} = \mathbf{u}$

- $|p|^{+C} = \{[s]_C \mid s \in |p|^+\}$

- $|p|^{-C} = \{[s]_C \mid s \in |p|^-\}$

Intuitively, a congruent structure treats all the elements of C as a single state.

Lemma 7.5. Let M and C be as above. Then M^C is a model.

Lemma 7.6. Let M^C be as above. For any state u in M^C, if there is no $s \in C$ such that $s \sqsubseteq u \sqsubseteq \bigsqcup C$, then for no $s \in C$ is $s \equiv_C u$.

We now form a congruence relation on our canonical model, transforming the latter into a congruent canonical model. Note that, since states in the canonical model are sets of sentences, the set of all such states is trivially closed under arbitrary fusions and pairwise difference; and we can always take a set of canonical model states S and close it under convexity and pairwise fusion. We use the resulting set of states, C, to form our convex canonical model.

Lemma 7.7 (Congruent models). Let M and C be as in definition 7.10. We form the congruent model M^C. Then:

$$M^C, s \Vdash_e A \text{ iff there is some } u \in s \text{ such that } M, u \Vdash_e A.$$

Corollary 7.8. Let $\mathfrak{M} = \langle\!\langle \mathfrak{S}, \subseteq, |\cdot|^+, |\cdot|^- \rangle\!\rangle$ be the canonical model, and $C \subseteq \mathfrak{S}$ be convex and closed under $\cup$. Form the congruent canonical model $\mathfrak{M}^C$. Then $\mathfrak{M}^C, s \Vdash_e A$ iff $s \cap \mathcal{S}A \neq \emptyset$.

Now for the characterisation theorem, which says the following. Suppose we have an entailment from premises Γ to conclusion A. Then, for any selection X from the premises, we must be able to find a selection y from the conclusion which lies between some specific $x \in X$ and X itself, in this sense: $x \subseteq y \subseteq \bigcup X$. If we think of selections as describing specific truth-grounds, then an entailment holds when, for any collection of truth-grounds for the premises, some truth-ground for the conclusion lies in-between one and all of those premise truth-grounds. That's what the theorem says.

To illustrate the idea, consider the entailment: $p, r \vDash_e (p \vee q) \wedge r$. The selections for p and r are just $\{p\}$ and $\{r\}$, neither of which is a selection from $(p \vee q) \wedge r$. But $\{\{p\}, \{r\}\}$ is the only selection from the premise-set $\{p, r\}$ and $\{p, r\}$ is a selection from the conclusion. This gives the inclusion relationship $\{p\} \subseteq \{p, r\} \subseteq \bigcup\{\{p\}, \{r\}\}$, which satisfies the theorem's condition on entailment, hence $p, r \vDash_e (p \vee q) \wedge r$.

Theorem 7.9 (Characterisation of $\vDash_e$). $\Gamma \vDash_e A$ if and only if, for any $X \in \mathcal{S}\Gamma$, some $y \in \mathcal{S}A$ and some $x \in X$: $x \subseteq y \subseteq \bigcup X$.

Now let's consider compactness and decidability of exact entailment. We cannot meaningfully express compactness in terms of satisfiability (i.e., by saying that any set of formulae is satisfiable iff all its finite subsets are), since as we have already noted, any set of formulae is satisfiable in the truthmaking semantics. (Just consider the state which simultaneously truthmakes and false makes each primitive p.) So compactness should be understood in terms of entailment:

Theorem 7.10 (Compactness). If $\Gamma \vDash_e A$ then $\Delta \vDash_e A$ for some finite $\Delta \subseteq \Gamma$.

Theorem 7.11 (Decidability). For finite Γ, it is decidable whether $\Gamma \vDash_e A$.

That concludes the logical investigation into exact truthmaking and exact entailment.

7.5 Inexact Truthmaking

An inexact truthmaker for $\langle A \rangle$ is one which guarantees $\langle A \rangle$'s truth, in the sense that it contains an exact truthmaker for $\langle A \rangle$ (§7.2). In this way, an inexact truthmaker is sufficient for a proposition's truth, but perhaps without being that in virtue of which the truth is true. I'll use '$s \Vdash_i A$' to abbreviate 'state s is an inexact truthmaker for A' and '$s \dashv\vert_i A$' for 'state s is an inexact falsemaker for A'.

We want to understand inexact truthmaking so that $s \Vdash_i A$ if and only if there is some $u \sqsubseteq s$ such that $u \Vdash_e A$ (and similarly for inexact falsemaking). Below, I'll give a direct, recursive definition of the $\Vdash_i$ relation. Before that, let's investigate the effect this clause has on inexact truthmaking (given our definition of exact truthmaking from §7.3). First, and most obviously, inexact truthmaking will satisfy (HEREDITY). For suppose s is an inexact truthmaker for $\langle A \rangle$ and $s \sqsubseteq u$. Then there is some exact truthmaker $t \sqsubseteq s$ for $\langle A \rangle$, hence $t \sqsubseteq u$, and so u too is an inexact truthmaker for $\langle A \rangle$ (and similarly for inexact falsemaking).

As a consequence, the inexact semantics can be stated more simply than the exact semantics. Suppose s is an inexact truthmaker for $A \wedge B$. Then there is some $u \sqsubseteq s$ which exactly truthmakes $A \wedge B$, and

INEXACT TRUTHMAKING   227

hence there are u_1, u_2 such that $u = u_1 \sqcup u_2$, $u_1 \Vdash_e A$, and $u_2 \Vdash_e B$. Then $u_1 \sqsubseteq s$ and $u_2 \sqsubseteq s$, and so u is an inexact truthmaker for both A and B individually. So we obtain the usual clause for conjunction for inexact truthmaking:

$$s \Vdash_i A \wedge B \text{ iff } s \Vdash_i A \text{ and } s \Vdash_i B$$

(This is implicit in van Fraassen 1969, 485–6.)

As a consequence, we also obtain the more familiar clause for disjunction for inexact truthmaking:

$$s \Vdash_i A \vee B \text{ iff } s \Vdash_i A \text{ or } s \Vdash_i B$$

As before, our falsemaking clause for conjunction parallels the truthmaking clause for disjunction, and the falsemaking clause for disjunction parallels the truthmaking clause for conjunction. So the unusual clauses we established for exact truthmaking (and falsemaking) simplify to standard clauses in the inexact semantics.

It is best to define inexact truthmaking directly, in terms of these simplified semantic clauses. We can then show that inexact truthmaking satisfies (HEREDITY) and that inexact truthmakers always include exact truthmakers for a given proposition. Now let's make all of this precise. We use the language, $\mathscr{L}$, of definition 7.1 and frames as in definition 7.13. Inexact truthmaking is then defined as follows.

Definition 7.11 (Inexact models). An *inexact truthmaking model* is a structure $\langle\!\langle S, \sqsubseteq, |\cdot|^+, |\cdot|^- \rangle\!\rangle$ where $\langle\!\langle S, \sqsubseteq \rangle\!\rangle$ is a frame (definition 7.2) and $|\cdot|^+$ and $|\cdot|^-$ are $\sqsubseteq$-upwards-closed valuation functions from primitive sentences $\mathscr{P}$ to 2^S: if $s \in |p|^+$ and $s \sqsubseteq u$, then $u \in |p|^+$ (and similarly for $|p|^-$).

Definition 7.12 (Inexact truthmaking and falsemaking). Given an inexact truthmaking model $M = \langle\!\langle S, \sqsubseteq, |\cdot|^+, |\cdot|^- \rangle\!\rangle$ (which I'll leave implicit), *inexact truthmaking* $\Vdash_i$ and *inexact falsemaking* $\dashv\!\Vdash_i$ relations are then defined by double recursion as follows:

228   THE LOGIC OF TRUTHMAKING

$$s \Vdash_i p \quad \text{iff} \quad s \in |p|^+$$
$$s \dashv\vdash_i p \quad \text{iff} \quad s \in |p|^-$$
$$s \Vdash_i \neg A \quad \text{iff} \quad s \dashv\vdash_i A$$
$$s \dashv\vdash_i \neg A \quad \text{iff} \quad s \Vdash_i A$$
$$s \Vdash_i A \wedge B \quad \text{iff} \quad s \Vdash_i A \ \& \ s \Vdash_i B$$
$$s \dashv\vdash_i A \wedge B \quad \text{iff} \quad s \dashv\vdash_i A \ \text{or} \ s \dashv\vdash_i B$$
$$s \Vdash_i A \vee B \quad \text{iff} \quad s \Vdash_i A \ \text{or} \ s \Vdash_i B$$
$$s \dashv\vdash_i A \vee B \quad \text{iff} \quad s \dashv\vdash_i A \ \& \ s \dashv\vdash_i B$$

Given this definition, it is easy to see that inexact truthmaking satisfies the heredity condition:

Theorem 7.12 (Heredity for inexact truthmaking). For any states $s, u \in S$: if $s \Vdash_i A$ and $s \sqsubseteq u$, then $u \Vdash_i A$. And similarly, if $s \dashv\vdash_i A$ and $s \sqsubseteq u$, then $u \dashv\vdash_i A$.

Proof: By a standard induction on A. ∎

We can combine exact and inexact truthmaking (and falsemaking) in a single model. We do this by basing both the exact and the inexact valuation functions on the same underlying function, as follows.

Definition 7.13 (Combined models). A *combined model* is a structure $\langle\!\langle S, \sqsubseteq, |\cdot|^+, |\cdot|^-\rangle\!\rangle$ where $\langle\!\langle S, \sqsubseteq\rangle\!\rangle$ is a frame and $|\cdot|^+$ and $|\cdot|^-$ are arbitrary functions from primitive sentences $\mathscr{P}$ to 2^S. We then define the exact and inexact valuation functions as follows:

- $|p|_e^+ = \{s \sqcup u \mid s, u \in |p|^+\}$ and $|p|_e^- = \{s \sqcup u \mid s, u \in |p|^-\}$
- $|p|_i^+ = \{u \mid \exists s \in |p|^+, s \sqsubseteq u\}$ and $|p|_i^- = \{u \mid \exists s \in |p|^-, s \sqsubseteq u\}$

The exact and inexact truthmaking and falsemaking relations are then as before, with $\Vdash_e$ and $\dashv\vdash_e$ defined relative to $|\cdot|_e^+$ and $|\cdot|_e^-$ (definition 7.3), and $\Vdash_i$ and $\dashv\vdash_i$ defined relative to $|\cdot|_i^+$ and $|\cdot|_i^-$ (definition 7.12).

Note that, by this definition, $|p|^+ \subseteq |p|_e^+ \subseteq |p|_i^+$ and $|p|^- \subseteq |p|_e^- \subseteq |p|_i^-$, for every primitive p. It is then easy to see that the two notions of truthmaking are related as intended:

Theorem 7.13. Let M be a combined model. Then $M, u \Vdash_i A$ iff there is some $s \sqsubseteq u$ such that $M, s \Vdash_e A$.

Proof: By a standard induction on A. ∎

Now let's turn to the notion of entailment we get from the inexact semantics. We'll see that it corresponds to a familiar entailment relation.

Definition 7.14 (Inexact entailment). Γ inexactly entails A, written $\Gamma \vDash_i A$ iff, for any inexact model M and any state s of M, $M, s \Vdash_i A$ whenever $M, s \Vdash_i B$ for each $B \in \Gamma$.

Inexact equivalence is defined as two-way inexact entailment.

Inexact entailment corresponds to *first-degree entailment* (Anderson and Belnap 1963), the provable $\to$-free implications of the relevant logic **R**. First degree entailment, $\vdash_{\text{fde}}$, is the smallest reflexive and transitive deducibility relation obeying the following rules (where 'A/B' should be read as an occurrence either of 'A' or of 'B'):

$$A \wedge B \vdash_{\text{fde}} A/B \qquad A/B \vdash_{\text{fde}} A \vee B$$

$$\frac{A \vdash_{\text{fde}} B \quad A \vdash_{\text{fde}} C}{A \vdash_{\text{fde}} B \wedge C} \qquad \frac{A \vdash_{\text{fde}} C \quad B \vdash_{\text{fde}} C}{A \vee B \vdash_{\text{fde}} C}$$

$$A \wedge (B \vee C) \vdash_{\text{fde}} (A \wedge B) \vee (A \wedge C) \qquad A \dashv\vdash_{\text{fde}} \neg\neg A$$

$$\neg(A \wedge B) \dashv\vdash_{\text{fde}} \neg A \vee \neg B \qquad \neg(A \vee B) \dashv\vdash_{\text{fde}} \neg A \wedge \neg B$$

This provides a sound and complete proof system for inexact entailment:

Theorem 7.14. $A \vdash_{\text{fde}} B$ iff $A \vDash_i B$.

Proof: It is sufficient to note that the inexact semantics is equivalent to Dunn's system **BN** (Dunn 2000), which defines an entailment relation $\vDash_{1,0}^{\text{BN}}$, and that $A \vDash_i B$ iff $A \vDash_{1,0}^{\text{BN}} B$. The proof then follows Dunn 2000, 13–14. ∎

This result was (in effect) first noticed by van Fraassen (1969). He proves that his fact-based approach provides a semantics for Anderson and Belnap's *tautological entailment* relation (Anderson and Belnap 1962), which is equivalent to first-degree entailment. Anderson and Belnap defined tautological entailment in a syntactic way (but not in the proof-theoretic way given above, although the two approaches are equivalent). Van Fraassen was the first to find a philosophical semantics for it. (Belnap (1967) gives a formal semantics for tautological entailment using matrices. But, unlike van Fraassen's approach, Belnap's approach says little about what the tautological entailment relation means.)

7.6 Chapter Summary

I've given a formal semantics for exact truthmaking (§7.3) and for inexact truthmaking (§7.5). The former results in a highly unusual logic, in which conjunctions do not entail their conjuncts. I presented a characterisation theorem for exact entailment (as well as decidability and compactness results) in §7.4. Inexact truthmaking, by contrast, provides a semantics for first-degree entailment (§7.5).

IV Propositions and Paradoxes

8

The Nature of Propositions

What kind of entity are truths? I shall argue that they are propositions (§8.1). To understand what propositions are, we must investigate their nature. Given what I've said previously about truth and grounding, a characterisation of their nature is easy to give (§8.2). But finding a theory of what propositions are which respects that nature is much harder. I'll argue that existing theories of propositions cannot account for their nature (§§8.2–8.4). A better account is to analyse propositions in terms of their possible truthmakers (§8.5). I investigate whether this is metaphysically tenable (§8.6) and what it tells us about the notion of same-saying *(§8.7).*

8.1 Roles for Propositions

THERE ARE TRUTHS out there. Some are known, some unknown. Some are more important than others. Some have been given names, such as 'Fermat's Last Theorem', but most have no special name. All obey the T-scheme. Truths can be quantified over, named, and counted; they bear properties; and they stand in relations to other things. In short, they are entities. But what kind of entity are they?

Many truths could have been falsehoods, had things turned out differently in certain ways. Such truths possess the property *being true* merely contingently. It is no part of what they are, metaphysically speaking, that they possess *being true*. When we talk about a truth, we are talking about some entity whose identity is fixed independently of whether it is, in fact, true or false. We are talking about a *truthbearer*, something which possesses either *being true* or *being false*, and which in fact possesses the former.

I'm going to argue that the truthbearers are propositions. (That should come as no surprise, given what I said in §1.2.) More precisely, I'm going to argue that there is a certain theoretical role, *bearer of truth or falsity*, which can't be filled by sentences, by utterances, by beliefs, or by any other entity of that ilk. I use 'proposition' to pick out the entities that play that theoretical role. That isn't an exercise in defining propositions into existence. It is a substantive issue whether the theoretical role is played by sentences, utterances, beliefs, or something else; and it is a further substantive issue whether any kind of entity instantiates the theoretical role, if sentences, utterances, and beliefs do not.

Part of the task, therefore, will be to say what kind of entity, metaphysically speaking, a proposition is. We need an account of propositions, independently of their specification as bearers of truth, which makes it clear how they play that theoretical role. But first of all, what is the argument that the theoretical role is not played by sentences, utterances, or beliefs? It is simple: there are more truths than there are natural language sentences, utterances, or beliefs; and so these entities do not play that role. (We have already met arguments along these lines in §1.2 and §2.4.)

Some truths have never been uttered or believed, and never will be. No one has ever articulated π's full decimal expansion, and no one ever will, because it's infinitely long. So there's a truth about π's full decimal expansion which can't practically be uttered or believed. So there are, in fact, more truths than there are utterances or beliefs. Similarly, there are more truths than there are physical sentence tokens. But 'sentence' is often taken to mean an abstract type, rather than its physical tokens. One may even hold that a type can exist even if no tokens of it do. One may take a sentence to be an abstract structure built from the primitive vocabulary of the language in question, such that every possible well-formed structure built from the primitive vocabulary exists. On that view, there will exist infinitely many sentences. We can even allow infinitely long sentences, specifying details with infinite precision.

But still, there are more truths than there are sentences (qua abstract structures), because there are truths we don't have the primitive vocabulary to express. I can't say what those truths are, due to lack of vocabulary. Even allowing for infinitely long, infinitely precise sentences, some states of the world can't be described. Take Max Black's perfectly symmetrical universe (Black 1952), containing nothing but two spheres. Of each sphere, it's true that it exists. These are different truths, since it's possible for one sphere but not the other to exist. But we have no natural language way of picking out just one of those spheres. There are truths about this hypothetical symmetrical universe that we can't express. So, there are more truths than there are natural language sentences.

When we talk about *truths*, as a metaphysical kind, we are not talking about sentences (or utterances, or beliefs). The theoretical role *bearer of truth or falsity* is not played by sentences, utterances, or beliefs. But it must be played by some class of entity. Truths are entities; *being true* is a property; for each truth, there is an entity possessing *being true*. Those entities, whatever they are, are propositions.

Of course, it's important to talk of sentences, utterances, and beliefs as being true or false. We aim at true belief, for example. We should understand such talk in terms of the proposition expressed by the sentence, utterance, or belief in question. A true sentence, utterance, or belief is one which expresses a true proposition. In this sense, propositions are the *primary* bearers of alethic values. Sentences, utterances, and beliefs can be said to be true (or false) derivatively on the proposition expressed. But strictly speaking, the truth (or falsehood) is the proposition expressed; the sentence, utterance, or belief is the way of expressing it.

Now let's say a bit more about the theoretical roles philosophers typically associate with the category *proposition*. Philosophers speak of the 'propositional attitudes', by which they mean, attitudes expressed by 'that'-clauses: *believing that, desiring that, hoping that, fearing that*, and so on. These are often analysed as relations between a cognitive agent and a proposition. One motivation for this move is that you and I can believe the same thing: we might both believe that global warming is currently the biggest existential threat facing humankind. What is that thing we both believe? The proposition *that global warming is currently the biggest existential threat facing humankind*.

Moreover, we can take different attitudes to the same content. Suppose you believe that global warming has reached the point of no return for humanity, whereas I fear that global warming has reached the point of no return for humanity but hope it isn't so. I fear what you believe, hope the negation of what you believe, and don't definitely believe either what you believe or its negation.

Another role often associated with propositions is this: they are the entities expressed by an utterance of a meaningful sentence. Alternatively, they are what a speaker expresses by making a meaningful utterance. They are *what is said* (by a speaker making an utterance). You and I can say the same thing, using different sentences, perhaps in different languages. And we can say different things using the same sentence: if we both utter 'I'm the author of *What Truth Is*', one of us says something true, one something false.

There's some reason to think that these three theoretical roles— *bearer of truth or falsity*, *object of the attitudes*, *what a speaker says*—converge. We see that reason in phrases like, 'I don't believe what he's saying' and 'what you said is true'. Taken literally, they imply that one kind of entity plays all three theoretical roles.

But equally, there are reasons for thinking that no one kind of entity plays all of these roles. We can say the same thing as one another without believing ourselves to be doing so. Anna says 'Ruth Barcan first came up with the concept of rigid designation'; Bec says 'No, it was Ruth Marcus'; 'No', replies Anna, 'it was definitely Ruth Barcan'. They have different beliefs (else their reply, 'No ...', makes no sense). But, since Ruth Barcan and Ruth Marcus are the same person, they were saying the same thing as one another, albeit in different ways. 'Stop arguing, you're saying the same thing!' is the appropriate interjection. We can't have the same belief in different ways, however. Anna's belief is different from Bec's: that's precisely why they take themselves to be in a dispute. (It's why each says 'no' in reply to the other, for example.) So we should not align *what is said* with *object of the attitudes*. They differ extensionally.

That argument is a bit quick. There's a use of 'belief' which does seem to allow the same belief to be held in different ways:

(8.1) Anna and Bec both believe Ruth Barcan to be the person who first came up with the concept of rigid designation (although Bec wouldn't put it like that).

(8.2) Of Ruth Barcan, both believe that she was the person who first came up with the concept of rigid designation (although Bec wouldn't put it like that).

These are *de re* uses of 'believes'. Each reports what Anna and Bec believed of Ruth Barcan, but does not report the way in which they thought of her: as Ruth Barcan or as Ruth Marcus. These *de re* uses (unlike the more common way of reporting beliefs) support the inference:

(8.3) a believes b to be F;

(8.4) $b = c$;

(8.5) Therefore, a believes c to be F.

But note, however, that this *de re* use of 'believes' doesn't make the reported content fully transparent: it does not support substitution of co-referring terms in the infinitival clause, 'to be —'. We cannot reason as follows:

(8.6) a believes b to be such that Rbc;

(8.7) $c = d$;

(8.8) × Therefore, a believes b to be such that Rbd.

So, even in the special case of infinitival belief reports, it would be a mistake to align their objects with *what is said*. In what follows, I'm going to focus on the usual case of *that*-clause belief reports.

I've argued that no one kind of object plays all three of the theoretical roles, *primary bearer of truth or falsity*, *object of the attitudes*, and *what a speaker says*. In particular, *object of the attitudes* does not align, extensionally, with either *bearer of truth or falsity* or with *what a speaker says*. There are good reasons to align the first and the third role, however, which I'll come back to in §8.7.

I've already reserved the term 'proposition' for the entities that occupy the first of these theoretical roles: propositions are the bearers of truth and falsity. So, on this usage, attitudes such as belief are not relations between agents and propositions. (If you think that 'proposition' should be reserved only for the objects of attitudes such as belief, that's fine: read me as talking about some other kind of entity. I'm interested in the entities that bear alethic properties, *truth* and *falsity*, which I'm calling 'propositions'.)

What should we say about belief and the other attitudes, if they are not relations between cognitive agents and propositions? For the purposes of this investigation into truth, I'm not that fussed what we say. But it's a good question. Here are some options we could take.

We may take a belief to be a three-place relation between an agent (the believer), a proposition (the belief's content), and a mode of presentation of that content. That mode of presentation may be a Fregean sense, or it may be what Salmon (1986) calls a 'guise'. (I have no idea what a 'guise' is, but from the job description, it sounds a lot like a Fregean sense. I also have no idea what a Fregean sense is, metaphysically speaking.) Richard's (1990) view is somewhat similar: the objects of belief are enhanced propositions, enriched with representational elements. On Crimmins's (1992) view, belief reports contain contextually contributed *unarticulated constituents*, which refer to ideas (or idea-types) in the believer's mind (see also Crimmins and Perry 1989).

My preferred view is rather different. I prefer to think in terms of a cognitive agent's total belief state, given by a set of epistemic possibilities, some of which are epistemically accessible from others for the agent in question. Metaphysically, those epistemic possibilities are worlds, some of which are (metaphysically and logically) impossible worlds. That approach allows us to account for agents who believe that Fermat's Last Theorem is false (without believing absurdities, like 0 = 1), and it allows us to treat agents as believing that 1 + 1 = 2 without thereby believing that Fermat's Last Theorem is true. In short, the approach is *hyperintensional*. I rattle on about the ins and outs of this approach in my previous book, *The Impossible* (Jago 2014). Have a look there if you're interested.

That's all I'll say here about belief. I'll come back to *what is said* in §8.7. Spoiler alert: I'll argue there that the account of propositions (qua bearers of truth and falsity) that I'm proposing is also good for analysing *what is said*. Before that, I want to discuss the leading theories of what propositions are. They say that propositions are metaphysically primitive entities (§8.2), sets of possible worlds (§8.3), or structured entities of some kind (§8.4). I'll argue that none of these theories captures what a proposition is. I'll offer a better approach in §8.5.

8.2 The Nature of Propositions

What are propositions? That is a question about their nature. On the approach I proposed in chapter 6, we can rephrase the question as: what is the real definition of *proposition*? The answer I gave in §8.1 was: they are the primary bearers of *truth* and *falsity*. I interpret that as a claim about the nature of propositions: propositions are the entities that, by their very nature, are true or false, depending on how things are.

Let's add to that picture the analysis of *truth* and *falsity* developed throughout this book. To be true is to have a truthmaker. To be false is to have a falsemaker (§2.7). That is the very nature of truth and falsity: it is what those properties are, metaphysically speaking. Given that it is the properties *truth* and *falsity* themselves that feature in the real definition of *proposition* (§6.3), we can substitute 'made true' for 'true' and 'made false' for 'false' in our analysis of what propositions are. This gives us:

(8.9) Propositions are the entities that, by their very nature, are made true or made false, depending on how things are.

That's the nature of *proposition* in general. In the case of a specific proposition, its nature is to be made true, or made false, in a specific way:

(PROP) The proposition *that A* is the entity that, by its very nature, is made true or made false, depending on whether things are such that *A*.

In other words, the nature of a specific proposition ⟨A⟩ must establish an essential link between ⟨A⟩ itself and the states of affairs *that A* or *that ¬A*, were they to exist. The nature of proposition ⟨A⟩ is to depend on whichever state of affairs obtains, such that it would be true were *that A* to obtain, and would be false were *that ¬A* to obtain. So, as a first pass, there is a counterfactual element to the proposition's nature.

We now need to find a metaphysical account of propositions which captures this nature. In general, the nature of an entity tells us what it is, metaphysically speaking (as an individual or as a kind). So we are looking for a metaphysical account of what propositions are which, in and of itself, does justice to (PROP).

To illustrate the challenge, consider the theory on which propositions are metaphysically basic, primitive entities (Merricks 2015). Here, 'primitive' means *metaphysically unanalysable*. Propositions are not to be understood as constructions from sets, states of affairs, sentences, or any other category of entity. *Proposition* is a *sui generis* metaphysical category. Propositions, on this account, are structureless. Propositions neither contain nor are parts of one another. That they represent what they do is a brute metaphysical fact. In short, there is no metaphysical analysis of *proposition* to be had. That is what it means to say they are metaphysically primitive.

So, on this account, there is no metaphysically informative answer to the question, *what are propositions?* All we can say is that they are not entities of this kind, or of that kind. They have no nature. (Or, at most, their nature is to be of the kind *proposition*, and not to be of the kind *set*, *state of affairs*, and so on.) But if propositions have no nature beyond this, then we cannot account for (PROP). A defender of this account may insist that propositions represent, and that they are true or false depending on how things are. She may insist that they do so necessarily, if she is happy to accept brute necessary connections. But she cannot insist that propositions have a substantial nature, for metaphysically primitive entities have no substantial nature (§6.3). So the primitivist approach to propositions cannot account for (PROP).

A similar conclusion applies to the pleonastic account of propositions (Schiffer 2003), which we met in §1.2. As Schiffer uses the term, calling an entity 'pleonastic' makes reference to our knowledge of its existence and identity conditions. We know about fictional characters on the basis of genuinely referential claims, such as 'Buck Mulligan isn't as well known as certain of Joyce's other characters, such as Molly Bloom' (Schiffer 2003, 51). Similarly, according to Schiffer, we know about propositions, and can individuate them, on the basis of *that*-clauses. But to say that propositions are pleonastic entities is not to say anything about their metaphysical nature. Indeed, for Schiffer, propositions are *sui generis* abstract entities (Schiffer 2003, 96), just as they are for Merricks (2015). They have no metaphysical nature. And as a consequence, Schiffer's account is unable to accommodate (PROP).

To account for (PROP), we can't treat propositions as metaphysically primitive entities. We need to spell out their nature, and that amounts to a metaphysical story of what they are (§6.3). There are two main approaches in the literature. The first takes propositions to be (structureless) sets of possible worlds (§8.3); the second takes propositions to be structured entities of some kind (§8.4). But, I'll argue, neither approach does justice to (PROP).

8.3 Sets of Possible Worlds

In this section, I discuss the account on which propositions are sets of possible worlds (Lewis 1986; Stalnaker 1984, 1976a,b). On this approach, the proposition $\langle A \rangle$ is the set of all possible worlds according to which it is the case that A. (Alternatively, the worlds which are such that, were they actual, then it would be the case that A.) This story comes with a ready-made account of what logically complex propositions are. $\langle A \wedge B \rangle$ is simply the set of worlds $\langle A \rangle \cap \langle B \rangle$ and, similarly, $\langle A \vee B \rangle = \langle A \rangle \cup \langle B \rangle$, $\langle \neg A \rangle = \langle A \rangle^c$ (the set-theoretic complement of the set $\langle A \rangle$, on the domain of all possible worlds), and $\langle A \rightarrow B \rangle = \langle A \rangle^c \cup \langle B \rangle$. As a consequence, necessarily equivalent propositions are identical (Stalnaker 1976a, 9).

The approach also has a neat characterisation of truth: proposition $\langle A \rangle$ is true at world w just in case $w \in \langle A \rangle$ and true (simpliciter) just in case the actual world is a member of $\langle A \rangle$. Truth reduces to set-membership. Simple!

It's often argued that these entities are hopeless in accounting for the contents of attitudes such as belief. And so they are: one can believe something without thereby believing everything that's logically equivalent to it. But, since I'm not taking propositions to be the objects of the attitudes, I'm not going to argue against the view on those grounds.

The sets-of-worlds account implies something interesting about the nature of propositions, qua *being the bearers of truth-values*. The membership of any set is part of its nature: it is of $\{a, b, c\}$'s nature to have a, b, and c (but no more) as members. So, if world w is a member of set-of-worlds proposition $\langle A \rangle$, then it is of $\langle A \rangle$'s nature to have w as a member. And if truth-at-w amounts to having w as a member, then it will be of $\langle A \rangle$'s nature that it is true-at-w.

Nevertheless, the nature of a proposition, as set out by (PROP) above, is not merely to bear truth-values. Their nature is to be made true or false by specific entities. It's of the very nature of the proposition *that Bertie is snuffling* that it would be made true by the state of affairs *that Bertie is snuffling*, were it to exist, and would be made false by the state of affairs *that Bertie isn't snuffling*, were that state to exist. The sets-of-worlds approach can't capture this feature.

One way to make that case is by considering the nature of sets in more detail. There is a simple and compelling account of the nature of sets, which is independent of anything I've said so far. The nature of a set X is given entirely by the facts about its membership, the membership of its members, and so on. Let $\in^*$ be the transitive closure of the membership relation $\in$, so that $x \in^* X$ iff there is a membership chain $X_1 \in \cdots \in X_n$ (for $n > 1$) where $x = X_1$ and $X = X_n$.

On this view, the nature of a set-of-worlds proposition is given entirely by the facts about its membership: that it contains such-and-such worlds. But we can't in general get from such facts to facts about a proposition's possible truthmakers. Here's one attempt. We take the state of affairs *that B* to be a truthmaker for $\langle A \rangle$ when all worlds in $\langle A \rangle$ represent that B. This approach will correctly imply that $\langle$Bertie is snuffling$\rangle$ would be made true by state of affairs *that Bertie is snuffling*. But it also implies, incorrectly, that $\langle$Bertie is snuffling$\rangle$ would be made true by any state of affairs *that Bertie is snuffling* $\vee$ *B*, for any B. (That's because any possible world which represents that A thereby represents that $A \vee B$.) It also implies, again incorrectly, that $\langle$Bertie is snuffling$\rangle$ would be made true by any necessary state of affairs, such as *that* $1 + 1 = 2$.

We can avoid these consequences by focusing just on the logically strongest states of affairs represented by all possible worlds in the proposition. This approach implies that $\langle$Bertie is snuffling$\rangle$ would be made true by any state of affairs *that Bertie is snuffling* $\wedge$ *B*, for any logically necessary B. But, as pointed out in §7.2, $\langle$Bertie is snuffling$\rangle$ is not true in virtue of such states of affairs. Rather, it's true just in virtue of the state of affairs *that Bertie is snuffling*. In the terminology of chapter 7, *that Bertie is snuffling* $\wedge$ *B* is an inexact truthmaker for $\langle$Bertie is snuffling$\rangle$, which is to say that it contains a genuine, exact truthmaker for $\langle$Bertie is snuffling$\rangle$. It is the exact, true-in-virtue-of notion that is relevant to (PROP). We can't extract this notion from the sets-of-possible-worlds approach. When B is necessary, possible worlds cannot distinguish between A and $A \wedge B$. The distinction we need is *hyperintensional*, drawing a line between logically equivalent contents. Possible worlds are simply too indiscriminate for that job.

Sets of possible worlds cannot correctly account for the nature of propositions. A similar argument shows that the approach cannot account for the actual properties of propositions (whether we take those properties to be essential or accidental). Consider these two propositions:

(8.10) ⟨Puss exists⟩

(8.11) ⟨Puss exists ∧ 3 exists⟩.

Puss alone truthmakes (8.10). But Puss on her own does not truthmake (8.11). Puss isn't the only part of our ontology relevant to whether (8.11) is true or false: the number 3 is too. It's in virtue of the existence of Puss and the existence of the number 3, not merely in virtue of Puss, that (8.11) is true. (8.10) is truthmade by Puss alone, whereas (8.11) is not truthmade by Puss alone. Hence (8.10) stands in a relation to Puss which (8.11) does not and so, by Leibniz' law, (8.10) and (8.11) cannot be one and the same proposition. But they are one and the same proposition, according to the sets-of-possible-worlds view. Hence, the sets-of-possible-worlds view cannot be correct.

Here's yet another way of making the point, this time without bringing in necessary existents or mathematical entities. If ⟨Puss is stretching⟩ is true, then it is truthmade by a state of affairs involving Puss. And, given that Puss isn't Bertie, it isn't truthmade by any state of affairs involving just Bertie. Similarly, if Puss isn't stretching, then ⟨¬Puss is stretching⟩ is truthmade by a state of affairs involving Puss, not Bertie.

So whatever is the case,

(8.12) ⟨Puss is stretching ∨ ¬Puss is stretching⟩

is truthmade by a state of affairs involving Puss, not Bertie. Similarly,

(8.13) ⟨Bertie is barking ∨ ¬Bertie is barking⟩

is truthmade by a state of affairs involving Bertie, not Puss. Yet (8.12) and (8.13) are logically equivalent and so, if the sets-of-possible-worlds story is correct, they are one and the same proposition. But they cannot be one and the same proposition, for (8.12) and (8.13) are truthmade by different states of affairs.

It's worth noting that these arguments don't require the full, heavy-duty notion of truthmaking for which I argued in previous chapters. For the argument involving (8.10) and (8.11), all we need to assume is that existential propositions ⟨∃xFx⟩ are made true by each of their instances: each particular thing that's F. That's a very weak assumption. It doesn't assume truthmaker maximalism, or the existence of states of affairs, or even the existence of properties.

For the argument involving (8.12) and (8.13), all we need to assume is that ⟨Puss is stretching⟩ and ⟨Bertie is barking⟩ are both true, and are made true by different parts of the world. Then (8.12) and (8.13) differ in what actually makes them true, and hence are distinct propositions. The conclusion follows irrespective of what, if anything, would truthmake ⟨¬Puss is stretching⟩ and ⟨¬Bertie is barking⟩, were they true.

8.4 Structured Propositions

An alternative to the sets-of-worlds view is to take propositions to be structured entities, built from the semantic values of lexical items. We met this view in §1.2, and saw that it comes in two flavours: *Russellian* (King 1995, 1996; Salmon 1986, 2005; Soames 1987, 2008) and *Fregean*. The former takes the constituents of propositions to be particulars, properties, and relations; the latter takes them to be Fregean senses.

I've argued elsewhere (Jago 2014, chapter 3) against this view of propositions. In short, it doesn't respect facts about meaning: it requires certain sentences which have the same meaning to express distinct propositions. I won't repeat the argument here. Instead, I want to focus on how well the structured proposition approach accounts for the nature of propositions. I'll argue that it cannot.

Consider the propositions expressed by:

(1.11) Bertie snuffles

(1.12) Bertie loves Anna

According to King (1995, 1996, 2012), these propositions are the structures:

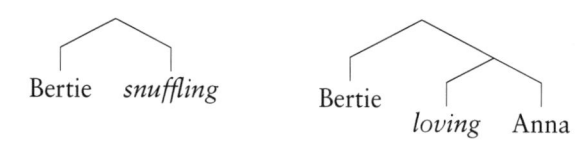

    Bertie *snuffling*   Bertie *loving* Anna

Now here's the problem. Why should these structures be the kind of thing that's made true or false, whereas

    1 2   me you

are not? What's so special about the structure involving Bertie and *snuffling*? (Note that it makes no difference to this worry whether we take these structures to be set-theoretic or some other kind of tree-like entity.)

A first attempt at an answer is: because the Bertie-*snuffling* tree is a representation, and representations are true or false, depending on how things are. That answer will need to be qualified, since not all representations are true or false. The mug-shot on this book's jacket represents me (on a good day), yet it isn't true or false. On the other hand, saying that the tree is a representation *that* such-and-such is question-begging. We're asking, in effect, why a given tree structure should count as a proposition, and hence why we should treat that tree structure, but not others, as having content at all. So it won't help to give a reply in terms of the content the tree supposedly has.

Here's another attempt, from King (1995), to explain why certain trees count as truth-apt representations, and hence as propositions:

humans were able to determine that objects possess or instantiate various properties; that is, they were able to detect that the relation of instantiation obtained. And presumably, their having made vocalizations consisting of concatenated words ... somehow resulted in this concatenation, a sentential relation, representing the relation of instantiation between object and property. Thus sentential relations between words came to stand for relations in much the same way that the words themselves came to stand for objects and relations. (King 1995, 524)

King's idea is that us humans came to associate certain structures with the *instantiation* relation. In particular, in a structure concatenating a property F and a particular a, the structure itself, King's 'sentential relation', represents *instantiation*. If so, King's thought runs, the structured entity as a whole represents a instantiating F: 'by having its constituents configured a certain way in the proposition, the proposition represents its constituents as being related in a certain way in the world' (King 1995, 525).

That last step doesn't follow. A structure may represent a, F, and *instantiation*, without representing a instantiating F. On King's account, the structure

does exactly that. So it can't be merely that a given structure has *instantiation* as its semantic value. It must be that the structure in question conveys that the things thereby structured are related by the *instantiation* relation. Let's take that to be King's view.

A consequence is that such structures represent *instantiation* merely contingently. That they do so is grounded in human activity, on King's view. Had humans behaved differently, those same structures could have represented something else entirely, or nothing at all. And had there been no humans, there would have been no representation-conferring activity, and hence those structures would not have been propositions at all. King endorses this consequence:

for propositions to exist, there must be vehicles consisting of lexical items standing in some (sentential) relation, where these lexical items bear semantic relations to propositional constituents. It seems to me doubtful that such vehicles existed prior to the existence of humans ... prior to the existence of humans (or whatever) there were no propositions (and thus, given that propositions are the things that are true and false, nothing was true or false). (King 1995, 522)

This view won't help answer our question about the nature of propositions. We want a theory which conforms to (PROP), and (PROP) entails a necessary link between a given proposition and the possible entities which would make it true, were they to exist. But on King's view, the proposition ⟨Rab⟩ could have been the proposition ⟨Rba⟩ (had we used sentential structures to present the order of arguments differently), and need not have existed at all. So, on this view, there is no necessary link between the state of affairs *that Rab* and ⟨Rab⟩'s truth.

Quite independently of this worry about the nature of propositions, King's view is difficult to maintain (although see King 1994 for a defence). It entails rejection of the T-scheme. It implies that, prior to there being any humans, it was not true that there were no humans. Let's set out the argument more carefully. If propositions are true relative to a time of evaluation, then the T-scheme instance

(8.14) ⟨There are no humans ↔ ⟨there are no humans⟩ is true⟩

doesn't exist, and hence is not true, at any time in the past when there were no humans. (Perhaps this isn't so bad, if you already think propositions can come into existence and go out again.)

A stronger worry along these lines is that certain T-scheme instances come out false on King's account. We get such instances via the *truth substitution* principle, which allows ⟨⟨A⟩ is true⟩ to be substituted anywhere for any instance of ⟨A⟩. (The T-scheme is then derivable from ⟨A ↔ A⟩). Using substitution, the following is a theorem:

(8.15) ⟨In 1 million BCE, there were no humans ↔ In 1 million BCE, ⟨there are no humans⟩ was true⟩.

On King's account, ⟨there are no humans⟩ did not exist, and hence was not true, in 1 million BCE. So the right-hand side is (now) false. But the left-hand side is (now) true, since there were no humans in 1 million BCE, and so the biconditional is (now) false. Consequently, we should reject King's explanation of how certain structures come to bear truth-values, and his account of propositions with it. The more general conclusion to be drawn is that the structured propositions view cannot account for (PROP), and should be rejected on that basis.

(Of course, as King (1995, 524) points out, any theory must explain how sentences come to represent what they do, and a story along the lines of the one he tells sounds plausible. But in the case of sentences, it is unproblematic to take the relation to be contingent. A given string of symbols or sounds could have meant something else, or nothing at all. So an explanation like King's can be used to explain the relationship between a sentence and the proposition it expresses (if any), but should not be used to explain that proposition itself, or why it should count as a proposition at all.)

8.5 Propositions as Truthmaker Conditions

It's common to identify propositions with truth-conditions. If the theory accepts classical logic, a truth-condition thereby specifies a falsity-condition. Those who treat propositions as entities need to explain what kind of entity they mean by a *condition*. Suppose we are interested in whether something meets condition X in such-and-such situations, and suppose we are interested only in getting a yes-no answer for each such situation. We naturally treat that condition as a function from the situations to the answers, *yes* or *no*. Mathematically, such functions are *characteristic functions*, and each such function defines a set, containing all and only the input entities for which the function's output is *yes*. It is then both very natural and mathematically elegant to identify the condition itself with a set of situations.

In the case of a truth-condition, the input situations are possible worlds and the outputs are *true* or *false*. So we identify a truth-condition with a set of possible worlds. But, as we saw above (§8.3), propositions are not sets of possible worlds. They are more discriminating than truth-conditions. A given proposition's nature is not merely to be true or false at a given world, but rather to be made true or made false by specific ways things could be. Propositions are not truth-conditions: they are *truthmaker conditions*.

If we continue to identify conditions with characteristic functions, then we'll treat truthmaker conditions as functions from entities to *yes* or *no*, depending on whether that entity is a truthmaker for the content in question. Or, more simply, we can identify this characteristic function with the set it defines, so that truthmaker conditions are sets of entities. (Typically, we'll think in terms of states of affairs. But we don't want to restrict this category, since any entity x whatsoever is a truthmaker for ⟨x exists⟩.) So, as a first pass, propositions are sets of entities (of any kind), and we think of those entities as truthmakers for that proposition.

This is just an approximation to my final theory. But already, it allows us to say something further about the truthmaking relation: it is intimately related to set membership. On this simple first-pass theory, an entity x is a truthmaker for a proposition ⟨A⟩ if and only if x is a member of ⟨A⟩. As the theory develops, this relationship will develop somewhat, but the truthmaking relation will remain intimately tied to set membership. We can then say that a proposition is true (at a world) iff one of its members exists (at that world). This isn't intended as a conceptual analysis of *truth*, or of the meaning of 'is true': it's a metaphysical theory of what property *truth* is. As promised way back in the Introduction, the metaphysics of truthmaking can be analysed without prior appeal to the property or concept of truth.

Why, on this approach, are sets suitable bearers of truth and falsity? Why are they suitable vehicles for representation? (These are worries I raised against the structured propositions account in §8.4.) Identifying propositions with truthmaker conditions leads directly to the analysis of truthmaking in terms of set-membership.

The members of a set, recall, are essential to it. So our theory implies that it's essential to a proposition that it has the truthmakers it has. Add to this our analysis of truth in terms of truthmaking, and our theory implies that it's essential to a proposition that it is true (at a world) when one of its members exists (at a world). That's why, on this approach, sets are suitable bearers of truth and falsity. And, for the same reason, they count as representations: they are, by their nature, true or false in virtue of how things are.

Using this (simplified) analysis, we can answer the questions left hanging at the end of §6.5, concerning the logical properties of the *truthmaking* relation. We saw there that truthmaking isn't transitive, but we couldn't settle the questions of (ir)reflexivity and (a)symmetry. (That's because we can't argue from the logical properties of *grounding* to the logical properties of *truthmaking*.) Now we can settle those questions. Truthmaking is irreflexive, asymmetrical, and non-transitive, because set-membership is. (Truthmaking isn't intransitive, because set-membership isn't: $x \in \{x,y\} \in \{\{x,y\},x\}$ and $x \in \{\{x,y\}\}$, for example. We might think of $\{x,y\}$ as the proposition *that either x or $\{x,y\}$ exists*.)

Here's a further advantage of the view. Any account of truth, whether of the property or the concept, must explain why the T-scheme plays such a central role in our understanding. (Mumford (2007) and Scharp (2013) reject the T-scheme, but that is precisely why their accounts are hard to swallow.) For the deflationist, the T-scheme provides an implicit definition of truth (§1.1); for an alethic pluralist like Wright, the T-scheme is one of the central platitudes governing what counts as a truth-predicate (§1.5). We saw in §2.7 that identifying truth with truthmaking allows one to derive the T-scheme from basic principles about truthmaking. But when we add our understanding of propositions as truthmaker-conditions, the T-scheme reveals itself as a more basic principle still, going deeper even than 'mere' logical equivalence, as follows.

Given our analysis of *being true*, $\langle \langle A \rangle$ is true$\rangle$ is identical to the existential proposition $\langle \exists x \ x \text{ truthmakes } \langle A \rangle \rangle$, which we identify with the set of all its witnesses: all truthmakers for $\langle A \rangle$. So $\langle \langle A \rangle$

is true⟩ is identical to ⟨A⟩ itself. (This result will remain even as we refine our analysis of propositions below.) The T-scheme reveals itself as an informative identity statement between propositions. To put things another way, stating that such-and-such is true *just is* stating such-and-such. One is saying the same thing, expressing precisely the same proposition twice, using different words. (I'll return to the topic of same-saying in §8.7.) In this way, the T-scheme captures a deep fact about the metaphysical nature of propositions about truth.

(If only the deflationist could avail herself of this machinery! She could then avoid the worries I raised for her in §1.3 and §1.4. But she can't, as the argument requires first identifying the properties *being true* and *having a truthmaker*. That's a paradigmatically substantial, non-deflationist view of truth.)

There's something of the *redundancy theory* in this result: both say that ⟨A⟩ and ⟨⟨A⟩ *is true*⟩ are identical. (Button (2014) discusses a version of the redundancy theory which has some affinities with my approach.) Ramsey (1927) defends the idea that the proposition ⟨A⟩ *is true* is identical to ⟨A⟩:

> the propositional function p is true is simply the same as p, as e.g. its value 'Caesar was murdered is true' is the same as 'Caesar was murdered'. (Ramsey 1927, 158)

Ramsey infers from this that 'there is really no separate problem of truth but merely a linguistic muddle' (1927, 157). Not so. We got this analysis of propositions only via a metaphysical analysis of the property *being true* in terms of truthmaking. We can still talk about that property directly, without ascribing it, as when we say 'the property *being true* is such-and-such'. The property is the semantic value of the predicate 'is true', and as such plays a role in the meaning of sentences ascribing truth. The sentence "'A' is true' need not mean exactly the same as 'A': sentences differing in meaning may nevertheless express the same proposition. (I say more about meaning and propositions in §9.9.)

Frege (1956) makes a similar point to Ramsey, arguing that 'predicating [truth] is always included in predicating anything whatever' (Frege 1897/1979, 129), and that 'the sentence 'I smell the scent of violets' has the same content as the sentence 'it is true that I smell the scent of violets'" (Frege 1918/1977, 88). Frege infers that *truth* is a primitive concept, for 'nothing is added to the thought by my ascribing to it the property of truth' and that 'the meaning of the word 'true' seems to be altogether *sui generis*' (Frege 1918/1977, 88). Asay (2013a,b) takes this as a compelling argument for a *primitivist* theory of (the concept of) truth.

Insofar as the content expressed by 'A' is just the proposition ⟨A⟩, I agree with Frege (and Asay) that adding 'is true' adds nothing to the content expressed. But I don't see why this should imply that the meaning of 'is true' is *sui generis*. 'Is true' has *being true* as its semantic value, and that property has a substantial metaphysical analysis, in terms of truthmaking, and ultimately in terms of set-membership.

The approach also deals swiftly with another worry raised against using truthmaker theory to analyse truth. Asay (2014) considers *alethic states of affairs*, of the form *that proposition ⟨A⟩ is true*, or [⟨A⟩ *is true*]. If ⟨A⟩ has a truthmaker, *t*, then [⟨A⟩ *is true*] also exists. Asay then poses a dilemma. Either *t* and [⟨A⟩ *is true*] are necessarily connected, or they're not. If they are, then there's a 'dubious' necessary connection to be explained. If they're not, then *t* can't be a truthmaker for ⟨A⟩ after all, on pain of contradiction. Necessary connections between distinct existences require justification. But in this case, says Asay, 'there is no such justification'. So 'metaphysical substantivism about truth is either contradictory or unmotivated' (Asay 2014, 158).

This is hardly a dilemma: given (NECESSITATION) (§3.1), *t* must necessitate the existence of [⟨A⟩ is true]. Asay demands an explanation of how they are necessary connected, 'in spite of being fully distinct' (2014, 158). Here it is. [⟨A⟩ is true] contains two entities: ⟨A⟩ and *being true*. The former is a set containing *t*. The latter is an existential property, demanding that a member of ⟨A⟩ exist. If *t* exists, that existential demand is met, and so [⟨A⟩ is true] exists. The mistake in the argument was to think that *t* and [⟨A⟩ is true] are *fully* distinct. Although *t* is not directly a constituent of [⟨A⟩ is true], it is nevertheless a member of a constituent of [⟨A⟩ is true]. Compare: *x* necessitates the existence of the state of affairs [$x \in \{\ldots, x, \ldots\}$]. There's no mystery to this connection, for x is a member of a constituent of [$x \in \{\ldots, x, \ldots\}$]. The case of alethic states of affairs is directly analogous.

Now let's develop this central idea of propositions as sets of truthmakers into a workable theory. We don't want to identify a proposition with the set of its actual truthmakers only. We want the proposition to be a condition on what would make it true, were it to exist. So the entities in question will have to include merely possible, as well as actual, entities (just as the sets-of-possible worlds view appeals to merely possible worlds). Just how to make sense of this thought is not at all straightforward. Propositions actually exist. They are sets, and so their members actually exist too. But by definition, merely possible entities do not actually exist. Several responses to this problem are available: I'll discuss them in §8.6.

I've said, as a first pass, that propositions are sets of their possible truthmakers. That makes sense when each of a proposition's truthmakers is a single entity. But that isn't always the case. Propositions can be made true by pluralities. ⟨There are pugs⟩ is made true by each individual pug, but also by pairs of pugs, triples of pugs, and, quite generally, by pug pluralities of any size. The set of all possible pugs leaves out these pug-plurality truthmakers. We can't represent pluralities by including all their members in the proposition. If we did, we would incorrectly treat each member of a truthmaking plurality as a full truthmaker for the claim in question. We would thereby interpret ⟨there are at least three pugs⟩ as the set of all possible pugs, and hence as identical to ⟨there is at least one pug⟩. But clearly, the latter can be true without the former.

Instead, we can represent pluralities through their mereological sums. ⟨There are pugs⟩ is the set of all possible pugs and all possible pug sums. ⟨There are at least three pugs⟩ is the set of all possible three-or-more-pug sums. This way, we treat each member of a set as a (possible) full truthmaker for that proposition. Likewise, we treat each proper part of each member as a (possible) partial truthmaker for that proposition.

A set of possible truthmakers is a truthmaker condition. But we might also want propositions to encode information about their possible falsemakers. So understood, propositions are truth-and-falsity-maker conditions. We can identify each of these with a set of possible truthmakers plus a set of possible falsemakers. Call the former single-set notion a *single proposition* and the latter double-set notion a *double proposition*. We might equivalently characterise a double proposition as a pair of single propositions. One very nice feature of double propositions is that (in the notation from chapter 7), if $\langle A \rangle$ is the pair $|A|^+, |A|^-$, then $\langle \neg A \rangle$ is simply the pair $|A|^-, |A|^+$. So $|\neg A|^+ = |A|^-$ and $|\neg A|^- = |A|^+$.

Double propositions are a good way to distinguish between necessarily false propositions. When $\langle A \rangle$ and $\langle B \rangle$ are distinct propositions, we want to distinguish between $\langle A \vee \neg A \rangle$ and $\langle B \vee \neg B \rangle$. (The inability to do this was part of the criticism of sets-of-worlds account in §8.3.) But by the same token, we should also distinguish between the necessarily false propositions $\langle A \wedge \neg A \rangle$ and $\langle B \wedge \neg B \rangle$. We can't do this by identifying propositions with sets of possible truthmakers (since both sets are empty). Double propositions are a neat solution to the issue. Although $\langle A \wedge \neg A \rangle$ and $\langle B \wedge \neg B \rangle$ have precisely the same possible truthmakers (none), they differ in their possible falsemakers. On our analysis, a falsemaker for $\langle A \wedge \neg A \rangle$ is whatever truthmakes either $\langle A \rangle$ or $\langle \neg A \rangle$ (or both). Such entities need truthmake neither $\langle B \rangle$ nor $\langle \neg B \rangle$. So, although $|A \wedge \neg A|^+$ coincides with $|B \wedge \neg B|^+$, in general $|A \wedge \neg A|^-$ will differ from $|B \wedge \neg B|^-$.

Not every set counts as a single proposition, and not every pair of sets counts as a double proposition. Nevertheless, the conditions on such sets are quite relaxed. A single proposition $\langle A \rangle$ must be *downwards closed* with respect to grounding. If $x \in \langle A \rangle$ and y is a possible full ground for x, then $y \in \langle A \rangle$ too. (Note that the criterion here makes use of the dyadic notion of grounding: as above, pluralities of partial grounds are represented as their sum. So, in particular, we can have $x \sqcup y \in \langle A \rangle$ without $x \in \langle A \rangle$.)

We may require that single propositions be upwards-closed with respect to mereological summation: if $x, y \in \langle A \rangle$ then $x \sqcup y \in \langle A \rangle$. If we do that, then we commit ourselves to impossible entities. If $\langle A \rangle$ has a possible truthmaker x and $\langle \neg A \rangle$ a possible truthmaker y, then $\langle A \vee \neg A \rangle$ contains both x and y and so, by the sum closure condition, also contain $x \sqcup y$. But $x \sqcup y$ is a truthmaker for $\langle A \wedge \neg A \rangle$! This is an entity that can't possibly exist. It is a sum of incompatible entities, from different possible worlds. If we want to avoid commitment to such entities, we should restrict the sum closure principle to possible entities: if $x, y \in \langle A \rangle$ and $x \sqcup y$ possibly exists, then $x \sqcup y \in \langle A \rangle$. (Below, I'll offer a reason for wanting such entities in the theory.)

We may also want to ensure that single propositions are convex: if $x, z \in \langle A \rangle$ and there is a y such that $x \sqsubseteq y \sqsubseteq z$, then $y \in \langle A \rangle$. (Fine (2017b) discusses convexity in relation to content; Fine and Jago (2017) discuss convexity in the context of truthmaker semantics.)

If a set satisfies these conditions, then it counts as a single proposition. That allows many, many arbitrary sets to count as propositions. Take the closure of an arbitrary set, $\{x_1, \ldots, x_n\}$, under the conditions just listed. This is the proposition *that x_1, or ..., or x_n exists*. Since the set is upwards-closed under mereological summation, this disjunction can be made true in virtue of any of its disjuncts, or any combination of them, being made true. But there may be additional ways to characterise this set. In general, if the closure of $x_1, \ldots, x_n$ is all the possible truthmakers for A, then that set is the proposition *that A*. So in many cases, there will be multiple complimentary ways to characterise a given proposition.

These conditions apply to single propositions, and they apply equally to each component, $|A|^+$ and $|A|^-$, of a double proposition. In addition, we had better rule out any possible entity being in both sets of a double proposition. If some possible x were a member of both $|A|^+$ and $|A|^-$, then it would be possible for both $\langle A \rangle$ and $\langle \neg A \rangle$ to be true simultaneously. But this isn't possible, so no possible entity can be in the overlap of $|A|^+$ and $|A|^-$. ($|A|^+$ and $|A|^-$ may overlap only if we accept impossible entities.)

There is a serious metaphysical worry facing double propositions. We might identify the double proposition $\langle A \rangle$ with an ordered pair, $\langle\!\langle |A|^+, |A|^- \rangle\!\rangle$. But we might instead identify it with $\langle\!\langle |A|^-, |A|^+ \rangle\!\rangle$.

Which identification is correct? For the purposes of our semantics, either approach is fine. But our interest is predominantly in the metaphysics of propositions. We want to know what they are, metaphysically speaking. One choice is right, one wrong, and there's no way we can say which.

(If we identify ordered pairs with sets, we face an additional issue. We can code the pair $\langle\!\langle x, y \rangle\!\rangle$ as $\{\{x\}, \{x, y\}\}$, or as $\{\{b\}, \{a, b\}\}$, or as $\{a, \{a, b\}\}$, $\{b, \{a, b\}\}$, or as $\{\{0, a\}, \{1, b\}\}$. Why think that the one we pick gets the nature of propositions right, rather than the others?)

If you don't see a problem here, try this. Consider the pair, $\langle\!\langle \{that\ Bertie\ is\ snuffling\}, \{that\ Bertie\ isn't\ snuffling\} \rangle\!\rangle$. Assume (for the moment) that this is a proposition. Is it *that Bertie is snuffling*? Or is it *that Bertie isn't snuffling*? Why that one? There cannot be any intrinsic differences in the composition of those sets to mark the difference, for the negation of a proposition $\langle A \rangle$ consists in those very same sets, $|A|^+$ and $|A|^-$, but with the order switched: $|\neg A|^+ = |A|^-$ and $|\neg A|^- = |A|^+$. So it seems we need to stipulate which set in the pair comes first, the truthmakers or the falsemakers. Yet there's nothing in the nature of propositions, or the nature of *truth*, which dictates any priority between truth and falsity. The problem is insoluble.

If we cannot make metaphysical sense of double propositions, then we will have to make do with single propositions. But then we must face again the issue of distinct but necessarily false propositions, raised above. How should we distinguish them? The problem, as we saw it above, is that necessarily false propositions have no possible truthmakers. So to distinguish them, we must drop the restriction to possible entities. We allow propositions to include states of affairs which couldn't possibly obtain, as well as those that could.

Above, we met one way to have impossible entities in our ontology. Where we have possible states of affairs *that A* and *that ¬A*, we also have their mereological sum. We take sums of states of affairs to be their conjunction. This gives us the (necessarily non-obtaining) state of affairs *that $A \wedge \neg A$*. This state of affairs *that $A \wedge \neg A$* is distinct from *that $B \wedge \neg B$* whenever *that A* and *that B* are distinct states of affairs. And that in turn is enough to distinguish $\langle A \wedge \neg A \rangle$ from $\langle B \wedge \neg B \rangle$.

Other impossible cases are not explained so easily. Take the necessarily false proposition ⟨1 = 2⟩. One might think that the very identities of those numbers, 1 and 2, are what make this false. So what would an impossible truthmaker for ⟨1 = 2⟩ look like? One suggestion is: the (necessarily non-obtaining) state of affairs *that* $\{1,2\}$ *is a singleton*. For, were $\{1,2\}$ a singleton, 1 would be identical to 2. But this gets things the wrong way around. The identities of its members make a set the set it is. It isn't the properties of the set that fix the identities of its members.

Another approach is to take the impossible truthmakers for ⟨1 = 2⟩ to be a state of affairs universally quantifying over properties: *that, for any F, F*1 *iff F*2. But again, this gets the explanation the wrong way around. It isn't that $a = b$ because a and b share all their properties; rather, any property of a is a property of b because $a = b$.

A better approach is available for those who take mathematical entities to be identical to points in a structure. Then, the identity of 1 and 2 is given by relational, structural facts. The (necessarily non-obtaining) state of affairs *that* 1 = 2 would be a conjunction of structural facts, identifying the 1-role with the 2-role. Just how this is done (and whether it is plausible) will depend on the details of one's particular structuralist theory.

If there are necessarily existing primitive entities, whose identities are not metaphysically analysable or grounded in more basic facts, then this kind of approach will not cover all cases. We will then be forced to admit some strange ontology. Perhaps there is an *identity* relation, so that *that* 1 = 2 involves the instantiation of *identity* with 1 and 2. That's an ugly solution since, for most everyday metaphysical purposes, no *identity* relation is required. Facts of identity are given by the identical entities themselves (which is to say, by each and every thing).

The double propositions account has a much more elegant solution to offer. It treats ⟨1 = 2⟩ as the empty set (since nothing could make 1 = 2) paired with $\{1,2\}$ (since 1 and 2 alone make it the case that 1 ≠ 2). So each account on offer—double propositions, or single propositions with impossible states of affairs—has its benefits and its drawbacks. The former requires us to stipulate, in what would seem an *ad hoc* way, which set in each pair is to count as the truthmakers, which the falsemakers. The latter will probably require the introduction of some dubious ontology. Such is the way in metaphysics. I'll put my money on single propositions (with impossible states of affairs).

Before moving on, there is one further issue to discuss. We have identified propositions with sets, and we think of the members of those sets as the (actual, possible, or impossible) truthmakers for those propositions. This faces an immediate difficulty with propositions such as:

(8.16) ⟨Propositions exist⟩

(8.17) ⟨Sets exist⟩

One might expect the truthmakers for (8.16) to be all propositions, and truthmakers for (8.17) to be all sets. In fact, that's what our truthmaking clause for existential propositions in general seems to say. But this is incompatible with (8.16) and (8.17) themselves being sets. Since (8.16) is a proposition, it would contain itself, contrary to the axiom of regularity (which rules out circular membership chains, $x \in \cdots \in x$. Similarly, if (8.17) is a set, then it would contain itself; but it cannot.

One may respond that some versions of set theory—non-well-founded theories—allow sets to contain themselves as members (Aczel 1988). I'm not tempted by that route. For one thing, I'm not sure we can make metaphysical sense of non-well-founded sets, given that sets are grounded by their members. For another, our theory of propositions shouldn't dictate what fundamental mathematical theories should look like.

Even if we set these worries to one side, (8.17) is simply too big to be a set. If it contained all its truthmakers, it would be the set of all sets. But, on pain of contradiction, there can be no such set. There's a similar worry for (8.16). For each entity x, there exists the proposition ⟨x exists⟩. The possible truthmakers for this are x itself (plus x's grounds). But (8.16) purports to contain all such sets, and hence purports to be at least as large as the set of all sets. There cannot be such a set.

We might respond with a theory that accepts proper classes, bigger than any set. But then we face the issue: how do we assert the existence of such classes? We are assuming that the proposition ⟨x exists⟩ is a set-or-class with x as a member. But proper classes are, by definition, members of no set-or-class. So if x is a proper class, then there is no proposition (qua set-or-class) asserting its existence.

These issues run deep. But they're a problem for everyone (who believes in sets). Even if you think there's no such thing as propositions, you still need to explain how the sentences

(8.18) There are sets

(8.19) All sets have ∅ as a subset

get to be true. These truths require a domain of quantification, which contains all the entities quantified over by those truths. But, on the face of it, both sentences quantify over all sets. That would imply a domain of quantification—a set—containing all sets, which is impossible. (If you want to escape by taking the domain of quantification to be a proper class, just change 'set' to 'class' to re-introduce the problem.)

Somehow, we meaningfully talk about sets using 'all sets' without thereby including all sets in the domain of quantification. The domain of 'all sets' can't include the domain of quantification itself. Similarly, the domain of 'some set' can't include the domain of quantification itself. That seems to be a fact about how the quantifiers work. Their semantics allows 'all sets' and 'some set' to range over all sets except the set specifying that very range.

I propose that the same goes for the quantifiers in (8.16) and (8.17). Those quantifiers range over all sets, except the very sets specifying those ranges. But those range-specifying set are precisely (8.16) and (8.17), respectively. So neither (8.16) nor (8.17) quantifies over itself, and hence neither is a truthmaker for itself. Both are genuine propositions, on this account. This avoids both the self-membership and the cardinality worry. And, importantly, the result is a consequence of the general semantics for the quantifier 'there are *Fs*'. This is a theoretical cog prior to our account of what propositions are. There is no need to fiddle with our theory of propositions.

8.6 What are Merely Possible States of Affairs?

I've claimed that propositions are sets, or pairs of sets, of possible (and perhaps impossible) entities. Typically, these entities are states of affairs. Or rather, we're treating them as states of affairs, but allowing that some of them do not (and perhaps could not) obtain. But what on earth is a state of affairs that does not obtain? Here are three potential options:

(OPTION 1) There exist merely possible concrete states of affairs, making up other possible worlds. 'Obtaining' (relative to world *w*) means existing at (as part of) world *w*. Non-obtaining states of affairs (relative to our wolds) are otherworldly states of affairs.

(OPTION 2) Some states of affairs do not exist (but remain legitimate objects of quantification). The obtaining states of affairs are those that exist.

(OPTION 3) There exist 'ersatz' states of affairs, in addition to the concrete ones. An ersatz state of affairs obtains when it corresponds to some concrete state of affairs.

These approaches are modelled on the main options in the metaphysics of possible worlds. The first takes its cue from the genuine modal realism of Lewis (1986), McDaniel (2004), and Yagisawa (2010). On this approach, all possible worlds are ontologically on a par with our own. The second is a broadly Meinongian approach, defended (in the case of worlds) by Priest (2005). The third approach is based on ersatz modal realism, on which possible worlds other than our own are actually existing ersatz representations.

If you don't like genuine modal realism about possible worlds, then you're going to hate the corresponding genuine realist view about possible states of affairs. All of the worries we have with genuine modal realism—principally, with its central thesis that there exist entities beyond the actual entities—apply equally to genuine realism about possible states of affairs. And, to make things worse, the view has issues of its own.

In fact, there seems to be a quick knock-down argument against genuine realism about possible states of affairs. I'm not wearing a hat, but I could have been. Both states of affairs, *that I'm wearing a hat* and *that I'm not wearing a hat*, are possible. According to genuine realism about possible states of affairs, all possible states of affairs exist, are real, and have the same ontological status. So, on that view, reality includes both states of affairs, *that I'm wearing a hat* and *that I'm not wearing a hat*. Reality is inconsistent! And since the existence of a state of affairs makes the corresponding proposition true, the contradictory propositions ⟨I am wearing a hat⟩ and ⟨I am not wearing a hat⟩ are both true.

One may respond that those possible states of affairs are parts of distinct possible worlds. No possible world contains both of them (because, although they're each possible, they aren't jointly possible). What's possible is whatever obtains at some possible world. So the contradiction, I'm wearing a hat and not wearing a hat, isn't possible. Consistency is restored.

This response is no solution. A genuine realist (either about possible worlds or about possible states of affairs) needs some standpoint from which she can assert her thesis. But there is no possible world which contains all those entities in which she believes. They are distributed across all the possible worlds. So, if we insist strictly that what's possible is whatever obtains at some possible world or other, then genuine realism (either about worlds or about states of affairs) is ruled impossible from the get-go.

To assert her thesis, a genuine realist cannot take the standpoint of this or that world only. She wants to describe all of modal space in one go. But she also wants what she says to be possible. So she needs a sense of possibility which isn't restricted to the goings on at some possible world or other. Divers (1999) has a good suggestion: when talking about modal space at large, both 'possibly, A' and 'necessarily, A' have the same content as just 'A'. That way, she may take her thesis to be true, necessarily true, and possibly true, even though no possible world realises her ontology as a whole. (I raise worries about Divers's approach in Jago 2016a.)

Nevertheless, genuine realism about possible states of affairs is still stuck with contradictory states of affairs, even though the contradiction does not obtain at any particular possible world. A contradiction $A, \neg A$ entails any B whatsoever. This is disastrous: genuine realism about states of affairs will entail arbitrary sentences, including the negation of the very view being put forward.

Note that the general problem here does not depend on having negative states of affairs in the ontology. Suppose there's no (actual or possible) negative states of affairs at all. Nevertheless, I could be wearing a completely red hat, and I could be wearing a completely green hat. Those possible states of affairs are metaphysically incompatible. If both exist, as genuine realism entails, then reality is impossible. And we can't be having that.

Some philosophers embrace, rather than shy away from, contradictions. *Dialethists* hold that there are, in fact, true contradictions, but that these don't entail arbitrary conclusions. That is, they reject the *explosion principle*: $A, \neg A \vDash B$. But this move won't help in the current situation. If all possible states of affairs exist, then any possible truth is true. The problem isn't to do with our logic entailing arbitrary truths; it's to do with our ontology making arbitrary (possible) propositions true.

The second option mooted above is Meinongian in spirit. It allows that some entities do not exist. On this view, it makes sense to talk about and quantify over entities which lack existence. The suggestion is that merely possible states of affairs be placed in this category.

To avoid the problems faced by the genuine realist, the Meinongian must allow that some states of affairs do not act as truthmakers. Rather, she will say, only the existing ones make anything true. For if all states of affairs act as truthmakers, and there are contradictory (but non-existent) states of affairs, then there are true contradictions (simpliciter), and we are back to the problems from above. So the Meinongian should say that an entity is a truthmaker only if it exists.

But then, what makes it true that some states of affairs don't exist? In general, the truthmakers for such propositions are their instances. So the only candidate truthmakers for

(8.20) ⟨Some states of affairs do not exist⟩

are states of affairs that do not exist. But we've just debarred all such states of affairs from acting as truthmakers. So (8.20) has no truthmakers. It's false. This entails that all states of affairs exist, contrary to the Meinongian view. Meinongianism about possible states of affairs is a non-starter.

Ersatz states of affairs avoid these worries. They count as states of affairs just as rubber ducks count as ducks, which is to say, not at all. They themselves do not constitute something's being the case, for they merely represent real states of affairs. So they do not make propositions true (other than propositions about the existence of ersatz states of affairs).

What kind of entity are they? The simplest approach is that the ersatz state of affairs representing *that Fa* is the ordered pair containing F and a themselves, in that order: $\langle\!\langle F, a \rangle\!\rangle$. Such entities look very similar to the set-theoretic, Russellian versions of structured propositions (§1.2, §8.4), you might think. And you'd be right. But then our current notion of propositions, understood in terms of sets of ersatz states of affairs, inherits the problems of the structured propositions account (§8.4). Neither approach captures the essential link between a given proposition and the entities that would make it true or false, were they to exist.

An adequate solution to our problem should be 'ersatz', in the sense that the entities standing for merely possible states of affairs cannot be genuine states of affairs. But they cannot be 'mere' representations of states of affairs, for these will not maintain the essential link we require between a proposition and its would-be truthmakers.

My suggestion is this. States of affairs have natures. These natures provide us with a way of talking meaningfully about states of affairs that do not obtain. We can talk about the nature of *that a is F*, even if there is no state of affairs *that a is F*, just as we can talk about the nature of the round square, or of my merely possible sister. This in turn gives us a way to make sense of 'non-obtaining states of affairs'. We should understand the idea as picking out a nature which corresponds to no actual state of affairs. Let's say that a state-of-affairs nature is *realised* when there exists a corresponding state of affairs.

We should then view (single) propositions as sets of *natures* of states of affairs. Since these natures actually exist, we then have no trouble explaining how propositions actually exist. A (single) proposition is true when one of its members is realised. Importantly, this approach maintains the essential link between a proposition and its would-be truthmakers, as follows. A proposition (qua set) is essentially linked to its members and each of its members (qua state-of-affairs nature) is essentially linked to a (possible or impossible) state of affairs.

How might we understand the natures of states of affairs? That will depend on our preferred account of states of affairs (chapter 4). Here is one tentative suggestion, built on the *fundamental tie* view (§4.1) which incorporates both a positive and a negative fundamental tie §5.6). On that view, states of affairs (both positive and negative) have constituents, tied together (positively or negatively) to form a unified whole. The identities of these states of affairs are given by the identities of their constituents plus the kind of tie involved. The nature of *that a is F* is to be the positive state of affairs involving *a*'s possessing *F*; and similarly, the nature of *that a isn't F* is to be the negative state of affairs involving *a*'s not possessing *F*. In general, the nature of a state of affairs involves the nature of its constituents, plus the nature of the tie involved.

My suggestion is that these are unified, structured wholes, just as the corresponding states of affairs are. The nature of *that a is F* involves the natures of *a* and of *F*, bound together by the nature of the positive tie. (And similarly for the nature of *that a isn't F*.) These states-of-affairs-natures are not themselves states of affairs. The nature of *that a is F* does not make it true that *a* is *F*. That requires the concrete state of affairs *that a is F* to exist, which is typically a contingent matter. The nature of *that a is F*, by contrast, is a necessary existent. This allows these natures to play the role described above, as members of propositions.

8.7 Same-Saying and Aboutness

We utter declarative sentences to say things to one another. What we thereby communicate is not the utterance itself, since we can say the same thing in different ways. As Frege says:

> If someone wants to say the same today as he expressed yesterday using the word "today", he must replace this word with "yesterday". ... The case is the same with words like "here" and "there". (Frege 1956, 296)

Similarly, two people can say the same thing about someone or something in different ways. If I'm talking to Anna about her knitting, I'll use 'your knitting', she'll use 'my knitting', and others might use 'her knitting' or 'Anna's knitting' to say the same thing: *that Anna's knitting is great*.

In these examples, the concept of *saying* is used in the sense of *what is communicated*, as opposed to the particular way in which that content is communicated. The examples so far all involve indexical terms ('I', 'you', 'today', 'yesterday'). A similar phenomenon occurs with co-denoting names. Utterances of 'Hesperus is a planet' and 'Phosphorus is a planet' say the same thing in the sense that each is about the same thing. Suppose Anna and Bob are arguing, Anna insisting that *that planet now visible* is Hesperus, whereas Bob insists that it's Phosphorus. There's clearly a sense in which they're not really disagreeing at all, for they are both correctly identifying the planet they see.

Nevertheless, in this case, both parties are genuinely informed when they come to learn that the planet is correctly called both 'Hesperus' and 'Phosphorus'. What they lacked was *a posteriori* knowledge, not linguistic competence. This shows that the notion *what is said* in an utterance does not align with the meaning of the utterance, or with the speaker's beliefs, or with common knowledge in the conversation.

The question I want to address in this section is: in general, under what conditions do utterances of two sentences '*A*' and '*B*' say the same thing? (Alternatively, under what conditions do speakers of those utterances say the same thing as one another?) A particularly interesting instance of this question occurs when '*A*' and '*B*' are logically related in certain ways. The question then becomes: which logical operations preserve same-saying? We would like answers to the following kind of question:

(8.21) Does '$A \vee (B \wedge C)$' say the same as '$(A \vee B) \wedge (A \vee C)$'?

(8.22) Does '$A \wedge A$' say the same as 'A'? How about '$A \vee A$'?

(8.23) Does '$\neg\neg A$' say the same as 'A'?

(8.24) Does '$\neg(A \wedge B)$' say the same as '$\neg A \vee \neg B$'?

Call this general form of question *the logical same-saying issue*. To my knowledge, the issue hasn't been discussed in the same-saying literature. (These kinds of question are often discussed in the *relevant logic* literature, under the question of *content* (e.g. Brady 2006). I'll say more on the connection between same-saying and relevant logic below.)

Here's a condition any suitable answer to the general same-saying question should meet:

(ABOUTNESS) *A* says the same as *B* only if *A* and *B* are about the same thing(s).

I'll assume we have a fairly good grip on words, or sentences, 'being about the same thing'. 'Hesperus'-sentences and 'Phosphors'-sentences are both about the planet Venus (perhaps amongst other things). Roughly, sentences are about the things to which their words refer. We might characterise 'Bertie is snuffling' as being about Bertie and *snuffling*, or we might characterise it as being about whether Bertie is snuffling. (I take these to be distinct but complementary ways of talking about *aboutness*.)

'*A*' and '*B*' can be about precisely the same things and yet not say the same as one another. 'Bertie is snuffling' and 'Bertie is not snuffling' are both about Bertie and *snuffling* (or about whether he is snuffling), yet each says the opposite of the other. That's why (ABOUTNESS) is formulated as a necessary but insufficient condition for same-saying. I'll say a little more on the *aboutness* relation below.

The simplest answer to the general same-saying question is this:

(SAMESAYING) *A* says the same as *B* iff $\langle A \rangle = \langle B \rangle$

Whether that's plausible depends on one's account of propositions. On the sets-of-possible-worlds view (§8.3), it isn't plausible at all. Saying that $1 + 1 = 2$ is clearly not the same as saying that properties exist, or that Bertie is either snuffling or not. But all are necessary truths, and hence captured by the same set of possible worlds. For similar reasons, the sets-of-possible-worlds view fails (ABOUTNESS).

Neither is (SAMESAYING) plausible on the structured propositions view (§8.4). For on that view, 'Bertie is snuffling and wheezing' expresses a distinct proposition from 'Bertie is wheezing and snuffling', and yet these are two ways to say the same thing about Bertie. But the view does satisfy (ABOUTNESS). Structured propositions are about (some or all of) their constituents, and so sentences expressing the same proposition are guaranteed to be about the same things.

I'm going to argue that (SAMESAYING) is correct, so long as we understand propositions as truthmaker conditions, as I suggested above (§8.5). This approach provides a plausible general answer to the same-saying question. I'll also argue that a truthmaker-based approach provides the only adequate answer to the logical same-saying issue. And finally, a truthmaker-based approach affords us a simple characterisation of the things a proposition is about.

If propositions are truthmaker-conditions, then (SAMESAYING) gets the same-saying cases involving indexicals and co-referring names right. The possible truthmakers for 'today is sunny' are defined by taking 'today' fixed in the context of utterance. If today is Monday 4th April 2016, then the relevant states of affairs capture all the possible ways in which Monday 4th April 2016 could be sunny. The same goes for 'yesterday was sunny', uttered on Tuesday 5th. Its possible truthmakers are the same. The two sentences express the same truthmaker condition, and so (SAMESAYING) predicts, correctly, that they say the same thing. The same goes for the 'Hesperus'/'Phosphorus' and the 'my'/'your'/'her' cases.

More interesting is what the truthmaker-condition account says about the logical same-saying issue. It seems clear that distinct but logically related sentences can be used to say the same thing, *in virtue of the logical relation between them*. Any utterance of 'it's warm and sunny' says the same thing as an utterance of 'it's sunny and warm' in the same context. In general, in the same context, utterances of '$A \land B$' and '$B \land A$' say the same thing.

We cannot explain this feature in terms of the necessary equivalence of '$A \land B$' and '$B \land A$' (or their equivalence in classical logic), because there are equivalent sentences, utterances of which do not say the same thing in a given context. Consider a mathematical example:

(8.25) I can colour in any map with just three colours, so that no two adjacent areas have the same colour.

(8.26) I can take one lemon and one orange, and thereby end up with three more fruits than I started.

Both claims are mathematically impossible, and hence (classically) equivalent. Yet utterances of (8.25) and (8.26) do not say the same thing. Each speaker claims to be able to do *different* (and, unbeknownst to them, impossible) things. The same holds of logical examples:

(8.27) The Liar is both true and false.

(8.28) Claims about large cardinal numbers are neither true nor false.

Here, both statements are classically unsatisfiable (and so classically equivalent), yet they say very different things. Suppose that (8.27)'s speaker is a dialethist, such as Priest (1979, 1987), who diverges from classical logic in rejecting the explosion principle (that everything follows from a contradiction). And suppose (8.28)'s speaker is a mathematical intuitionist, such as Dummett (1978, 1993), who rejects excluded middle. It is absurd to think that, in stating their different philosophical positions, they say the same thing as one another. So it is not the case that, in uttering any two classically equivalent sentences, the speakers thereby say the same thing as one another.

A much better account of the logic of same-saying is given by *exact truthmaker equivalence* (§7.3). Recall that A and B are exactly equivalent when they share all their truthmakers (in all truthmaker models). This account predicts that, for each of the following pairs (a/b), utterances of them (in a common context) say the same:

(8.29a) It's cold and wet

(8.29b) It's wet and cold

(8.30a) Cath or Dave will turn up, and Ed will turn up

(8.30b) Either Cath and Ed will turn up, or else Dave and Ed will

(8.31a) Either Cath doesn't like Dave or she doesn't like Ed

(8.31b) Cath doesn't like both Dave and Ed

These pairs are intuitively clear cases of same-saying. So exact equivalence looks to be in good standing as an analysis of same-saying.

There are other notions of logical equivalence that get these results correct. *First-degree entailment* (Anderson and Belnap 1963) (which we met in §7.5, and which corresponds to *inexact* truthmaking) also verifies these equivalences, whilst distinguishing between classically equivalent contents. Indeed, relevant logics in general are often seen as ways to preserve content from premises to conclusion in an entailment. (Brady (2006) develops a semantics for a (weak version of) relevant logic in terms of *content inclusion*, for example.) If that's right, then one might expect relevant equivalence to amount to sameness of content, which should in turn amount to same-saying.

But first-degree entailment (and hence relevant logics) do not provide a good account of either same-saying or sameness of content. First-degree entailment treats both $A \land (A \lor B)$ and $A \lor (A \land B)$ as being equivalent to A. But these equivalences do not preserve what is said. Just consider:

(8.32) Bertie is snuffling, and either he's snuffling or Puss is stretching.

(8.33) Either Bertie is snuffling, or he's snuffling and Puss is stretching.

Neither says (just) that Bertie is snuffling, so neither says the same as 'Bertie is snuffling'. Neither is just about Bertie (and whether he's snuffling); both are also about Puss (and whether she's stretching). So again, given (ABOUTNESS), neither (8.32) nor (8.33) says the same as 'Bertie is snuffling'. So relevant equivalence is not a good criterion for same-saying.

This point is powerful, since just about every logic treats both $A \land (A \lor B)$ and $A \lor (A \land B)$ as being equivalent to A. The truthmaker semantics for exact entailment is one of the few systems that draws semantic distinctions between these sentences. So we have a strong argument in favour of analysing same-saying in terms of exact equivalence. Moreover, given the view of propositions as truthmaker-conditions, $\langle A \rangle$ and $\langle B \rangle$ are exactly equivalent iff $\langle A \rangle = \langle B \rangle$. So '$A$' and '$B$' say the same thing (in a context) iff $\langle A \rangle = \langle B \rangle$, just as (SAMESAYING) says.

The truthmaker approach to propositions and same-saying also allows for a neat characterisation of a sentence's or proposition's *subject matter*. This is what that sentence or proposition is about. Recall from above that we can say that 'Bertie is snuffling' is about whether Bertie is snuffling, or that it is about Bertie and *snuffling*. These ways of talking are complementary each to the other. Taking the former way as our starting point, we identify what a sentence or proposition is about with a set of states of affairs. We then define the objects and properties it is about as those that appear as constituents of any of those states of affairs.

There are a number of ways we can implement the first step. The simplest would be to identify the subject matter of a sentence with the proposition it expresses. But this will give us the strange result that 'A' and '$\neg A$' have different and indeed incompatible subject matters (since the truthmakers for 'A' and '$\neg A$' do not overlap). But this is the wrong result. 'A' and '$\neg A$' are incompatible precisely because they say opposite things about the same subject matter.

We improve matters by taking the subject matter of 'A' to be the set of all its possible truthmakers and falsemakers: $|A|^+ \cup |A|^-$. (If we adopt the double proposition account from §8.5, then we obtain A's subject matter by 'flattening' $\langle A \rangle$ into a single set, $|A|^+ \cup |A|^-$.) This approach gives the correct results for negation: A and $\neg A$ coincide on their subject matter.

This approach still gives strange results, however. It allows that $A \wedge B$ and $A \vee B$ can have different subject matters. They differ in their truthmakers (and falsemakers) because conjunction pairwise sums together elements from $|A|^+$ and $|B|^+$, whereas disjunction takes their union, $|A|^+ \cup |B|^+$. This gives incorrect results for subject matter. Both $A \wedge B$ and $A \vee B$ are about whatever A is about, plus whatever B is about. They differ in what they say about that subject matter, but not in the subject matter itself.

There are two ways we can avoid this result. One is to take A's subject matter to be given by all the atomic parts of its truthmakers and falsemakers:

$$\{x \mid x \sqsubseteq \bigsqcup (|A|^+ \cup |A|^-) \;\&\; x \text{ is atomic}\}$$

The other is to take A's subject matter to be the sum of all its truthmakers and falsemakers, $\bigsqcup(|A|^+ \cup |A|^-)$. Both approaches give similar results, given that:

$$\bigsqcup\{x \mid x \sqsubseteq \bigsqcup (|A|^+ \cup |A|^-) \;\&\; x \text{ is atomic}\} = \bigsqcup(|A|^+ \cup |A|^-)$$

This approach to subject matter allows us to make sense of notions like *content inclusion* (Fine 2017a,b; Yablo 2014). If we identify A's subject matter with $\bigsqcup(|A|^+ \cup |A|^-)$, then A's subject matter includes B's just in case:

$$\bigsqcup(|B|^+ \cup |B|^-) \sqsubseteq \bigsqcup(|A|^+ \cup |A|^-)$$

This notion of inclusion, based on subject matter, ignores whether that subject matter is being affirmed or denied. So, for example, $A \wedge B$'s subject matter will include $\neg A$'s, even though the latter content is incompatible with the former.

We can define a notion of content inclusion which avoids this consequence, taking A's content to include B's just in case:

$$\bigsqcup |B|^+ \sqsubseteq \bigsqcup |A|^+ \text{ and } \bigsqcup |B|^- \sqsubseteq \bigsqcup |A|^-$$

On this account, $A \wedge B$'s content includes A's content, even though $A \wedge B$ does not exactly entail A. We also have that $A \vee B$'s content includes A's content (so content inclusion need not preserve truth).

Content inclusion can in turn be used to explain *partial truth*. The intuitive idea is that 'Wittgenstein was one of the greatest female philosophers' is partly true (since he was one of the greatest philosophers), but not wholly true (since he wasn't female). A simple take on partial truth has it that $\langle A \rangle$ is (at least) partly true when it content-includes some (wholly) true $\langle B \rangle$. (Fine (2016) gives an alternative in terms of *analytic containment*, based on Angell 1989.)

Finally, let's return to *aboutness*. We will analyse what a sentence is about (in a context) in terms of what the proposition it expresses is about. So what, precisely, is a proposition $\langle A \rangle$ about? Let's write $Ab\langle A \rangle$ for the set of things $\langle A \rangle$ is about. According to Merricks (2007), 'a truth must be *about* its truthmaker' (2007, 32). On that view, $Ab\langle A \rangle$ is the set of $\langle A \rangle$'s truthmakers, $|A|^+$. (So, on our view of single propositions, $Ab\langle A \rangle = \langle A \rangle$.)

This view, however, implies that false propositions aren't about anything. Perhaps the intended view is that propositions are about their *possible* truthmakers. But even then, necessary falsehoods will be about nothing. That hardly seems any better. Moreover, as already noted, Merricks's view has the bizarre consequence that $\langle A \rangle$ and $\langle \neg A \rangle$ are not about the same things (and, when $\langle A \rangle$ is logically contingent, there is nothing which both $\langle A \rangle$ and $\langle \neg A \rangle$ are about). Merricks's view also has the consequence that $\langle A \vee B \rangle$ is about things which $\langle A \wedge B \rangle$ is not about (since $|A \wedge B|^+ \subseteq |A \vee B|^+$ but, in general, $|A \wedge B|^+ \neq |A \vee B|^+$). We should avoid each of these consequences.

Merricks argues that truthmaker theorists are compelled to say that propositions are about their truthmakers, 'for only then would the existence of a truthmaker for a truth imply that there is something that that truth is about' (2007, 26). But that inference is clearly faulty. All that's required is that $Ab\langle A \rangle$ be some function of $\langle A \rangle$'s possible truthmakers (and perhaps possible falsemakers too). That is enough for the possible existence of truthmakers to imply that $\langle A \rangle$ is about something.

Aboutness and subject matter are intimately related. We could take $\langle A \rangle$ to be about each part of its subject matter. On that view, $\langle A \rangle$ is about all of its possible truthmakers and falsemakers, plus all combinations thereof. It may be more natural, however, to restrict $Ab\langle A \rangle$ to the atomic parts of $\langle A \rangle$'s subject matter: all of the possible states of affairs which would contribute to $\langle A \rangle$'s truth or falsity, were they to exist. (This avoids the implication of the previous suggestion that a contingent proposition $\langle A \rangle$ is somehow about *whether $A \wedge \neg A$*.)

An even better approach takes $\langle A \rangle$ to be about the *constituents* of the proper parts of its subject matter. These are the properties and the (natures of) particulars which make up those possible states of affairs. On this approach, ⟨Bertie is snuffling⟩ is equally about Bertie and about *snuffling*. Is it also about *that Bertie is snuffling*? We may admit an inclusive notion of aboutness on which it is, as well as a restricted notion on which it is not (so that the former properly includes the latter). Since both are defined in terms of ⟨A⟩'s subject matter, nothing much hangs on which notion we use.

This approach has a clear advantage over its main rival, which comes from the theory of structured propositions (§8.4). On the Russellian version of that approach, an atomic proposition is a structured complex containing particulars, properties, and relations, and is about those very entities. On the Fregean version, the constituents are Fregean senses, descriptive conditions, or property clusters, which uniquely pick out particulars, properties, and relations, and which are about those particulars, properties, and relations. Rasmussen (2014) defends a variant of the latter view.

On this view, conjunctive Russellian propositions contain the *conjunction* function (or whatever we take to be the semantic value of '∧'), disjunctive Russellian propositions contain the *disjunction* function, and so on. Similarly for logically complex Fregean propositions and senses or properties uniquely denoting those functions. As a consequence, conjunctions will be about the *conjunction* function, disjunctions about the *disjunction* function, negations about *negation*, and so on. This is unpalatable. ⟨Anna is singing and Liz is dancing⟩ is about Anna, Liz, singing, and dancing; it isn't also about *conjunction*. We can't avoid this consequence by, as it were, plucking entities from the analysis. For some propositions are about *conjunction*: ⟨*conjunction* is a logical operator⟩ is one.

The account I've offered here does a good job of explaining why ⟨*conjunction* is a logical operator⟩ is about *conjunction*, whereas ⟨Anna is singing and Liz is dancing⟩ is not. The former is made true by a state of affairs involving *conjunction* as a constituent, whereas the latter is not. The latter is a conjunctive state of affairs, the sum of its conjuncts. But mereological sums do not involve some further constituent, the *mereological sum* operation.

This analysis of *aboutness* agrees with Merricks's on the issue of existential propositions. He says '*that a human exists* stands in the *aboutness* relation to me because, first, it is—in the more familiar sense of 'about'—'about humans', and second, I am a human' (2007, 152). In general, an existential proposition will be about each of its witnesses. (In effect, this approach does not distinguish between an existential and the corresponding infinite disjunction. We're committed to that result, given our analysis of propositions in terms of truthmakers and falsemakers.) But it's not clear to me whether this is the right result.

It's not clearly the wrong result. For one thing, we sometimes use existentials to talk about particular things. Anna, glass of Pedro Ximenez in hand, is joyously singing along to the *Cabaret* soundtrack. '*Someone's* having fun', I shout through the door. My utterance is clearly about Anna. The same considerations apply if definite descriptions are understood as existentially quantified phrases. 'The greatest rock band is playing' is about Ziggy and the Spiders from Mars, not merely about the properties *greatest rock band* and *playing*. (Dissenters may substitute Led Zeppelin.)

These examples show that existential propositions are sometimes about their witnesses. Note that their effectiveness does not depend on the uniqueness of their designation: on finding Anna and Liz singing along to *Caberet*, I can say 'someone's having fun' to talk about both Anna and Liz. Given the choice between a theory on which existentials are always about their witnesses, and a theory on which they never are, I'll take the former.

It's worth noting that, in these examples, the proposition's *actual* truthmaker plays an important role. 'The greatest rock band' could—in some deeply musically impoverished possible world—have picked out my high-school punk band. But 'the greatest rock band is playing' isn't about that particular rabble. Interestingly, our theory does allow a special role for actual truthmakers.

Recall that (what I've been calling) 'non-actual states of affairs' are to be understood in terms of states-of-affairs-natures (§8.6). So, given any true proposition's subject matter, its actual truthmaker(s) stand apart, ontologically, as the parts which are genuine states of affairs. So we can devise a notion of *aboutness*, call it *about*$_@$, which focuses on the constituents of genuine states of affairs found in a proposition's subject matter. Note one happy implication of this approach: 'the greatest rock band are playing' is not about$_@$ my high-school punk band, even though it is an actual entity which could have been the greatest rock band.

There is clearly much more to be said about aboutness, subject matter, and the various notions of content inclusion. Yablo (2014) discusses these concepts in detail, offering a fine-grained possible worlds-based account. (Osorio-Kupferblum (2016) summarises and critically discusses Yablo's approach.) Simchen (2012) discusses the modal properties of the *aboutness* relation. My suggestion here is that the truthmaker approach offers a natural and elegant way to account for these concepts.

8.8 Chapter Summary

I've argued that neither the sets-of-worlds approach (§8.3) nor the structured propositions approach (§8.4) can account for the metaphysical nature of propositions, as set out in (PROP) (§8.2). Instead, I proposed to treat propositions as *truthmaker conditions* (§8.5): sets of possible (and perhaps impossible) entities. I argued that we can understand merely possible states of affairs in terms of their (actually existing) natures (§8.6). This approach gives us a powerful way to understand semantics notions including *same-saying* and *aboutness* (§8.7).

9

Dealing with Liars

In this final chapter, I want to investigate what the theory of truth developed so far tells us about the Liar paradox (and other paradoxes involving truth). I'll begin by reviewing the paradox (§9.1) and why it is such a difficult issue to solve (§9.2). I'll then argue that approaches which weaken the underlying logic (§§9.3–9.5), or restrict or alter the T-scheme (§9.6), are not good options. Instead, I'll argue that our account of propositions from chapter 8 already provides an adequate solution: there is no proposition for the Liar sentence to express (§9.8). I discuss the consequences of this view for meaning and logic in §9.9.

9.1 The Liar

WE CAN HARDLY tell a convincing story about what truth is without mentioning the paradoxes it seems to generate. On the face of it, adding a way of talking about truth to a consistent theory is easy. We simply add a predicate 'is true', and rules to the effect that '*A* is true' is true just in case *A* is true. But that simple addition is often enough to render the initial theory absurd.

In this section, I'll introduce some of the paradoxes of truth (or, as they're often called, the *semantic paradoxes*). Then I'll look at potential solutions to the paradoxes. My own will appear in §9.8. Some of this material will be a little technical. That's partly because (as with any paradox) we need to be very careful with our reasoning, and partly because making each step of reasoning explicit can often shed light on where potential solutions lie. If you're unfamiliar with modern proof theory (and in particular the sequent calculus), there's a short introduction in appendix 10. (If you're looking for a proper introduction to proof theory, Restall (2016) is a great philosopher-friendly resource.)

The most famous semantic paradox of all is the Liar. In its simplest form, it concerns a sentence saying of itself that it is false, like this:

(L) This sentence is false.

The problem then is: is (L) true or false? First suppose that it's true. Then what it says is the case. But (L) says that (L) is false, so we infer that (L) is false, contradicting our original assumption. So suppose instead that (L) is false. Then what it says is incorrect. But (L) says that (L) is false. If this is incorrect, then (L) must be true, contradicting our assumption. In short, (L) is a problem: if it's true then it's false, and if it's false then it's true. But presumably, it must be either true or false, and cannot be both. That's the (simple version of the) Liar paradox. It's an old problem. (Dutilh Novaes (2008, 2011) discusses mediaeval solutions to the Liar, for example.) And it's very hard to solve.

On first encountering the Liar, many people have the feeling of a conjuring trick. So we need to be especially careful, both in our formulation of the Liar sentence, and in our reasoning about it. Let's begin with a look at the Liar sentence itself. It is designed to say something of itself, which it does by referring to itself using the demonstrative phrase, 'this sentence'. That seems clear enough. An alternative way to formulate a Liar sentence is using a name, say, 'L_1', which we stipulate to be a name for the following sentence:

(L_1) L_1 is false.

Then L_1 refers to itself, and says of itself that it's false.

A popular reaction at this point is that there's something dodgy about a sentence referring to itself. How can a name, like 'L_1', refer to a sentence which includes that very name? But the worry here is easily overcome. For one thing, there are self-referring sentences which are clearly true. Here are some examples:

(9.1) This sentence contains five words.

(9.2) This is an English sentence.

(9.3) Sentence (9.3) contains the word 'word'.

Take a moment to check whether (9.1) is correct. You probably just counted the words in (9.1). If you did, then you clearly understand what it means. Notice that you counted the words in *that very sentence*. No one seems to be puzzled about which sentence (9.1) is talking about. The same goes for the other examples. So self-reference, either via a name or via the demonstrative 'this sentence', is not in general a problem. As Jenkins and Nolan (2008) say, 'it seems unlikely that what features the object language has matters much at all for whether there are Liar-like paradoxes around' (2008, 72).

A more refined version of the self-reference worry goes like this. We might be able to formulate self-referential sentences in a messy language like English, but can we do so in a precise, formal language? The answer is yes, we can, so long as we have a suitable bag of tricks for naming sentences. Here's one (very precise) way to name sentences: we assign each symbol an integer and come up with some numerical function which takes in the sequence of integers corresponding to the symbols in a given sentence and outputs a unique integer. We then treat that integer as a name for that sentence.

(One way to do this is via the *Gödel number*, gS, of the sentence S. The technical details aren't important, so long as we can always recover the sentence from its number. We can in the case of Gödel numbering, due to the unique prime factorisation theorem.)

Now suppose our language contains the ability to express what we've just done (that is, names for the integers, plus arithmetical predicates). Then it's a mathematical fact that that language contains self-referential sentences An, where n is an integer which corresponds to that very sentence. This holds for any open sentence Ax with one free variable. So, in particular, there is a sentence '$\neg \text{True}(n)$', where n codes that very sentence. Indeed, if $\ulcorner A \urcorner$ is the numeral which codes sentence A and Bx is any open sentence with one free variable, we can show that a suitable arithmetical theory $\mathcal{T}$ in that language has theorems of the form $B(\ulcorner A \urcorner) \leftrightarrow A$. As an instance, $\neg \text{True}(\ulcorner A \urcorner) \leftrightarrow A$ is a theorem of $\mathcal{T}$.

The second point to make, in response to self-reference worries, is that Liar-like paradoxes can arise without self-reference. The easiest case to consider is the following pair of sentences:

(9.4) The sentence below is false.

(9.5) The sentence above is true.

If (9.4) is true, then (9.5) is false, and so (9.4) is false: contradiction. If (9.4) is false, on the other hand, then (9.5) is true, and so (9.4) is true: contradiction. Neither sentence is self-referential, but the two together behave like a Liar sentence.

We can generate similar cases without cycles of reference at all, as pointed out by Yablo (1993). Consider an infinite sequence of sentences, $S_1, S_2, \ldots$, each saying that all subsequent sentences in the sequence are false. Each sentence has the form:

(S_n) For every $m > n$, sentence S_m is false.

Suppose S_n is true. Then S_{n+1} is false, so for some $m > n + 1$, S_m is true. But then S_n is false: contradiction. On the other hand, if S_n is false, then for some $m > n$, S_m is true. Reasoning as before (with S_m in place of S_n), S_m must be false: contradiction.

And finally, we can generate Liar-like paradox without (strictly speaking) referring to sentences at all. We can do so by describing, or quantifying over, certain sentences. Consider the following sentences:

(9.6) The sentence written on my board is false.

(9.7) Some sentence written on my board is false.

(9.8) All sentences written on my board are false.

Suppose I write (9.6) on my board, so that it's the only sentence there. Then it describes itself, and we get a Liar paradox via the usual reasoning. Similarly for (9.7) and (9.8), if each is the only sentence written on my board.

These cases (9.6)–(9.8) are particularly curious, since whether they are paradoxical depends on what else is written on my board. They are all *contingent Liar sentences*. If (9.6) isn't the only sentence on my board, then it's simply (and non-paradoxically) false. (That's assuming that truth-conditions for 'the F' require a unique F. If there's indeterminacy when 'the F' is not uniquely satisfied, then (9.6) is indeterminate. Either way, we don't get a Liar-like situation.) Similarly, whether (9.7) or (9.8) is paradoxical depends on whether there are other sentences on my board (and whether they are true or false). Indeed, all three sentences might all be written on my board together without generating a Liar-like situation.

It's certainly curious that a sentence can be unproblematic when written on a crowded board but then, as the other sentences are rubbed off, that very same sentence becomes paradoxical. Contingent liars are especially tricky to solve for theories that say Liar-like sentences are meaningless or that one cannot make a genuine statement by uttering one of them. Goldstein (1985) suggests a view along these lines:

> No competent speaker would seriously assert that the very statement he is making is not true. ... If someone seriously wished to *assert* one of [the Liar-type sentences] we should have to declare him semantically incompetent ... We can attach no sense to what the person who flouts our semantical principles says; he uses our words but does not use them our way. What he utters—his sentences—may be in perfect grammatical order, but *what he means* is inaccessible to us. (Goldstein 1985, 12)

Contingent Liars show that this cannot be right. To test a student, I might write some sentences on my board and ask her, which are true? She thinks some are true, some false. I correct her by uttering (9.8).

That's clearly a meaningful conversational move, containing a genuine assertion via my token of (9.8). It clearly doesn't matter whether I speak (9.8) or write it down—I could have emailed (9.8) to the student later on. But if so doing produces a meaningful utterance, it is absurd to think that writing (9.6) on my board would not likewise produce a meaningful utterance. And it cannot matter whether there are other sentences on the board. The domain of quantification does not affect what a quantified sentence means. The domain of quantification plays a role in the truth-condition of the utterance, not in what the utterance means.

Neither can we pin the problem (in all cases) on some rational failing of the speaker. After a long argument after a conference, I declare 'everything we've said so far today is false'. But, unbeknownst to me, the clock has just ticked past midnight, so that my statement is, at that point, the only one made by either of us on that day. It thus quantifies over a singleton domain containing only that very utterance, and paradox results. I may be to blame for talking shop past midnight or for not knowing what time it is. But neither is a rational error, in the way Goldstein suggests. Neither is the kind of error which would prevent my utterance from making a meaningful statement.

Contingent Liars show that (contingently) paradoxical sentences can be meaningful, and can be used with the intention of making a genuine statement. The view I'll develop in §9.8 has some similarities with Goldstein's later approach (Goldstein 2000, 2001). The point I want to underline here is that we cannot solve the Liar by claiming that it is (always, or in some situations) meaningless.

9.2 The Liar's Revenge

Once we accept that the Liar is meaningful, and that self-reference is not to blame, a common approach is to deny that the Liar must be either true or false. The form of the standard Liar reasoning suggests this move: after all, we establish that the Liar is true if false, and false if true. To get a contradiction from these conditionals, we further assume that the Liar is either true or false. But given that this assumption leads to paradox, it's natural to think that the Liar cannot be either true or false. It receives no truth-value, on this view. This is what Parsons (1984, 143) calls the *standard solution*.

The standard solution faces a severe difficulty. It seems to assert the following:

(9.9) Liar-like sentences are neither true nor false.

But now consider a variant on the standard Liar sentence:

(L^+) This sentence is not true.

This is the *strengthened* Liar sentence. It faces the same initial problem as the standard Liar: if it's true, then it's not true; and if it's not true, then it's true. So the standard solution will claim that (L^+) is neither true or false. This implies that (L^+) is not true. However, that's precisely what (L^+) says! So it appears that (L^+) is true, after all. For each of the Liar-like sentences in §9.1 above, there is a corresponding strengthened sentence, got from replacing 'is false' with 'is not true'. Similar problems apply to them all.

This is the *revenge* phenomenon. If a purported solution says that the Liar lacks some property P, then the revenge sentence takes the form,

(9.10) This sentence lacks property P.

That solution then seems to entail that the revenge sentence is true and, for many choices of P, this conclusion conflicts with that sentence's lacking the property P.

The issues here can be complex and subtle. To investigate them, it helps to have a specific view of truth on the table. Perhaps the most influential view which supports the standard solution is Kripke's 'Outline of a Theory of Truth' (1975). Kripke's is a formal theory of truth: an attempt to specify a consistent (or at least, a non-trivial) theory containing a truth-predicate and suitable rules for it.

Kripke's approach can be seen as an existence proof that a truth-predicate can, consistently, be contained in the object language (contrary to Tarski 1976). The idea is to construct a model in stages. In the first stage, sentences not containing the truth-predicate are classified into two groups: *true* and *false*. In each subsequent stage, we make True($\ulcorner A \urcorner$) true (or false) iff we previously made A true (or false). We repeat until we reach a fixed point (after infinitely many iterations). Some sentences (including the Liar) are assigned no truth-value in this fixpoint construction. Such sentences are neither true nor false: Kripke calls them *ungrounded*. But Kripke is able to show that True($\ulcorner A \urcorner$) is assigned the same status as A itself: each is true, false, or truth-valueless just in case the other is. (Sher (2002) discusses the details in an accessible way.)

The theory is formally consistent. But, as Kripke is well aware, the standard revenge problem persists. Ungrounded sentences are neither true nor false, hence not true. So, reflecting on the fixpoint construction, we can truthfully say of some ungrounded sentence A that A is not true (according to the model). But the model disagrees: if A is ungrounded, then so are True($\ulcorner A \urcorner$) and ¬True($\ulcorner A \urcorner$). So our model treats a truth about itself, that A is not true, as being ungrounded.

This discussion raises an important point: in an adequate philosophical theory of truth, we want the theory's decisions on the extensions of 'true' and 'false' to agree with what is true or false, according to the theory. In other words, we expect the theory's treatment of its own predicates, 'true' and 'false', to agree with our metalinguistic uses of 'true' and 'false', which we use to describe the theory. But this is not so in Kripke's fixpoint construction. (Related approaches to the Liar face similar revenge problems: see Jenkins 2007, 2008.)

The issue for Kripke's approach is not one of formal inconsistency. Rather, it is that we still have a notion of truth which cannot be captured in full in the object language. So in the end, Kripke accepts what McGee (1989, 531) calls *Tarski's commandment*:

(9.11) Thou shall not develop the semantics of a language within the language itself, but in an essentially richer metalanguage.

The problem with the commandment, of course, is that we also want a semantics for *English*, which contains its own truth-predicate. Kripke's approach doesn't give us a semantics for such a language. We need to look beyond the standard solution to the Liar.

9.3 Embracing Contradictions

We have tried to avoid saying that the Liar is both true and false. This has proved hard. So one option is to accept instead that the Liar is both true and false. This is the *dialetheist* solution to the Liar (Priest 1979, 1987, 2010). Dialetheism allows that some sentences are both true and false, but denies that, as a consequence, all sentences are true. That principle is at the core of classical logic: if any sentence were both true and false, then all would be true. Dialetheists thus deny classical logic. In its place, they adopt a *paraconsistent* notion of consequence, on which the inference from $A, \neg A$ to arbitrary conclusions B is not warranted. (This classically valid inference, $A, \neg A \vDash B$, is often called the *explosion principle*; paraconsistent logics, which reject the principle, are said to be non-explosive.)

A dialetheist distinguishes sharply between contradiction and absurdity. A paradox is a seemingly acceptable set of premises which nevertheless lead to absurdity. But since (by dialetheist lights) contradictions are not necessarily absurdities, the usual Liar reasoning does not establish a genuine paradox. It would be absurd to infer arbitrary conclusions from the Liar. But to make this step, we would need the principle that contradictions entail arbitrary conclusions, which is precisely what paraconsistent logicians (including dialetheists) reject. The dialetheist thus finds no issue in the standard Liar reasoning. The Liar sentence must be either true or false, and if it is either, it is both. Fine: it is both, replies the dialetheist; what's wrong with that? So long as we do not infer, further, that every B is true, no absurdity has been derived.

Whether it is conceptually coherent to assert and accept the dialetheist position is a tricky matter. It turns, in part, on the function we associate with expressing a negation. If the function of an assertion ¬*A* is to reject *A*, then dialetheism looks to be irrational. For then, the dialetheist who asserts a contradiction *A*, ¬*A* will be both accepting and rejecting the content of *A*, and that is surely rationally impermissible. But the dialetheist denies that this is the function of negation. In general, she claims, asserting (or accepting) ¬*A* is not the same as rejecting (or denying) *A*.

The issues are complex, and beyond the scope of my treatment here. My own view is that we need some way of signalling our rejection of a content in language, and, as a matter of empirical fact, our way of doing that is by saying 'no' and 'not' (Jago 2014). But I won't assume or argue for that view here.

The problem for the dialetheist—even if we assume the general view to be coherent—is that there are paradoxes of truth, similar to the Liar, on which dialetheism doesn't make any headway. One is Curry's paradox. Pick some sentence *B*, as clearly false or absurd as you like. The Curry sentence for *B* is:

(C) If (C) is true, then *B*.

The Curry paradox purports to prove *B*, as follows. First, we prove (C) by conditional proof, by assuming the antecedent and deriving the consequent. Assume that (C) is true. (This is (C)'s antecedent.) Then, by the T-scheme, (C) and, by *modus ponens*, *B*. Discharging the assumption, we've proved (C). So by the T-scheme, (C) is true and, by *modus ponens*, *B* follows (under no assumptions). So we've proved *B*, where *B* can be any sentence whatsoever! (Bimbo (2006) formulates more paradoxes along these lines.)

It won't help to claim that (C) is both true and false. For then it's true, and *B* with it. So dialetheism makes no progress on the problem. Neither will it help to point out that, by dialetheist lights, the material conditional *A* ⊃ *B* does not obey *modus ponens*. (That's because *A* ⊃ *B* is defined as ¬*A* ∨ *B*. When *A* is both true and false, both A and $\neg A \vee B$ are true, but this does not guarantee that B is true.) (C) is formulated using the English 'if ... then', which obeys *modus ponens*. All that's needed for the Curry paradox is *conditional proof* and *modus ponens* (which together encapsulate the meaning of 'if ... then') plus the T-scheme.

The Curry paradox is a problem for everyone, not just dialetheists. Both are paradoxes of truth. Neither arise without a truth predicate (or something similar), and once we have a device suitable for generating one, the other appears too. They need a unified solution. Dialetheism isn't that solution.

Let's look at matters another way. What principles should we reject to block each of these paradoxes? We can formulate the paradoxical reasoning (in each case) in a formal proof system, and then try to pinpoint the proof rules at fault. I'll use a sequent proof system, since this forces us to make explicit proof-theoretic moves which other systems have a tendency to bury in their notation. (Appendix 10 sets out a sequent system for classical logic.)

The dialetheist targets the classical rules for negation:

$$\frac{\Gamma \vdash A, \Delta}{\Gamma, \neg A \vdash \Delta} (\neg \text{L}) \qquad \frac{\Gamma, A \vdash \Delta}{\Gamma \vdash \neg A, \Delta} (\neg \text{R})$$

These allow a sentence to be moved from left to right, or vice versa, with the addition of a negation symbol. The dialetheist rejects these rules because (together with weakening) they allow us to prove arbitrary conclusions from contradictions, as follows:

$$\frac{\dfrac{A \vdash A}{A, \neg A \vdash} (\neg \text{L})}{A, \neg A \vdash B} (\text{KR})$$

Rejecting both ($\neg$L) and ($\neg$R) is a well-motivated move, given dialetheism, if we read $\Gamma \vdash \Delta$ as saying that it would be bad (rationally incoherent) for us to accept all the Γs whilst rejecting all the Δs (Restall 2005). Here, *acceptance* and *rejection* are rational attitudes one may take to a proposition. (They correspond to the outward speech-acts of *assertion* and *denial*.) On that interpretation, ($\neg$L) says that denying A amounts to the same as accepting $\neg A$, and ($\neg$R) says that denying $\neg A$ amounts to the same as accepting A. But dialetheists deny this: they hold that negation is not a marker for rejection or denial. For the dialetheist, denying A and accepting $\neg A$ are fundamentally different rational moves.

Without ($\neg$L) and ($\neg$R) (or equivalent) rules, one cannot move proof-theoretically from contradiction to arbitrary conclusions. So although the Liar still proves a contradiction, it does not prove arbitrary conclusions, according to the dialetheist account. But dropping ($\neg$L) and ($\neg$R) does nothing to block the Curry paradox reasoning.

It's easy to see why it doesn't: the Curry sentence doesn't involve negation, and so the reasoning goes through even in the absence of ($\neg$L) and ($\neg$R). So dropping ($\neg$L) and ($\neg$R) alone is ineffective. Arbitrary conclusions can still be proved in a system containing rules for the truth-predicate.

Dialetheists may argue that, while dropping ($\neg$L) and ($\neg$R) alone is not sufficient to avoid the problem, it is nevertheless part of the solution. On this view, further rules need to be dropped. Since the Curry paradox is essentially a puzzle concerning the conditional, one possible move is to revise the rules for $\rightarrow$ (as well as those for $\neg$):

$$\frac{\Gamma \vdash A, \Delta \quad \Gamma', B \vdash \Delta'}{\Gamma, \Gamma', A \rightarrow B \vdash \Delta, \Delta'} (\rightarrow\text{L}) \qquad \frac{\Gamma, A \vdash B, \Delta}{\Gamma \vdash A \rightarrow B, \Delta} (\rightarrow\text{R})$$

Using these rules, plus the rules for truth, (T-IN) and (T-OUT), which allow us to move from A to True($\ulcorner A \urcorner$) and vice versa, we can derive arbitrary B using the Curry sentence as follows. First, we prove the Curry sentence:

$$\cfrac{\cfrac{\cfrac{\cfrac{\cfrac{\cfrac{C \vdash C}{C \vdash \text{True}(\ulcorner C \urcorner)}(\text{T-IN}) \quad B \vdash B}{C, \text{True}(\ulcorner C \urcorner) \rightarrow B \vdash B}(\rightarrow\text{L})}{C, C \vdash B}(\text{T-OUT})}{C \vdash B}(\text{WL})}{\text{True}(\ulcorner C \urcorner) \vdash B}(\text{T-IN})}{\vdash \text{True}(\ulcorner C \urcorner) \rightarrow B}(\rightarrow\text{R})$$

Let this proof be Π. It derives $\text{True}(\ulcorner C \urcorner) \to B$, which is identical to just C. We then derive B as follows:

$$\dfrac{\dfrac{\Pi}{\vdash \text{True}(\ulcorner C \urcorner) \to B} \qquad \dfrac{\dfrac{\Pi}{\vdash C}}{\vdash \text{True}(\ulcorner C \urcorner)}\,(\text{T-IN}) \qquad B \vdash B}{\dfrac{\text{True}(\ulcorner C \urcorner) \to B \vdash B}{\vdash B}\,(\text{CUT})}\,(\to\text{L})$$

Rejecting ($\to$L) and ($\to$R) will block this reasoning.

In general, the story is that, if we're facing a paradox formulated using a certain connective, we should revise or reject the rules for that connective. But there are several problems with this. First, it looks *ad hoc*. The Liar and the Curry paradox are similar paradoxes. They're both paradoxes making essential use of *truth*. We'd like a unified solution. Second, this approach is at risk of constantly chasing the tail of further paradoxes. We change such-and-such rules to avoid one paradox. But another crops up. We revise our rules again, always weakening our logic. What guarantee do we have that the revisions are ever enough?

Third, there are versions of the Curry paradox which don't involve any (object language) connectives. Beall and Murzi (2013) discuss the *Validity Curry paradox*. Let '*Val*' be an object-language predicate, with '$Val(\ulcorner A \urcorner, \ulcorner B \urcorner)$' expressing that the argument from 'A' to 'B' is valid. Then we should expect the following principle to hold:

(VAL-IN) If $A \vdash B$ then $\vdash Val(\ulcorner A \urcorner, \ulcorner B \urcorner)$

Moreover, if we know that the argument from A to B is valid, then we should expect to be able to reason from A, plus this fact, to B:

(VAL-OUT) $A, Val(\ulcorner A \urcorner, \ulcorner B \urcorner) \vdash B$

These principles together give us

(9.12) $\vdash Val(\ulcorner A \urcorner, \ulcorner B \urcorner)$ iff $A \vdash B$

But this principle generates a kind of Curry paradox. We consider a sentence V saying 'the argument from this sentence to an absurdity $\bot$ is valid'. In biconditional form:

(9.13) $\quad V \leftrightarrow Val(\ulcorner V \urcorner, \ulcorner \bot \urcorner)$

We then reason from (9.13) to $\bot$ as follows. Assume V. *Modus ponens* then gives us $Val(\ulcorner V \urcorner, \ulcorner \bot \urcorner)$, from which (VAL-OUT) gives us $\bot$. Discharging the assumption, we've shown $V \vdash \bot$. So by (VAL-IN), we infer $Val(\ulcorner V \urcorner, \ulcorner \bot \urcorner)$. So *modus ponens* on (9.13) gives us V, from which (VAL-OUT) gives us $\bot$.

This shows that, in theories strong enough to derive (9.13), a Curry-style paradox arises, given only *modus ponens* plus (VAL-IN) and (VAL-OUT). Weakening or rejecting the introduction rules for $\rightarrow$ won't help avoid this worry. To many, this suggest that we need to look elsewhere in our logical systems to find a suitable solution.

9.4 The Non-Contractive Approach

If restricting the logical rules governing $\neg$ and $\rightarrow$ isn't the way to solve the paradoxes, where else can we turn for a solution? In certain proof systems, there is an obvious candidate: the *structural* proof rules. Whereas logical proof rules govern the behaviour of the logical constants, structural proof rules govern other aspects of proof construction, such as whether the order or repetition of premises matters.

In a natural deduction system, structural rules are often implicit in the notation for opening and closing sub-proofs. A sequent system, by contrast, makes these structural rules explicit. (See appendix 10.) And, as it happens, there are several structural rules which crop up in each bit of paradoxical reasoning. These are the *identity* (ID), (CUT), and *contraction* (WL, WR) rules, shown in figure 9.1.

So, the thought runs, one of these must go. It can't be (ID), since without it, we have no proofs at all. (A proof is a tree with an

$$\frac{}{A \vdash A} \text{ (ID)} \qquad \frac{\Gamma, A \vdash \Delta \quad \Gamma' \vdash A, \Delta'}{\Gamma, \Gamma' \vdash \Delta, \Delta'} \text{ (CUT)}$$

$$\frac{\Gamma, A, A \vdash B, \Delta}{\Gamma, A \vdash B, \Delta} \text{ (WL)} \qquad \frac{\Gamma, A \vdash B, B, \Delta}{\Gamma, A \vdash B, \Delta} \text{ (WR)}$$

Figure 9.1: STRUCTURAL RULES

instance of (ID) at each leaf.) And it can't be (CUT), since either (CUT) makes no different at all, or else it does, in which case it allows indispensable chaining of sub-proofs. So, the culprit must be contraction: contraction must go! Beall and Murzi (2013), Shapiro (2011), and Zardini (2011) adopt an approach along these lines. Non-contractive systems have also been studied by Alechina and Van Lambalgen (1996), Grišin (1982), Petersen (2000), Restall (1994), and Rogerson and Restall (2004).

(The reasoning above is a bit too quick. Greenough (2001) rejects (ID) and Cobreros et al. (2013), Ripley (2015), and Weir (2005) reject (CUT). I'll say a little more about these—on the face of it crazy—moves in §9.5. For now, let's assume that (ID) and (CUT) are mandatory, so that the only option in the neighbourhood is to reject (WL) and (WR).)

The *non-contractive* approach to the paradoxes, NC, adopts all the usual proof rules, except (WL) and (WR). (In the absence of contraction, classically equivalent formulations of the rules for ∧, ∨ and → are not equivalent. We needn't go into the details here. I'll formulate NC in terms of the 'multiplicative' rules.) In NC, one cannot derive absurdities from the Liar or Curry sentences. One cannot reason to the empty sequent in these cases. Validity-Curry is blocked. And, since the Liar and Curry sentences are not assigned some special alethic value, revenge sentences do not occur (as they often do when we say, for example, that the Liar is neither true nor false). So NC seems to offer a robust solution to the paradoxes.

Contraction asserts that repetition of a premise or conclusion makes no difference to the proof. How could that be denied? The non-contractive theorist has two options. She may offer an explanation of what logical consequence is which explains why contraction should be rejected. Or she may refrain from giving an explanation, and instead hold that dropping contraction is justified because so doing blocks the paradoxes more successfully than other approaches.

Let's begin with the former option. Here's three broad ways to understand logical consequence, as captured by '⊢'. First, we understand 'Γ ⊢ A' in terms of a *rational licence* to move from premises or assumptions Γ to conclusion A. When we derive Γ ⊢ A, we have an 'inference ticket' to move from Γ to A. (This approach makes best sense in a single-conclusion setting, where just one sentence may appear on the right.) A second approach reads Γ ⊢ Δ as saying that it would be bad (rationally incoherent) for us to accept all the Γs whilst rejecting all the Δs (Restall 2005). Here, *acceptance* and *rejection* are rational attitudes one may take to a proposition, corresponding to the outward speech-acts of *assertion* and *denial*. A third approach is the familiar semantic one, on which it is impossible for the conclusion (or, in a multiple conclusion setting, for all conclusions) to be false when the premises are all true.

To what extent do any of these ways of understanding logical consequence give us traction on the issue of dropping contraction? The 'inference ticket' gives us none. It understands consequence proof-theoretically: a derivation Γ ⊢ A provides us with a licence to move from Γ to A. On this view, our accepted proof rules provide inferential permissions. But whether such-and-such proof rules should be accepted is precisely our question. So this approach won't help.

The acceptance-and-rejection approach gives us an independent handle on which rules are acceptable, to the extent that we have an independent grip on what it is rationally incoherent to accept and reject simultaneously. Acceptance is a relation to a proposition. If one accepts A, then one stands in that relationship to A until one cancels that acceptance. A further thought or utterance token of 'A' thus has no effect on that relationship: one is no more and no less in the acceptance relation to A after the second token than after the first. The same goes for rejection. But then, Γ, A, A ⊢ B, Δ captures precisely the same 'rational position' as Γ, A ⊢ B, Δ, which in turn captures precisely the same rational position as $\Gamma, A \vdash B, B, \Delta$. They are one and the same position, notated differently. So there is no question, on this understanding of logical consequence, of rejecting contraction.

Finally, the semantic (truth-theoretic) account of consequence is unequivocal: A's being true 'twice over' is nonsense; it's either true (full stop) or it's not true. If each of Γ, A, A is true, then each of Γ, A is true; and likewise, if each of B, B, Δ is false, then so is each of B, Δ. Each amounts to one and the same situation. So, as before, there is no alethic gap between the upper and lower contraction sequents. There is no question, on this understanding of logical consequence, of rejecting contraction.

There are certainly other interpretations of proof systems which reject contraction. In linear logic (Girard 1987), for example, sentences represent *resources*. Each occurrence of 'A' in a proof represents a use of an A-resource. What follows from the double use of a resource might not follow from a single use of it. So, in this setting, contraction is clearly not justified. But there is no prospect for understanding logical consequence in general in terms of resource use. Linear logic was designed for a representational purpose, with sentence-tokens as resources. Tokens, so understood, are not truth-apt. So we cannot capture argumentation in general using linear logic.

No current way of understanding logical consequence comes anywhere near supporting a contraction-free system. As NC theorists Beall and Murzi (2013) concede,

> What may be needed, if Structural Contraction is to be abandoned, is a new metaphysical account of validity—one for which the rejection of Structural Contraction is perfectly natural'. (Beall and Murzi 2013, 164)

But, as they go on to say, 'little has been done along these lines' (2013, 164). (And for what it's worth, I can't see any alternatives to the above approaches which would improve the NC theorist's claims.)

Instead, the NC theorist will need to hold that logical consequence is whatever the best system of proof rules says it is. And she will argue from the presence of the paradoxes to the absence of contraction in the best system of rules. There is a clear cost here: we then cannot use an independent understanding of logical consequence as a criterion on good rules of inference. That brings with it worries about the justification of the other rules in the system. Moreover, it's not clear that NC does provide the best overall approach to the paradoxes. Dropping contraction has logical implications which need to be taken into account in the overall evaluation of NC. I'll consider two such implications, concerning *modus ponens* and *cumulative reasoning*.

There's a variety of principles one might mean by '*modus ponens*'. One might mean that the sentence

(9.14) $A \wedge (A \rightarrow B) \rightarrow B$

is valid. Or one might mean that a certain argument, from A and $A \rightarrow B$ to B, is valid, so that the sequent $A, A \rightarrow B \vdash B$ is derivable. Or one might mean that, whenever one can infer both A and $A \rightarrow B$ from some assumptions, then one can infer B from those assumptions. This is expressible as:

$$\frac{\Gamma \vdash A, \Delta \qquad \Gamma \vdash A \rightarrow B, \Delta'}{\Gamma \vdash B, \Delta, \Delta'} \text{ (MMP)}$$

NC has no problem with the sentence and rule forms of *modus ponens*, but it cannot accommodate (MMP). That's because (MMP) gets us (nearly all instances of) contraction. Let Π be a derivation of $\Gamma, A \vdash A$ from $A \vdash A$, using however many instances of (KL). Then we reason (from the contraction premise, $\Gamma, A, A \vdash B, \Delta$) as follows:

$$\frac{\dfrac{\dfrac{\Gamma, A, A \vdash B, \Delta}{\Gamma, A \vdash A \rightarrow B, \Delta} (\rightarrow \text{R}) \qquad \dfrac{\Pi}{\Gamma, A \vdash A}}{\Gamma, A \vdash B, \Delta}}{} \text{ (MMP)}$$

(This isn't quite full contraction, since the above derivation requires a non-empty succedent, B, Δ, whereas full contraction operates in addition on sequents with an empty succedent, from $\Gamma, A, A \vdash$ to

$\Gamma, A \vdash$. But it's contraction enough to infer absurdities from the Liar and Curry sentences. So NC can't accept (MMP).)

Giving up on (MMP) is a real cost to a theory. It is bizarre for someone to accept (rule) *modus ponens*, and yet to think that the consequences one is entitled to draw need not be closed under that rule. Indeed, a *formal theory* is usually defined as a set of sentences closed under *modus ponens* (and perhaps other rules too). For the NC theorist, by contrast, it is illegitimate to require theories to be closed under *modus ponens*.

The NC theorist may reply that, since (MMP) contains a large dose of contraction, it was part of her proposal all along that (MMP) be rejected. It is no extra objection, to the NC theorist, to point out that NC rejects (MMP). But this reply misses its mark. The objection draws out a problematic consequence of rejecting contraction. If rejecting (MMP) is indeed problematic, as I have argued, then the NC approach is in trouble.

Here is another problematic consequence of rejecting contraction: the resulting system fails to satisfy *cautious cut*,

$$\frac{\Gamma \vdash A \quad \Gamma, A \vdash B}{\Gamma \vdash B} \quad \text{(CCUT)}$$

This is an important form of transitivity, used frequently when we reason *cumulatively*. Here's something we often do (particularly in philosophy and mathematics). We begin with some assumptions. We reason from them, deriving some intermediate conclusion, A. We then add that intermediate conclusion to our assumptions, and reason to some further conclusion, B. It seems clear that the further conclusion follows from our original assumptions: after all, all we added to derive B was the intermediate conclusion, A, which already follows from our original assumptions.

That final step of reasoning is precisely what (CCUT) allows, but which is disallowed in NC. David Ripley makes the point:

> Sustained ordinary reasoning, where it involves lemmas, involves them on the model of cumulative reasoning: as things

that, once established, can be drawn on *repeatedly* in combination with any other available information, *including* the very information appealed to in establishing them. (Ripley 2015, 324)

But NC cannot 'accommodate this in the obvious way' and so 'owe[s] a story about the failure of this important transitivity property' (Ripley 2015, 324).

As NC contains the regular (CUT) rule, we may still infer from $\Gamma \vdash A$ and $\Gamma, A \vdash B$ to $\Gamma, \Gamma \vdash B$. In other words, if our assumptions lead us to an intermediate conclusion, which together with those assumptions leads us to a further conclusion B, then our assumptions *twice over* lead us to B. But it's no good the defender of NC downplaying the difference between $\Gamma, \Gamma \vdash B$ and $\Gamma \vdash B$. Her whole project is premised on there being an important, crucial difference between assumptions Γ taken on their own and assumptions taken twice over, Γ, Γ.

In short, it is very hard to see how any notion of logical consequence could motivate dropping contraction. Moreover, in dropping contraction, NC theories are not closed under *modus ponens*, and do not permit cumulative reasoning. On balance, dropping contraction is not a good way to respond to the paradoxes.

9.5 Other Substructural Approaches

Contraction is not the only structural rule implicated in paradoxical reasoning. The other potential structural culprits are (ID) and (CUT). Both have been questioned in response to the paradoxes: Greenough (2001) rejects (ID), whereas Ripley (2015) rejects (CUT). Greenough's idea is that 'liar sentences are ... not legitimately supposable' (Greenough 2001, 118). If supposing that A is not a correct rational move, then we cannot be right to derive anything on the supposition that A—not even A itself. In such cases, Greenough rejects $A \vdash A$.

For Greenough, (ID) is acceptable only when A is *supposition-apt*:

A sentence A fails to be supposition-apt if, for all sentences B, one can establish that

(i) ⊢ $A \to B$, and
  (ii) ⊢ $\neg(A \to B)$

(Greenough 2001, 123, notation changed.)

Here, '⊢' denotes proof 'in classical logic (plus the rules of truth-introduction and truth-elimination)' (Greenough 2001, 123). However, this test treats every A as supposition-inapt. This system (with Liar-like sentences) is trivial, and so any B can be derived, including both $A \to B$ and $\neg(A \to B)$. It won't help to focus on a system without the truth rules, for then the Liar will fail the test and be judged supposition-apt. Greenough suggests we might need to restrict to the classical rules which 'are beyond reproach' (2001, 123): all but (ID). But without the use of (ID), nothing is provable; and to restrict (ID) only to supposition-apt sentences begs the question.

There can't be a formal test for supposition-inaptness. If there were, we could formally establish that A is supposition-inapt (if it is). In particular, we could formally establish, and hence assert, that 'this sentence is supposition-inapt' is supposition-inapt. But then we have asserted that very sentence, and so it must be supposition-apt: contradiction. If there are supposition-inapt sentences (in Greenough's specific sense), then there can't be a formal test for them.

There's a simple way to capture what's right about Greenough's proposal. To suppose something is to stand in a relation to a proposition. So where there's no proposition, there's no supposing. In particular, if 'A' (in a given context) does not express a proposition, then a mental or speech act involving a token of 'A' cannot result in a supposition. I'll say more on the idea in §9.8.

There's little to be said for holding (ID) to blame for paradoxical reasoning. Let's instead consider what happens if we drop (CUT). Weir (2005), Cobreros et al. (2013), and Ripley (2015) make this move. The system NT (for 'non-transitive') contains all the classical rules listed in appendix 10, except for (CUT). (NT, unlike NC, doesn't draw a distinction between multiplicative and additive connectives: the rules for each are inter-derivable, given the presence of contraction and weakening.)

It will come as no surprise that NC must reject (CCUT), given that (CCUT) is a form of transitivity. NC must also reject (MMP), for, as Ripley notes, (MMP) 'brings almost every instance of cut with it' (2015, 316), using just weakening (the ' : ' lines) and (MMP):

$$\frac{\dfrac{\Gamma, A \vdash \Delta}{\vdots} \quad \dfrac{\Gamma', A \vdash B, \Delta'}{\vdots}}{\dfrac{\Gamma, \Gamma', A \vdash \Delta \quad \Gamma, \Gamma' \vdash A \to B, \Delta'}{\Gamma, \Gamma' \vdash \Delta, \Delta'}} \text{ (MMP)}$$

So (MMP) replicates the effects of (CUT) on sequents with a non-empty succedent (just as it replicates the effects of contraction on sequents with a non-empty succedent). And that's far too much transitivity for the NT theorist to accept.

From one point of view, NT trumps NC, since both are non-transitive systems (in the sense of 'transitivity' captured by (CCUT)), yet NT gets to keep contraction. But it isn't clear to me how much of an advantage that is, in the absence of transitivity. Failing to close theories under *modus ponens*, and failing to allow for cumulative reasoning, is just as much a problem for either approach. Moreover, the independent ways of understanding logical consequence discussed above support (CUT)) just as much as they support contraction. So, as I see it, NT and NC are (roughly) as badly off as one another.

9.6 Restricting The T-scheme

In all of the truth-theoretic paradoxes, the T-scheme (or the corresponding rules) play a crucial role. If all other options for avoiding the paradoxes look to be flawed, then we must consider whether we should amend, restrict, or altogether drop the T-scheme (or the corresponding rules). That's the topic of this section.

The overriding problem with the suggestion is that the T-scheme (or rules) appear to be *constitutive* of our concept of truth. Armed only with what we mean by 'truth', we thereby know that we can infer 'it is true that A' from 'A' and vice versa. This is most readily apparent given the usual semantic characterisation of logical consequence in terms of preservation of truth: there then seems to be no gap between ⟨⟨A⟩ is true⟩ and ⟨A⟩ itself. The theory of truth developed so far in this book supports this analysis, of course. But it isn't required by any means: just about any acceptable metaphysical analysis of what *truth* is entails that the T-rules are valid.

Nevertheless, theorists have attempted to reject the T-scheme. One approach is to restrict the scheme, so that it holds only for certain sentences or propositions. We met an example of this approach back in §1.4, when discussing the dialetheist's response to the Liar. Horwich (1998), for example, holds that 'certain instances of the equivalence scheme [(T-PROP)] are not to be included as axioms in the minimal [i.e. deflationist] theory' (Horwich 1998, 42).

For this move to be theoretically viable, one must propose some property (of sentences, or propositions), possessed only by those sentences or propositions which satisfy the T-scheme. This property might be *being grounded*, or *expressing a proposition*, or something else entirely. To be completely neutral, call it *being OK*. Then, having analysed this property, the theorist says that only the OK sentences (or propositions) satisfy the T-scheme. If we put this in terms of sentences, we get the *sententially restricted T-scheme*:

(SRT) $OK(\ulcorner A \urcorner) \to (True(\ulcorner A \urcorner) \leftrightarrow A)$

Bacon (2015) argues convincingly that replacing the standard T-scheme with (SRT) will not help avoid paradox. The problem (which he demonstrates formally) is with the revenge sentence, R, which says of itself that it is not true if it's OK:

(R) $R \leftrightarrow (OK(\ulcorner R \urcorner) \to \neg True(\ulcorner R \urcorner))$

By diagonalisation, any suitable arithmetical theory $\mathcal{T}$ will prove R. If $\mathcal{T}$ is classical and contains all instances of (SRT), then $\mathcal{T}$ includes theorems that are provably not OK (Bacon 2015, 308–9, theorem 1.1). But surely, if a theory proves some sentence A, then A must be OK (by the lights of that theory). But if we accept that much (so that we can infer from $\vdash_{\mathcal{T}} A$ to $\vdash_{\mathcal{T}} OK(\ulcorner A \urcorner)$), then the theory is inconsistent (Bacon 2015, 309, corollary 1.2).

This result rules out theories which attempt to solve the paradoxes by restricting the T-scheme to sentences satisfying a given property. In particular, it seems to rule out 'no proposition' views, on which the Liar (and related sentences) do not express a proposition. Such theories seem committed to the T-scheme, restricted to sentences which express a proposition. But then Bacon's argument goes through, with 'expresses a proposition' in place of 'is OK'. The positive view I'll develop in §9.8 is a 'no proposition' view. I'll argue in §9.9 that my view escapes Bacon's conclusion. But for now, our conclusion is that a theory can't solve the Liar merely by restricting the T-scheme.

A more radical response to the paradoxes is to junk the T-scheme altogether. But this is clearly unsatisfactory, as it stands. Our concept of truth plays a useful (and perhaps ineliminable) theoretical role. Scharp (2013) addresses that worry by offering a *replacement theory* of truth. He argues that truth is an inconsistent concept, and so must be replaced. Since there's no single consistent concept that can do all the things we want truth to do, Scharp's theory contains two replacement concepts, *descending truth*, **D**, and *ascending truth*, **A**. Each validates just one direction of the T-scheme:

(DT) $D(\ulcorner A \urcorner) \to A$

(AT) $A \to A(\ulcorner A \urcorner)$

In particular, **D** is defined axiomatically and **A** is then introduced by setting $A(\ulcorner A \urcorner) =_{df} \neg D(\ulcorner \neg A \urcorner)$. We can thus account for the theoretical uses of truth and the T-scheme, according to Scharp. Since we can't account for all such uses in terms of a unified concept, *truth*, we account for each of those uses either in terms of **D**-truth or in terms of **A**-truth.

This approach fares badly in comparison with those discussed above. The converse to (AT) cannot hold, else **A** would coincide with truth, and hence (on Scharp's analysis) be inconsistent. Since Scharp's underlying logic is classical, this gives us instances of $\neg(A \to A(\ulcorner A \urcorner))$

and hence $\mathbf{A}(\ulcorner A \urcorner) \wedge \neg A$, for some A. But from this, we can infer $\mathbf{A}(\ulcorner A \urcorner) \wedge \mathbf{A}(\ulcorner \neg A \urcorner)$: the A-truths are inconsistent.

As a consequence, Scharp has to deny that the A-truths are closed under logical consequence (which, for Scharp, is classical). If they were closed, then we would be able to derive $\mathbf{A}(\ulcorner B \urcorner)$ for arbitrary B. And the problem would not be limited to A-truths only. From $\mathbf{A}(\ulcorner \neg B \urcorner)$, we can infer $\neg \mathbf{D}(\ulcorner B \urcorner)$ for arbitrary B. Descending-truth would be a necessarily empty concept. And indeed, Scharp does not take the A-truths to be closed under logical consequence (Scharp 2013, 151).

Scharp's project then faces a deep problem. If the A-truths may fail some logical rule, why not say the same about *truth*? The logic of A-truths must be non-explosive: we cannot (on pain of absurdity) infer from $\mathbf{A}(\ulcorner A \urcorner) \wedge \mathbf{A}(\ulcorner \neg A \urcorner)$ to $\mathbf{A}(\ulcorner B \urcorner)$, for arbitrary B. But if that logic is suitable for governing a concept of truth, why not accept the dialetheist account (§9.3), without the need to replace truth at all? Alternatively, we might point to the validity-Curry paradox (§9.3) as evidence that the logic of A-truths lacks some structural rule: either *contraction* or (CUT). But if we accept that move, then why not accept either the non-contractive (§9.4) or non-transitive (§9.5) approaches to truth, without Scharp's replacement?

In short, whatever Scharp says about the logic of A-truths, we could accept a similar story about *truth*. That option will trump Scharp's theory, since it maintains a unified concept of truth. Moreover, as we saw above, all such options are dubious. So we should reject Scharp's replacement approach.

9.7 The Undecidability Approach

Stephen Barker (2014) presents a novel approach to solving semantic paradoxes, including the Liar and its variants, and the Curry paradox. His approach is based around the concept of *alethic undecidability*. His approach, if successful, renders futile all attempts to assign semantic properties (*truth*, *falsity*, gap, or glut) to the paradoxical sentences, whilst leaving classical logic fully intact. And, according to Barker, even the T-scheme remains valid, for validity is not undermined by undecidable instances.

Barker takes as his starting point a version of the truthmaker principle, which he formulates as:

(9.15) If a sentence is true (or false), then it is true (or false) in virtue of non-alethic facts (Barker 2014, 201).

A *non-alethic fact* is a state of affairs not involving the properties *truth* or *falsity*: *that students drink* is one such fact, whereas *that the proposition ⟨that students drink⟩ is true* is not, since the latter involves the property *being true*.

Truth or falsity requires a sentence to connect, eventually, to non-alethic facts. Barker (2014, 202) offers two examples of this connection failing. Consider the following infinite sequence of sentences:

(R_1) Sentence (R_2) is true.

(R_2) Sentence (R_3) is true.

(R_3) Sentence (R_4) is true.

⋮

Or, consider the *truth-teller* sentence:

(T) Sentence (T) is true.

In each case, no sentence has the right kind of connection to non-alethic facts. They are *ground-unspecifiable* (Barker 2014, 203). Notice that there's nothing paradoxical about such cases: we can consistently assign them all the value *true*, or all the value *false*. But Barker claims, based on (9.15), that we should not, for truth or falsity require the kind of connection to non-alethic reality that's missing in each case.

Barker then argues as follows:

> Ground-unspecifiable sentences are undecidable with respect to their grounding status. Given [9.15]—which says that all alethic properties must be grounded—it follows that such sentences are undecidable with respect to their alethic properties. ... Call this undecidability with respect to alethic properties *alethic-undecidability* or *A-undecidability* for short. (Barker 2014, 206)

As a consequence, for each example sentence above, it is undecidable whether it 'is either true or false, lacks truth and falsity, is both true and false, and so on' (Barker 2014, 206). Alethic undecidability thus implies unassertability: 'we cannot assert, in principle, whether they are true, false, either true or false, neither true nor false, both true and false, and so on' (Barker 2014, 201).

Barker applies this reasoning to the (strengthened) Liar sentence, (L^+) and the Curry sentence, (C). The claim is that both (L^+) and (C) are ground-unspecifiable, hence A-undecidable. Moreover, according to Barker (2014, 208–9), all attempts at 'revenge' fail under this analysis. So, for example:

(R^u) Sentence (R^u) is A-undecidable

is ground-unspecifiable, hence A-undecidable (Barker 2014, 208). But this result doesn't imply that (R^u) is true, since for any A-undecidable sentence, we're banned from saying whether it 'is either true or false, lacks truth and falsity, is both true and false, and so on' (Barker 2014, 206). That, at least, is Barker's story.

Below, I'll demonstrate that Barker's approach is flawed. I'll do so using only A-decidable reasoning from A-decidable premises. That guarantees our conclusions will likewise be A-decidable, and hence assertable. That's because valid reasoning (from finite premises, at least) preserves A-decidability. For if the premises are A-decidable, then so is their conjunction; and if the reasoning is valid, then the conditional from the conjoined premises to the conclusion is valid, hence A-decidable. Since logical proof is one way to decide the truth of a statement, that conditional itself must be A-decidable; and a conditional with an A-decidable antecedent must have an A-decidable consequent. It follows that A-decidable reasoning from A-decidable premises results in A-decidable conclusions.

My case against Barker will be in two steps. First, we can in certain cases establish (in an A-decidable way) facts about a sentence's dependencies. I'll then argue that reasoning in this way allows us to reinstate the (strengthened) Liar paradox. We can establish, in an A-decidable way, certain facts about dependency between entities, including sentences like (L^+) and (C). We can use these facts to build directed *dependency graphs* for the sentences in question. The idea is simple: when entity e_1 depends on e_2, we put an arrow from the e_1 node to the e_2 node in our graph.

For full generality, we would need to capture different senses of dependency. (An entity may depend on another for its *existence*; but in the case of sentences, we often talk about S_1 depending on S_2 for its *truth*.) We could capture different dependency relations in our graphs with different colour arrows. Full generality would also require us to capture the distinction between full and partial dependency. $(A \wedge B) \vee C$'s truth depends on the truth of A, B, and C, but in different ways: C is a full ground, whereas A and B are individually mere partial grounds, but jointly a full ground, for $(A \wedge B) \vee C$. We can track the difference using an AND-OR graph structure, familiar from the technical literature.

We needn't go into the details here, however, as the cases we're interested in—(L^+), (C), and each (R_i)—involve simple one-one dependencies. Their graphs are as follows:

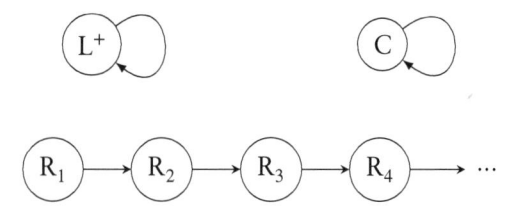

We may interpret an edge $A \longrightarrow B$ as saying that A's truth-value depends on B's truth-value; or alternatively, as saying that the fact *that A* depends on (or obtains in virtue of) the fact *that B* (obtaining). For our purposes, it doesn't matter.

Let's focus on the finite graph for (L$^+$). It's clear that the process of associating a sentence like (L$^+$) with its graph is algorithmically decidable, given the facts (i) that the only referring term in (L$^+$) is '(L$^+$)'; and (ii) that '(L$^+$)' refers only to (L$^+$). Fact (i) concerns syntax only, and so is clearly A-decidable. Fact (ii) is about reference. It would be absurd to suggest that the reference-facts are A-undecidable in these cases. For that would imply that we can't assert that (L$^+$) is self-referential, and hence that the set-up to the paradoxes cannot even be stated. Putting these points together, the association of (L$^+$) with its graph is A-decidable. (Similarly for (C) and its graph.)

Given that these graphs are determinate, finite structures, we can clearly make determinate statements about them. We can say, for example, that both (L$^+$)'s and (C)'s graph consists of a single node, and that neither graph has a leaf node. And from such facts, we can infer further facts about (L$^+$)'s and (C)'s dependencies: that (L$^+$) does not depend on (C), for example. And crucially, we infer such facts from A-decidable premises using only A-decidable reasoning, hence our inferred conclusions are themselves A-decidable.

One class of facts we can determine, using this kind of reasoning, concern whether given nodes correspond to alethic or to non-alethic facts. Since nodes are sentences, this amounts to a syntactic check for the predicates 'is true' and 'is false'. Clearly, that check is A-decidable. (And even if we thought the class of alethic predicates was open-ended, or otherwise A-undecidable, it's clear that 'is true' and 'is false' are alethic predicates. So we clearly have a sufficient condition for a node's representing an alethic fact.) This allows us to infer, A-decidably, that (L$^+$)'s graph's sole node states an alethic fact, and hence that no node in the graph states a non-alethic fact. Such inferences will be crucial in the argument below.

The worry for Barker's proposal goes like this. (L$^+$)'s graph contains no non-alethic nodes. All its nodes are alethic nodes, expressing alethic facts. So (L$^+$)'s dependencies involve only alethic facts. But by (9.15), no alethic fact grounds any sentence's truth. So (L$^+$) has no alethic ground. It is ungrounded. So by (9.15), it is not true. This conclusion was inferred from A-decidable premises using only A-decidable reasoning, and so it is A-decidable that (L^+) is not true. We can then reason (A-decidably) in the usual way to a contradiction.

Barker (2014, 204–5) considers a related argument along these lines, and argues that it does not work: 'to infer ... that $[(L^+)]$ is ungrounded from that fact is to forget the infinite deferment of grounding' (Barker 2014, 204), involving 'an infinite series of interpretative stages' (Barker 2014, 6). In the analogous case of the truth-teller, (T), he argues that

> ... at each stage, no grounding condition is specified. But there is always a further interpretative stage after any given stage. ... Since [(T)] at no stage can be held up as the source of [(T)]'s failing to be grounded, we cannot say that [(T)] is ungrounded on the basis that no sentence at any interpretive stage describes a non-alethic condition. (Barker 2014, 205)

Barker's reasoning here is faulty. We can infer general conclusions about (T)'s dependencies. The reasoning via (T)'s graph allows us to infer (A-decidably) that no node in (T)'s graph states a non-alethic condition, and hence (A-decidably) that (T) does not depend on any non-alethic fact. We don't need to enter into Barker's infinite sequence of interpretive stages: we need only the premises that (i) '(T)' refers (only) to (T) and (ii) (T) contains 'is true' and hence states an alethic fact. That is sufficient information to build the dependency graph and conclude that (T) does not depend on any non-alethic fact, and hence is ungrounded.

Exactly the same goes for (L^+), with paradoxical consequences. Given that (i) '(L^+)' refers (only) to (L^+) and (ii) (L^+) contains 'is true' and hence states an alethic fact, we can build (L^+)'s dependency graph and determine, A-decidably, that it contains only alethic nodes. So, A-decidably, (L^+) is not grounded by any non-alethic fact and hence, by (9.15), is not true. It is A-decidable that (L^+) is not true. Then (L^+) is assertible and apt for inclusion in standard logical reasoning. But that reasoning quickly leads to absurdity: we can assert the Liar equivalence ((L^+) is true iff it is not true), from which it follows that (L^+) is both true and not true. The paradox has not been blocked.

In this section, I've argued that we can, in certain cases, draw clear, A-decidable conclusions about a sentence's alethic dependencies. From clear facts about a sentence's syntax and reference of its terms, we can build dependency graphs, and reason about a sentence's dependencies. In particular, we can determine, A-decidably, that (L^+) is ungrounded, hence not true; but this quickly results in absurdity. So, A-decidably, we must reject Barker's proposal.

9.8 The No Proposition Approach

My response to the Liar is simple: there is no Liar proposition. The Liar sentence doesn't say anything. There's nothing said by that sentence to be true or false. Ditto for the Curry sentence, the truthteller, and all their revenge sentences. The approach is beautifully simple. It's not *ad hoc*. And it's immune to revenge paradoxes. That's what I'll claim in this section.

The view is that there is no Liar proposition. The Liar sentence does not express any proposition because, given what the Liar means, there is no proposition to be expressed. The view isn't that the Liar is meaningless. Every word in the Liar is meaningful; they're put together in a perfectly grammatical way; and there's no category mistake involved in predicating falsity (or lack of truth) to a certain sentence. So the Liar sentence is perfectly meaningful. Rather, the view is that there's simply no Liar proposition to be expressed. (How can it be meaningful if it doesn't express a proposition? I'll return to this point below.)

It's not the Liar's fault: it tries to say something, but the world doesn't cooperate. Recall that a proposition is a truthmaker condition: a set of (natures of) possible states of affairs. But the world doesn't provide possible truthmaker conditions for the Liar. There are no possible states of affairs that could truthmake or falsemake the Liar. To see this, suppose (for *reductio*) that s truthmakes (L). Without loss of generality, suppose further that nothing that grounds s also truthmakes (L). (There must be such a state if (L) has truthmakers at all.) Then s involves (L) itself and the property *being false*. On our analysis, *being false* is an existential property, and so is grounded by an instance, s', a truthmaker for (L). But given that grounding is irreflexive, $s' \neq s$, contradicting our assumption. So, there are no possible truthmakers for (L).

(This argument bears a resemblance to Barker's approach to the paradoxes (§9.7) in terms of the 'infinite deferment of grounding' (Barker 2014, 204–5). The phenomenon he describes captures a deep insight into the Liar pathology. But it is best understood in terms of there being no truthmaker-condition, and hence no proposition, to be expressed.)

That conclusion is entailed purely by our analysis of what the properties *truth* and *falsity* are. So, there's no proposition to be expressed by the Liar sentence. That conclusion is entailed purely by our analysis of what propositions are. Neither of those bits of theorising appeal to truth-theoretic paradoxes in general or to Liar-like considerations in particular. That's why this approach to the Liar is not *ad hoc*.

To bring this point out further, consider what we should say about the *Truth-teller* and *No truthmaker* sentences:

(TT) This sentence (TT) is true.

(NTM) This sentence (NTM) has no truthmaker.

The interesting feature of the Truth-teller (in contrast to the Liar) is that, as far as logic is concerned, it may be true, it may be false. Logic alone won't help us. But neither can any empirical matter settle whether the Truth-teller is true. It's completely unsettled, both logically and empirically, what the Truth-teller's truth-value is. One way to interpret this baffling feature is by thinking of it as an *ungrounded* truth (if true) or an ungrounded falsehood (if false). This is the line Sorensen (2001) takes. But this option would be disastrous for the truthmaker maximalist! The Truth-teller poses a deep problem for maximalists.

If propositions are truthmaker-conditions, then there is no Truth-teller proposition: (TT) fails to express a proposition, simply because there's no proposition to be expressed. The reasoning is the same as in the case of the Liar. This result is instructive in dealing with the Liar. The Truth-teller is logically consistent, and yet it is treated in the same manner as the Liar. So it is not contradiction or paradox that drives this approach to the Liar. The general metaphysical analysis of the property *being true* rules out certain states of affairs from existing, and consequently rules out the existence of certain propositions.

(Rodriguez-Pereyra (2015) thinks that the Truth-teller shows that *grounding* is not irreflexive, for 'if (TT) is true, the fact that (TT) is true grounds the fact that (TT) is true' (2015, 525, notation changed). But since there is no such proposition, there is no such fact, and so this is no counterexample to *grounding*'s irreflexivity.)

The same can be said of the No-truthmaker sentence (NTM). If false, then it has no truthmaker; but if it has no truthmaker, it appears to be true. If so, it is a truthmakerless truth, contrary to maximalism (Milne 2005). The response is as before: our theory of propositions implies that (NTM) expresses no proposition. But that doesn't make (NTM) true, for being truth requires a proposition to be expressed.

Rodriguez-Pereyra (2006a) agrees that (NTM) does not express a proposition (despite rejecting this solution in the case of the Truth-teller (2015)). But he argues for this on the grounds that (NTM) is Liar-like. Paradox drives his reasoning. This leaves him hostage to the response that (NTM) is not Liar-like (Milne 2013); see Barrio and Rodriguez-Pereyra 2015 for further discussion. Better, I think, to have a theory of propositions which provides a unified solution to the Liar, Truth-teller, No-truthmaker sentence, and similar examples.

What does the *no proposition* approach say about the Liar sentence, if that sentence expresses no proposition? It is not true. It is not false. The answer is the same for any sentence—and indeed, for any entity whatsoever—which doesn't express a proposition. 'Get me a shrubbery!' is not true, not false. 'Whusindgyaohnjkxvb' is not true, not false. My trusty MacBook is not true, not false. Truth and falsity are complementary properties (lacking one entails possessing the other) for the domain of propositions. Derivatively, they are complementary properties for the domain of sentences which express propositions. As far as truth and falsity are concerned, propositionless sentences might as well be nothing at all.

If that sounds like the standard 'neither true nor false' response to the Liar, well, it is and it isn't. It isn't the same solution as *three-valued* responses to the Liar, which posit a third truth-value, *neither true nor false* (or *undecided*, or *unsettled*, or what have you). From an alethic point of view, propositionless sentences have no value at all. They don't receive some alternative value. That's because propositions are the primary bearers of alethic values, and so if there's no proposition, then there's no value-bearing.

The key distinguishing feature of the *no proposition* approach— and what really sets it apart from the standard response to the Liar—is how it deals with the revenge problem. The issue for the standard response is this. If the (strengthened) Liar sentence is neither true nor false, then it's not true; but that's precisely what the sentence says, so it's true. But it cannot be true, so the 'neither true nor false' option was illusory. The *no proposition* approach blocks that argument. The Liar sentence expresses no proposition, so says nothing at all. In particular, it doesn't say that it isn't true. So, from claiming that the sentence isn't true, we can't infer that it is true on the grounds of what it says.

What about the purely proof-theoretic revenge argument? This argument first derives the extended Liar (from zero assumptions), and then derives arbitrary conclusions. To address this argument, we first need to address the general issue of what logic looks like, given the *no proposition* approach. I'll devote §9.9 below to the issue. (Spoiler alert: the worry doesn't arise.)

What about other revenge arguments? Typically, a revenge argument for a theory about the Liar can be formulated in terms of what the Liar sentence lacks, according to that theory. In our case, this is the property *not expressing a proposition*. So consider this sentence:

(9.16) (9.16) does not express a proposition.

That can't be true. If it were, (9.16) does not express a proposition, and hence (9.16) is not true: contradiction. But it's consistent that (9.16) is false. If (9.16) is false, then (9.16) expresses a proposition, hence a false proposition; and if (9.16) expresses a proposition at all, it expresses a false one. So one logically consistent stance to take is this: (9.16) is false, because it expresses a (false) proposition.

Can (9.16) express a proposition? I don't think so. Suppose it did: call this proposition p. Then the state of affairs s of (9.16)'s expressing p is a falsemaker for p. So p plays a role in fixing s's identity. (If states of affairs are non-mereological sums, then s contains p as a non-mereological part). But, given our analysis of propositions, s also plays a role in fixing p's identity (s is a member of a member of p). I don't think that that's possible: if x plays a role in making y what it is, then x's identity must be fixed prior to y's. So there is no proposition *that (9.16) expresses no proposition*, and hence no proposition for (9.16) to express. The correct view, then, is that (9.16) is neither true nor false.

But wait! If (9.16) doesn't express a proposition, then surely I shouldn't assert that (9.16) doesn't express a proposition, since there's nothing to assert? That's partly right. What I can't do is say what I want to say using (9.16), since, given the argument above, (9.16) doesn't say anything. But I can say what I want to say using some other sentence, such as this one:

(9.17) The previous example sentence does not express a proposition.

That sentence isn't (type) identical to (9.16), since they differ syntactically. Does (9.17) express a proposition? Of course! The argument used above, showing that (9.16) doesn't express a proposition, does not apply to (9.17).

This example involving (9.16) and (9.17) brings out a crucial, and bizarre, feature of the *no proposition* approach. The latter sentence expresses a proposition about the former sentence, which is just like the latter, except that it contains the name '(9.16)' in place of the description 'the previous example sentence'. They are co-denoting terms, picking out the very same sentence, (9.16). Yet (9.17) says something, whereas (9.16) says nothing.

This strange phenomenon also occurs with the contingent Liar sentences, (9.6), (9.7), and (9.8), which we met in §9.1. Whether (9.6), (9.7), or (9.8) is paradoxical depends on what else is written on my board. So, on my analysis, whether (9.6), (9.7), or (9.8) expresses a proposition depends on what else is written on my board. How could this be?

For a sentence to express a proposition, the sentence and the rest of reality have to cooperate. A proposition, as a truthmaker condition, cannot exist unless certain states of affairs could exist. Where there is no possibility of those states of affairs existing, the proposition we want won't exist. When the world won't cooperate with a sentence, that sentence simply can't express a proposition. This isn't due to some defect in the sentence's meaning, or in extra linguistic contextual factors. Rather, it's due to a limitation on what non-linguistic reality is like. But what non-linguistic reality is like includes contingent facts about what's written on my board. So we shouldn't be so surprised when we learn that it's contingent whether (9.6), (9.7), or (9.8) express a proposition. It is much harder to explain this phenomenon if we consider only facts about meaning.

9.9 Meaning and Logic

I've argued that some meaningful sentences, including the Liar, fail to express a proposition, and hence do not say anything. There's two questions I want to address in this section. How are such sentences meaningful, if they do not say anything? And what becomes of logic, if meaningful sentences can fail to express a proposition? I'll begin with the question of meaning.

A sentence's meaning isn't the proposition it expresses. We know that independently of the 'no proposition' view. I argued in §8.1 that propositions (as I've defined them here) are not the objects of belief. But a sentence's meaning must be at least as fine-grained as the objects of belief. Suppose not. Then there are sentences 'A' and 'B' with the same meaning, such that, possibly, a believes that A but not B. But then 'a believes that A' means the same as 'a believes that B', yet they differ in truth in the same situation. That's impossible.

A key principle in semantics is that the theory of meaning must be compositional: the meaning of the whole (a sentence) must be a function of the meaning of the parts (the individual words, together with their syntactic structure). The guiding idea is that, given these functions, one can plug in their arguments (including worlds, times, and so on) and arrive at a truth-value.

We can take the meaning of a sentence to be a syntactically structured entity containing those functions. Such entities are similar to the structured entities discussed in §8.4, except they contain meanings, not referents or Fregean senses (Cresswell 1985; Lewis 1970). These entities are not propositions. They lack sufficient information to play that role. The meaning of 'I'm in Nottingham now' is not a proposition, for absent completing contextual information about the speaker and time, it can't be evaluated for truth. But given enough completing information, a structured meaning typically determines a proposition, which is true or false at a world.

That's what happens when things go well. But sometimes things don't go well. Sometimes, the function that's supposed to take in the meanings of the component words and output a proposition goes wrong. That function is partial: it isn't defined for all possible combinations of inputs. That's to say that, for some combinations of meanings, the semantic function gives no proposition as output.

This is precisely what happens in the case of the Liar. Each of its words has a meaning, and together these meanings comprise a structured meaning for the Liar sentence as a whole. But, given this structured meaning as input, the semantic function gives no output. When, in general, does this happen? We can't say. There is no finite axiomatisation of the semantic function. If there were, we could generate a revenge-style paradox (using the sentence 'the semantic function gives no output for this sentence', for example). That's how sentences can be meaningful, and yet fail to express a proposition.

Now we turn to the question of logic. Logic is the study of logical consequence. Logical consequence is a guarantee of truth preservation from premises to conclusion (in virtue of the logical structure of premises and conclusion). Since propositions are the primary bearers of truth and falsity, (sets of) propositions are the relata of the logical consequence relation. So, from this standpoint, a sentence's failing to express a proposition is quite incidental to the question of logical consequence. Holding that such-and-such sentence fails to express a proposition does not require any revision to the usual logical rules: they are just as we learned them.

To illustrate: my MacBook does not logically entail my MacBook. But this is no counterexample to the reflexivity of logical entailment (A entails A). For to say that logical entailment is reflexive is to say that every proposition entails itself. So the fact that such-and-such sentence expresses no proposition cannot have any influence on the reflexivity of entailment. The same goes for the other formal features of entailment.

Exactly the same goes for the T-scheme and the associated rules for truth, which say that $\langle A \rangle$ is equivalent to $\langle \langle A \rangle$ is true$\rangle$. If it turns out that the name '$\langle A \rangle$' is empty—that is, if the sentence 'A' doesn't express a proposition—then so is '$\langle \langle A \rangle$ is true$\rangle$'. So there is no possibility of $\langle A \rangle$ being true without $\langle \langle A \rangle$ is true$\rangle$ being true, or vice versa.

Indeed, as we saw in §8.5, the T-scheme goes deeper than 'mere' logical equivalence. For $\langle \langle A \rangle$ is true$\rangle$ is identical to the existential proposition $\langle \exists x \; x \; \text{truthmakes} \; \langle A \rangle \rangle$, which we identify with the set of all (natures of) possible truthmakers for $\langle A \rangle$, which is none other than $\langle A \rangle$ itself. The T-scheme is an informative identity statement between propositions. So, far from rejecting the T-scheme, the approach here treats it as a central principle of the theory of truth, holding with the strongest form of necessity.

The discussion above assumes the semantic notion of logical consequence (or entailment), in terms of necessary truth preservation.

The alternative view is to characterise logical consequence in terms of proof rules, thought of as instructions for manipulating symbols. But there are independent reasons for rejecting the proof-theoretic approach. The first is that it cannot deal with the paradoxes. Nontrivial proof-theoretic accounts must restrict the T-scheme or else be logically revisionary. But, given the arguments in §§9.3–9.6, all such moves are highly unattractive.

The second reason for rejecting pure proof-theoretic accounts is that they have a hard time justifying their chosen rules. Suppose we adopted the following inference rules (Prior 1960):

$$\frac{\Gamma, A/B \vdash \Delta}{\Gamma, A \text{ tonk } B \vdash \Delta} \text{ TONK L} \qquad \frac{\Gamma \vdash A/B, \Delta}{\Gamma \vdash A \text{ tonk } B, \Delta} \text{ TONK R}$$

(The 'A/B' notation indicates a rule with one exactly of 'A' and 'B' in that place.) They quickly allows us to derive any conclusion from any premise, as follows:

$$\frac{\dfrac{A \vdash A}{A \vdash A \text{ tonk } B} \quad \dfrac{B \vdash B}{A \text{ tonk } B \vdash B}}{A \vdash B}$$

Clearly, the *tonk* rules do not define a genuine connective. But why not? Purely proof-theoretic answers have been offered; but the jury is out on whether any can be made to work. If we characterise logical consequence in semantic terms, as I'm suggesting, then the problem doesn't arise. Connectives aren't defined by proof rules. They are defined semantically. Proof rules then attempt to mimic their semantic behaviour.

We should not understand proof rules as coming with a proviso, 'provided Γ, Δ all express propositions'. If we did, (ID) would say:

(9.18) If 'A' expresses a proposition, then A is a logical consequence of A.

But this is false. If 'A' expresses no proposition, then neither does the consequent, and hence the conditional is not true. Rather, proof theory is formulated by quantifying over propositions. We say: *for all propositions A, B, ..., we may use the following rules* .... That done, everything else stays as normal. We can then use all the classical rules we know and love, including the usual rules for truth. So no proof rule needs to be rejected, so long as we understand the metavariables, $A, B, \ldots$ as ranging over propositions.

Similarly, I am not proposing a restriction to the T-scheme, saying:

(9.19) If 'A' expresses a proposition, then ('A' is true iff A)

That approach would come a cropper, given Bacon's argument (2015), which we met in §9.6. Rather, the T-scheme holds in full generality: for every proposition $\langle A \rangle$, we have $\langle \langle A \rangle$ is true$\rangle$ iff $\langle A \rangle$. Indeed, as I argued above, this is really just an identity statement, given our metaphysical analysis of what propositions are. The same goes for the proof rules for 'is true'.

In almost all contexts, this understanding of proof theory (including the rules for truth) makes no difference at all. Meaningful sentences nearly always express a proposition. Uses of Liar sentences (and the truth-teller, the Curry sentence, and so on) outside philosophical discussions of truth are rare. When we teach logic, we almost always focus on languages without their own truth-predicate, reserving talk of truth for the strictly richer metalanguage. In any of these contexts, it would be uncommon to use a meaningful sentence that doesn't express a proposition.

Compare that situation with the one proposed by the the dialetheist (§9.3), non-contractive (§9.4), or non-transitive (§9.5) approaches discussed above. On those views, we're banned from making certain inferences, in any context. The dialetheist bans *reductio* and *disjunctive syllogism*, both of which are useful in practical (as well as theoretical) contexts. I can't find my keys. I know from experience that they're either still in my door or at the bottom of my bag. I check my bag: not there. So, I infer, they're still in my door. That's a practically useful instance of *disjunctive syllogism*. Practical instances of *reductio* abound. Similarly, both transitivity and contraction are practically indispensable.

The approach I've offered here is, as far as I can see, the only genuine, non-*ad hoc* solution to the paradoxes that is immune to revenge. It is also the only one which leaves logic as we know it, for all practical purposes.

9.10 Chapter Summary

I've argued that we shouldn't try to solve the Liar (and the other semantic paradoxes) by revising our logic. The dialetheist (§9.3) approach alone does not solve all the paradoxes, and both the non-contractive (§9.4) and non-transitive (§9.5) approaches would force us to give up patterns of reasoning that are essential in philosophy and mathematics. Nor can we solve the paradoxes by restricting or replacing the T-scheme (§9.6), or by claiming Liar sentences are undecidable (§9.7). I then argued that the account of propositions from chapter 8 already provides a solution: there is no proposition for the Liar sentence to express (§9.8). This approach is non-*ad hoc*, and is immune to revenge problems. It allows us to say that the Liar sentence is meaningful (as it surely is), even though it does not express a proposition (§9.9). Logic, understood as specifying relations between propositions, is not affected by the theory. So understood, all the usual (classical) proof rules remain valid, including the rules for *truth* (§9.9).

Appendix
Proof Theory

A *sequent* is a statement of the form Γ ⊢ Δ, where Γ and Δ are (possibly empty) lists of sentences. We read this as 'Γ proves Δ'. We understand the sentences in Γ (the premises) conjunctively and the sentences in Δ (the conclusions) disjunctively. In semantic terms, we might understand 'Γ ⊢ Δ' as saying that, if all the premises in Γ are true, then one of the conclusions in Δ must be true.

The *sequent calculus* (Gentzen 1934) gives us a system of rules for manipulating sequents like this. Those rules can be divided into *logical rules* (figure 10.1), which specify how the logical connectives work, and *structural rules* (figure 10.2), which tell us how to manipulate sequents in a derivation. Most of the rules come in a *left* (L) and *right* (R) version, telling us how to do something to the *left* or to the *right* of the '⊢' symbol in the sequent.

A derivation of a sequent Γ ⊢ Δ is a tree with Γ ⊢ Δ at its root (i.e., at the bottom) and an instance of (ID) at each leaf (the top end of each branch). In practice, proofs are constructed bottom-up, beginning with the sequent to be proved and working upwards, applying the rules from lower sequent to upper sequent(s). In each case, (ID) is the goal.

The structural rules in figure 10.2 are *identity* (ID), (CUT), *weakening* ((KL) and (KR)), *contraction* ((WL) and (KR)), *exchange* (or *permutation*, (EL) and (ER)). (The naming of these rules goes back to *combinatory logic* (Curry 1930), in which the **K** combinator corresponds to weakening (**K**$xy = x$) and the **W** combinator to contraction (**W**$xy = xyy$).)

$$\frac{\Gamma \vdash A, \Delta}{\Gamma, \neg A \vdash \Delta} \; (\neg\text{L}) \qquad \frac{\Gamma, A \vdash \Delta}{\Gamma \vdash \neg A, \Delta} \; (\neg\text{R})$$

$$\frac{\Gamma, A \vdash \Delta \quad \Gamma', B \vdash \Delta'}{\Gamma, \Gamma', A \vee B \vdash \Delta, \Delta'} \; (\vee\text{L}) \qquad \frac{\Gamma \vdash A/B, \Delta}{\Gamma \vdash A \vee B, \Delta} \; (\vee\text{R})$$

$$\frac{\Gamma, A/B \vdash \Delta}{\Gamma, A \wedge B \vdash \Delta} \; (\wedge\text{L}) \qquad \frac{\Gamma \vdash A, \Delta \quad \Gamma' \vdash B, \Delta'}{\Gamma, \Gamma' \vdash A \wedge B, \Delta, \Delta'} \; (\wedge\text{R})$$

$$\frac{\Gamma \vdash A, \Delta \quad \Gamma', B \vdash \Delta'}{\Gamma, \Gamma', A \to B \vdash \Delta, \Delta'} \; (\to\text{L}) \qquad \frac{\Gamma, A \vdash B, \Delta}{\Gamma \vdash A \to B, \Delta} \; (\to\text{R})$$

Figure 10.1: LOGICAL RULES

$$\frac{}{A \vdash A} \; (\text{ID}) \qquad \frac{\Gamma, A \vdash \Delta \quad \Gamma' \vdash A, \Delta'}{\Gamma, \Gamma' \vdash \Delta, \Delta} \; (\text{CUT})$$

$$\frac{\Gamma \vdash \Delta}{\Gamma, A \vdash \Delta} \; (\text{KL}) \qquad \frac{\Gamma, A, A \vdash B, \Delta}{\Gamma, A \vdash B, \Delta} \; (\text{WL}) \qquad \frac{\Gamma, A, B \vdash \Delta}{\Gamma, B, A \vdash \Delta} \; (\text{EL})$$

$$\frac{\Gamma \vdash \Delta}{\Gamma \vdash B, \Delta} \; (\text{KR}) \qquad \frac{\Gamma, A \vdash B, B, \Delta}{\Gamma, A \vdash B, \Delta} \; (\text{WR}) \qquad \frac{\Gamma \vdash C, D, \Delta}{\Gamma \vdash D, C, \Delta} \; (\text{ER})$$

Figure 10.2: STRUCTURAL RULES

If sequents are defined over lists or sequences of sentences Γ and Δ, then (EL) and (ER) guarantee that the order of sentences doesn't matter. Alternatively, we can define sequents over *multisets* of sentences, in which each element may occur one or more times but order doesn't matter, so that the *exchange* rules become redundant. (We can treat a multiset Γ as a standard set Δ coupled with a function ## : $\Delta \longrightarrow \mathbb{N}$, with ##$x$ telling us how many occurrences of x appear in Γ.) If we use either lists or multisets, *contraction* tells us to ignore repetition. Alternatively, we can build this feature in by using sets of sentences Γ, Δ, which ignore both order and repetition of sentences. Then, the *exchange* and *contraction* rules come for free.

Bibliography

Achourioti, T., Galinon, H., Fernández, J. M., and Fujimoto, K. (eds) (2015). *Unifying the Philosophy of Truth*, Springer, Dordrecht.

Aczel, P. (1988). *Non-well-founded sets*, CSLI Lecture Notes Vol. 14, CSLI, Stanford.

Adams, R. (1974). Theories of actuality, *Noûs* 8(3): 211–31.

Alechina, N. and Van Lambalgen, M. (1996). Generalized quantification as substructural logic, *Journal of Symbolic Logic* 61(03): 1006–44.

Anderson, A. and Belnap, N. (1962). Tautological entailments, *Philosophical Studies* 13(1): 9–24.

Anderson, A. and Belnap, N. (1963). First degree entailments, *Mathematische Annalen* 149(4): 302–19.

Angell, R. B. (1989). Deducibility, entailment and analytic containment, *Directions in Relevant Logic*, Springer, pp. 119–43.

Anjum, R. L. and Mumford, S. (2014). Powers as causal truthmakers, *Disputatio* 4: 5–31.

Anscombe, E. (2000). Making true, *Royal Institute of Philosophy Supplement* 46: 1–8.

Armstrong, D. (1997). *A World of States of Affairs*, Cambridge University Press, Cambridge.

Armstrong, D. (2003). Truthmakers for modal truths, in H. Lillehammer and G. Rodriguez-Pereyra (eds), *Real Metaphysics: Essays in Honour of D. H. Mellor*, Routledge, London, pp. 12–24.

Armstrong, D. (2004). *Truth and Truthmakers*, Cambridge University Press, Cambridge.

Armstrong, D. M. (1978). *Universals and Scientific Realism: Nominalism and Realism* Vol. 1, Cambridge University Press, Cambridge.

Armstrong, D. M. (1980). *Universals and Scientific Realism: A Theory of Universals* Vol. 2, Cambridge University Press, Cambridge.

Armstrong, D. M. (1989). *Universals: An Opinionated Introduction*, Westview Press, Boulder, CO.

Armstrong, D. M. (1991). Classes are states of affairs, *Mind* 100: 189–200.

Armstrong, D. M. (2010). *Sketch for a Systematic Metaphysics*, Oxford University Press, Oxford.

Asay, J. (2012). A truthmaking account of realism and anti-realism, *Pacific Philosophical Quarterly* 93(3): 373–94.

Asay, J. (2013a). Primitive truth, *Dialectica* 67(4): 503–19.

Asay, J. (2013b). *The Primitivist Theory of Truth*, Cambridge University Press, Cambridge.

Asay, J. (2014). Against truth, *Erkenntnis* 79(1): 147–64.

Asay, J. and Baron, S. (2012). Unstable truthmaking, *Thought: A Journal of Philosophy* 1(3): 230–8.

Audi, P. (2012a). A clarification and defense of the notion of grounding, in F. Correia and B. Schnieder (eds), *Metaphysical Grounding*, Cambridge University Press, Cambridge, pp. 101–21.

Audi, P. (2012b). Grounding: Toward a theory of the in-virtue-of relation, *Journal of Philosophy* 109(12): 685–711.

Ayer, A. (1936). *Language, Truth and Logic*, Victor Gollancz, London.

Bacon, A. (2015). Can the classical logician avoid the revenge paradoxes?, *Philosophical Review* 124(3): 299–352.

Bar-On, D., Horisk, C. and Lycan, W. G. (2000). Deflationism, meaning and truth-conditions, *Philosophical Studies* 101(1): 1–28.

Barker, S. (2014). Semantic paradox and alethic undecidability, *Analysis* 74(2): 201–09.

Barker, S. and Jago, M. (2012). Being positive about negative facts, *Philosophy and Phenomenological Research* 85(1): 117–38.

Barker, S. and Jago, M. (2017). Material objects and essential bundle theory, *Philosophical Studies*, doi 10.1007/s11098-017-0990-6.

Baron, S., Miller, K., and Norton, J. (2014). Groundless truth, *Inquiry* 57(2): 175–95.

Barrio, E. and Rodriguez-Pereyra, G. (2015). Truthmaker maximalism defended again, *Analysis* 75(1): 3–8.

Beall, J. and Murzi, J. (2013). Two flavors of Curry's paradox, *Journal of Philosophy* 110(3): 143–65.

Beebee, H. and Dodd, J. (2005a). Introduction, *Truthmakers: The Contemporary Debate*, Oxford University Press, pp. 1–16.

Beebee, H. and Dodd, J. (eds) (2005b). *Truthmakers: The Contemporary Debate*, Oxford University Press, Oxford.

Belnap, N. (1967). Intensional models for first degree formulas, *Journal of Symbolic Logic* 32(1): 1–22.

Bennett, K. (2011a). By our bootstraps, *Philosophical Perspectives* 25(1): 27–41.

Bennett, K. (2011b). Construction area (no hard hat required), *Philosophical Studies* 154(1): 79–104.

Bennett, K. (2011c). Truthmaking and case-making, *Philosophy and Phenomenological Research* 83(1): 187–95.

Berkeley, G. (1710/1995). *A Treatise Concerning the Principles of Human Knowledge*, ed. K.P. Winkler, Hackett, Indianapolis.

Bernstein, S. (2016). Grounding is not causation, *Philosophical Perspectives* 30(1): 21–38.

Bigelow, J. (1988). *The Reality of Numbers: A Physicalist's Philosophy of Mathematics*, Oxford University Press, Oxford.

Bigelow, J. (1996). Presentism and properties, *Philosophical Perspectives* 10: 35–52.

Bimbo, K. (2006). Curry-type paradoxes, *Logique et Analyse* 49(195): 227–40.

Black, M. (1952). The identity of indiscernibles, *Mind* 61: 153–64.

Bliss, R. (2014). Viciousness and circles of ground, *Metaphilosophy* 45(2): 245–56.

Bliss, R. L. (2013). Viciousness and the structure of reality, *Philosophical studies* 166(2): 399–418.

Bliss, R. and Priest, G. (forthcoming). *Reality and its Structure*, Oxford University Press, Oxford.

Bliss, R. and Trogdon, K. (2016). Metaphysical grounding, in E. N. Zalta (ed.), *Stanford Encyclopedia of Philosophy*, https://plato.stanford.edu/archives/win2016/entries/grounding/.

Bradley, F. H. (1897). *Appearance and Reality: A Metaphysical Essay*, Clarendon Press, Oxford.

Brady, R. (2006). *Universal Logic*, CSLI Publications, Stanford, CA.

Briggs, R. (2012). Truthmaking without necessitation, *Synthese* 189(1): 11–28.

Burge, T. (1992). Frege on knowing the third realm, *Mind* 101: 633–50.

Button, T. (2013). *The Limits of Realism*, Oxford University Press, Oxford.

Button, T. (2014). The weight of truth: Lessons for minimalists from Russell's 'Gray's Elegy' argument, *Proceedings of the Aristotelian Society* 114: 261–89.

Cameron, M. A. (2015). Is ground said-in-many-ways?, *Studia Philosophica Estonica* 7(2): 29–55.

Cameron, R. (2008). How to be a truthmaker maximalist, *Noûs* 42(3): 410–21.

Cameron, R. (2010). Truthmaking for presentists, in K. Bennett and D. Zimmerman (eds.), *Oxford Studies in Metaphysics*, Vol. 6, Oxford University Press, Oxford, pp. 55–100.

Carnap, R. (1934). *Logische Syntax der Sprache*, Springer, Vienna.

Casati, R. and Varzi, A. (1994). *Holes and other Superficialities*, MIT Press, Cambridge, MA.

Cheyne, C. and Pigden, C. (2006). Negative truths from positive facts, *Australasian Journal of Philosophy* 84(2): 249–65.

Church, A. (2009). Referee reports on Fitch's 'A Definition of Value', in J. Salerno (ed.), *New Essays on the Knowability Paradox*, Oxford University Press, Oxford, pp. 13–20.

Clark, M. J. and Liggins, D. (2012). Recent work on grounding, *Analysis* 72(4): 812–23.

Cobreros, P., Égré, P., Ripley, D. and Van Rooij, R. (2013). Reaching transparent truth, *Mind* 122: 841–66.

Cotnoir, A. (2009). Generic truth and mixed conjunctions: Some alternatives, *Analysis* 69(3): 473–79.

Cresswell, M. J. (1985). *Structured Meanings*, MIT Press, Cambridge, MA.

Crimmins, M. (1992). *Talk About Belief*, MIT Press, Cambridge, MA.

Crimmins, M. and Perry, J. (1989). The prince and the phone booth: Reporting puzzling beliefs, *Journal of Philosophy* 86: 685–711.

Curry, H. B. (1930). Grundlagen der kombinatorischen logik, *American Journal of Mathematics* 52(4): 789–834.

Dasgupta, S. (2014a). On the plurality of grounds, *Philosopher's Imprint* 14(20), 1–28.

Dasgupta, S. (2014b). The possibility of physicalism, *Journal of Philosophy* 111(9/10): 557–92.

David, M. (2016). The correspondence theory of truth, in E. N. Zalta (ed.), *The Stanford Encyclopedia of Philosophy*, https://plato.stanford.edu/archives/fall2016/entries/truth-correspondence/.

Demos, R. (1917). A discussion of a certain type of negative proposition, *Mind* 26(1): 188–96.

DeRosset, L. (2013). Grounding explanations, *Philosopher's Imprint* 13(7): 1–26.

Divers, J. (1999). A genuine realist theory of advanced modalizing, *Mind* 108(430): 217–40.

Dodd, J. (2013). Deflationism trumps pluralism, in Pedersen and Wright (eds.), *Truth and Pluralism: Current Debates*, Oxford University Press, Oxford pp. 298–322.

Dowe, P. (2009). Absences, possible causation, and the problem of non-locality, *Monist* 92: 24–41.

Dummett, M. (1978). *Truth and Other Enigmas*, Harvard University Press, Cambridge, MA.

Dummett, M. (1993). *The Seas of Language*, Oxford University Press, Oxford.

Dummett, M. (1996). *Frege and Other Philosophers*, Oxford University Press, Oxford.

Dunn, J. M. (2000). Partiality and its dual, *Studia Logica* 65: 5–40.

Dutilh Novaes, C. (2008). A comparative taxonomy of medieval and modern approaches to liar sentences, *History and Philosophy of Logic* 29(3): 227–61.

Dutilh Novaes, C. (2011). Lessons on truth from mediaeval solutions to the liar paradox, *The Philosophical Quarterly* 61(242): 58–78.

Dyke, H. (2007). Tenseless/non-modal truthmakers for tensed/ modal truths, *Logique et Analyse* 50(199): 269–87.

Edwards, D. (2009). Truth-conditions and the nature of truth: Resolving mixed conjunctions, *Analysis* 68: 143–49.

Epstein, B. (2015). *The Ant Trap: Rebuilding the Foundations of the Social Sciences*, Oxford University Press, Oxford.

Farennikova, A. (2013). Seeing absence, *Philosophical Studies* 166(3): 429–54.

Fine, K. (1977). Postscript, in A. Prior and K. Fine (eds.), *Worlds, Times and Selves*, MIT Press, Amherst, MA, pp. 116–61.

Fine, K. (1994). Essence and modality: The second philosophical perspectives lecture, *Philosophical Perspectives* 8: 1–16.

Fine, K. (1995). Senses of essence, in Walter Sinnott-Armstrong, Diana Raffman, and Nicholas Asher (eds.), *Modality, Morality, and Belief: Essays in Honor of Ruth Barcan Marcus*, Cambridge University Press, Cambridge, pp. 53–73.

Fine, K. (2001). The question of realism, *Philosophers' Imprint* 1: 1–30.

Fine, K. (2005). *Modality and Tense: Philosophical Papers*, Oxford University Press, New York.

Fine, K. (2012a). Counterfactuals without possible worlds, *Journal of Philosophy* 109(3): 221–46.

Fine, K. (2012b). Guide to ground, in F. Correia and B. Schnieder (eds.), *Metaphysical Grounding: Understanding the Structure of Reality*, Cambridge University Press, Cambridge, pp. 37–80.

Fine, K. (2012c). The pure logic of ground, *Review of Symbolic Logic* 5(1): 1–25.

Fine, K. (2014). Truth-maker semantics for intuitionistic logic, *Journal of Philosophical Logic* 43(2–3), 549–77.

Fine, K. (2015). Subject matter. Talk given at Yablo on Aboutness workshop, Hamburg, 3 August.

Fine, K. (2016). Angellic content, *Journal of Philosophical Logic* 45(2): 199–226.

Fine, K. (2017a). A theory of truth-conditional content I: Conjunction, disjunction and negation, *Journal of Philosophical Logic* 46(6), 625–74.

Fine, K. (2017b). A theory of truth-conditional content II: Subject-matter, common content, remainder and ground, *Journal of Philosophical Logic* 46(6), 675–702.

Fine, K. and Jago, M. (2017). Exact truthmaker logic, unpublished draft.

Fitch, F. (1963). A logical analysis of some value concepts, *Journal of Symbolic Logic* 28(2): 135–42.

Fox, J. (1987). Truthmaker, *Australasian Journal of Philosophy* 65(2): 188–207.

Frege, G. (1897/1979). Logic, in K. F. Hermes, H. and F. Kaulbach (eds.), *Posthumous Writings*, University of Chicago Press, Chicago, pp. 126–51.

Frege, G. (1904/1980). Letter to Russell, 13.11.1904, in G. Gabriel, H. Hermes, F. Kambartel, C. Thiel, and A. Veraart (eds.), *Gottlob Frege: Philosophical and Mathematical Correspondence*, Blackwell, Oxford, pp. 160–66.

Frege, G. (1918/1977). Thoughts, *Logical Investigations*, Blackwell, Oxford.

Frege, G. (1956). The thought: A logical inquiry, *Mind* 65(259): 289–311.

Gaifman, H. (2006). Naming and diagonalization, from Cantor to Gödel to Kleene, *Logic Journal of IGPL* 14(5): 709–28.

Gentzen, G. (1934). Untersuchungen über das Logische Schließen, *Mathematische Zeitschrift* 39: 176–210.

Gettier, E. (1963). Is justified true belief knowledge?, *Analysis* 23(6): 121–3.

Girard, J.-Y. (1987). Linear logic, *Theoretical Computer Science* 50(1): 1–102.

Gödel, K. (1931). Über formal unentscheidbare Sätze der Principia Mathematica und verwandter Systeme I, *Monatshefte für Mathematik und Physik* 38(1): 173–98.

Goldstein, L. (1985). The paradox of the liar: A case of mistaken identity, *Analysis* 45(1): 9–13.

Goldstein, L. (2000). A unified solution to some paradoxes, *Proceedings of the Aristotelian Society* 100(1): 53–74.

Goldstein, L. (2001). Truth-bearers and the liar—a reply to Alan Weir, *Analysis* 61(270): 115–26.

Green, K. (2009). Necessitating nominalism, *Acta Analytica* 24(3): 193–6.

Greenough, P. (2001). Free assumptions and the liar paradox, *American Philosophical Quarterly* 38(2): 115–35.

Griffith, A. M. (2014). Truthmaking and grounding, *Inquiry* 57(2): 196–215.

Griffith, A. M. (2015). Towards a pluralist theory of truthmaking, *Erkenntnis* 80(6): 1157–73.

Griffith, A. M. (2017). Social construction and grounding, *Philosophy and Phenomenological Research*, doi: 10.1111/phpr.12376.

Grišin, V. N. (1982). Predicate and set-theoretic calculi based on logic without contractions, *Mathematics of the USSR-Izvestiya* 18(1): 41–59.

Hand, M. (2009). Performance and paradox, in J. Salerno (ed.), *New Essays on the Knowability Paradox*, Oxford University Press, Oxford, pp. 284–301.

Haslanger, S. (2004). Future genders? Future races?, *Philosophic Exchange* 34(1): https://digitalcommons.brockport.edu/ phil_ex/vol34/iss1/1.

Hawley, K. (2011). Trivial truthmaking matters, *Philosophy and Phenomenological Research* 83(1): 196–202.

Heil, J. (2003). *From an Ontological Point of View*, Oxford University Press, Oxford.

Hornsby, J. (2005). Truth without truthmaking entities, in H. Beebee and J. Dodd (eds.), *Truthmakers: The Contemporary Debate*, Clarendon Press, Oxford, pp. 33–47.

Horwich, P. (1998). *Truth*, 2nd edition, Blackwell, Oxford.

Ingram, D. (2016a). The virtues of thisness presentism, *Philosophical Studies* 173(11): 2867–88.

Ingram, D. (2016b). Thisnesses, propositions, and truth, *Pacific Philosophical Quarterly*, doi: 10.1111/papq.12181.

Jackson, F. (1994). Armchair metaphysics, in M. Michael and J. O'Leary-Hawthorne (eds), *Philosophy in Mind: The Place of Philosophy in the Study of Mind*, Kluwer, Dordrecht, pp. 23–42.

Jago, M. (2009). The conjunction and disjunction theses, *Mind* 118: 411–15.

Jago, M. (2010). Closure on knowability, *Analysis* 70(4): 648–59.

Jago, M. (2011). Setting the facts straight, *Journal of Philosophical Logic* 40: 33–54.

Jago, M. (2012). The truthmaker non-maximalist's dilemma, *Mind* 121: 903–18.

Jago, M. (2014). *The Impossible*, Oxford University Press, Oxford.

Jago, M. (2016a). Advanced modalizing problems, *Mind* 125: 627–42.

Jago, M. (2016b). Essence and the grounding problem, in M. Jago (ed.), *Reality Making*, Oxford University Press, Oxford, pp. 99–120.

Jansson, L. (2016). Explanatory asymmetries, ground, and ontological dependence, *Erkenntnis* pp. 1–28.

Jenkins, C. S. (2007). True, false, paranormal and designated: A reply to Beall, *Analysis* 67(1): 80–83.

Jenkins, C. S. (2008). The importance of being designated: A comment on Caret and Cotnoir, *Analysis* 68(299): 244–7.

Jenkins, C. S. (2009). The mystery of the disappearing diamond, in J. Salerno (ed,), *New Essays on the Knowability Paradox*, Oxford University Press, Oxford, pp. 302–19.

Jenkins, C. S. (2013). Explanation and fundamentality, in M. Hoeltje, B. Schnieder, and A. Steinberg (eds.), *Varieties of Dependence*, Philosophia, Munich, pp. 211–42.

Jenkins, C. S. (2011). Is metaphysical dependence irreflexive?, *Monist* 94(2): 267-76.

Jenkins, C. S. and Nolan, D. (2008). Liar-like paradox and object language features, *American Philosophical Quarterly* 45(1): 67-73.

Kant, I. (1781/1998). *Critique of Pure Reason*, ed. P. Guyer and A.W. Wood, Cambridge University Press, Cambridge.

Kim, J. (1998). *Mind in a Physical World*, Cambridge University Press, Cambridge.

King, J. (1995). Structured propositions and complex predicates, *Noûs* 29(4): 516-35.

King, J. (1996). Structured propositions and sentence structure, *Journal of Philosophical Logic* 25(5): 495-521.

King, J. C. (1994). Can propositions be naturalistically acceptable?, *Midwest Studies in Philosophy* 19(1): 53-75.

King, J. C. (2012). Structured propositions, in E. N. Zalta (ed.), *The Stanford Encyclopedia of Philosophy*, http://plato.stanford.edu/archives/win2012/entries/propositions-structured/.

Koslicki, K. (2012). Varieties of ontological dependence, in F. Correia and B. Schnieder (eds.), *Metaphysical Grounding: Understanding the Structure of Reality*, Cambridge University Press, Cambridge, pp. 186-213.

Koslicki, K. (2015). The coarse-grainedness of grounding, in K. Bennett and D. Zimmerman (eds.), *Oxford Studies in Metaphysics* Vol. 8, Oxford University Press, Oxford, pp. 306-44.

Koslicki, K. (2016). Where grounding and causation part ways: Comments on Schaffer, *Philosophical Studies* 173(1): 101-12.

Kripke, S. (1975). Outline of a theory of truth, *Journal of Philosophy* 72: 690-716.

Kukso, B. (2006). The reality of absences, *Australasian Journal of Philosophy* 84(1): 21-37.

Ladyman, J. and Ross, D. (2007). *Every Thing Must Go: Metaphysics Naturalized*, Oxford University Press, New York.

Lange, M. (2004). A note on scientific essentialism, laws of nature, and counterfactual conditionals, *Australasian Journal of Philosophy* 82(2): 227-41.

Lewis, D. (1970). General semantics, *Synthese* 22(1): 18-67.

Lewis, D. (1971). Counterparts of persons and their bodies, *Journal of Philosophy* 68(7): 203-11.

Lewis, D. (1986). *On the Plurality of Worlds*, Blackwell, Oxford.

Lewis, D. (1991). *Parts of Classes*, Blackwell, Oxford.

Lewis, D. (1992). Critical notice of D. M. Armstrong's *A Combinatorial Theory of Possibility*, *Australasian Journal of Philosophy* 70(2): 211-24.

Lewis, D. (1993). Mathematics is megethology, *Philosophia Mathematica* 1(1): 3-23.

Lewis, D. (1999). A world of truthmakers?, *Papers in Metaphysics and Epistemology*, Cambridge University Press, pp. 215-20.

Lewis, D. (2001). Truthmaking and difference-making, *Noûs* 35(4): 602-15.

Lewis, D. (2003). Things qua truthmakers, in H. Lillehammer and G. Rodriguez-Pereyra (eds.), *Real Metaphysics*, Routledge, London, pp. 25-38.

Lewis, D. and Lewis, S. (1970). Holes, *Australasian Journal of Philosophy* 48(2): 206-12.

Lewis, D. and Rosen, G. (2003). Postscript to 'things qua truthmakers': Negative existentials, in H. Lillehammer and G. Rodriguez-Pereyra (eds.), *Real Metaphysics*, Routledge, London, pp. 39–42.

Liggins, D. (2008). Truthmakers and the groundedness of truth, *Proceedings of the Aristotelian Society* 108: 177–96.

Linsky, B. (2009). Logical types in arguments about knowability and belief, in J. Salerno (ed.), *New Essays on the Knowability Paradox*, Oxford University Press, Oxford, pp. 163–179.

Litland, J. (2017). Grounding ground, in K. Bennett and D. Zimmerman (eds.),*Oxford Studies in Metaphysics* Vol. 10, Oxford University Press, Oxford, pp. 279–316.

Lowe, E. J. (2012). Essence and ontology, in L. Novák, D. D. Novotn, P. Sousedík, and D. Svoboda (eds), *Metaphysics: Aristotelian, Scholastic, Analytic*, Ontos, Frankfurt, pp. 93–112.

Lowe, E. J. and Rami, A. (eds.) (2009). *Truth and Truth-Making*, Acumen, Stocksfield.

Lynch, M. P. (2001). A functionalist theory of truth, in M. Lynch (ed.), *The Nature of Truth: Classic and Contemporary Perspectives*, MIT Press, Cambridge, MA, pp. 723–749.

Lynch, M. P. (2004). *True to Life: Why Truth Matters*, MIT Press, Cambridge, MA.

Lynch, M. P. (2009). *Truth as One and Many*, Oxford University Press, Oxford.

Mares, E. (2004). *Relevant Logic: A Philosophical Interpretation*, Cambridge University Press, Cambridge.

Marques, T. (2016). This is not an instance of (E), *Synthese*, doi: 10.1007/s11229-016-1293-8.

Martin, C. B. (1996). How it is: Entities, absences and voids, *Australasian Journal of Philosophy* 74(1): 57–65.

McDaniel, K. (2004). Modal realism with overlap, *Australasian Journal of Philosophy* 82(1): 137–52.

McGee, V. (1989). Applying Kripke's theory of truth, *Journal of Philosophy* pp. 530–9.

Melia, J. (2005). Truthmaking without truthmakers, in H. Beebee and J. Dodd (eds), *Truthmakers: The Contemporary Debate*, Oxford University Press, Oxford, pp. 67–84.

Mellor, D. (2003). Replies, in H. Lillehammer and G. Rodriguez-Pereyra (eds.), *Real Metaphysics*, Routledge, London, pp. 212–38.

Mellor, D. (2009). Truthmakers for what?, in H. Dyke (ed.), *From Truth to Reality: New Essays in Logic and Metaphysics*, Routledge, New York, pp. 272–90.

Merricks, T. (2007). *Truth and Ontology*, Clarendon Press, Oxford.

Merricks, T. (2015). *Propositions*, Oxford University Press, Oxford.

Mill, J. S. (1889). *An Examination of Sir William Hamilton's Philosophy: And of the Principal Philosophical Questions Discussed in his Writings*, Longmans & Green, London.

Miller, K. and Norton, J. (2016). Grounding: It's (probably) all in the head, *Philosophical Studies* 174(12): 3059–81.

Milne, P. (2005). Not every truth has a truthmaker, *Analysis* 65(3): 221–4.

Milne, P. (2013). Not every truth has a truthmaker II, *Analysis* 73(3): 473–81.

Molnar, G. (2000). Truthmakers for negative truths, *Australasian Journal of Philosophy* 78(1): 72–86.

Moltmann, F. (2015). A truthmaker semantics for 'cases', http://cnrs.academia.edu/FriederikeMoltmann.

Moore, G. E. (1901). Truth and falsity, in J. Baldwin (ed.), *Dictionary of Philosophy and Psychology*, Macmillan, London, pp. 20–2.

Mumford, S. (2007). Negative truth and falsehood, *Proceedings of the Aristotelian Society* 107(1): 45–71.

Mumford, S. and Anjum, R. (2009). Double prevention and powers, *Journal of Critical Realism* 8(3): 277–293.

Mumford, S. and Anjum, R. L. (2011). *Getting Causes from Powers*, Oxford University Press, Oxford.

Noonan, H. (1991). Indeterminate identity, contingent identity and Abelardian predicates, *Philosophical Quarterly* 41(163): 183–93.

Osorio-Kupferblum, N. (2016). Aboutness, *Analysis* 76(4): 528–46.

Parsons, J. (2006). Negative truths from positive facts?, *Australasian Journal of Philosophy* 84(4): 591–602.

Parsons, T. (1984). Assertion, denial, and the liar paradox, *Journal of Philosophical Logic* 13(2): 137–52.

Pedersen, N. J. L. L. and Wright, C. (2013). Pluralist theories of truth, in E. N. Zalta (ed.), *The Stanford Encyclopedia of Philosophy*, http://plato.stanford.edu/entries/truth-pluralist/.

Percival, P. (1990). Fitch and intuitionistic knowability, *Analysis* 50: 182–7.

Petersen, U. (2000). Logic without contraction as based on inclusion and unrestricted abstraction, *Studia Logica* 64(3): 365–403.

Plantinga, A. (1974). *The Nature of Necessity*, Oxford University Press, Oxford.

Plantinga, A. (1976). Actualism and possible worlds, *Theoria* 42(1-3): 139–60.

Poggiolesi, F. (2016). On defining the notion of complete and immediate formal grounding, *Synthese* 193(10): 3147–67.

Priest, G. (1979). Logic of paradox, *Journal of Philosophical Logic* 8: 219–41.

Priest, G. (1987). *In Contradiction: A Study of the Transconsistent*, Martinus Nijhoff, Dordrecht.

Priest, G. (2005). *Towards Non-Being*, Clarendon Press, Oxford.

Priest, G. (2010). Inclosures, vagueness, and self-reference, in F. Berto, E. Mares, F. Paoli, and K. Tanaka (eds.), *Proceedings of the Fourth World Congress of Paraconsistency*.

Priest, G. (2014). *One*, Oxford University Press, Oxford.

Prior, A. (1960). The runabout inference-ticket, *Analysis* 21(2): 38–9.

Pritchard, D. (2005). *Epistemic Luck*, Oxford University Press, Oxford.

Pritchard, D. (2007). Anti-luck epistemology, *Synthese* 158(3): 277–97.

Pritchard, D. (2009). Safety-based epistemology: Whither now?, *Journal of Philosophical Research* 34: 33–45.

Putnam, H. (1979). How to be an internal realist and a transcendental idealist (at the same time), in R. Haller and W. Grassl (eds), *Language, Logic, and Philosophy: Proceedings of the 4th International Wittgenstein Symposium*, Hölder-Pichler-Tempsky, Vienna, pp. 100–8.

Putnam, H. (1981). *Reason, Truth and History*, Cambridge University Press, Cambridge.

Quine, W. V. O. (1948). On what there is, *Review of Metaphysics* 2(5): 21–38.

Quine, W. V. O. (1951). Ontology and ideology, *Philosophical Studies* 2: 11–13.

Quine, W. V. O. (1960). *Word and Object*, MIT Press, Cambridge, MA.

Quine, W. V. O. (1986). *Philosophy of Logic*, Harvard University Press, Cambridge, MA.

Quine, W. V. O. (1987). *Quiddities*, Harvard University Press, Cambridge, MA.

Ramsey, F. P. (1927). Facts and propositions, *Proceedings of the Aristotelian Society*, Supplementary Volume 7: 153–206.

Rasmussen, J. (2014). About aboutness, *Metaphysica* 15(1): 173–86.

Read, S. (1988). *Relevant Logic*, Blackwell, Oxford.

Read, S. (2000). Truthmakers and the disjunction thesis, *Mind* 109: 67–79.

Restall, G. (1994). On logics without contraction, PhD thesis, University of Queensland.

Restall, G. (1996). Truthmakers, entailment and necessity, *Australasian Journal of Philosophy* 74(2): 331–40.

Restall, G. (2005). Multiple conclusions, *Logic, Methodology, and Philosophy of Science: Proceedings of the twelfth International Congress*, pp. 189–205.

Restall, G. (2016). *Proof Theory and Philosophy*, manuscript in progress (March 2016), http://consequently.org/writing/ptp/.

Richard, M. (1990). *Propositional Attitudes*, Cambridge University Press, Cambridge.

Ripley, D. (2015). Comparing substructural theories of truth, *Ergo* 2(13), doi: http://dx.doi.org/10.3998/ergo.12405314.0002.013.

Rodriguez-Pereyra, G. (2005). Why truthmakers, in J. Dodd and H. Beebee (eds), *Truthmakers*, Oxford University Press, Oxford, pp. 17–31.

Rodriguez-Pereyra, G. (2006a). Truthmaker maximalism defended, *Analysis* 66(291): 260–4.

Rodriguez-Pereyra, G. (2006b). Truthmaking, entailment, and the conjunction thesis, *Mind* 115: 957–82.

Rodriguez-Pereyra, G. (2009). The disjunction and conjunction theses, *Mind* 118: 427–43.

Rodriguez-Pereyra, G. (2015). Grounding is not a strict order, *Journal of the American Philosophical Association* 1(3): 517–34.

Rogerson, S. and Restall, G. (2004). Routes to triviality, *Journal of Philosophical Logic* 33(4): 421–36.

Rosen, G. (2010). Metaphysical dependence: Grounding and reduction, in R. Hale and A. Hoffman (eds.), *Modality: Metaphysics, Logic, and Epistemology*, Oxford University Press, Oxford, pp. 109–36.

Routley, R., Plumwood, V., and Meyer, R. K. (1982). *Relevant Logics and their Rivals*, Ridgeview Publishing Company, Atascadero, CA.

Russell, B. (1903). *The Principles of Mathematics*, George Allen and Unwin, London.

Russell, B. (1904/1980). Letter to Frege, 12.12.1904, in G. Gabriel, H. Hermes, F. Kambartel, C. Thiel, and A. Veraart (eds.), *Gottlob Frege: Philosophical and Mathematical Correspondence*, Basil Blackwell, Oxford, pp. 166–70.

Russell, B. (1905). On denoting, *Mind* 14: 479–93.

Russell, B. (1905/1994). The nature of truth, in A. Urquhaut (ed.), *The Collected Works of Bertrand Russell*, Vol. 4, Routledge, London, pp. 492–506.

Russell, B. (1906). On the nature of truth, *Proceedings of the Aristotelian Society* 7: 28–49.

Russell, B. (1912). *The Problems of Philosophy*, Williams and Norgate, London.

Russell, B. (1940). *An Inquiry into Meaning and Truth*, George Allen and Unwin, London.

Russell, B. (1985). The philosophy of logical atomism, in D. Pears (ed.), *The Philosophy of Logical Atomism*, Open Court, La Salle, IL, pp. 35–155.

Russell, B. (1989). *Logic and Knowledge*, Unwin Hyman, London.

Russell, B. (2003). *Russell on Metaphysics: Selections from the Writings of Bertrand Russell*, ed. Stephen Mumford, Routledge, London.

Russell, B. (2009). *The Philosophy of Logical Atomism*, Routledge, Oxford.

Russell, G. (2007). The analytic/synthetic distinction, *Philosophy Compass* 2(5): 712–29.

Russell, G. (2008). *Truth in Virtue of Meaning: A defence of the Analytic/Synthetic Distinction*, Oxford University Press, Oxford.

Saenz, N. (2014). The world and truth about what is not, *Philosophical Quarterly* 64(254): 82–98.

Salmon, N. (1986). *Frege's Puzzle*, MIT Press, Cambridge, MA.

Salmon, N. (2005). *Metaphysics, Mathematics, and Meaning*, Oxford University Press, New York, NY.

Schaffer, J. (2009). On what grounds what, in D. Chalmers, D. Manley, and R. Wasserman (eds), *Metametaphysics*, Oxford University Press, Oxford.

Schaffer, J. (2010a). The internal relatedness of all things, *Mind* 119: 341–76.

Schaffer, J. (2010b). The least discerning and most promiscuous truthmaker, *Philosophical Quarterly* 60(239): 307–24.

Schaffer, J. (2010c). Monism: The priority of the whole, *Philosophical Review* 119(1): 31–76.

Schaffer, J. (2012). Grounding, transitivity, and contrastivity, in F. Correia and B. Schnieder (eds.), *Metaphysical Grounding: Understanding the Structure of Reality*, Cambridge University Press, Cambridge, pp. 122–38.

Schaffer, J. (2016a). Grounding in the image of causation, *Philosophical studies* 173(1): 49–100.

Schaffer, J. (2016b). Social construction as grounding; or: Fundamentality for feminists, a reply to Barnes and Mikkola, *Philosophical Studies*, 174(10): 2449–65.

Scharp, K. (2013). *Replacing Truth*, Oxford University Press, Oxford.

Schiffer, S. (2003). *The Things We Mean*, Oxford University Press, Oxford.

Schnieder, B. (2010). A puzzle about 'because', *Logique et Analyse* 53(211): 317–43.

Schnieder, B. (2011). A logic for 'because', *Review of Symbolic Logic* 4(3): 445–65.

Schnieder, B. (2015). The asymmetry of 'because', *Grazer Philosophische Studien* 91(1): 131–64.

Shapiro, L. (2011). Deflating logical consequence, *Philosophical Quarterly* 61(243): 320–42.

Shapiro, S. (2009). Truth as one and many, by Michael P. Lynch, *Notre Dame Philosophical Reviews*, https://ndpr.nd.edu/news/24169-truth-as-one-and-many.

Sher, G. (2002). Truth, the liar, and Tarski's semantics, in D. Jacquette (ed.), *A Companion to Philosophical Logic*, Blackwell, Oxford, pp. 143–63.

Sher, G. (2015). Truth as composite correspondence, in D. Achourioti, K. Fujimoto, H. Galinon, and J. Martinez (eds.), *Unifying the Philosophy of Truth*, Springer, Dordrecht, pp. 191–210.

Sher, G. (2016). Substantivism about truth, *Philosophy Compass* 11(12): 818–28.

Sider, T. (2003). *Four-dimensionalism: An Ontology of Persistence and Time*, Oxford University Press, New York.

Sider, T. (2013a). Against parthood, in K. Bennett and D. Zimmerman (eds.), *Oxford Studies in Metaphysics* Vol. 8, Oxford University Press, Oxford, pp. 237–93.

Sider, T. (2013b). Bennett on grounding ground, seminar handout, http://tedsider.org/teaching/ground/ground.html.

Simchen, O. (2012). *Necessary Intentionality: A study in the Metaphysics of Aboutness*, Oxford University Press, Oxford.

Simons, P. (2005). Negatives, numbers, and necessity: Some worries about Armstrong's version of truthmaking, *Australasian Journal of Philosophy* 83(2): 253–61.

Simpson, M. (2014). Defending truthmaker non-maximalism, *Thought* 3(4): 288–91.

Skiles, A. (2014). Is there a dilemma for the truthmaker non-maximalist?, *Synthese* 191(15): 3649–59.

Skyrms, B. (1981). Tractarian nominalism, *Philosophical Studies* 40(2): 199–206.

Soames, S. (1987). Direct reference, propositional attitudes and semantic content, *Philosophical Topics* 15(1): 47–87.

Soames, S. (2008). Why propositions cannot be sets of truth-supporting circumstances, *Journal of Philosophical Logic* 37(3): 267–76.

Sorensen, R. (2001). *Vagueness and Contradiction*, Oxford University Press, Oxford.

Sosa, E. (1999a). How must knowledge be modally related to what is known?, *Philosophical Topics* 26(1–2): 373–84.

Sosa, E. (1999b). How to defeat opposition to Moore, *Philosophical Perspectives* 13: 141–153.

Sosa, E. (2009). *A Virtue Epistemology: Apt Belief and Reflective Knowledge*, Vol. 1, Oxford University Press, Oxford.

Sosa, E. (2011). *Reflective Knowledge: Apt Belief and Reflective Knowledge*, Vol. 2, Oxford University Press, Oxford.

Stalnaker, R. (1976a). Possible worlds, *Noûs* 10(1): 65–75.

Stalnaker, R. (1976b). Propositions, in A. MacKay and D. Merrill (eds.), *Issues in the Philosophy of Language*, Yale University Press, New Haven, pp. 79–91.

Stalnaker, R. (1984). *Inquiry*, MIT Press, Cambridge, MA.

Stoljar, D. and Damnjanovic, N. (1997). The deflationary theory of truth, in E. N. Zalta (ed.), *The Stanford Encyclopedia of Philosophy*, https://plato.stanford.edu/archives/fall2014/entries/truth-deflationary/.

Tahko, T. E. (2013). Truth-grounding and transitivity, *Thought: A Journal of Philosophy* 2(4): 332–40.

Tallant, J. (2009). Ontological cheats might just prosper, *Analysis* 69(3): 422–30.

Tappolet, C. (1997). Mixed inferences: A problem for pluralism about truth predicates, *Analysis* 57: 209–10.

Tarski, A. (1976). *The Concept of Truth in Formalised Languages*, Clarendon Press, Oxford.

Thompson, N. (2016a). Grounding and metaphysical explanation, *Proceedings of the Aristotelian Society* 116(3): 395–402.

Thompson, N. (2016b). Metaphysical interdependence, in M. Jago (ed.), *Reality Making*, Oxford University Press, Oxford, pp. 38–56.

Trogdon, K. (2013). An introduction to grounding, in M. Hoeltje, B. Schnieder, and A. Steinberg (eds.), *Varieties of Dependence: Ontological Dependence, Grounding, Supervenience, Response-Dependence*, Philosophia Verlag, Munich, pp. 97–122.

Turner, J. (2016). *The Facts in Logical Space: A Tractarian Ontology*, Oxford University Press, Oxford.

van Fraassen, B. (1969). Facts and tautological entailments, *Journal of Philosophy* 66(15): 477–87.

Vetter, B. (2015). *Potentiality: From Dispositions to Modality*, Oxford University Press, Oxford.

Vitola, A. (1998). For a deflationary conception of truth, PhD thesis, Rutgers University, New Brunswick.

von Solodkoff, T. (2012). Straightening priority out, *Philosophical studies* 161(3): 391–401.

Weir, A. (2005). Naive truth and sophisticated logic, in J.C. Beall and B. Armour-Garb (eds.), *Deflationism and Paradox*, Oxford University Press, Oxford, pp. 218–49.

Williamson, T. (1993). Verificationism and non-distributive knowledge, *Australasian Journal of Philosophy* 71(1): 78–86.

Williamson, T. (2000). *Knowledge and its Limits*, Oxford University Press, Oxford.

Williamson, T. (2009). Probability and danger, *The Amherst Lecture in Philosophy* 4: http://www.amherstlecture.org/williamson2009/.

Wilsch, T. (2015). The nomological account of ground, *Philosophical Studies* 172(12): 3293–312.

Wilson, J. (2014). No work for a theory of grounding, *Inquiry* 57(5–6): 535–79.

Wilson, J. (2016a). Grounding-based formulations of physicalism, *Topoi*, doi: 10.1007/s11245-016-9435-7.

Wilson, J. (2016b). The unity and priority arguments for grounding, in K. Aizawa and C. Gillett, *Scientific Composition and Metaphysical Ground*, Springer, Dordrecht, pp. 171–204.

Wilson, A. (2017). Metaphysical causation, *Noûs*, doi: 10.1111/nous.12190.

Wittgenstein, L. (1921/1922). *Tractatus Logico-Philosophicus*, Routledge & Kegan Paul, London.

Wright, C. (1992). *Truth and Objectivity*, Harvard University Press, Harvard, MA.

Wright, C. (1996). Précis of truth and objectivity, *Philosophy and Phenomenological Research* 56(4): 863–8.

Wright, C. (2001). Minimalism, deflationism, pragmatism, pluralism, in M. Lynch (ed.), *The Nature of Truth: Classic and Contemporary Perspectives*, MIT Press, Cambridge, MA, pp. 751–87.

Wright, C. (2003). *Saving the Differences: Essays on Themes from Truth and Objectivity*, Harvard University Press, Cambridge, MA.

Wright, C. (2013). A plurality of pluralisms, in N. Pedersen and C. Wright (eds.), *Truth and Pluralism: Current Debates*, Oxford University Press, Oxford, pp. 123–53.

Yablo, S. (1992). Mental causation, *Philosophical Review* 101(2), 245–80.

Yablo, S. (1993). Paradox without self-reference, *Analysis* 53(4): 251–52.

Yablo, S. (2014). *Aboutness*, Princeton University Press, Princeton, NJ.

Yagisawa, T. (2010). *Worlds and Individuals, Possible and Otherwise*, Oxford University Press, New York.

Zalta, E. N. (1989). Singular propositions, abstract constituents, and propositional attitudes, in J. Almog, J. Perry, and H. Wettstein (eds.), *Themes from Kaplan*, Oxford University Press, Oxford, pp. 455–78.

Zardini, E. (2011). Truth without contra(di)ction, *Review of Symbolic Logic* 4(4): 498–535.

Index: Authors

Adams, Robert Merrihew, 164
Anderson, Alan Ross, 230
Armstrong, David, 2, 3, 53–4, 72, 105–12, 123, 146–9, 151, 162, 167–8, 181–2, 209
Asay, Jamin, 253
Audi, Robert, 185, 187–9

Bacon, Andrew, 301–2, 318
Barker, Stephen, 149, 155–6, 193, 303–9
Beall, JC, 291, 295
Beebee, Helen, 160
Belnap, Nuel, 230
Bennett, Karen, 197–8
Bliss, Ricki, 202

Cameron, Ross P., 88, 141–4, 171
Carnap, Rudolf, 35, 36
Casati, Roberto, 152
Cheyne, Colin, 136–8
Church, Alonzo, 50
Cobreros, Pablo, 299
Cotnoir, A. J., 43–4
Crimmins, Mark, 238

Demos, Raphael, 135–6
Divers, John, 263
Dodd, Julian, 160, 168
Dowe, Phil, 152

Dummett, Michael, 67, 270
Dunn, J. Michael, 229
Dyke, Heather, 166

Égré, Paul, 299

Fine, Kit, 60, 164–6, 188, 211, 217–26, 273
Fitch, Frederic B., 50
Fox, John, 177
Frege, Gottlob, 27, 58, 252

Gödel, Kurt, 35–6
Goldstein, Laurence, 283
Green, Karen, 86
Greenough, Patrick, 298–9
Griffith, Aaron M., 204

Haslanger, Sally, 187
Horwich, Paul, 26, 30, 37, 75–6

Jansson, Lina, 202
Jenkins, Carrie, 202

King, Jeffrey C., 27, 245–9
Kripke, Saul, 285–7

Lewis, David, 82, 125, 139–41, 152, 242, 261
Lewis, Stephanie, 152
Litland, Jon, 199
Lowe, Edward Jonathan, 188
Lynch, Michael, 47–50

Martin, Charles Burton, 54
McDaniel, Kris, 261
Melia, Joseph, 60, 63, 73, 107
Mellor, David Hugh, 91, 161
Merricks, Trenton, 56–7, 61, 161, 240, 273–6
Milne, Peter, 311
Molnar, George, 150–1
Mumford, Stephen, 149
Murzi, Julien, 291, 295

Noonan, Harold W., 170

Parsons, Josh, 138, 150
Pigden, Charles, 136–8
Plantinga, Alvin, 164
Priest, Graham, 202, 270, 287
Prior, Arthur, 317

Quine, Willard van Orman, 22

Ramsey, Frank P., 22, 252
Read, Stephen, 182
Restall, Greg, 178–84, 294
Richard, Mark, 238
Ripley, David, 297, 299–300
Rodriguez-Pereyra, Gonzalo, 57–61, 168, 180, 202, 204, 210–15, 311
Rosen, Gideon, 140–1, 166, 185, 188, 190
Russell, Bertrand, 27, 55, 82, 105, 133, 135–6

Salmon, Nathan U., 238, 245
Schaffer, Jonathan, 144–6, 185–6, 202
Scharp, Kevin, 302–3
Schiffer, Stephen, 26, 241
Sider, Theodore, 196
Simpson, Matthew, 96–7
Skiles, Alexander J., 99, 101
Skyrms, Brian, 113–5
Soames, Scott, 245
Sosa, Ernest, 97–9
Stalnaker, Robert, 242
Stoljar, Damnjanovic, 20

Tahko, Tuomas E., 204
Tappolet, Christine, 43
Thompson, Naomi, 202
Turner, Jason, 116–22, 156

van Fraassen, Bas, 212, 217, 222, 230
van Rooij, Robert, 299
Varzi, Achille, 152
Vetter, Barbara, 166

Weir, A.J., 299
Williamson, Timothy, 99
Wilsch, Tobias, 193
Wilson, Alastair, 186
Wright, Cory, 40, 50, 76

Yablo, Stephen, 192, 282
Yagisawa, Takashi, 261

Index: Terms

Abelardian predicate, 170
aboutness, 267, 272–7, *see also* subject matter
absence-necessitators, 86, 132–4
absences, 86, 88, 93, 95, 132–4, 149–55
    perception of, 152–4
acceptance, 289, 294
actual, 141–4
actualism, 129–30
actually, 136–8
alethic pluralism, 39–47
alethic undecidability, 303
analytic, 20, 22, 24, 160, 168–70, *see also* truthmakers for analytic truths
assertion, 289

because, 75
being true, *see* truth (property of)
beliefs, 237–8
Bradley's regress, 106

causation, 151–2, 186
cause, 70–1
cautious cut, 297
characteristic functions, 249
co-reference, 269
composition
    mereological, *see* mereology
    non-mereological, 112–13

congruence, 223–4
conjunction principle, 180, 208, 210, 212, 217
content inclusion, 273
contradiction, 287, 290
convex set, 222–3
correspondence, 3, 4, 40–3, 47, 49–51, 78
counterfactuals, 97, 167
counterpart, 139, 141
cumulative reasoning, 297
Curry paradox, 288–92, 303, 305, 306

De Morgan Laws, 43, 44
deflationism, 19–40, 66
denial, 289
derivation, 321
diagonal function, 35, 36
dialetheism, 263, 287–92, 318
disjunction principle, 178–9, 208, 212–15, 217
dispositions, 56, 145, 166

entailment, *see* logical consequence
    first-degree, *see* FDE
entailment principle, 210
entailment thesis, 83, 177–84

entities
   fundamental, 144, 151
   impossible, 256–9
equivalence scheme (ES), 19–23, 37, 75, *see also* T-prop
essence, 166, 167, 189, 200, 201
   intrinsic, 143
   of falsity, 239
   of logical concepts, *see* grounding
   of material objects, 195
   of truth, 239
eternalism, 170
exact entailment, 217–26
exact truthmaker equivalence, 219, 270
exact truthmaking, 12, 209–26, 243
existence, 150
explanation, 76, 145, 198, 199
explosion principle, 263, 287

facts, *see* states of affairs
falsemakers, 74, 82, 217, 254
falsemaking, 74
falsity, 74, 91–2, 234–5, 238–40, 249, 250, 254, 257, 303–5, 310, 311
FDE, 229, 271
fixed point theorem, 36
Fregean sense, 33, 238
functionalism about truth, 47, 49
fundamental tie, 105–13

Gödel numbering, 281
Gettier Problems, 94–101
ground-unspecifiable, 304
grounding, 57–61, 184–206, 255
   and essence, 188–9, 196–202
   and truthmaking, 57–61, 185
   as a connective, 60–1
   as a relation, 59, 88, 184–200
   conditions, 191, 195–8
   grounding, 196–201
   logical cases of, 186–7
   logical properties of, 202–6
   material objects, 195
   standard view of, 202

hyperintensionality, 239, 244, 269

idealism, 55, 66
identity determination, 20, 33
identity relation, 258
in virtue of, *see* explanation
incompatibility, 135
indexicals, 269
inexact entailment, 229
inexact falsemaking, 227
inexact truthmaking, 12, 209–16, 226–30, 271
instantiation, 68–9, 106, 107, 247, *see also* Bradley's regress
'is true', *see* truth predicate

Jackson's thesis, 180

knowability paradox, 50
knowledge, 94–100

liar paradox, 20, 34–8, 280–319
   and grounding, 310
   and meaning, 283–4, 309
   contingent, 283
   no proposition approach, 309–14
   revenge, 284–5, 301, 312
   solutions to, 284–314
   strengthened, 285, 305
   substructural solutions to, 292–300, 318
   undecidability approach, 303–9

linear logic, 295
logical consequence
   accounts of, 294–5
   proof-theoretic, 316–18
logical rules, *see* sequent calculus

makes true, *see* truthmaking
material constitution, 152
maximalism, *see* truthmaker maximalism
meaning, 252, 267, 314, 315
Meinongianism, 261, 263
mereology
   atom, 147
   composition, *see* sum
   extensional, 109, 123, 125
   overlap, 109
   sum, 107–8, 124, 125, 146, 194, 200
   universalism, 108, 109, 123, 185
metaphysical causation, *see* causation
metaphysical dependence, *see* grounding
metaphysical explanation, *see* explanation
metaphysical interdependence, 202
minimalism, *see* deflationism
mixed conjunctions, 42–6
modal realism, 261–3, *see also* modality, possible worlds
modality, 139, 162, 167
Molinism, 56
monism about truth, 48–9
multiset, 321

nature, *see* essence
necessary connection, 110–11
necessitation, 84–95, 131, 139, 145–6, 253

necessity, 120–2, 161, 166, *see also* modality
negation, 44, 45, 288–9
negative existential, 82–5, 87, 89, 95, 131, 133–4, 137–8, 140, 149–50, 155
negative fundamental tie, *see* states of affairs (negative)
negative states of affairs, *see* states of affairs (negative)
nominalism, 56, 59, 62–7, 73, 118
non-well-founded set theory, 259
notation, 14–15
null state, 223

ordered pair, *see* sequences
orientation function, 116

paraconsistent logic, 287
paradox, *see* Curry paradox, liar paradox
parthood
   mereological, *see* mereology
   non-mereological, 112–13
particular, 68, 70, 105–6, 110
perception, 71–2, 152–4
phenomenalism, 54, 56
pluralism about truth, *see* alethic pluralism
possibility, 120–4, *see also* modality
possible worlds, 111, 124–6, 138, 207, *see also* modality
potentialities, 166, *see also* dispositions
predication, 118, 119
presentism, 56, 126, 145, 171
priority monism, 144
proper class, 260

properties, 20, 105–6, 110, 113, 127, 144, 171, 191, 192, 195, 202
    logically complex, 193
    nature of, 148, 187, 189–91
    negative, 157
property possession, *see* instantiation
propositional attitudes, 235, 238
propositions, 5, 24–31, 33, 44, 67, 90–3, 169, 205, 233–77, *see also* liar paradox
    as sets of truthmakers, 249–66
    as sets of worlds, 242–5, 268
    as truthmaker conditions, 249–61, 268–9, 309, 314
    double, 255–8
    Fregean, 28, 31, 245, 275
    nature of, 85, 189, 201, 239–61
    negative, 82, 90, 93, 135, *see also* negative existential
    Russellian, 31, 36, 205, 245, 275
    structured, 27–8, 31, 36, 204, 245–9, 268

quantification, 62, 63, 68, 71, 260

real definition, 188–91, 195
realism, 6–9, 54
rejection, 289, 294
relations, *see* properties
relevant logic, 182, 267, 271
Russell's paradox, 147

same-saying, 266–77
selection, 221

self-reference, 204, 205, 280–2
semantic function, 315
semantic value, 27, 32, 168, 245, 247, 252
sequences, 128–9
sequent calculus, 321–2
sets, 125–6, 128, 194, 259
states of affairs, 68–73, 76, 105–30, 151, 152, 157, 179, 193, 253, 261, 265, 304
    as truthmakers, 51–2, 54, 72–3, 147
    ersatz, 264–6
    fundamental tie account of, 105–13, 129, 193, 265
    geometrical account, 116–22, 156–8
    merely possible, 261–6
    mereological account of, 105, 122–30, 158–60
    nature of, 114, 119, 121, 265–6
    negative, 93, 95, 132, 133, 135, 149–60, 263, *see also* absences
    primitive, 105, 114, 121, 129–30, 193
    totality, 93, 95, 131–3, 146–7
strong supplementation, 109, 112
structural rules, *see* sequent calculus
subject matter, 142, 143, 272–4, *see also* aboutness
substantial theories of truth, 9, 38, 40, 49–52

T-equivalence, *see* T-scheme
T-prop, 25, 28–36
T-scheme, 19, 21, 40, 42, 75, 248, 251, 252, 288, 301–2, 316, 318

TATM, *see* truth as truthmaking
tautological entailment, 230
time, 170
totality relation *Tot*, 146–9
truth, 19–52, 58, 75, 83, 90, 101, 233, 235, 242, 273, 311
    as truthmaking, 4, 48–51, 74–8
    concept of, 21, 58, 176
    domains of, 40–5, 47
    generic property, 41, 43, 46–7, 49
    grounding, *see* truthmaking, grounding
    hecceitistic, 171
    nature of, 33, 188, 195, 201
    negative, *see* proposition (negative), negative existential
    predicate, 21, 38, 40, 42, 75, 76, 252, 253, 279, 286, 318
    property of, 20, 32, 38, 41, 42, 46, 49, 58, 74–8, 195, 201, 233–5, 250, 252, 275, 311
    rules for, 290, 316
    theories of, 3, 22, 43, 47, 49, 76–8, 252, 286, 302–3
truth-teller, 304, 310
truthbearers, 233–9, *see also* propositions
truthmaker condition, 254
truthmaker maximalism, 76, 81–102, 131, 149, 211, 311
    parsimonious, 134–46
truthmaker monism, 144–6
truthmaker necessitarianism, *see* necessitation
truthmaker non-maximalism, 81–7, 89–92, 96–101

truthmaker principle, 53–61, 304
truthmaker semantics, 207–30
    exact, *see* exact truthmaking, exact entailment
    inexact, *see* inexact truthmaking, inexact entailment
truthmakers, 48, 51, 55, 59, 61, 74, 81, 84, 89–92, 102, 131, 139–46, 169, 201, 208–10, 243, 276
    exact, *see* exact truthmaking
    for analytic truths, 102, 131, 160, 168–70
    for counterfactual truths, 54, 131, 167–8
    for general truths, 83, 132, 133
    for modal truths, 131, 160–7, *see also* modality
    for necessary truths, 102, 161
    for negative existentials, 82, 84, 131–3, 138–40, *see also* negative existential
    for temporal truths, 131, 170–1
    inexact, *see* inexact truthmaking
    minimal, 209, 215
truthmaking, 1–5, 48–51, 53–61, 74–8, 131, 135–6, 161, 175–206, 210, 250
    and grounding, *see* grounding
    as a relation, 72–4
    as logical entailment, 182–4
    as necessity, 177–84

truthmaking (cont.)
   exact, *see* exact
      truthmaking
   inexact, *see* inexact
      truthmaking
   logical properties of, 202–6
   without truthmakers, 60,
      63, 72

universal, *see* properties

unrestricted composition, *see*
   mereology
   (universalism)

ways, 60–2, *see also* properties,
   modality
what is said, 266–72
whole, *see* mereology
world, *see* possible worlds

zero-grounded, 199

The manufacturer's authorised representative in the EU for product safety is Oxford University Press España S.A. of el Parque Empresarial San Fernando de Henares, Avenida de Castilla, 2 - 28830 Madrid (www.oup.es/en)

Printed and bound by CPI Group (UK) Ltd, Croydon, CR0 4YY